NHIE STRUCTURAL SYSTEMS & BUSINESS

NHIE STRUCTURAL SYSTEMS & BUSINESS

Bruce A. Barker

NHIE Structural Systems & Business

Copyright © 2019 by Examination Board of Professional Home Inspectors, Inc. (EBPHI) All rights reserved. No part of this book may be reproduced or retransmitted in any form or by any means without the written permission of the copyright holder.

Publisher's Cataloging-in-Publication Data

Bruce A. Barker

NHIE home inspection manual volume 2 / Bruce A. Barker

Includes bibliographic references and index.

ISBN 13: 978-0-9964518-2-6

1. Housing- Standards --Popular works. 2. Building laws--Popular works. 3. Dwellings--Design and construction--Standards--Popular works. I Title.

Disclaimer of Liability

Every effort has been made to ensure the accuracy of the material contained in this book. The author, EBPHI, and printer assume no liability whatsoever for any loss or damages caused by the use or interpretation of the material in this book. The author, EBPHI, and printer disclaim liability to any and all parties for any and all losses or damages including, but not limited to, incidental and consequential damages and losses or damages caused by deficiencies, errors, or omissions contained in this book regardless of whether such deficiencies, errors, or omissions result from negligence or any other cause or theory. The author, EBPHI, and printer recommend that the reader consult the local building official and qualified professionals before and during all projects.

The information in this book addresses topics that may appear in the National Home Inspector Examination (NHIE). No representation is made that the information in this book constitutes a complete list of topics that may appear in the NHIE. Review questions are examples of the types of questions that may appear in the NHIE. Purchase of this book and study of the information herein is not a guarantee that the purchaser will pass the National Home Inspector Examination or any other examination.

ACKNOWLEDGMENTS

TECHNICAL REVIEWER

Thomas G. Lauhon

ILLUSTRATIONS

Bruce A. Barker

PHOTOGRAPHS

The Bilco Company

Bruce A. Barker

Mike Casey

Bob Davidson

Jennifer Davidson

Alden Gibson

David Grudzinski

Bryck Guibor

Jim Katen

Thomas G. Lauhon

Don Lovering

Sioux Chief Manufacturing Co.

Randy Sipe

Welmoed Sisson

Skip Walker

REFERENCES

American Heritage Dictionary of the English Language
Fifth Edition

Dictionary of Architecture and Construction, Fourth Edition
Cyril M. Harris

Garner's Modern American Usage 2003
Bryan A. Garner

InspectAPedia
www.inspectapedia.com
Daniel Friedman

International Residential Code 2018
International Code Council, Inc

National Electrical Code 2017
National Fire Protection Association

TABLE OF CONTENTS

1: SITE CONDITIONS 1
- INSPECTION SCOPE 1
- SITE CONDITIONS TERMS 1
- RETAINING WALLS 2
  - Introduction 2
  - Construction 3
  - Defects, Safety, Standards 7
- GRADE AND DRAINAGE 8
  - Introduction 8
  - Common Drainage Systems 10
  - Defects and Standards 12
- VEGETATION 13
  - Introduction 13
  - Defects, Safety, Standards 14
- DRIVEWAYS, WALKWAYS, AND PATIOS 15
  - Driveway 15
  - Walkway 16
  - Patio 17
  - Construction 17
  - Defects, Safety, Standards 19
- POOL AND SPA ACCESS BARRIERS 21
  - Introduction 21
  - Fences and Walls 22
  - Gates 23
  - House Walls 23
  - Defects and Standards 24

2: EXTERIOR COMPONENTS 28
- INSPECTION SCOPE 28
- EXTERIOR COMPONENT TERMS 28
- EXTERIOR WALL COVERINGS AND RELATED TRIM 29
  - Introduction 29
  - Adhered Masonry Veneer 30
  - Aluminum Siding (also Steel Siding) 34
  - Asbestos Cement Siding 35
  - Brick Veneer (also Natural Stone) 36
  - Fiber Cement Siding 42
  - Hardboard (Composite Wood) Siding 46
  - Insulbrick Siding 48
  - Stucco – Cement 48
  - Stucco – EIFS 50

Vinyl Siding 51
Wood Structural Panel Siding 53
Wood Siding 54
Wall Covering Trim 56
FLASHING AND SEALANTS **58**
Keeping Water Out of the House 58
Wall Penetration Flashing 58
Defects, Standards 61
EAVES AND ASSOCIATED TRIM **62**
EXTERIOR DOORS **64**
Hinged Doors 64
Sliding (Patio) Doors 67
Bulkhead Doors 67
Door Safety Issues 68
Defects and Standards 71
EXTERIOR WINDOWS **73**
Defects and Standards 78
Window Safety Issues 80
STOOPS AND PORCHES **85**
Introduction 85
Construction 85
Defects, Safety, Standards 87
BALCONIES **89**
Introduction 89
Construction 89
Defects, Safety, Standards 91
DECKS **92**
Introduction 92
Construction 92
Defects, Safety, Standards 105
GARAGE VEHICLE DOORS AND DOOR OPERATORS **114**
Garage Vehicle Doors 114
Vehicle Door Operators 118

3: ROOF COMPONENTS 122

INSPECTION SCOPE **122**
STEEP SLOPE ROOF COVERINGS **122**
Introduction 122
Asbestos Cement Shingles 122
Asphalt (Fiberglass, Composition) Shingles 123
Concrete and Clay Tiles 127
Fiber Cement Roofing 131
Metal Shingles 132

Metal Panels	134
Slate Shingles	136
Synthetic Component (Polymer) Roof Coverings	139
Wood Shingles and Shakes	139
Ice Dams	143

LOW SLOPE ROOF COVERINGS 144
Introduction	144
Built-Up Roof Membranes (BURs)	144
Mineral-Surfaced Roll Roofing	146
Modified Bitumen Roofing	147
Polyurethane Foam Roofing	150
Single-ply Membrane Roofing	152

ROOF DRAINAGE SYSTEMS 155
Gutters (Steep Slope Roof Drainage)	155
Low Slope Roof Drainage	157

ROOF FLASHING 159
Roof Penetration Flashing	159
Sidewall and Headwall Flashing	161
Defects, Safety, Standards	163

SKYLIGHTS 165

4: STRUCTURAL COMPONENTS 170

INSPECTION SCOPE 170
STRUCTURAL COMPONENT TERMS 170
FOUNDATIONS 174
Forces Affecting Houses	174
Footings, Piles, Piers, and Columns	176
Basement Foundation	181
Crawl Space Foundation	192
Slab-on-Grade Foundation	192
Slab-on-Stem Wall Foundation	193
Slab Foundation Reinforcement	194
Slab Foundation Defects and Standards	195

FLOOR SYSTEM 196
Introduction	196
Dimensional Lumber Floor Systems	197
Wood I-Joists and Engineered Wood (Floors and Roofs)	207
Floor Trusses	212

WALL SYSTEM 215
Introduction	215
Fireblocking and Fire Separation	216
Foam Plastic Materials	219
Wood-Framed Wall Systems	220

Concrete Masonry Unit (CMU) and Structural Brick Wall Systems 230
Insulating Concrete Forms Wall Systems 233
Structural Insulated Panel Wall Systems (SIPS) 234
Uncommon Wall Materials and Systems 235

ROOF AND CEILING SYSTEM 238
Introduction 238
Roof Styles 239
Dimensional Lumber Roof Systems 240
Typical Construction Techniques 241
Truss Roof Systems 254
Wood I-Joists and Engineered Wood Roof Systems 261
Attic Access 261

5: INSULATION AND VENTILATION 266

INSPECTION SCOPE 266
INTRODUCTION TO INSULATION AND VENTILATION 266
Insulation 266
Ventilation 267
INSULATION AND VENTILATION TERMS 268
HOW INSULATION WORKS 269
HOW VAPOR RETARDERS WORK 272
THE HOUSE AS A SYSTEM 273
COMMON TYPES OF INSULATION 277
Batt Insulation 277
Loose Fill/Blown-in Insulation 278
Sheet/Rigid Insulation 279
Spray Foam Insulation 280
Other Insulation Types 281
ENERGY EFFICIENCY AND MOISTURE MANAGEMENT COMPONENTS ... 288
Water-Resistive Barriers (WRBs) 288
Radiant Barriers 289
Fenestration 290
Recommended Energy Efficiency Values 291
MECHANICAL VENTILATION AND EXHAUST 292
Mechanical Ventilation Systems 292
Whole-house Fans 297
Local Exhaust Systems 298
ATTIC VENTILATION 307
Ventilated Attics 307
Unventilated (Closed) Attic 312
CRAWL SPACE VENTILATION 314
Ventilated Crawl Spaces 314
Unventilated (Closed) Crawl Spaces 318
BASEMENT WALL INSULATION 320

6: THE HOUSE INTERIOR 324

INSPECTION SCOPE 324
INTERIOR WALL AND CEILING FINISHES 325
INTERIOR DOORS 331
- Cased Openings 331
- Hinged Swinging Doors 331
- Sliding Doors, Pocket Doors, and Bifold Doors 333

FLOOR COVERINGS 334
- Introduction 334
- Carpet 335
- Laminate and Engineered Wood 336
- Linoleum and Vinyl 338
- Tile and Stone 339
- Wood 341

STAIRWAYS AND LANDINGS 343
- Introduction 343
- Stairways 343

HANDRAILS AND GUARDS 350
- Handrails 350
- Guards 352

CABINETS AND COUNTERTOPS 354
- Cabinets 354
- Countertops 357

SMART HOME TECHNOLOGY 359

7: ANALYSIS AND REPORTING 363

INSPECTION SCOPE AND LIMITATIONS 363
- Inspection Scope 363
- Inspection Limitations 364

STANDARDS OF PRACTICE (SOP) 365
REPORT WRITING 366
- Communication 366
- Report Formats 366
- Deficiency Statements 367
- Deficient Conditions 371
- System and Component Descriptions 374
- Inspection Limitation Statements 379
- Other Report Contents 382

INSPECTION TOOLS 384
THE INSPECTION PROCESS 389

8: PROFESSIONAL RESPONSIBILITIES 395

BUSINESS LAW 395
Introduction 395
Dealing with Dissatisfied Clients 395
Types of Home Inspector Liability 398

INSPECTION AGREEMENTS (CONTRACTS) 401
Introduction 401
Contract Basics 401
Contract Contents (Required) 403
Contract Contents (Optional) 404

INSURANCE 407
Introduction 407
Bond 407
Errors and Omissions Insurance (E&O) 407
General Liability Insurance (GL) 408
Worker's Compensation Insurance 408
Homeowner's Insurance 409
Vehicle Insurance 409

HOME INSPECTION ETHICS 409
Introduction 409
Conflicts of Interest 410
Ethical Reporting 411

STARTING A HOME INSPECTION BUSINESS 412
Introduction 412
The Business Plan 412
Types of Business Ownership 413
Government Licensing and Registration 414
Accounting and Financial Management 416

HOME INSPECTION MARKETING 419
Introduction 419
What is Marketing? 419
Marketing the Intangible 420
Features and Benefits 420
Elements of a Marketing Plan 420
Marketing Resources 421

GLOSSARY 423

INDEX 445

1: SITE CONDITIONS

INSPECTION SCOPE

A home inspection involves more than inspecting the house itself. The condition of components around the house, and the condition of the land itself, is important information for clients. The condition of components like driveways, walkways, and patios is in scope, and should be reported like any other in scope component. Grade of the land and drainage of water away from the house and ultimately off the property is essential for the long term integrity of the house and property. Home inspectors should carefully inspect these site conditions and report visible deficiencies. The condition of components like retaining walls and vegetation is in scope of a home inspection only insofar as their condition is likely to have an adverse impact on the house.

The condition of structures that are not attached to the house (auxiliary structures) is **out of scope** of a home inspection, except for the condition of detached garages and carports. In practice, some inspectors inspect auxiliary structures as a courtesy to their client. Some inspectors charge an additional fee to inspect these auxiliary structures, especially if the structures are served by utilities. Be sure to report if auxiliary structures are on the property, and report whether or not you inspected these structures.

Inspection of **swimming pool and spa access barriers** is **out of scope** of a home inspection; however, some home inspectors inspect these components because of the significant safety implications of absent and improperly installed access barriers. Home inspectors should either inspect these access barriers, or specifically disclaim inspection in the report and recommend that a qualified specialist inspect the access barriers.

SITE CONDITIONS TERMS

The area around a house has many terms that a home inspector should know and be able to use. Here are some of the most common terms that a home inspector should know. Some of these definitions have been altered to conform to usage in residential construction.

> **Barrier, access (child):** a fence, wall, house wall, or similar structure that is designed to limit access to the pool or spa area by unauthorized persons, especially children. A natural barrier such as a large body of water, a hill, or a cliff may also serve as a barrier, with approval.
>
> **Culvert:** a below ground passage that allows water to flow, usually through a large diameter metal or concrete pipe. In residential construction, a culvert may be located at the end of a driveway to permit water to flow in a swale under the driveway.
>
> **Deadman:** a buried component, such as a railroad tie or landscape timber, that serves as an anchor to keep a retaining wall from rotating; a deadman is connected to the retaining wall using a tieback.

Drainage (storm water): a system intended to capture water and direct it away from the house and ultimately off the property. A drainage system may include components such as gutters and downspouts, swales, underground drains, and grading.

Driveway: a private road that is intended for vehicle use between a public road and a building.

Grade: the elevation or level of the ground outside the house.

Grading: the act of moving soil or other material to form a desired elevation on the property. The term is often used in conjunction with drainage to describe shaping land to affect water flow.

Landscape (garden) block: a manufactured (precast) solid concrete block used to construct a landscape wall.

Landscape wall: a short height structure (usually 2 feet or less) that holds soil or fill on one side and keeps it from moving beyond the wall; a short-height retaining wall.

Patio: a flat outdoor recreational area adjacent to a house, often, but not always, on grade.

Retaining wall: a structure that holds soil or other fill on one side and keeps it from moving beyond the wall; usually applied to walls more than 2 feet tall.

Swale: a depression or channel in the soil intended to direct water in a particular direction.

Tieback: a device used to resist the lateral force on a retaining wall. See **Deadman**.

Walkway: a private path on private property that is intended for pedestrian use.

RETAINING WALLS

Introduction

A retaining wall is a structure that holds earth or other fill on one side and keeps it from moving beyond the wall. Retaining walls are used to keep earth behind the wall from eroding, and to add additional level space to a sloping lot. Retaining walls are usually in scope of a home inspection only insofar as their failure might negatively impact the house. In practice, many home inspectors inspect most or all retaining walls on the property because repair and replacement of retaining walls can be expensive, and because clients often expect inspection of retaining walls. Home inspector's reports should disclaim retaining walls not inspected, and should recommend that they be inspected.

A retaining wall may be any height. Wall height is often measured from the top of the footing. Retaining walls more than 4 feet tall with no horizontal support at the top, and retaining walls that retain a lateral load, may require an engineer approved design and a permit to construct. Retaining walls less than about two feet tall are sometimes called **landscape walls** or garden walls.

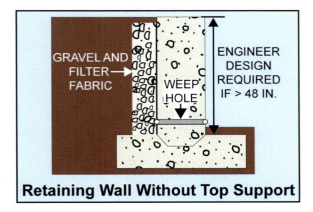
Retaining Wall Without Top Support

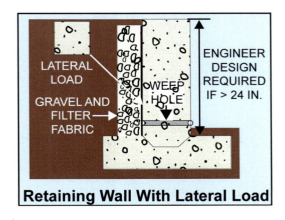
Retaining Wall With Lateral Load

Wood Retaining Wall is Supporting a Lateral Load. Wall is Likely Too Tall For Wood. Wall is Near Failure.

Lateral Load On the Failing Wood Retaining Wall.

Construction

Common Materials Common retaining wall materials include wood, masonry (concrete blocks and bricks), natural stone (rubble), poured concrete, and precast (landscape, garden) blocks. Landscape block walls may not be reinforced or tied together (pinned), and sometimes do not have a footing. Their height may be limited by the manufacturer to around two or three feet. A gabion retaining wall is a wire basket or cage filled with natural stone or rubble. Gabion retaining walls are less common.

Landscape Block Retaining Wall.
Wall is Likely Too Tall For This Material. No Footing is Visible Footing. Wall is Failing.

Typical Natural Stone (Rubble) Retaining Wall.

Wood retaining walls may be constructed using preservative treated landscape timbers or railroad ties that are treated with creosote (a black tar-like material) or a similar material. Landscape timbers are available in many sizes from 3x5 inches to 8x8 inches. Railroad ties are usually about 7x9 inches. Walls made from wood may be limited to four feet tall in some areas. Preservative treated wood should be a category that is rated for ground contact (UC4A or higher). Wood preservative treatment cannot be determined by looking at the wall. The only visual means to determine wood preservative treatment is by the tag attached to the wood. Wood retaining walls have a typical service life of between ten and twenty years depending on materials used, drainage, and soil conditions.

**Typical Landscape Timber Retaining Wall.
Rectangle At Lower Left is a Tieback.**

Wood May Not Be UC4A. Note the Significant Lateral Load.

Masonry retaining walls are usually built using concrete masonry units (CMUs, also called concrete blocks). Walls built using bricks are possible, but are less common. CMU cells in taller walls should be grouted (filled with mortar) and if grouted should be reinforced with steel. CMU cells in shorter walls may be built with the cells left hollow. Walls built with bricks are usually not reinforced, so they should be shorter. Be careful not to describe CMU walls covered with brick veneer as brick walls.

Poured concrete retaining walls are built by erecting metal or wood forms and pouring concrete between the forms. Metal bars called ties are usually placed between the forms to hold the forms together. The forms are usually removed after the concrete has hardened. Reinforcing steel should be placed horizontally in taller walls. The ties sometimes project from the wall. This is mostly a cosmetic issue with retaining walls; however, the rust can cause the ties to expand and cause cracks. Reinforcing steel should also be placed in the footings and project vertically into the wall. This helps tie the wall to the footing and helps the wall resist horizontal movement (sliding) and to a lesser extent resist rotation and other wall failures.

<u>**Construction Techniques**</u> Masonry and concrete retaining walls should be constructed on a poured concrete footing that is reinforced with steel as appropriate. Wood, garden block, and rubble walls may be constructed on compacted sand or gravel if adequate drainage is established so that water does not undercut the footing, and if the walls are not over approximately four feet tall. Remember that walls over four feet tall may require an engineered design. Even if an engineered design is not required, it is a good idea.

Retaining walls taller than about four feet should have structural components to help reduce wall failure caused by forces such as water pressure and frost heave. Wood retaining walls should have large nails (spikes) to secure each course to the next. Retaining walls may have vertical posts located on the outside of the wall (buttresses and shoring) to secure the wall. A more aesthetically pleasing means to secure the wall involves installing horizontal lumber buried in the retained soil. Horizontal lumber consists of two parts. The part that connects with the retaining wall is a tieback. The tieback runs several feet under the retained dirt and is connected to a deadman anchor that is installed perpendicular to the tieback.

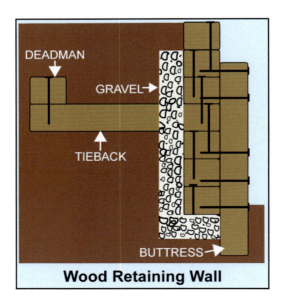

Wood Retaining Wall

Structural components that help reduce wall failure in masonry and concrete walls include vertical and horizontal reinforcing rods embedded in grout (masonry walls) or in the concrete. Reinforcing rods are not usually visible for inspection. Footings for concrete and masonry walls may be unusually wide to help provide additional failure resistance (known as cantilever retaining walls).

**Concrete Block Wall is Failing.
No Reinforcing Rods are Visible. No Grout is Visible in Cells.**

Drainage Most retaining walls should have a means to drain water that accumulates behind the wall. Lack of drainage can cause the wall to rotate, crack, bow, slide, or deteriorate because of pressure from retained wet soil, or from frost heave. Wood and rubble walls will usually drain water through the natural spaces between the members. Masonry and concrete walls should have openings, called **weep (drain) holes**, near the bottom of the wall. The quantity, size, and location of weep holes will vary based on site conditions.

Weep holes can be reduced in size or completely blocked by dense fill, such as clay, placed directly behind the wall. A layer of gravel covered by filter fabric should be placed directly behind the wall. Taller walls and walls where water may be a problem may need drainage pipe at the footing in addition to weep holes. Drainage components such as gravel and filter fabric are not usually visible for inspection.

Retaining walls may be drained using footing drains similar to those found around basement foundation walls. The footing drain terminations should be visible at the end of the wall. Retaining walls with footing drains are uncommon in residential construction.

Defects, Safety, Standards

Typical Defects Typical defects that home inspectors should report include:

1. deterioration, rot, insect damage (usually wood walls),
2. spalling and efflorescence (masonry and concrete walls, usually an indication of water management problems),
3. rotation (wall leaning out from the retained material),
4. bowing (part of the wall protrudes out from the rest of the wall),
5. cracking (usually masonry and concrete walls),
6. sliding (parts or all of the wall move laterally),

7. lack of visible reinforcement (no tiebacks in wood walls),
8. support undercut (soil eroded under wall or footing),
9. too tall for material used (usually garden block and wood walls),
10. lack of visible weep holes, weep holes are blocked, no gravel and filter fabric has been installed to facilitate drainage through weep holes,
11. components are loose or are not secured in place.

Safety Issues Retaining walls rarely present safety issues; however, a retaining wall with a walking surface on one side and a drop of more than 30 inches on the other side may be a reportable fall hazard, regardless of whether a guard is required.

Standards (1) manufacturer's instructions for garden block and other precast and manufactured retaining wall systems; (2) IRC 2018 R404.4 (retaining walls); (3) American Wood Protection Association Standard U1-16 specifications for preservative treated wood; (4) local and state governments and homeowner associations may have regulations about issues such as retaining wall design, construction, and location.

GRADE AND DRAINAGE

Introduction

The grade and the drainage system around a house consists of two complementary components. **Grade must be established near the home to:** (1) separate framing and wall covering materials from earth and hard surfaces such as driveways, and (2) divert water away from the foundation. Grade must be established on land near the house to make sure water flows away from the house and toward appropriate points either on or off the land. We address separation between building materials, earth, and hard surfaces in the wall covering section.

Establishing and maintaining means to divert water away from the foundation is essential for several reasons. **Water** that enters into crawl spaces and basements **can damage wood structural members, insulation, and finish materials, and can provide moisture for fungal growth. Moist soil** near the foundation can provide a hospitable environment for some wood destroying organisms including **termites.** Moist soil contributes to problems such as frost heave and soil expansion.

Water can severely damage the foundation walls, footings, and concrete slabs causing problems including cracks, bulging, rotation, lifting, and deterioration. Water pressure against the foundation walls is a common cause of foundation damage. Water that freezes near the foundation can expand causing frost heave.

Water can cause some unstable soils (such as **expansive clays**) to expand and contract. Soil expansion against foundation walls increases pressure on the foundation that can cause damage similar to water pressure. Soil expansion under the foundation can lift the foundation and with it the entire house. Soil contraction under the foundation can cause the foundation to sink and with it the entire house. Damage from water pressure can occur almost anywhere. Damage from unstable soils is more common in certain areas of the country such as the Southwest.

Natural slope away from the foundation is the ideal means for diverting water away from the foundation. Other means of diverting water (such as swales and underground drains) are acceptable if natural slope is not practical because of nearby structures, impediments such as hills and vegetation, or because the natural slope of the land is toward the foundation. **Earth should slope away from the foundation at least 6 inches in the first 10 feet.** Hard surfaces, such as concrete, should slope away between at least ⅛ - ¼ inch per foot. When earth slopes toward the foundation, swales or other grading systems should be established such that water is diverted around the foundation.

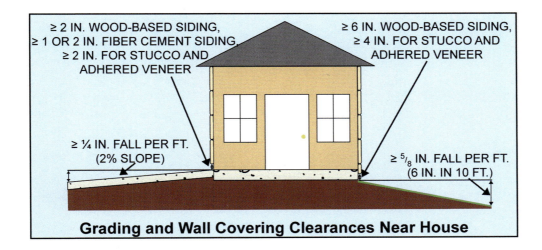

Grading and Wall Covering Clearances Near House

Examples of Grade Improperly Sloping Toward House.

Land should be graded so that water is not diverted on to neighboring land unless the water flow is part of the natural grade. For example, water from a higher lot may flow on to a lower lot, but the higher lot should be graded so that the water's impact on the lower lot is minimized to the extent practical. Houses on low-lying land often have water problems, including flooding basements, flooding crawl spaces, and erosion. Home inspectors should be aware of a house's position relative to surrounding land and may wish to report potential water problems caused by runoff from neighboring land.

It is possible to have too much slope away from the house as well as too little. It is also possible to have too much slope toward the house. Steep slopes are prone to landslides that can cause major damage. The distance between a house and the beginning of a downward slope should usually be 40 feet or H/3, where H is the height of the slope, whichever is less. The distance between a house and the beginning of an upward slope should usually be 15 feet or H/2, whichever is less. Reporting houses that do not meet these guidelines is a judgment call. The foundation may have been designed to allow placement closer to the slope or the building official may have approved the placement. Absent visible defects caused by excessive slopes near the house, a warning in your report may be all that is necessary.

Common Drainage Systems

Drainage swales are often established to channel water to a desired location. A swale is a depression or channel in the soil. A swale can be shallow and covered with grass or whatever surrounding landscaping materials are used. A swale can be deeper and lined with stones, in which case it is sometimes called a dry bed.

Example of a Dry Bed (Left) and a Swale (Right).

Underground drainage systems are sometimes used where drainage swales are impractical or where natural water flow causes erosion, such as on steep hills. Underground drains are sometimes called **French Drains**. Underground drains for older homes may be constructed using clay tiles. Flexible corrugated plastic pipe, usually 4 inches diameter, is often used for newer homes.

Underground Drain Downspout Connection (Left) and Drain Termination (Right).

Channel Drains (Left) and Catch Basins (Right) that are Connected to Underground Drains Can Be Used When Swales are Impractical.

Water entering underground drains may come from several sources. Water often comes from a gutter downspout. Water may be captured above ground in a component called a **catch basin** or in a hole filled with stones called a **dry well.** Water may flow from a sump pump or in rare cases from an underground water source. People occasionally connect foundation drains to underground drains. While often not visible, this connection is a significant defect that can cause water to back up into the basement or crawl space.

Water flows inside the underground drain and discharges at an appropriate location such as at the street or into a swale, creek, or drainage easement. The discharge pipe is usually terminated to the open air (sometimes called daylighting). In cases where there is not enough slope for an open air termination a device sometimes referred to as a **bubbler** is used. A bubbler opens above ground to let water flow out and closes when the water flow stops.

Sump pumps are occasionally used in exterior drainage systems when storm water must be pumped up for discharge. The sump pump is located in a pit or catch basin that receives surface water or water from underground pipes and mechanically discharges the water to an appropriate location.

12   1: Site Conditions

Defects and Standards

Typical Defects Typical defects that home inspectors should report include:

1. earth or hard surface slopes toward the foundation,
2. depressions in soil at the foundation caused by soil settlement, recent foundation work, or recently modified landscaping,
3. gutter and downspout problems including blockage, damage, deterioration, improper slope, downspouts discharge too close to foundation,
4. foundation drains blocked or damaged (only above ground terminations are usually visible),
5. changes to swale slope caused by plant roots or by modified landscaping,
6. debris in swale blocking water flow,
7. underground drains blocked (blockage is often not visible, but debris may be visible at the termination point),
8. underground drain termination point blocked or not visible,
9. earth or mulch at the foundation too close to or above wall coverings,
10. planting boxes installed above the foundation,
11. soil settled in utility trenches,
12. soil erosion,
13. evidence of water and drainage problems on lots at bottom of hills or in low-lying areas.

Inspectors Should Report Poor Drainage When Visible.

Standards (1) IRC 2018 R401.3 (drainage), R403.1.7 (footings near slopes), R801.3 (roof drainage/gutters); (2) local governments and homeowner associations often have regulations about drainage and grading issues.

VEGETATION

Introduction

Vegetation on the property includes all plant materials, such as trees, shrubs, grass, and other ground covers. Vegetation is usually in scope of a home inspection only insofar as it may affect the house. Issues such as **vegetation condition** and the **appropriateness of the plant** for its location are **out of scope**. For example, a dead tree that could fall on the house is usually a reportable condition. A shrub that might grow too large for the space where it's planted is usually not a reportable condition.

Plants should be selected and planted so that when the plant is fully grown there is adequate distance between the branches and leaves of the plant and the wall coverings and roof of the house. Plants that touch wall coverings and the roof can physically damage these components, and can retain moisture against these components. Damage and moisture can cause the wall coverings and the roof to deteriorate, and can create conditions for fungal growth. Vines should not be allowed to grow on wall coverings, especially wood wall coverings, for the same reasons. Vines that grow on trellises near the house may be acceptable if the trellises are far enough from the wall coverings.

Trees should be selected and planted so that when the tree is fully grown the limbs and roots will not cause damage. Tree roots can extend at least as far as the tree canopy when the tree is fully grown. **Tree limbs can physically damage the wall coverings and roof coverings** and can drop debris that can block gutters and hasten deterioration of roof coverings. Tree limbs and entire trees can fall during high wind, heavy snow, and ice storms. **Tree roots can damage the foundation** and can also damage underground plumbing, such as the building sewer pipe and the septic system drainage field. Tree roots can, and often do, uplift and damage solid horizontal surfaces such as walkways, driveways, and patios (especially those constructed of materials such as pavers). This uplift can cause significant trip and fall hazards.

Consideration should also be given to the location of overhead wires, such as the electricity service drop, telephone, and broadband cable, when selecting and planting trees. Tree limbs can damage these wires and utility companies may prune trees that could damage their wires. Utility contractor pruning can severely damage the tree, and may eventually kill the tree.

Plants, especially turf grasses and foundation plants, should not be planted where water from irrigation systems will be necessary to maintain the plants. Water from spray irrigation heads can direct water toward wall coverings and cause damage. Excess plant watering and irrigation system leaks can direct water toward the foundation and can cause problems as discussed in Grade and Drainage. The best strategy is often to plant nothing near the foundation or to plant drought-tolerant native plants that do not require watering.

Trees are sometimes supported by metal guy wires when they are new or are damaged. Support wires can cause injury if someone runs into them. Metal guy wires should be avoided or at least clearly marked so accidental contact is less likely, especially in the dark.

Plants and plant litter that are too near the house can be a fire danger in areas that are prone to wildfires. Defensible space of up to 100 feet around the home is recommended, and may be required, in wildfire areas.

Plants that provide shade for HVAC condensers can improve the efficiency of the condenser, but plants should not be located so close that the plant interferes with air circulation around the condenser. Clearance between a condenser and plants is based on the condenser manufacturer's instructions. At least **1 foot around the sides** is a typical guideline.

Defects, Safety, Standards

Typical Defects Typical defects that home inspectors should report include:

1. plants touching wall coverings or roof coverings,
2. tree limbs overhanging the roof,
3. visibly dead, diseased, and distressed trees that are near the house,
4. cracked or uplifted walkways, driveways, patios, retaining walls, and similar components that may be caused by vegetation,
5. tree limbs near overhead utility wires,
6. trees leaning toward the house,
7. trees supported by metal guy wires,
8. plants are too close to HVAC condensers.

Safety Issues (1) plants that obscure visibility from driveways and intersecting streets can be a traffic safety hazard, (2) plants that obscure visibility at the front of the house can be a security hazard because they provide cover for burglars.

Standards (1) local governments and homeowner associations may have regulations about issues such as tree removal and the types and locations of plants; (2) local agricultural extension service offices and local nurseries often have information about recommended native plants; (3) local Master Gardener programs can be a good source of free advice about landscaping issues.

Plants Should Be At Least One Foot From the House.

1: Site Conditions

Trees Should Not Touch House or Lean Toward House.

Limbs Should Not Be Above Electrical Service or Utility Drop Wires, or Hang Over the House.

This Type of Cracking and Uplift is Often Caused by Tree Roots.

DRIVEWAYS, WALKWAYS, AND PATIOS

Driveway

A driveway is a private road that is intended for vehicle use between a public road and a building. Residential driveways should provide safe and convenient vehicle access including access for delivery vehicles. The recommended minimum width of a straight one-lane residential driveway is 10 feet. The recommended minimum width of a straight two-lane residential driveway is 20 feet. These minimum widths should be increased by at least 1 to 2 feet where the driveway curves and if the driveway is surrounded on either side by a wall or a steep slope. A driveway should flare out on each side where it terminates on a public road to keep the vehicle on the driveway when it turns on to the public road.

Garages with side and rear entry doors require space in front of the garage to turn the car for garage entry and exit. The typical recommended minimum depth in front of these garages is 20 feet. This minimum depth may be inconvenient for long cars and trucks that may require additional maneuvering to enter and exit the garage.

Driveways and walkways occasionally run above water and drainage easements, which are often shallow and wide swales. Corrugated metal pipes (culverts) are sometimes installed under driveways and walkways. Inspecting culverts is usually considered part of the grade and drainage inspection. Inspection of structural systems such as bridges is not usually considered part of inspecting driveways and walkways, although many home inspectors will report obvious visible structural defects.

Culvert Serving a Swale Running Under a Driveway.

Walkway

A walkway is a private path on private property that is intended for pedestrian use. This definition distinguishes a walkway from a sidewalk, which is a paved path adjacent to a public road and intended for public use. Sidewalk maintenance is the homeowner's responsibility in some communities and the government's responsibility in other communities. Homeowners are sometimes held liable for dangerous sidewalk conditions, so inspecting sidewalks for slip and trip hazards is usually a good idea.

Residential walkways should provide safe and convenient access to the house. The minimum recommended width of a residential walkway that will allow two people to walk side-by-side is 48 inches. Narrower walkways are common and are not necessarily deficient; however, walkways less than 36 inches wide that serve the main door of the home may be a fall safety hazard, especially at night. The minimum recommended width for walkways intended for wheelchair access is 60 inches.

When walkways contain steps, the steps should comply with rules for stairways including maximum riser height and minimum tread depth. Steps with greater than the minimum tread depth are safer for walkway steps because these steps provide more walking surface. Walkway steps with four or more contiguous risers should have a handrail like interior stairways.

Patio

A patio is a flat outdoor recreational area adjacent to a house. While usually located on grade and at the rear of a house, a patio could be located on any side of the house and could be raised above grade. Patios that are more than 30 inches above surrounding grade should have guards installed. A patio that is completely surrounded by walls on four sides is sometimes called a courtyard.

**Typical Patio.
Note the Patio Level Relative to the House. This Patio is Above the Wood Floor Framing. Extensive Wood Deterioration was Observed in the Crawl Space.**

Construction

Common Materials Common driveway and walkway materials include concrete, asphalt (blacktop), soil, gravel, flagstone, and pavers made from masonry units (bricks) or concrete. Common patio materials include concrete, flagstone, and pavers. Concrete patios are sometimes covered with tile or other finish materials, such as outdoor carpet. Concrete can be stamped and colored to provide the appearance of flagstone and pavers. Carpet is sometimes used to conceal cracked concrete.

Walkways are occasionally made using pressure treated wood or railroad ties. These materials are common when a walkway consists of different levels on a steep lot where the walkway forms a long stairway. Pressure treated wood smaller than 4x4 inches may not be rated for ground contact. Walkways made from wood can deteriorate in wet climates and may reach the end of their service life rapidly.

Construction Techniques Driveways, walkways, and patios rely on the soil and the base materials underneath to provide support and to resist settlement, uplift, and cracking. Preparation of this subbase is important for avoiding problems, and lack of proper subbase preparation is a common reason for problems. Driveways, walkways, and patios should be placed on compacted, dry soil which has had the top soil and vegetation removed.

Concrete driveways, walkways, and patios should be at least 3 ½ inches thick. **Crack control joints** should be installed in these structures at about 10 foot intervals and at depth of about ¼ of the slab thickness. Crack control joints are grooves installed soon after the concrete is poured. They allow the concrete to crack at the joint instead of cracking randomly in the slab. Cracks in control joints are normal and are not usually a deficiency unless the cracks are very wide or there is vertical displacement. **Isolation joints** should be installed where the driveway and walkway meet and where the driveway or where the walkway meets other structures such as the house or a column. Isolation joints are often made from asphalt impregnated fiberboard. Isolation joints reduce cracking by allowing the concrete and adjacent materials to move at a different rate.

Many concrete defects can be traced to an improper concrete mix, and to improper placing, finishing, and curing of the concrete. Concrete should not be placed when the temperature will fall below 32° F. within 24 hours. Spalling (popping of the surface layer) is a common result of concrete that freezes before it cures. Spalling can also be caused by freeze/thaw cycles and by deicing chemicals. Improper finishing techniques can cause problems, such as dusting (powdery material on the concrete's surface). Crazing (numerous small surface cracks) can be caused by concrete that dries too quickly (in hot weather) and by concrete that has too much water in the mix.

Asphalt (blacktop) driveways and walkways should be between at least 2 and 4 inches compacted (installed) thickness. Crack control and isolation joints are not necessary for asphalt driveways and walkways.

Many asphalt defects can be traced to improper use and maintenance. Asphalt softens when the temperature rises, so heavy vehicles and even cars can leave tire tracks. Turning wheels while the vehicle is stationary can be especially damaging. Asphalt cracks are inevitable and can be made worse in areas with freeze/thaw cycles. Regular sealing of asphalt is a necessary maintenance procedure to help reduce expansion of common cracks. Gasoline and especially diesel fuel can disintegrate asphalt.

Proper subbase preparation is essential for the long-term performance of driveways, walkways, and patios made from flagstone and pavers. Improperly installed flagstone and pavers are likely to shift and settle creating a trip hazard and places where water can accumulate. A subbase consisting of compacted gravel (a crusher run) and compacted sand is usually specified by manufacturers. Special polymeric sand may be used to fill the spaces between the flagstone and pavers in a manner similar to grout between ceramic tiles.

Driveways, walkways, and patios should slope away from the house and should not impede water flow. They should not be placed above the foundation level at or above the framing level. Hard surfaces such as these should slope away from the house at least ¼ inch per foot. It is common to install walkways several feet from the house, in which case a foundation planting area is often created between the house and the walkway. The walkway should be installed so that water flows over the walkway and is not trapped behind it. An alternative to water flowing over the walkway is installing a catch basin and a pipe running under the walkway.

Defects, Safety, Standards

Typical Defects
Typical defects that home inspectors should report include:

1. surface slopes toward the house or has inadequate slope away from the house,
2. cracking, crazing, delamination, dusting, popouts in concrete,
3. cracking and damage in asphalt,
4. surface is uplifted, usually caused by tree roots and expansive soil,
5. surface settled, usually caused by improper soil compaction and expansive soil,
6. ruts and thin gravel coverage in soil and gravel,
7. erosion and voids any surface,
8. sand soft or absent around flagstones and pavers,
9. flagstones and pavers loose, unstable, or damaged,
10. surface coverings (carpet, tiles, etc.) cracked or deteriorated,
11. evidence of ponding water exists (slip on ice hazard),
12. edging materials such as bricks (trip hazard) loose and deteriorated,
13. walkway is higher than foundation planting bed (water trapped near foundation).

There is no agreed upon standard for what constitutes a reportable crack in concrete driveways, walkways, and patios. **A common guideline** is that cracks that exceed ¼ inch in width or vertical displacement should be considered for reporting.

Refer to the Slab-on-Stem Wall Foundation section for more about concrete defects.

Safety Issues
A common defect of driveways, walkways, and patios is when one section is higher than the adjacent section. This creates a trip and fall hazard. **There is no agreed upon standard** for what constitutes a reportable trip hazard. **A common guideline** is that a ½ inch height difference between adjacent sections should be considered for repair.

Another common defect is standing water in depressions. This creates a slip and fall hazard, especially if the water freezes in the winter. **A common guideline** is that ⅜ inch of standing water after 24 hours should be considered for repair. Depressions are often difficult to detect unless there is water in the depression. Visible stains or algae on flat surfaces can be a clue that water remains in the stained area. The stains are often soil left after the water evaporates.

Accidents are possible where the view of oncoming traffic is restricted and where the driveway intersects with a high-traffic road. Possible safety issues include a driveway that enters the road at a blind curve or at a steep hill and a driveway where vision is restricted by plants. While not specifically required, home inspectors may wish to alert clients to these types of safety issues.

Driveways with a steep slope up or down can present challenges for clients. Vehicles that are long or low to the ground can scrape on driveways that transition quickly from a flat surface to a steep slope when the vehicle enters or leaves the driveway, or when the vehicle enters or leaves the garage. Steep slopes can be a safety issue and a convenience issue in areas subject to snow and ice. Cars and people may slip on steep surfaces. Driveways with a steep slope toward the garage can direct water into the garage.

Standards (1) local governments and homeowner associations may have regulations about issues such as driveway and walkway width, materials, and construction.

**This Part of the Driveway is Sliding Down the Hill.
The Large Rocks are Clues that there May Be Erosion and Drainage Issues.**

Sometimes Erosion or Settlement is Clearly Visible.

**Poor Base Compaction and Road Salt
May Be the Causes of This Spalling and Cracking.**

There are At Least Two Trip Hazards in This Walkway.

POOL AND SPA ACCESS BARRIERS

Introduction

Inspecting pool and spa access barriers is out of scope of a home inspection; however, some inspectors observe these components during the home inspection. This is especially true in areas where pools and spas are common. Around 400 children die and around 5,100 children are treated in emergency rooms annually due to pool related accidents, so it is important that inspectors either inspect these barriers or specifically disclaim inspection and recommend inspection by a qualified specialist.

Regulations regarding pool and spa access barriers vary significantly between jurisdictions. Differences include component specifications, effective dates when components were required, and requirements to retrofit existing pools and spas. Specifications presented in this book come from nationally recognized sources, but these specifications will vary between jurisdictions.

It is important to note that inspection of pool and spa access barriers involves inspection for the **presence and condition** of the components. Home inspectors should **not** report about the **adequacy** of the barriers or about **whether the barriers comply** with local, state, or federal regulations. Adequacy means whether or not the barriers are sufficient or capable of performing its intended functions.

Fences and Walls

The objective of fences and walls around pools and spas is to **keep unauthorized persons, especially children, out of the pool and spa area.** The fence or wall should, at least, conform to the specifications in the illustration. It is important to note the location of horizontal members. Horizontal members should either be at least 45 inches apart or they should be located on the pool side of the barrier.

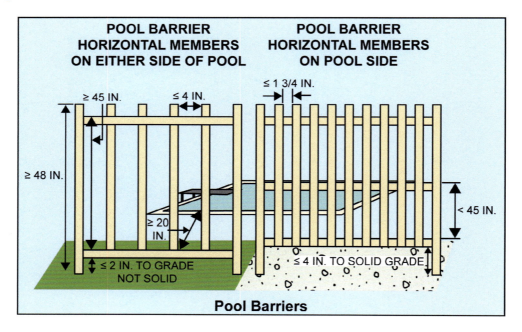

Pool Barriers

A fence or a wall that allows a person to climb the fence or wall should not be installed. Objects that provide something a person could use to access the pool area over the fence or wall should not be installed. Chain link or lattice fences should have openings not more than 1¾ inches wide. Walls should not have protrusions that a person could use to grasp and scale the wall. A bench, a pot, or a similar object that a person could use to climb over the fence or wall should not be near the fence or wall. A climbable tree that a person could use to climb over the fence or wall should not overhang the fence or wall. Issues such as trees, pots, and similar objects often occur on adjacent property. The home inspector should alert clients to these issues even if the client cannot affect conditions on the adjacent property.

Gates

Two common gate types allow access into a pool and spa area. Pedestrian gates are usually single gates. Double gates are usually intended to allow vehicle or pedestrian entry. A single gate should be self-closing and self-latching. A double gate should be self-latching, but self-closing is not required. Both types of gates should swing away from the pool. Gates should, at least, conform to the specifications in the illustration.

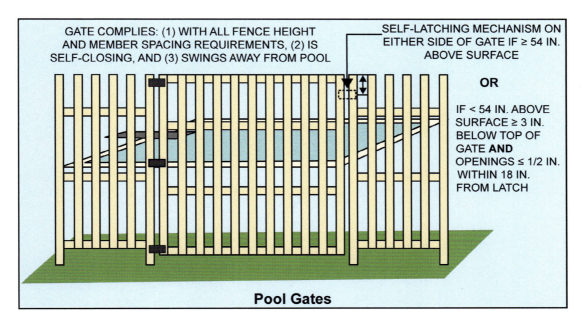

Pool Gates

House Walls

A house wall is frequently part of the access barrier system. Openings in the wall that provide access to the pool or spa should be equipped with some mechanism that either restricts unauthorized access to the pool or sounds an alarm if access is attempted. This includes openings such as the garage service door. **A door should be self-closing and self-latching.** This function is often disabled or not functioning properly on sliding doors. It is recommended, but not always required, that the door lock be at least 54 inches above the floor and that the door swing into the house. It is recommended, but not always required, that a window latch be at least 54 inches above the floor or that the window opening size be limited to 4 inches or less. An approved alarm may be substituted in place of the door and window requirements and recommendations.

Openings such as pet doors should not provide access to the pool area. Children can crawl through these openings.

Defects and Standards

Typical Defects Typical defects that home inspectors should report include:

1. absent, damaged, or deteriorated fence, wall, or gate,
2. low fence, wall, or gate, or low gate latch,
3. large openings in or under fence, wall, or gate,
4. climbable fence, wall, or gate,
5. single gate or door not self-closing and self-latching, or mechanism not functioning properly,
6. gate swings in toward the pool,
7. disabled door alarm,
8. pet door allows access to pool.

Standards (1) 2018 International Swimming Pool and Spa Code; (2) Virginia Graeme Baker Pool and Spa Safety Act (federal law, mostly applies to commercial pools); (3) local and state regulations; (4) Consumer Product Safety Commission (CSPC) pool safety guidelines.

**This Fence is Climbable.
Horizontal Supports are Less Than 48 Inches Apart and the Vertical Supports are More Than 1¾ Inches Apart.**

Lumber On the Other Side Could Be Used to Climb Over the Fence.

Someone Could Easily Fit Through the Space Between These Two Fences.

This Fence is Too Low.

1: Site Conditions

**These Gates Could Easily Be Opened or Climbed.
Gate in Right Photo Swings In Toward Pool.**

Please visit https://nationalhomeinspectorexam.org/prepare-for-the-exam/ and take advantage of the practice quizzes. The questions in the practice quizzes are designed to reflect the difficulty of the questions on the actual exam. The questions on the practice quizzes are not questions on the National Home Inspectors Exam. Passing the practice quizzes does not guarantee that you will pass the National exam. You will still need to study all topics to be prepared for the National exam.

2: EXTERIOR COMPONENTS

INSPECTION SCOPE

Exterior components that are in scope of a home inspection include the visible and accessible wall coverings (cladding), trim, eaves, wall penetration flashing and sealants, windows and doors, including the garage vehicle door and any operator, decks, balconies, stoops, porches, and associated steps, handrails, and guards.

Exterior components, such as wall coverings and trim, that are made from wood or wood composite materials should be covered with paint, stain, or some other type of coating. These **coatings** perform as **protection against deterioration** and as an **aesthetic feature**. Inspection of coatings is **in scope** of a home inspection if the coating appears **not to be performing its intended protective function**. This condition can be caused by deterioration, or by visibly poor application. Home inspectors are not required to report about the condition of these coatings unless they are visibly and significantly failing to perform their protective function.

EXTERIOR COMPONENT TERMS

The house exterior has many terms that a home inspector should know and be able to use. Here are some of the most common terms that a home inspector should know. Some of these definitions have been altered to conform to usage in residential construction.

Balcony: an outdoor platform that is located at the second story or above. A balcony may be supported by posts, or it may be cantilevered.

Bed molding: a thin decorative molding that covers the joint between the soffit and the frieze and between interior walls and ceilings; also used for shadow boxes and for other decorative purposes.

Bulkhead door: a horizontal or inclined door that provides access to an area under the house or to a storage area such as a cellar; sometimes referred to by the brand name Bilco.

Cantilever: a structural member (such as a floor joist) that extends horizontally beyond the vertical support (usually a wall) and has no other posts or supports.

Cornice: the exterior trim where the rafters and wall meet. Cornice usually encloses the eaves. Cornice often consists of the fascia, soffit, and bed molding.

Cornice return: the continuation of the cornice in a different direction, such as at a gable end.

Crown molding: a decorative molding that covers the joint between the soffit and frieze and between interior walls and ceilings; usually wider and more ornate than bed molding.

Deck: an outdoor recreational area that is usually, but not always, attached to the house. A deck is supported by posts. A deck is usually not covered. See **Balcony** and **Patio**.

Eaves: the extension of the rafters beyond the exterior wall of the buildings. See **Cornice**.

EIFS: an acronym for Exterior Insulation and Finish System, a type of wall covering that looks like stucco. EIFS is not stucco and should not be described as such.

Fascia (eaves): vertical trim at the end of the eaves, usually part of the cornice.

Frieze: vertical trim that connects or covers the top course of wall covering with the bottom of the cornice. A frieze board usually hides the termination of wall covering, such as brick and stone.

Lintel (angle iron): a horizontal structural component that carries a load from above. Lintels are used in masonry construction over openings, such as windows and doors. Lintels are usually made from L-shaped steel, but may be made from steel reinforced concrete, or from wood.

Porch: an outdoor area that is attached to the house. Porches are usually covered, which is a way to distinguish a porch from a deck.

Soffit (eaves): the horizontal trim that covers the rafters, usually part of the cornice.

Stoop: a small platform that serves as a landing on the exterior side of a door.

Veneer: a decorative surface applied over the exterior walls of a house. The term is usually applied to wall coverings such as brick and natural stone.

Wall covering (cladding): a non-load-bearing material or assembly that is applied over the exterior walls of a house.

Water (weather)-resistive barrier (WRB): a material that resists penetration of liquid water; usually describes materials such as asphalt-impregnated building paper (e.g., #15 felt) and house wraps.

Wythe (withe): (1) a course of masonry (usually brick) that separates flues in a masonry chimney; (2) a vertical masonry wall that is one masonry unit thick. A typical brick veneer wall is one wythe thick.

EXTERIOR WALL COVERINGS AND RELATED TRIM

Introduction

An **exterior wall covering** (cladding) is a **non-load-bearing** material or assembly that is applied over the exterior walls of a house. **Houses built using wood-frame and light-gauge steel construction need a wall covering to shed liquid water.**

Wall coverings are often referred to as **veneers**. There are three categories of veneers. Most wall covering veneers are attached veneers, so called because the veneer is attached to the house with fasteners. All types of siding, and exterior insulation and finish system (EIFS), are **attached veneers**. Brick and natural stone are **anchored veneers**. Anchored veneers are supported directly on the foundation, or on reinforced framing, and are anchored to the house walls to prevent the veneer from rotating away from the structure. Stucco and artificial and some natural stone are **adhered veneers**, so called because the components are attached to the house walls with mortar that acts as a "glue" to adhere the components to the wall.

Houses built using materials such as structural brick and stone, concrete masonry units (concrete blocks), and insulated concrete forms do not need an exterior wall covering. A water-repellant material, such as stucco may be applied directly to the exterior walls of the house, or a coat of paint may be applied as a water-repellant material. In these cases, the stucco or paint is a coating, not a wall covering. A wall covering such as brick may be installed as a wall covering over structural materials. Log home exterior walls are usually stained, sealed, or painted, and usually do not have a separate wall covering.

Exterior wall coverings serve two functions. Their first function is to **shed liquid water** and keep it from entering into the home. Their second function is to **protect any water-resistive barrier** (WRB) that may be present under the wall covering. Of course, exterior wall coverings also serve an important architectural and aesthetic function, but these issues are out of scope of a home inspection.

Exterior wall coverings shed water, but are not water-resistive barriers. It must be assumed that water will get behind wall coverings; therefore, another line of defense is required. This second, and most important, line of defense is the water-resistive barrier, and flashing under the wall covering. When the water-resistive barrier and flashing are properly installed, **water that gets behind the wall covering should drain down the water-resistive barrier and out of the weep holes or other openings.**

The exterior wall coverings that home inspectors are most likely to encounter are discussed in this section. This is not a discussion of all exterior wall coverings.

Adhered Masonry Veneer

Adhered masonry veneer (AMV) is usually a manufactured material made to look like natural stone and sometimes like brick. It is installed by setting the material in a mortar bed applied to wire lath placed over sheathed wood-framed walls and a water-resistive barrier, using techniques similar to those used to install stucco. AMV has been available since the 1960s, though it is most common on homes built since the mid-1980s. This material is also called artificial stone, cultured stone, and manufactured stone. Cast stone is a different product. Do not describe artificial stone as natural stone, cast stone, or brick.

Typical Adhered Masonry Veneer Installation.

Adhered veneer using natural stone is available. It is installed in a manner similar to artificial stone veneer and it can be difficult to distinguish between the two materials. The pigment layer of artificial stone may be only at the surface, so scraping a small inconspicuous area may sometimes distinguish between the two materials. Artificial stone has a more hollow sound when tapped, but this distinguishing method requires experience to use, and can yield an incorrect identification.

Adhered masonry veneer should be installed according to manufacturer's instructions. These instructions may vary based on the manufacturer, the type of material being installed, and the location of the house.

Adhered veneers are (artificial and natural) a known problematic wall covering. Problems are usually caused by **failure to install recommended flashing and sealants** around penetrations, such as windows and doors. Common installation guidelines include installing a backer rod and sealant around the perimeter of windows and doors, and installing header flashing above windows and doors. Problems are also caused by failure to install recommended weep screed, and failure to maintain recommended clearances between the adhered veneer and grade, and between adhered veneer and the roof. Home inspectors should carefully inspect adhered veneer installations.

Typical Defects
Typical defects that home inspectors should report include:

1. inadequate clearance above grade, hard surfaces, and roof coverings,
2. absent or improperly installed weep screed,
3. blocked weep screed drain holes,
4. absent and deteriorated flashing and sealant around doors, windows, other penetrations, and at transitions between wall coverings,
5. absent and improperly installed flashing and kick out flashing at wall intersections,
6. absent, loose, and damaged stones and mortar,
7. exposed lath,
8. veneer not fully embedded in mortar (not usually visible),
9. efflorescence on stone or mortar,
10. water on stone or mortar long after rain has ceased falling.

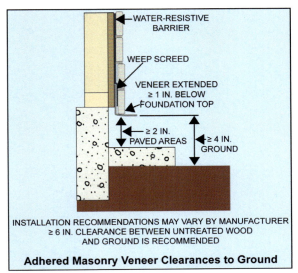

Adhered Masonry Veneer Clearances to Ground

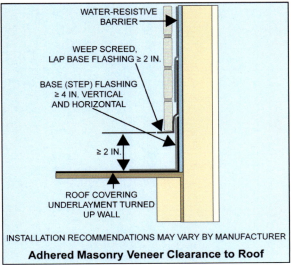

Adhered Masonry Veneer Clearance to Roof

2: Exterior Components

Adhered Veneer Too Close To Roof.

Adhered Veneer Too Close To Hard Surface.

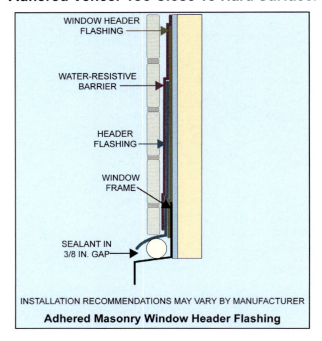
Adhered Masonry Window Header Flashing

Sealant Absent at Wall Covering Transition (Left) and at Window Jamb (Right).

Absent Flashing at Window Header.

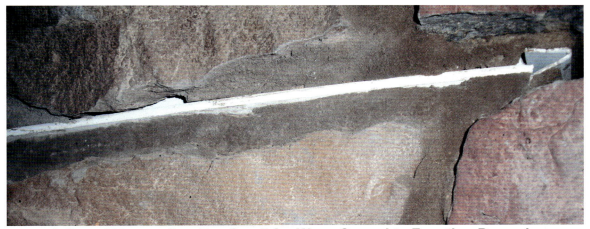

Adhered Veneer Gap Too Small for Weep Screed to Function Properly.

Standards (1) IRC 2018 Section R703; (2) Masonry Veneer Manufacturer's Association Guidelines; (3) manufacturer's instructions.

Aluminum Siding (also Steel Siding)

Aluminum siding and steel siding are most commonly seen as interlocking horizontal strips. They are also seen as vertical panels. Finishes include smooth and textured simulating wood. These types of siding should be installed by fastening the siding to sheathed walls covered by a water-resistive barrier. Aluminum siding was first available in the late 1940s and was most popular during 1950s and 1960s. It is currently available but rarely installed in many markets. Steel siding is uncommon on houses in most markets.

There is a widely held belief that metal wall covering and roof covering materials must be grounded or bonded. **There is no such requirement.** The mechanical and electrical connections between pieces of metal wall coverings and roof coverings are not sufficient to create a continuous current path to any grounding or bonding conductor connection point.

Typical Defects Typical defects that home inspectors should report include:

1. absent and deteriorated flashing and sealant around doors, windows, and other penetrations,
2. absent and improperly installed flashing and kick out flashing at wall intersections,
3. damaged and deteriorated siding and trim,
4. fading or pealing finish,
5. oxidation where bare metal is exposed,
6. buckling siding, often caused by siding being fastened too tightly against the wall.

Standards (1) IRC 2018 Section R703; (2) grounding/bonding of metal siding is not required by model codes, but may be required in some jurisdictions; (3) manufacturer's instructions.

Typical Aluminum Siding with Typical Damage.

Aluminum Siding Deteriorated by Contact with Concrete or Masonry.

Asbestos Cement Siding

Asbestos cement siding is most commonly seen as rectangular shingles measuring about 18 by 24 inches. It is also seen as horizontal lap siding. Finishes include smooth and textured. Thickness is about ⅛ inch. It was installed by fastening siding to sheathed walls, preferably over a water-resistive barrier. It was first available in the early 1900s and was most popular from 1920s to 1950s.

Asbestos was banned in most building products in 1973. This siding is no longer available, but some fiber cement siding manufacturers produce products that mimic some common types of asbestos cement siding. More information about asbestos products is available at: http://www2.epa.gov/asbestos/us-federal-bans-asbestos.

Inspection for and reporting of hazardous materials, such as asbestos, is out of scope of a home inspection. Most home inspectors, however, report the presence of suspected asbestos containing materials and recommend that the materials be tested to determine if asbestos is present. Asbestos abatement and containment protocols must be followed during cutting, sanding, and removal; these procedures can be costly.

Typical Defects Typical defects that home inspectors should report include:

1. absent and deteriorated flashing and sealant around doors, windows, and other penetrations,
2. absent and improperly installed flashing and kick out flashing at wall intersections,
3. damaged and deteriorated siding and trim,
4. fading or pealing finish,

Safety Issues **Asbestos is a known carcinogen when inhaled or ingested.** Asbestos is not a safety issue when intact and not frieable (airborne).

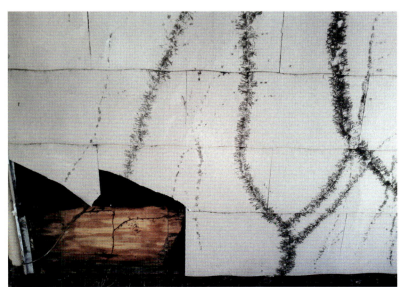

Typical Asbestos Cement Siding with Significant Damage.

Brick Veneer (also Natural Stone)

Brick and natural stone veneer are available in a wide variety of shapes, sizes, and colors. The most common brick is the **modular brick** which is 7⅝ inches long by 2¼ inches tall by 3⅝ inches deep. Queen and king size bricks are occasionally encountered. Natural stone is occasionally used as adhered masonry veneer. Refer to the Adhered Masonry Veneer section for more information.

Brick and natural stone have been used since ancient times and are still widely used, although natural stone has been replaced by adhered masonry veneer in many newer houses. Brick and natural stone are also called anchored veneer because the veneer is attached to the structural wall using metal wall ties.

If Supported on the Foundation, It is Probably Natural Stone Veneer.

**If Not Supported on the Foundation, It is Probably Adhered Veneer.
Note Absence of Weep Screed at the Transition Between Framing and Foundation.
Flashing Alone is Not Adequate.**

Brick and natural stone veneer are usually installed by placing the material on a structural support such as a foundation ledge or on a lintel (L shaped steel). Both veneer types must be installed over sheathed walls and a water-resistive barrier. They are typically installed with an air space between the material and the wall.

Brick and natural stone veneer may be supported by wood framing (except in high seismic risk zones). The veneer should be supported by a lintel when supported by framing. The lintel may be anchored to the studs using lag screws, or the lintel may bear on at least three rafters. Brick support details are often concealed during a home inspection. Home inspectors should look for cracks in the bricks and mortar, and for roof framing deformation as clues that brick support details may be improperly installed.

Bricks can expand due to changes in temperature and moisture. Brick veneer that is supported by different structural components may move at different rates. This expansion and movement can cause cracking. Expansion (movement) joints should be placed at various locations to accommodate expansion and movement. For example, an expansion joint should be installed where brick and stone veneer supported by framing meets veneer supported by the foundation.

An expansion joint is formed by omitting mortar from between bricks and filling the joint with a backer rod and sealant. Expansion joints are uncommon in residential construction; however, their absence can be the explanation for some cracks observed in brick veneer.

A steel lintel is usually installed to support the veneer above openings such as windows and doors. Each end of a lintel should bear on at least four inches of the supporting veneer; additional bearing distance is recommended for lintels over large openings such as garage vehicle doors. Lintels should be covered with a rust-resistant coating, such as paint. Rusted lintels may expand and cause cracks in the veneer around openings.

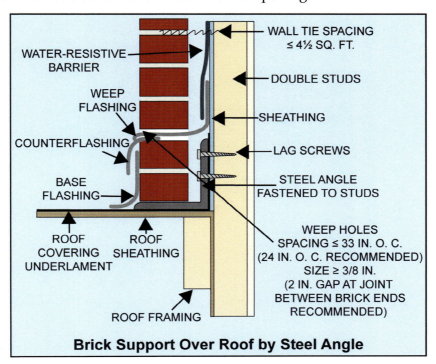

Brick Support Over Roof by Steel Angle

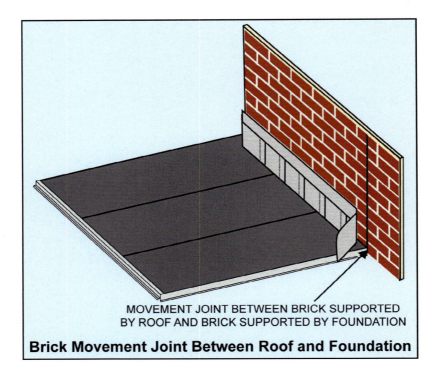

Brick Movement Joint Between Roof and Foundation

Mortar is used to bind brick and natural stone veneer to each other. Bed joints (horizontal joints) and head joints (vertical joints) are usually about ⅜ thick and may vary between ¼ and ½ inch thick. Joints are sometimes up to ¾ inch thick, especially the bed joint below the first course; however, joints this thick are subject to cracking.

Mortar joints are usually tooled for aesthetic reasons, and to help shed water. Joints that provide a shelf where water can collect (such as the raked and struck joints) are not recommended. Home inspectors should report the presence of these mortar joints, and should recommend monitoring for deterioration of bricks and mortar.

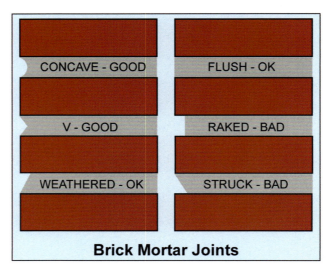

Brick Mortar Joints

The brick industry uses many terms to identify bricks when installed. The following illustration presents some of the most common terms.

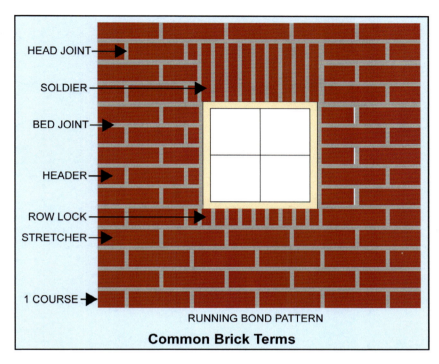

Common Brick Terms

Typical Defects Typical defects that home inspectors should report include:

1. absent and deteriorated flashing and sealant around doors, windows, and other penetrations,
2. absent and improperly installed flashing and kick out flashing at wall intersections,
3. cracked and deteriorated mortar,
4. cracks run through bricks and stone (often more serious than cracks in mortar),
5. different color mortar (evidence of repairs),
6. bricks and stone rotating away from the structure,
7. rusted lintels,
8. absent and improperly installed weep holes at currently required locations including foundation and above and below windows and doors (weep holes requirement is relatively recent), deteriorated or spalling brick and mortar,
9. improper mortar joints that may allow water to deteriorate brick and mortar,
10. efflorescence,
11. deformed lintels and framing,
12. absent movement joint where bricks are supported by different components (e.g., framing and foundation).

Standards (1) IRC 2018 Section R703; (2) Brick Industry Association Technical Notes; (3) manufacturer's instructions.

Acceptable Base and Counterflashing. Kick out Flashing is Too Small.

No Visible Counterflashing. Unacceptable Raked Mortar Joint.

White Powder is Efflorescence, a Clue That There May Be a Water Issue.

2: Exterior Components 41

Three Pictures Above Show Significant Brick Veneer Cracking.
Upper Left and Lower Pictures Show Cracks Seen on the Same Side of the House.
Upper Right Picture Shows Foundation Wall Crack on the Same Side of the House.

Weep Holes Should Be Above Grade.
Picture Courtesy of Welmoed Sisson

Different Color Mortar is a Clue That Repairs May Have Been Made.

Typical Rusted Lintel.

Fiber Cement Siding

Fiber cement siding is most commonly seen as horizontal lap siding. It is also seen as vertical panels and as horizontal strips that simulate wood shingles. Finishes include smooth and textured patterns that simulate wood. Thickness is between $^5/_{16}$ and ½ inch. It is installed by fastening siding to walls covered by a water-resistive barrier. Fiber cement siding has been available for about one hundred years. It was not until the mid-1980s that this siding became widely available in North America, and it has been increasingly popular since then. It is currently a widely installed wall covering. This siding is sometimes referred to by the brand name Hardie® after the company that first introduced it in the North American market. **It is not correct to use brand names to describe materials.** There are other fiber cement siding manufacturers.

Fiber cement siding should be installed according to manufacturer's instructions. These instructions will vary based on the manufacturer, the model of siding being installed, and the location of the house.

2: Exterior Components

Typical Defects Typical defects that home inspectors should report include:

1. inadequate clearance above grade, hard surfaces, and roof coverings (1 or 2 inches above hard surfaces and above roof coverings, 6 inches above grade, all clearances per manufacturer's instructions),
2. absent and deteriorated flashing and sealant around doors, windows, and other penetrations,
3. absent and deteriorated sealant at corner boards,
4. absent movement gap (about ¼ inch) at vertical surfaces (e.g., corner boards, penetrations) and at horizontal flashing,
5. absent blocks and head-flashing around wall penetrations such as exhaust duct terminations and hose bibbs,
6. absent and improperly installed flashing and kick out flashing at wall intersections,
7. damaged and deteriorated siding,
8. improperly installed fasteners (e.g., wrong fastener type, improper location, over and under driven),
9. excessively wavy or buckled siding,
10. absent or deteriorated paint at the bottom edge.

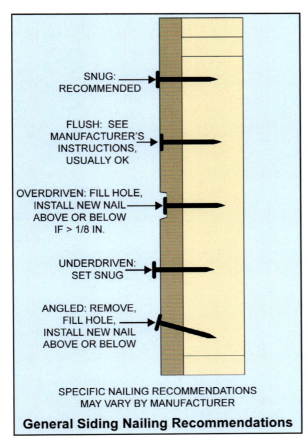

General Siding Nailing Recommendations

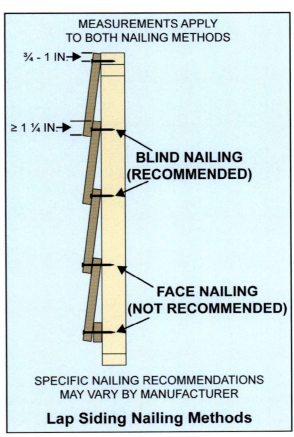

Lap Siding Nailing Methods

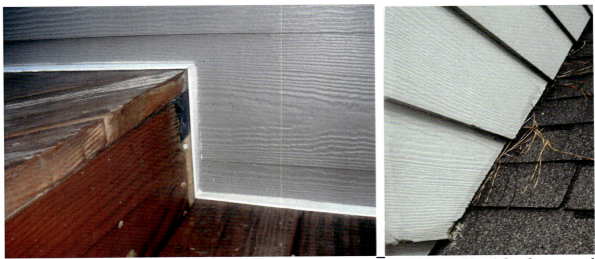
Fiber Cement Siding Should Have 1 or 2 Inches Clearance Above Hard Surfaces and Above Roof Coverings.

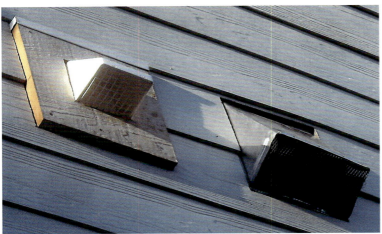
Wall Penetration Properly Blocked and Flashed (Left) and Improperly Installed (Right).

Penetrations Should Not Occur at Joints. Hose Bibbs Should Be Blocked and Flashed.

Nails in Wrong Location. Siding May Split.

Buckled Fiber Cement Siding. Possibly Installed Without Movement Gaps.

**Absent Caulk at Inside Corner Board.
No Movement Gap (About ¼ inch) at Inside Corner Board.**

<u>**Standards**</u> (1) IRC 2018 Section R703; (2) manufacturer's instructions.

Hardboard (Composite Wood) Siding

Hardboard siding is most commonly seen as horizontal lap siding. It is also seen as vertical panels and as horizontal strips that simulate wood shingles. Finishes include smooth and textured patterns that simulate wood. Thickness is about 7/16 inch. It should be installed by fastening siding to walls covered by a water-resistive barrier. This material was first available in the early 1900s and became widely available in the 1930s. It was most popular from 1940s through 1990s, and is experiencing a comeback in current construction. **Do not describe this material as plywood, oriented strand board, or wood siding.** Newer versions of material are sometimes called **composite wood** siding and **engineered wood** siding.

Hardboard siding should be installed according to manufacturer's instructions. These instructions will vary based on the manufacturer, the model of siding being installed, and the location of the house.

Some hardboard siding is manufactured using wood byproducts and binders. **Older versions of hardboard siding are a known problematic wall covering.** Many of the problems experienced with this siding were caused by improper installation, and by improper maintenance (painting and caulking). Class action lawsuits alleging product defects were filed against many manufacturers of this wall covering in the 1990s. These lawsuits were settled, and the recovery funds were exhausted many years ago.

Typical Defects Typical defects that home inspectors should report include:

1. inadequate clearance above grade, hard surfaces, flashing, and roof coverings (1 or 2 inches above hard surfaces and above roof coverings, 1 to 6 inches above grade, all clearances per manufacturer's instructions),
2. absent and deteriorated flashing and sealant around doors, windows, and other penetrations,
3. absent and deteriorated sealant at corner boards,
4. absent movement gap (about ¼ inch) at vertical surfaces (e.g., corner boards, penetrations) and at horizontal flashing,
5. absent and improperly installed flashing and kick out flashing at wall intersections,
6. damaged and deteriorated siding,
7. improperly installed fasteners (e.g., wrong fastener type, improper location, over and under driven),
8. excessively wavy or buckled siding,
9. absent or deteriorated paint at the bottom edge.

Standards (1) IRC 2018 Section R703; (2) manufacturer's instructions.

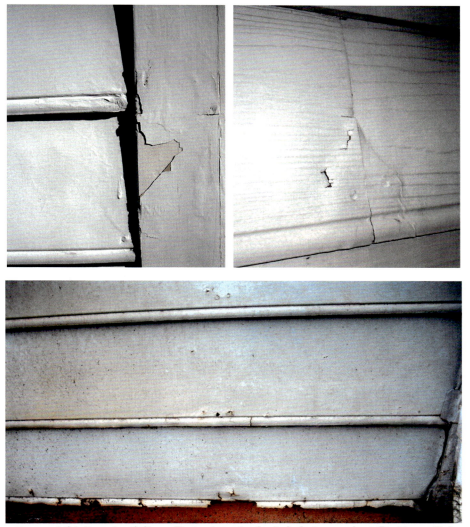
Hardboard Siding is Often Deteriorated at Joints and at Bottom Edges.

Example of Why Kick Out Flashing is Important.

Insulbrick Siding

Insulbrick siding is asphalt impregnated fiberboard that is embossed to simulate brick. It is most commonly seen as rectangular panels measuring about 48 by 24 inches. It is usually installed by fastening directly to wood plank sheathing without a water-resistive barrier. This material was available from the 1930s through the 1960s. It is common in some markets, mostly in Canada and the northern United States. This material is also called Insulstone and Insulwood.

Typical Defects Typical defects that home inspectors should report include:

1. inadequate clearance above grade, hard surfaces, and roof coverings,
2. absent and deteriorated flashing and sealant around doors, windows, and other penetrations,
3. absent and improperly installed flashing and kick out flashing at wall intersections,
4. damaged and deteriorated siding.

Standards This siding is no longer available, so there are no current standards for installation.

Stucco – Cement

Three-coat (also called hard coat) cement stucco is installed by applying scratch, brown, finish layers of Portland cement, sand, lime, and water on wire lath placed over a water-resistive barrier, such as building wrap, Grade D paper, or a liquid coating. **Two layers** of building wrap or paper are recommended because the stucco will adhere to the top layer and interfere with the drainage plane.

The total thickness of all three layers is approximately ⅞ inch. Two-coat cement stucco may be installed on masonry walls and eliminates the scratch coat, lath, and water-resistive barrier. Cement stucco installed since the 1980s often uses a colored finish coat that combines color and acrylics with the Portland cement.

Proprietary one-coat and two-coat cement stucco systems also exist, and are popular in some parts of the United States, such as the Southwest and parts of California. Most systems advertised as one-coat are really two-coat systems. These systems often consist of a water-resistive barrier under a Polystyrene, or other type of insulation board, that is covered by metal lath. One layer of a proprietary Portland cement-based product is applied over the lath to a thickness between ⅜ and ½ inch. A colored finish layer may be applied or the base layer may be painted. Painting may not be an approved method of finishing these systems; however, painting is a common finishing method in some markets. These systems are sometimes called hybrid stucco.

Three-coat stucco (two coats over masonry) has been used since ancient times, but is less common today in many markets. This material is also called exterior plaster.

Stucco, especially proprietary one-coat and two-coat systems, should be installed according to manufacturer's instructions. These instructions may vary based on the manufacturer, the type of system being installed, and the location of the house.

Evidence of water infiltration may not be visible during an inspection. Home inspectors may wish to report this limitation and recommend further evaluation.

One Type of One-Coat Stucco

<u>**Typical Defects**</u> Typical defects that home inspectors should report include:

1. inadequate clearance above grade, hard surfaces, and roof coverings (2 inches above hard surfaces and above roof coverings, 4 inches above grade, all clearances per manufacturer's instructions),
2. absent and deteriorated flashing and sealant around doors, windows, and other penetrations,
3. absent and improperly installed flashing and kick out flashing at wall intersections,
4. absent and improperly installed weep screed,
5. blocked weep screed drain holes,
6. cracks, especially at wall penetrations, and bulges, especially at the band joists,
7. damage,
8. efflorescence and spalling,
9. absent and improperly installed crack control and expansion joints,
10. trim slopes toward wall,
11. loose trim,
12. stucco is installed as a roof on a horizontal surface using a standard weather-resistant barrier; this allows water to enter and swell wood below causing stucco cracking.

<u>**Standards**</u> (1) IRC 2018 Section R703; (2) manufacturer's instructions.

Typical Stucco Crack at Wall Penetration.

Stucco Crack with Displacement.

Stucco Damage.

Too Close to Hard Surface.

All Pictures Above are One-Coat Stucco.

Stucco – EIFS

Exterior Insulation and Finish System (EIFS) is often thought of, and is sometimes described as, stucco. **EIFS is not stucco. It is a proprietary wall covering system that looks like stucco.**

Two EIFS systems exist. (1) The barrier system relies on installing all components exactly according to manufacturer's instructions, and relies on these components remaining sealed against water entry. Barrier systems are no longer allowed in many jurisdictions. (2) The drained system relies on the traditional combination of a water-resistive barrier and penetration flashing to provide a secondary drainage system for water that infiltrates behind the EIFS.

EIFS should be installed by applying a one layer synthetic finish coat over a fiber reinforced synthetic base coat applied on insulating sheathing that is attached to structural sheathing. A drained system adds a water-resistive barrier and integrated flashing between the structural sheathing and the insulating sheathing. EIFS has been available since the 1960s, and was most popular from the late 1970s to the early 1990s. It is still available and used today. EIFS is sometimes referred to by the brand name Dryvit®, after the company that first introduced it in the North American market. **It is not correct to use brand names to describe materials.**

EIFS should be installed according to manufacturer's instructions. These instructions may vary based on the manufacturer, the type of system being installed, and the location of the house.

Older (barrier) versions of EIFS are a known problematic wall covering. Many of the problems experienced with this wall covering were caused by improper installation. **Evidence of moisture intrusion is often concealed**; therefore, evaluation and invasive moisture testing by an EIFS specialist is a prudent recommendation, especially for barrier systems installed before the early 2000s. Class action lawsuits alleging product defects were filed against many manufacturers of this wall covering. These lawsuits were settled, and the recovery funds were exhausted many years ago.

<u>**Typical Defects**</u> Typical defects that home inspectors should report include:

1. inadequate clearance above grade, hard surfaces, and roof coverings,
2. absent and deteriorated flashing and sealant around doors, windows, and other penetrations,
3. absent and improperly installed flashing and kick out flashing at wall intersections,
4. absent and improperly installed weep screed,
5. blocked weep screed drain holes,
6. cracks, especially at wall penetrations, and bulges, especially at the band joists,
7. damage,
8. efflorescence and spalling,
9. thin base and finish coats, especially at edges and corners,
10. trim flat or slopes toward wall,
11. loose trim,
12. exposed mesh.

<u>**Standards**</u> (1) IRC 2018 Section R703; (2) manufacturer's instructions (must be followed precisely).

Vinyl Siding

Vinyl siding is most commonly seen as interlocking horizontal strips. It is also seen as vertical panels, and as strips that simulate wood shingles and shakes. It comes in many colors and finishes. It should be installed by fastening the siding to sheathed walls covered by a water-resistive barrier. This siding was first widely available in the 1960s and has been increasingly popular since then. It is currently one of the most widely installed wall coverings. This material is sometimes called polymer or polymeric siding.

Vinyl siding is relatively inexpensive and is virtually maintenance-free. It does, however, have some disadvantages. The color can fade over time, especially on sides of the house exposed to sunlight. Vinyl siding can be painted with paint made for this purpose, but once painted it must be repainted regularly. Vinyl siding is easily damaged. It can be a challenge to replace damaged pieces with matching material. Vinyl siding is known to warp when exposed to heat, and it can become brittle when exposed to extreme cold.

Vinyl siding should be installed according to manufacturer's instructions. These instructions may vary based on the manufacturer, the type of siding being installed, and the location of the house.

Typical Defects Typical defects that home inspectors should report include:

1. absent flashing and channel trim around doors, windows, and other penetrations,
2. inadequate clearance above grade, hard surfaces, and roof coverings,
3. inadequate lap at joints (about 1 inch),
4. inadequate space (about ¼ inch) at vertical trim to allow for expansion,
5. fastened too tight against wall; each piece should be free to move with expansion and contraction,
6. absent and improperly installed flashing and kick out flashing at wall intersections,
7. damage, deterioration, faded color,
8. absent starter course.

Standards (1) IRC 2018 Section R703; (2) manufacturer's instructions (must be followed precisely).

Vinyl Siding Should Have At Least ¼ Inch Clearance Above Hard Surfaces and Roofs.

Typical Minor Vinyl Siding Damage.

 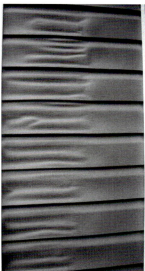

Vinyl Siding Will Melt and Warp. Cause of Left Picture is Heat From A Grill. Cause of Right Picture Warping is Reflection of Infrared From a Low E Window.

Vinyl Siding Joints Should Lap At Least 1 Inch.

Wood Structural Panel Siding

Wood structural panels used as siding are made from plywood. They are most commonly seen as 4x8 foot and 4x9 foot vertical panels. They come in a wide variety of textures and panel patterns. Thickness is between ⅜ and ½ inch. Panels should be installed by fastening siding to walls over a water-resistive barrier. Plywood was first available in the late 1800s, became widely available in the 1930s, and was most popular during 1940s through 1990s. It is currently available, but has a small share as siding in many markets. Do not describe this material as hardboard or wood siding. Plywood siding is often referred to as T1-11 because the indentations can be 1 inch wide and the raised section can be 11 inches wide. Wood structural panel siding comes in many different textures and panel patterns so the term T1-11 is not an accurate description of this material.

Wood structural panel siding should be installed according to manufacturer's instructions. These instructions will vary based on the manufacturer, the model of siding being installed, and the location of the house.

Typical Defects Typical siding defects that home inspectors should report include:

1. inadequate clearance above grade, hard surfaces, and roof coverings (2 inches above hard surfaces and above roof coverings, 6 inches above grade),
2. absent and deteriorated flashing and sealant around doors, windows, other penetrations, and at horizontal joints between sheets,
3. absent and improperly installed flashing and kick out flashing at wall intersections,
4. damaged and deteriorated siding; deterioration often found near the bottom edge of the siding,
5. improperly installed fasteners (e.g., wrong fastener type, improper location, over and under driven),
6. absent or deteriorated paint at the bottom edge.

Standards (1) IRC 2018 Section R703; (2) manufacturer's instructions.

Plywood is Deteriorated Because It is Too Close to Grade and Hard Surface.

Wood Siding

Wood siding comes in many styles, including planks, shingles, and shakes. Planks installed horizontally may be lapped (clapboard), or may have edge treatments such as rabbit, tongue-and-groove, and shiplap. Planks installed vertically may have wood strips covering vertical joints (board and batten). Shakes and shingles are the same as those used as roof coverings (See Roof Coverings). Thickness of plank siding is usually between $\frac{3}{8}$ and $\frac{1}{2}$ inch in modern installations, but may be different in older installations. Installation depends on the siding material. A water-resistive barrier is required under most of these materials for modern installations, but was often not used in older installations. These materials have been used since ancient times. They are still available, but are not widely used in many markets.

Wood siding should be installed according to manufacturer's instructions. These instructions will vary based on the manufacturer, the type of siding being installed, and the location of the house.

Typical Defects Typical defects that home inspectors should report include:

1. inadequate clearance above grade, hard surfaces, and roof coverings (2 inches above hard surfaces and above roof coverings, 6 inches above grade),
2. absent and deteriorated flashing and sealant around doors, windows, other penetrations,
3. absent and improperly installed flashing and kick out flashing at wall intersections,
4. damaged and deteriorated siding; deterioration often found near the bottom edge of the siding,
5. improperly installed fasteners (e.g., wrong fastener type, improper location, over and under driven),
6. absent or deteriorated paint at the bottom edge.

Standards (1) IRC 2018 Section R703; (2) manufacturer's instructions.

Wood Plank Siding Too Close to Grade.

Typical Wood Shingle Siding.

Wall Covering Trim

Trim associated with exterior wall coverings can be functional, decorative, or both. Functional trim provides a consistent and stable surface against which wall coverings can terminate. Sealants are more effective and last longer when applied to a consistent and stable surface. Examples of functional trim include inside and outside corner trim, channel trim used with vinyl siding, and various styles of moldings and casing around windows and doors, such as brick molding. Examples of decorative trim include pediments above doors and windows and other facing materials. Decorative trim is often installed on top of the wall covering. Decorative stucco trim is usually installed under the stucco coating. Modern stucco trim is usually made from foam. Stucco trim on older buildings is usually made from wood.

Trim that is made from the same material as the wall covering and that is required to be used when installing the wall covering is evaluated as part of the wall covering inspection. Examples of this trim include J and F channel trim for vinyl siding. Decorative trim that is integrated into the wall covering is also evaluated with the wall covering. Examples of this trim include projecting trim around windows and doors installed with stucco, and decorative trim (such as pediments) installed with vinyl siding.

Trim made of materials different from the wall covering is evaluated as a separate, but related, component. Examples of this trim include wood and composite wood corner boards installed with wood-based siding and fiber cement siding, moldings and casings around windows and doors, and all attached decorative trim such as pediments above doors and windows and pilasters at the sides of doors.

Trim is not required, except when specified by the wall covering manufacturer's installation instructions. Lack of trim where it is usually found, such as corner boards, may be an indication of deficient or amateur construction. These situations should be evaluated carefully, especially for signs of water infiltration.

Trim on buildings constructed before about 2000 is usually made from wood or wood-products and requires the same clearances to surfaces such as earth and concrete as any other wood product. Trim on recently constructed buildings may be made of engineered materials or PVC that look like wood but may not require the same clearances to surfaces as wood-based products.

Typical Defects Typical defects that home inspectors should report include:

1. inadequate clearance above grade, hard surfaces, and roof coverings,
2. absent and deteriorated sealant around doors and windows,
3. damaged and deteriorated trim; deterioration often found near the bottom edge of the trim,
4. trim slopes toward the house,
5. absent or deteriorated paint at the bottom edge.

Standards Manufacturer's instructions (for trim required by the wall covering manufacturer and for engineered trim).

Corner Boards are Often Unpainted on the Bottom Resulting in Deterioration. Corner Board on Right is Too Close to the Roof Covering, and is Deteriorated.

Watch for Trim Sloped Toward the House.

FLASHING AND SEALANTS

Keeping Water Out of the House

Water is a major cause of damage to houses. Building components that get wet and stay wet deteriorate and are prone to mold infestation. Homes built before the 1970s were more forgiving of occasional wetting because small amounts of water could dry before causing damage. Homes built since the 1970s may be tighter and more energy efficient, thus, water may stay on components longer and cause more damage. Homes built since 2000 are likely to be even tighter and less forgiving. Keeping water out of homes is increasingly important, and so is inspecting for properly installed and maintained flashing and sealants.

The function of flashing is to create an effective, long term, and maintenance-free barrier against water infiltration into the home. This distinguishes flashing from sealants such as caulk and roofing cement. Sealants require periodic replacement whereas properly installed flashing should function for a long time without replacement. **Sealants installed in place of flashing and sealants used to repair flashing are a reportable defect.**

We now know that flashing and sealants do not create a perfect barrier against water infiltration. Newer homes are supposed to be designed with a drainage system that assumes water will find its way past flashing, sealants, and other barriers. This is why flashing and sealants should be installed in conjunction with a water-resistive barrier that covers the protected area and creates a drainage plane. **Water that finds its way behind the flashing or sealants should drain down the flashing and the water-resistive barrier and out through weep holes or other outlets.**

Flashing should be installed, when practical, wherever an opening exists where water could enter the home. Flashing should also be installed wherever trim or other material projects from a wall. A sealant may be installed where flashing is not practical. Wall penetration flashing should be installed at doors and windows, where different wall covering materials meet, at horizontal seams in some wall covering materials, such as panel siding, and where vents and exhaust ducts penetrate a wall. Roof penetration flashing is installed where components such as plumbing vents, electrical cables, HVAC vents, and exhaust ducts penetrate the roof. Flashing is also installed around roof penetrations such as skylights. Sidewall and headwall flashing is installed where a vertical sidewall intersects a roof. This occurs at locations such as chimneys, at second story walls above first story roofs, and above bay windows. Valley flashing is installed on the roof where two descending slope roofs intersect. Roof flashing is discussed in the Roof Coverings chapter.

Wall Penetration Flashing

Description Window and door flashing in older homes is usually made from galvanized steel or aluminum. These materials are still used for components such as L flashing above window and door header trim, and Z flashing at the horizontal seam between panel siding. Wall penetration flashing around windows and doors in newer homes is often made from flexible plastic, such as polyethylene, or from composite materials.

Wall penetration flashing for appliance vents and exhaust ducts is made from materials appropriate for the application. Galvanized steel is the common material for gas vent flashing. Galvanized steel, aluminum, and plastic are the common materials for exhaust duct flashing. Flashing for appliance vents at walls and roofs is sometimes called a thimble. Flashing for exhaust duct wall terminations is sometimes called a cap.

Most flashing around windows and doors is not visible during a home inspection because it is concealed behind wall coverings. This flashing should include pan flashing at the window and door sill, jamb flashing along the sides, and header flashing at the top. Inspecting concealed window and door flashing involves looking for water stains and water damage, which indicates that the flashing is not installed or not properly installed.

<u>Visible Siding Flashing</u> **L flashing** above window and door header trim and **Z flashing** at horizontal seams between sheets of panel siding should be visible at siding such as cement fiber, hardboard, and wood. **J channel flashing** should be installed around windows, doors and other wall penetrations when vinyl siding and aluminum siding is used.

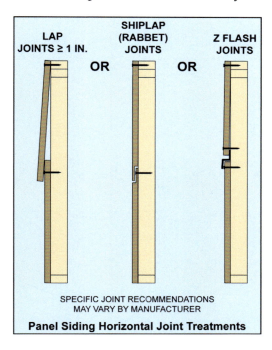

Panel Siding Horizontal Joint Treatments

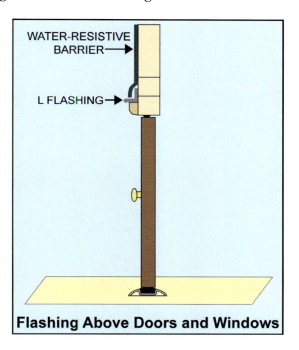

Flashing Above Doors and Windows

L Flashing Above a Garage Vehicle Door.

Vinyl J Channel Flashing.

Visible Brick Veneer Flashing **Flashing should be installed** and visible at several locations **when brick veneer wall covering is used**. Flashing locations should include at door headers and thresholds, at window headers and sills, at each floor level, and at the foundation. The flashing should extend past the brick just below the weep holes, but this is seldom done. **Weep holes** should be at least $3/16$ inch diameter and be located at least every 32 inches. In practice, brick veneer flashing in all recommended locations is uncommon, even in newer houses. Weep holes may be visible in some recommended locations, but there is usually no way to know if flashing is installed behind the brick.

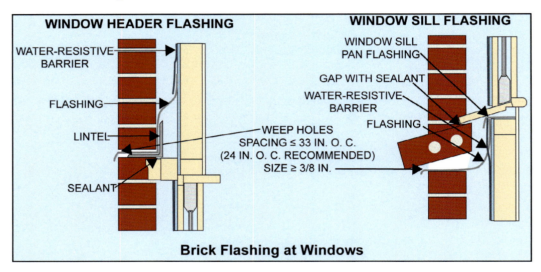

Brick Flashing at Windows

Weep Holes Above Door Header.

Visible Wall Covering Transition Flashing Flashing should be installed where one **wall covering material meets a different wall covering material**. An example is where siding or stucco meets brick veneer. The flashing should be visible at the transition, and should extend an inch or more over the lower wall covering. In practice, this flashing is uncommon, especially on older houses.

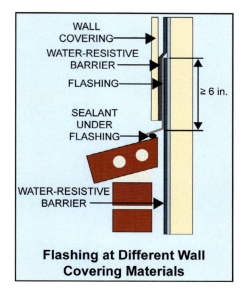

Flashing at Different Wall Covering Materials

Transition Flashing, Vinyl to Brick.

Other Wall Penetrations Exhaust ducts that penetrate a wall usually terminate in a cap. The cap flange should be set in a bed of sealant and the space between the opening and the cap should also be sealed. The space around plumbing pipes, condenser coolant tubes, electrical wires, light fixtures, and similar penetrations should be sealed. The sealant, if any, is not usually visible under wall coverings such as vinyl that use J channel flashing around wall penetrations.

Defects, Standards

Typical Defects Typical defects that inspectors should report include:

1. absent flashing,
2. flashing too small,
3. absent weep holes in brick,
4. damaged, deteriorated, or loose flashing,
5. gaps between flashing and sidewall or penetration; sealants used to repair these defects,
6. sealants substituted for flashing,
7. absent and deteriorated sealants where sealants should be installed.

Standards (1) IRC 2018 R703.4; (2) Brick Industry Association Technical Notes; (3) wall covering manufacturer's instructions.

Gap Between Flashing and Wall Covering at Headwall.

EAVES AND ASSOCIATED TRIM

The eaves are the extension of the rafters beyond the exterior wall of the house. Eaves are desirable because they provide a partial shield from solar radiation, and because they help divert water away from the exterior walls. Eaves are not required, and are not often present on houses a with low slope roof.

When the rafters are exposed, the eaves are called open eaves. When the rafters are enclosed, the eaves are called boxed eaves, closed eaves, or a boxed cornice.

A boxed cornice (eaves) consists of several trim components. The fascia is the vertical trim at the rafter end. The fascia is usually wood or a composite material. Wood, especially where vinyl or aluminum siding has been installed, may be covered by vinyl or aluminum. The soffit is the horizontal trim that encloses the rafter bottoms between the fascia and the house wall. The soffit is usually wood or plywood. When the wall covering is aluminum or vinyl, the wood soffit may be covered by aluminum or vinyl, or the soffit may be the made from aluminum or vinyl. The intersection of the soffit and house wall is often trimmed with bed molding or various styles of crown molding. With some wall coverings, such as brick, an additional vertical trim component, the frieze, may be installed between the building wall and the fascia to hide where the wall covering ends. A boxed cornice that changes direction at a gable roof end is called a cornice return, or a return.

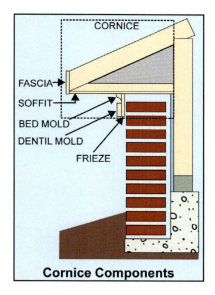

Cornice Components

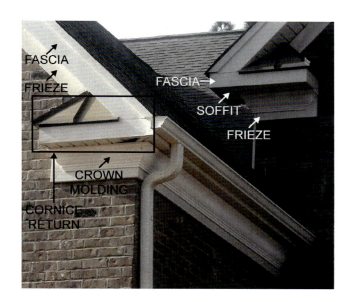

Typical Defects Typical defects that home inspectors should report include:

1. water stains and water damage,
2. absent, loose, damaged, and warped trim,
3. absent and deteriorated paint or other coating,
4. absent, damaged, and blocked ventilation screens,
5. openings that allow vermin entry,
6. trim penetrates wall covering creating a water entry point.

Standards (1) IRC 2018 R703.1 (soffit installation), R806 (attic ventilation); (2) manufacturer's instructions (for vinyl and aluminum).

Trim Penetrating Wall Covering is a Likely Water Intrusion Point.

Water Damaged Trim Can Be Difficult to See. Bubble in Paint Was the Clue to Probe.

EXTERIOR DOORS

Hinged Doors

Door Types, Styles, Materials **Hinged exterior doors** usually open in one direction, swing on three or four side-mounted hinges, and usually open at least 90°. A single door consists of one door (leaf) mounted in a frame. A double door consists of two doors (leaves) mounted in one frame. One side of a double door is usually held in place with surface bolts or with bolts built into the door stile. Exterior hinged doors are made in standard sizes. Height is usually 80 inches. Widths are usually from 24 to 36 inches in 2 inch increments.

Hinged doors are usually constructed using natural or engineered wood or using metal as a skin with an insulating foam core. Doors constructed using fiberglass, vinyl, and composite materials are also available.

Many common hinged door styles exist, including the flush (single) panel door, the raised-panel door (often six or eight panels), and doors containing various sizes and styles of glazing. A **French door** (casement door) is a hinged door that consists mostly of fixed glazing, usually divided into several (often nine or twelve) small pieces.

Less common door styles include the **jalousie door** (also seen as a window). This is a hinged door containing many horizontal panes of glazing that are opened and closed together with a crank. Jalousies are usually found in older homes in southern coastal areas. The **Dutch door** is a hinged door with a top leaf, and a bottom leaf, that open independently.

**Single Door with Sidelights and Transom (Left).
Double Door (French) with Eyebrow Transom (Right).**

Hinged Door and Frame Parts Hinged doors constructed from wood consist of parts including a top and bottom **rail**, a **stile** along each side, a vertical **mullion** (between panels, if any), and a lock rail near the center. Hinged doors made from other materials are often molded or routed to simulate stile and rail construction. Hinged doors usually have a sweep at the bottom to seal the area between the bottom rail and the threshold.

Hinged door frame parts consist of a **header** at the top, a **hinge jamb** on one side where the hinges are mounted, a **strike jamb** on the other side where the lock strike plate is mounted, and a sill at the bottom. A **threshold** is installed on top of the sill. An **astragal** (T-astragal) is attached to one side of a double door to seal the gap where the doors meet.

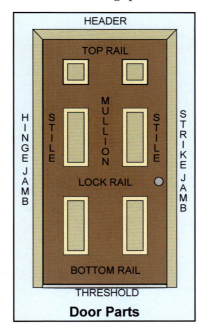

Door Parts

Installation Exterior doors are usually installed in a framed **rough opening** consisting of a **header** supported by **jack and king studs** appropriate for the door size. The rough opening size is specified by the door manufacturer. The rough opening is larger than the door on the top and sides to provide room for the door frame, and to allow the door to be installed plumb and square in the opening. The door frame is installed in the rough opening, checked for **plumb and square**, shimmed as necessary, and fastened to the frame. There should be an **even reveal** (gap) between the door and the frame of about ⅛ **inch** on all sides. The door should remain in place when partially open. Doors that move when partially open (a condition sometimes called ghosting) may be improperly installed, or the framed opening may have shifted position.

Doors are usually attached to wood framing using 16d casing nails driven through the shims and elsewhere through the header and jambs as required for secure attachment. Extra nails may be installed around the hinges and the lock strike plate for additional support at those vulnerable points. When doors come with pre-installed molding, such as brick mold, nails are also driven through the molding. Special attachment requirements may apply in high wind areas. Door manufacturers may have specific installation instructions including instructions for flashing around the door.

Threshold installation and sill installation are important for door operation and for sealing against the elements. The threshold and sill should be fully and firmly supported. Thresholds and sills that extend past the support may deform or break. **Pan flashing** and a generous bead of sealant should be installed under the sill to reduce water infiltration. This step is frequently omitted.

Doors should be flashed according to the door manufacturer's instructions. Absent instructions, doors should be flashed using properly installed header, jamb, and pan flashing that is integrated with the water-resistive barrier. Improper door flashing is common in buildings of all ages and is a common point for water infiltration. See the flashing section for details about proper door flashing.

Locks, Hardware, Accessories

A **hinge plate** is mounted on the door and on the frame jamb, usually in a recessed mortise. A pin connects the two plates and allows the door to swing. A pick-proof hinge is one that has caps on the top and bottom that prevent removal of the hinge pin. These hinges are recommended on doors that swing out to prevent removing the door by removing the hinge pins.

A door lock (**entry lock**) restricts entry through the door from the exterior by requiring a key or a combination to open the lock. A door lock is operated using a knob or handle. A **deadbolt lock** is a higher security lock that inserts a solid bolt into a reinforced strike plate and (ideally) into the strike jamb. A double-cylinder deadbolt requires a key to operate from both door sides. A single-cylinder deadbolt requires a key to operate from the exterior and uses a knob on the interior.

A kickplate (often a thin piece of brass) is sometimes installed on the bottom rail to reduce damage. Kickplates sometimes conceal damage to the bottom rail.

Most doors have some type of **weather stripping** that seals between the top and sides of the door and frame. Most doors also have a **threshold** and a **sweep** that seals at the bottom of the door.

Sliding (Patio) Doors

Description A sliding door moves on rollers inside a track that is the bottom of the door frame. Most sliding doors are large pieces of glazing surrounded by a frame made from metal, vinyl, or fiberglass. One side of the door is usually fixed and the other side is active; however, large sliding doors have more than one moving section. Sliding doors often are equipped with a sliding screen. Sliding doors are made in standard sizes. Height is usually 80 inches. The most common widths are five and six feet with other widths available, usually by special order.

Installation Sliding doors are installed like hinged doors. See Hinged Doors. Proper installation is important because sliding doors are heavy and minor installation errors can have a significant negative impact on door operation.

Typical Sliding Door.

Bulkhead Doors

Description A bulkhead door is a horizontal or inclined door that provides access to an area under the home or to a storage area, such as a cellar. These doors are sometimes referred to by the brand name Bilco. Modern bulkhead doors are often made from aluminum or steel. Older doors are often made from wood. Bulkhead doors often consist of two side-hinged doors, but may be a single top-hinged door.

**New Factory-built Metal Bulkhead Door (Left). Site-built Wood Bulkhead Door (Right)
Left Picture Courtesy of The Bilco Company.**

Installation Installation varies widely depending on the opening size, the area to which the door provides access, and the age of the door. Manufactured bulkhead doors should be installed according to manufacturer's instructions.

Door Safety Issues

Egress Door Every house should have at least one side-hinged door that is accessible from all parts of the house and opens directly to the outside, not through the garage. The door should be at least 36 inches wide and 80 inches tall. A landing or finished floor at least 36 inches wide by 36 inches deep should exist on both sides of the door; however, one step down is allowed on the exterior side. The egress door is usually the front door. Other exterior doors usually do not need to comply with these conditions.

Landings at Doors A landing or finished floor should exist on both sides of every exterior door. The landing should be at least as wide as the door and at least 36 inches deep in the direction of travel. The exterior landing may be not more than two risers below the door threshold if the door does not swing over the steps. Doors, except for screen and storm doors, should not swing over steps.

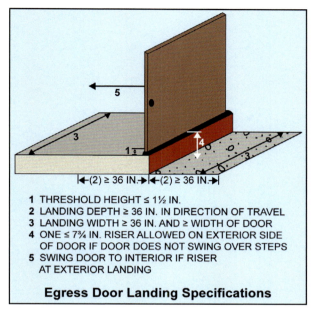

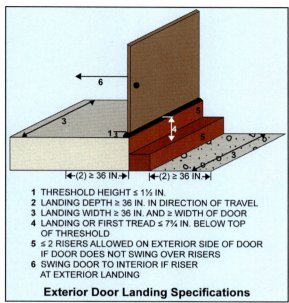

Safety Glazing In and Near Doors Most glazing in and near doors should be safety glazing. Glazing in all doors should be safety glazing, except for stained glass and similar decorative glass. Most glazing within 24 inches of either vertical edge of the door and less than 60 inches above a walking surface should be safety glazing. Note that this applies to approach from the interior and exterior side of the door. Exceptions to the 24 inch rule include glazing near the fixed panel of a glass door and glazing in a window that is separated from the door by a permanent barrier on both sides of the door. Safety glazing should be identified with a **permanent label etched in to one corner of the glazing.**

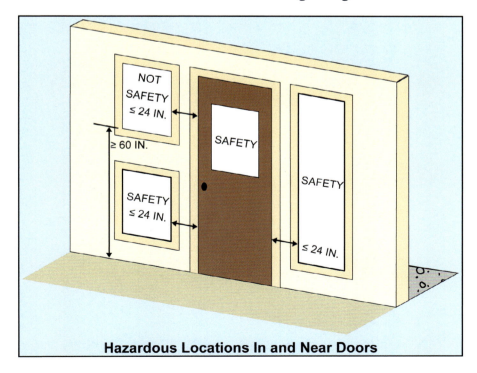

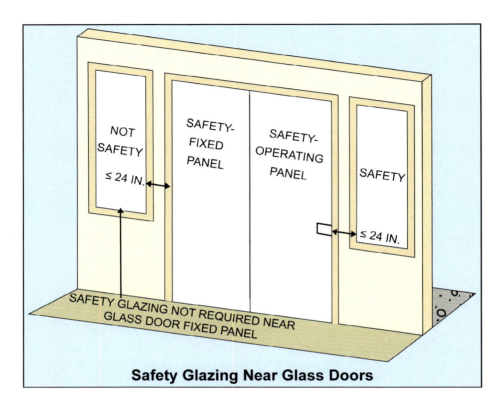

Safety Glazing Near Glass Doors

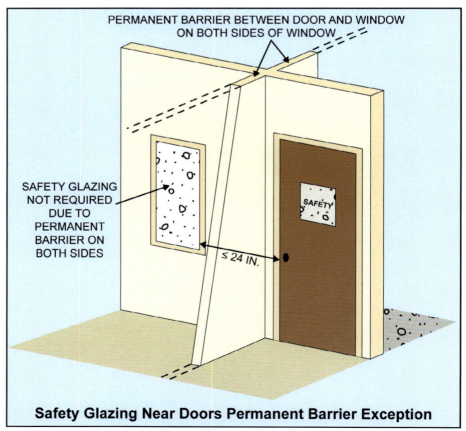

Safety Glazing Near Doors Permanent Barrier Exception

Defects and Standards

Typical Defects, Hinged Doors Typical defects that home inspectors should report include:

1. improper lock operation,
2. double cylinder deadbolt lock on egress door,
3. door sticks or rubs on frame (uneven or inadequate gap between door and frame),
4. light around door edges,
5. absent and damaged weather stripping, sweep, and threshold,
6. damaged door and glazing,
7. warped door,
8. water stains and water damage around door and under door,
9. deterioration due to water and sun, especially at the bottom,
10. loose, damaged, improperly operating bolts on the fixed side of double doors,
11. interior door is used as exterior door,
12. door not painted/sealed on all sides,
13. unsupported threshold,
14. door does not remain open.

Typical Defects, Sliding Doors Typical defects that home inspectors should report include:

1. improper lock operation,
2. difficult operation (often caused by deteriorated or fouled lower track and worn rollers),
3. damaged door and glazing,
4. absent and damaged weather stripping,
5. water stains and water damage around door and under door,
6. compromised hermetic seal between glazing panes,
7. door loose in frame,
8. frame loose or not square in opening,
9. blocked drain holes in lower track (water leaks into house),
10. absent, damaged, improperly operating screen,
11. unsupported lower track,
12. deteriorated lower track, especially when in contact with stucco.

Typical Defects, Bulkhead Doors Typical defects that home inspectors should report include:

1. water leaks through and around door,
2. no method to drain water that leaks through or around door,
3. difficult operation,

4. damaged door,
5. rot, rust, deterioration,
6. improper installation (e.g., door frame is not intended for embedment in concrete; door frame is not intended for attachment to preservative treated lumber),
7. blocked drainage channel.

Standards (1) IRC 2018 R311 (for door and landing requirements), R308 (safety glazing), and R703.8 (flashing); (2) manufacturer's instructions (for door installation and maintenance).

Threshold, Door, and Jambs are Water Damaged.

Water Stains on Floor at Door (Left). Water Damage on Subfloor Under Door (Right).

Door Finish Deteriorated. Can Be Difficult to Refinish Without Stripping to Bare Wood.

Bulkhead Doors Frequently Leak.

EXTERIOR WINDOWS

Window Types, Styles, Materials Windows can be divided into two broad categories. **Fixed (stationary) windows** contain glazing that does not move or open. Fixed windows provide light only. **Operable windows** contain at least one piece of glazing (a sash) that moves to allow air flow from outside. Operable windows provide both light and ventilation. Windows are manufactured in standard sizes that vary according to the window type.

Fixed windows can be any shape, but are usually rectangular. A rectangular window above a door is usually called a **transom window**. It is usually fixed, but may be operable. If the window is semicircular it is usually called a **fanlight window**. If the window has an oval shape it is usually called an **eyebrow window**. Windows at the sides of a door are usually called **sidelights**. A **Palladian window** is a three-part window with an arched sash in the middle and two smaller sashes on the sides. A **semicircular (roundhead) window** is a window with a semicircle on top.

A common operable window is the **double hung window**. Double hung means both sashes are operable, moving up and down. A common variant is the **single hung window,** where only the bottom sash is operable. **Sliding windows** usually have one movable sash that slides horizontally and one fixed sash. **Casement windows** are side-hinged windows that are operated by a crank and swing out. **Hopper windows** are hinged at the bottom and swing in. **Awning windows** are hinged at the top and swing out.

A **bay window** is any window that extends past the wall of the building. Most bay windows are cantilevered from the supporting structure below. Most are three-sided angled bay windows with one larger side parallel to the main wall and two smaller sides at about 45° angles to the larger side. A bay window with a semi-circular shape is usually called a **bow (compass) window.** A bow window can have as many as nine panes.

Individual windows are often joined to create double and triple windows, and windows with a semicircular top. A **mullion** separates the windows. The interior trim that covers the joint between the windows is also usually called mullion.

Original windows in older homes are constructed using wood. Windows in newer homes and replacement windows in older homes are constructed using natural or engineered wood, aluminum, fiberglass, and vinyl. Windows made with composite materials and various types of plastic are also available in new homes and as replacement windows.

Window glazing usually consists of one or more panes of glass. Glazing made of plastic blocks is also common, especially in bathroom windows where both light and privacy are desired. Single pane windows are common in older homes but are no longer allowed by energy codes. Double pane windows have been available since the 1930s and are the most common windows in homes built since the 1980s. Triple pane windows are available, but are very expensive.

Bay Window With Center Fixed Sash and Double Hung Windows on Sides (Left). Palladian Window With Casement Windows on Sides (Right).

**Bow Window (Left). Jalousie Window (Right).
Right Picture Courtesy of Welmoed Sisson**

Awning Window.

Window Energy Efficiency Window energy efficiency performance is determined by more than the number of panes. Air fills the space between panes of standard quality double pane windows. An inert gas (such as Argon) fills the space between higher quality double pane windows and many triple pane windows. Inert gas increases the window's energy efficiency by reducing convection currents between the panes that can increase the rate of heat transfer through the window. Over time, the **hermetic seal** between the panes degrades and allows moisture-filled air between the panes. This condition presents as streaks, spots, or condensation on the panes that cannot be removed from either accessible side. A window with a compromised hermetic seal will function normally in most respects, but its energy efficiency is reduced because of the convection currents.

Windows (and glazing in some doors) should have a **low emissivity (Low E) coating** in climates where cooling is predominant. This is a recent energy efficiency requirement, so this coating may be found in newer homes, and in homes with replacement windows. A Low E coating reflects infrared radiation while admitting visible light. Reflecting infrared radiation helps reduce solar heat gain through the glazing. This coating should be on the interior surface of the outside glazing pane in cooling climates (called glazing surface two). Low E coatings can help in heating climates by retaining heat loss at infrared frequencies. The Low E coating should be on the interior surface of the inside glazing pane in heating climates (called glazing surface three).

Window Sash and Frame Parts A **window sash** is the framework surrounding the window glazing. Like a door, a window sash consists of **stiles** on the sides, a **top rail** at the head jamb, and a **bottom rail** at the sill. Single and double hung windows have **meeting rails** where the two sashes meet. When a sash consists of individual glazing panes, the panes are held in place by bars. The vertical bars are sometimes called **muntins**. Decorative bars (grills) are sometimes installed in sashes containing a single glazing pane.

Glazing in older wood sashes is usually secured from the outside by small metal triangles called **glazier points** inserted between the glazing and the bars. The bars should then covered by **glazing putty,** not by caulk. Modern window glazing is usually secured to the frame by neoprene gaskets.

A **window frame** provides support for the window sash. Like a door, a window frame consists of a head jamb at the top, jambs on the sides, and a sill at the bottom. Some windows move on tracks. Hung windows move vertically on vertical tracks. Sliding windows move horizontally on horizontal tracks.

Windows may have trim installed to improve appearance and to cover the joint between the wall covering and the window frame. Windows in older houses are usually surrounded by trim called casing. The sill is covered by trim called a **sill**. The sash or tracks are held in place around the perimeter by trim called **stop**. Windows in some homes may have no trim installed. The header, jambs, and sill are wrapped with drywall.

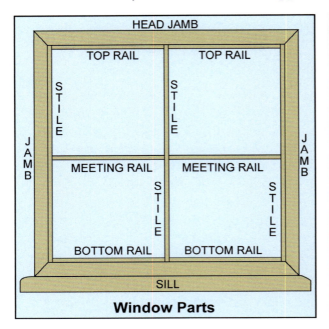

Installation Exterior windows are usually installed in a framed **rough opening** consisting of a header supported by **jack and king studs** appropriate for the window size. The window sits on a horizontal plate supported by **cripples**. The rough opening size is specified by the window manufacturer and varies by window type and material. The rough opening is larger than the window on the top and sides to provide room for the window frame, and to allow the window to be installed **plumb and square** in the opening. The window frame is installed in the framed opening, checked for plumb and square, shimmed as necessary, and fastened to the frame. The sashes should operate smoothly and should seal completely at the top, middle, and bottom.

Windows should be attached to structural components (usually wood framing) according to the window manufacturer's instructions. Attachment, flashing, and other installation instructions are usually on a sticker that comes with each window. Modern wood windows with pre-installed brick molding are usually attached using 16d casing nails driven through the brick molding. Aluminum and vinyl windows are usually attached using fasteners specified by the window manufacturer. These fasteners are driven through a **nailing flange** that surrounds the window. Windows in older buildings may be attached using a variety of attachment methods and fasteners.

Windows should be flashed according to the window manufacturer's instructions. Absent instructions, windows should be flashed using properly installed **header flashing, jamb flashing,** and **pan flashing** that is integrated with the water-resistive barrier. **Improper window flashing** is common in buildings of all ages and **is a common point for water infiltration**. Improper window flashing can be a common problem with replacement windows. See the flashing section for more details about proper window flashing.

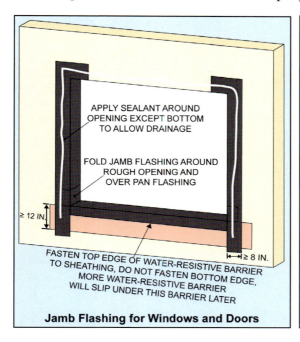

Jamb Flashing for Windows and Doors

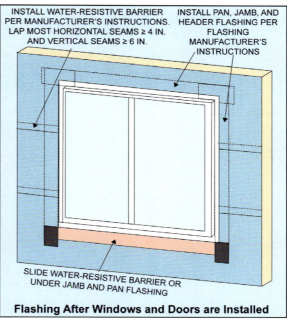

Flashing After Windows and Doors are Installed

Locks, Hardware, Accessories Hung window sashes move inside a track. Older window tracks are a groove mortised into the window frame. Modern window tracks are made from metal or plastic.

Sashes are heavy, can be difficult to open, and will not remain open without a means to hold them in place. The weight of sashes in older hung windows is counterbalanced by a system consisting of a sash cord or chain attached to the sash. The sash cord or chain is run through a pulley and is attached to a sash weight inside the window frame. Modern hung windows use a spring-loaded sash balance as the counterbalancing system.

A **sash lock** (sash fast) is usually installed where the sashes meet to secure them and to reduce air infiltration. Sash locks requiring a key are sometimes installed at a side stile to improve security. A rod or nail inserted into a hole drilled in the meeting rail serves a similar function.

Some hung windows have a **sash lift** (sash pull) to help occupants grip the sash to open it. The sash lift may be a metal finger hold mortised into the bottom rail or a metal hook, especially in older windows. Modern hung windows may have a groove routed into the bottom rail that serves as a sash lift.

Modern hung windows should have **weather stripping** installed on the top and bottom rails and at the meeting rails. Sliding windows should have weather stripping where the sash meets the frame (either on the sash stile or on the frame), and at the center stile where the sashes meet. Casement windows should have weather stripping at the header jamb and at the center meeting stiles. Weather stripping may be necessary at other locations depending on how the window is constructed.

Window Inspection Most standards of practice state that the home inspector should **operate at least one operable window in every room**. Many home inspectors operate all accessible windows. The home inspector should **exercise caution when operating windows**, especially those that are difficult to open. Attempting to force the window open can damage the window or the home inspector. Windows with broken springs or sash cords can close with some force and damage the window, or the home inspector's fingers.

Inspection of window energy features such as Low E and hermetic seals is out of scope of a home inspection. Most home inspectors report visible evidence of compromised hermetic seals, but it is sometimes difficult to know if the seals are compromised. Home inspectors should disclaim inspection of window energy features.

Windows are a common place to find water leaks. The home inspector should look carefully around every window, especially at the header, sill, and below the window.

Defects and Standards

Typical Defects Typical defects that home inspectors should report include:

1. stuck or difficult to operate sashes,
2. weak or broken sash balance springs,
3. damaged or broken sash cords,
4. damaged (broken) glazing,
5. damaged or deteriorated sash and frame (often by water infiltration or condensation),
6. compromised hermetic seal between multiple pane windows,
7. absent, loose, damaged, or improperly operating sash locks and other window hardware such as casement window crank handles,
8. absent or damaged weather stripping,
9. evidence of water infiltration around or near the window,
10. visible light around sash edges,
11. absent or damaged glazing putty or gaskets,
12. blocked bottom rail weep holes,
13. windows in showers not designed for water resistance from the inside.

Standards (1) IRC 2018 R303 (light and ventilation), R301.2.1.2 (opening protection in high wind zones), and R703.4 (flashing); (2) manufacturer's instructions (window installation and maintenance).

Casement Window With Deteriorated Frame, Not Visible Unless Window is Open.

Deterioration on Upper Sash Meeting Rail, Probably Caused By Condensation.

**Old-style Double Hung Window With Broken Sash Cord (Left).
Newer Double Hung Window with Broken Balance Spring Assembly (Right).**

Upper Left Sash With Failed Hermetic Seal.

Failed Hermetic Seal.

Window Safety Issues

Emergency Escape and Rescue Openings Emergency escape and rescue openings, hereinafter referred to as **escape openings**, are usually **required** in **sleeping rooms, basements,** and **habitable attics** to allow occupants to escape in an emergency, and to allow entry by rescue personnel. An escape opening may be a window or a door. The clear opening size of an escape window should be at least 20 inches horizontally, and 24 inches vertically with a clear opening area of at least 5.7 square feet (5 square feet **at grade level**), and the opening should be not more than 44 inches above the finished floor. An escape opening should be operable without a key, combination lock, special knowledge, or unusual force. Security bars on the outside of windows and security doors on the outside of doors that serve as escape openings should be operable from the inside. Requirements vary between jurisdictions.

Window Wells Window wells are usually **required** when any part of a window or opening (such as a ventilation opening) is **below grade**. Window wells that serve escape openings should be at least 36x36 inches. Window wells more than **44 inches below grade** should be equipped with a **ladder** or similar means that provide access. Window wells should be equipped with a means to drain water.

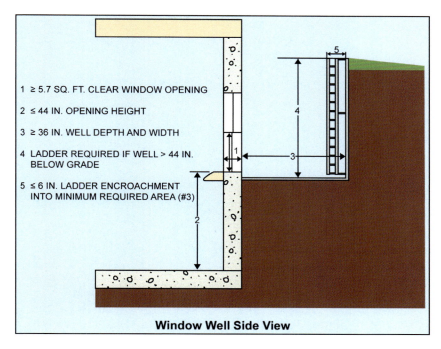

Window Well Side View

1 ≥ 5.7 SQ. FT. CLEAR WINDOW OPENING
2 ≤ 44 IN. OPENING HEIGHT
3 ≥ 36 IN. WELL DEPTH AND WIDTH
4 LADDER REQUIRED IF WELL > 44 IN. BELOW GRADE
5 ≤ 6 IN. LADDER ENCROACHMENT INTO MINIMUM REQUIRED AREA (#3)

Example of Window Well With Ladder.

Safety Glazing Identification Safety glazing should be identified with a permanent label etched in to one corner of the glazing. These labels are often difficult to see.

Safety Glazing In and Near Doors See door safety issues.

Safety Glazing Near Bathing and Swimming Areas Glazing less than 60 inches horizontally from water and with the bottom edge of the glazing less than 60 inches vertically from a walking surface should contain safety glazing. Bathing and swimming areas include bathtubs, showers, swimming pools, and spas. Glazing includes bathtub and shower surrounds.

Safety Glazing is Required In and Near Bathtubs and Showers.

Safety Glazing in Large Windows Windows containing **individual glazing panes** larger than 9 square feet should be equipped with safety glazing if all of the following are true: (a) the bottom edge of the glazing is less than 18 inches above the walking surface, and (b) the top edge of the glazing is more than 36 inches above the walking surface, and (c) the walking surface is within 36 inches of the glazing. A substantial bar or similar device may be used instead of safety glazing to protect the window. A substantial bar does not include grills and/or muntins.

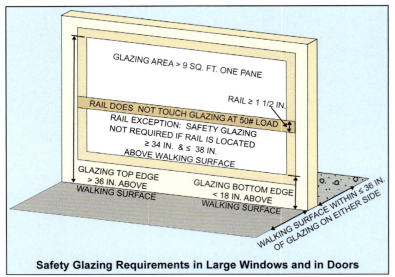

Safety Glazing is Required In Large Windows.

Safety Glazing Near Stairs Glazing in guards and rails should be safety glazing. Glazing in windows and doors near stairs should be safety glazing if: (a) the glazing is within 36 inches horizontally of the top landing or an intermediate landing or within 60 inches of the bottom tread, and (b) the bottom edge of the glazing is less than 36 inches above a landing or tread.

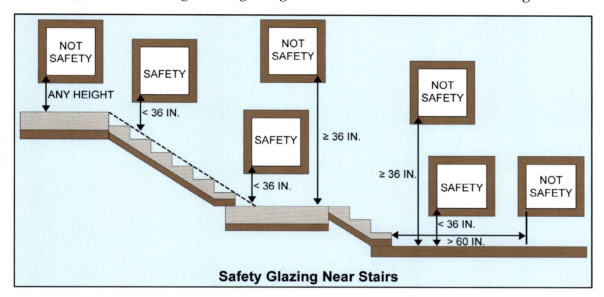

Safety Glazing Near Stairs

Safety Glazing Required In Left Window. Safety Glazing Required At Landing.
Safety Glazing Not Required In Right Window.

Operable Windows Near the Floor The opening size of an operable window should be limited to less than 4 inches if: (a) the bottom edge of the window opening is less than 24 inches above the interior floor, and (b) the bottom edge of the window opening is more than 6 feet above exterior grade. The method of limiting the opening size should not impede opening the window as specified for escape openings. This is a recent (IRC 2012) requirement.

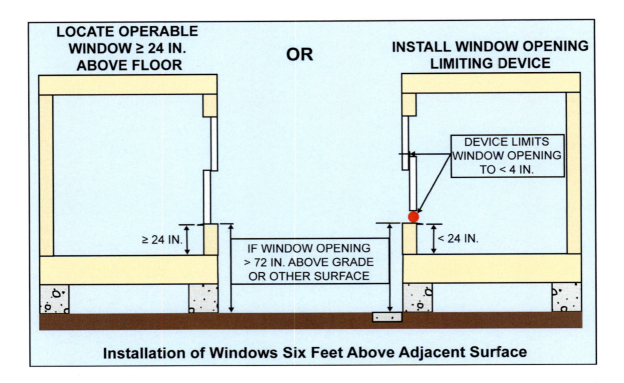

Example of Window Opening Limiting Device, Red Device In Upper Right Corner.

Standards (1) IRC 2018 R308 (safety glazing), R310 (escape openings and window wells), R312.2 (window fall protection). Local interpretation and enforcement of window safety standards varies. Standards regarding safety glazing locations have changed over time. Home inspectors should use good judgment when reporting about safety glazing in older houses. Refer to the definition of unsafe for more information.

STOOPS AND PORCHES

Introduction

A stoop is a small platform that serves as a landing on the exterior side of a door. A stoop is usually not much wider than the door it serves and may or may not be covered by a roof.

A porch is an outdoor area that is attached to the house. A porch is often covered by a roof, and is often open sided, but may be enclosed by insect screens or glazing including glass and acrylic panels. A porch frequently serves as a landing for a door. Stoops and porches are often raised above surrounding grade and have steps leading to them, but they will be on grade with slab-on-grade foundations.

Stoop and porch roofs are often shed roofs, but gable and hip roofs are sometimes used. The roofs are usually supported by columns.

Typical Stoop (Left) and Porch (Right).

Construction

Common Materials Common stoop and porch materials include concrete, masonry (bricks), concrete masonry units (blocks), stone, pavers like those used for patios, and wood. Stoops and porches are sometimes covered with finish materials such as bricks, pavers, or flagstones. Concrete can be stamped and colored to provide the appearance of flagstone or pavers.

Common stoop and porch roof column materials include wood posts (usually 6x6 or 4x4), boxed columns (wood posts, dimension lumber, or steel posts surrounded by trim lumber), masonry, metal, such as aluminum, various plastics, such as PVC, and manufactured hollow wood columns. These columns usually support beams that support the roof rafters.

Construction Techniques Stoop and porch construction depends on the material. Stoops and porches built using wood are usually wood decks and should be evaluated as such. Refer to the section on decks for more information.

Stoops and porches built using concrete and masonry should be built on an appropriate foundation. What constitutes an appropriate foundation depends on the climate zone where the house is located, and on the stoop or porch size. The bottom of the foundation should be below the local frost line. A small stoop and steps made entirely of concrete could be its own foundation if it bears on compacted soil and if the home is in a warm climate. A large stoop or porch usually needs a full foundation with footings and possibly foundation walls to transmit the load to undisturbed soil below the frost line. Stoops and porches are sometimes built without a foundation on backfill that has not been properly compacted and that settles over time. Failure to build a stoop or porch on an appropriate foundation is a common reason for defects such as settlement, rotation, heaving, and cracking.

Stoops and porches built using concrete and masonry may be built using one of several methods. The most straightforward method is to build a solid structure using one or more of the materials. For example, a stoop could be built using concrete blocks with bricks as the exterior decorative facing. This method works well for small stoops, but because it uses more materials, it costs more.

Less costly methods involve building a shell for a stoop or porch using concrete blocks or poured concrete walls. The shell may be covered with bricks or stucco to improve the appearance. The shell can be filled with soil or gravel and concrete poured over the material to form the top of the stoop or porch. The concrete may settle over time as the soil settles producing cracks and low areas. This problem can be reduced by compacting the soil and by using reinforcing bars to secure the concrete to the foundation. Another method is to leave the shell open and install sheets of corrugated metal over the open area under the shell and pour concrete on the metal. The metal needs support by steel lintels, piers, or both. Try to look inside these stoop and porch shells for defects such as rusted lintels and corrugated metal, improper supports, such as wood, and wood construction debris that could attract wood destroying organisms. In cold climates, this open shell can create an unconditioned space that opens to a basement. This cold room should be treated as unconditioned space. Still another stoop construction method is to build a precast concrete stoop off-site and deliver it to the site. A precast stoop should bear on a footing, or at least well-compacted soil, otherwise, it may rotate like a site-built stoop.

Columns supporting stoop and porch roofs should be an appropriate size and material to support the roof load. Determining this is usually out of scope for a home inspection, but defects such as bowing and deterioration can indicate an inappropriate column. Columns should be secured at the top, bottom, and where different materials (such as masonry and wood) intersect. This helps reduce the chance that the column will move under stress. Straps, anchors, and similar hardware are usually the appropriate means to secure columns. Fasteners such as nails are usually not adequate, but are common in older homes. Means used to secure columns are frequently concealed, especially with boxed columns.

2: Exterior Components   87

Defects, Safety, Standards

Typical Defects Typical defects that home inspectors should report include:

1. stoop/porch slopes toward the house or inadequately slopes away from the house,
2. stoop/porch moved, settled, or rotated, often caused by inadequate foundation, inadequate soil compaction, expansive soil, erosion, inadequate or no connection to the house foundation, and frost heave,
3. cracking, crazing, delamination, dusting, pop-outs in concrete,
4. stoop/porch uplifted, usually caused by tree roots, expansive soil, and frost heave,
5. erosion and voids under stoop and porch foundation,
6. materials loose, unstable, and damaged (trip hazard),
7. evidence of ponding water (slip on ice hazard) exists,
8. columns bowed or leaning,
9. columns rotted, rusted, or deteriorated (especially at the base and where columns meet other materials),
10. columns separating at hinge joint between different materials such as masonry and wood.

There is no agreed upon standard for what constitutes a reportable crack in concrete stoops, porches, and steps. **A common guideline** is that cracks exceeding ¼ inch in width or vertical displacement should be considered for repair.

There is no agreed upon standard for what constitutes a reportable separation between stoops, porches, steps and the house, and between steps and stoops and porches. **A common guideline** is that separation that exceeding 1 inch should be considered for repair; however, smaller separation distances should be considered for reporting because water leakage through the gap can cause further separation. Refer to the Slab on Stem Wall Foundation section for more about concrete defects.

Safety Issues Stoops and porches and any related steps are subject to rules involving risers, treads, handrails, guards, and landings. Refer to the section about decks for more information.

Standards Refer to the section about decks for more information.

Poorly Compacted Fill is the Probable Cause of This Porch Settlement and Cracking.

**This Porch Has Rotated. The Sealants are a Clue That Rotation May Be Active.
Picture Courtesy of Welmoed Sisson**

**Deteriorated Posts are a Common Defect.
Deteriorated Paint in the Left Photo is a Clue that Probing May Be Prudent.
The Uneven Surface and Cracking in the Right Photo Is a Clue that Wood Filler Has
Been Used for Repair. Wood Filler Is Visible in the Damaged Area in the Right Photo.**

BALCONIES

Introduction

A balcony is an outdoor platform that is located at the second story and above. Balconies are usually either self-supporting (cantilevered beyond the house wall) or are supported on one side by the house and by posts and beams on the outside. A balcony sometimes serves as the roof for either a porch or for conditioned space below. A balcony is often open above and on all sides, but it may be covered by a roof. Access to a balcony is through a door from the house. Balconies are not usually served by stairs. **Balconies that are attached to the house with a ledger and are supported by posts and beams on the outside are more like decks** and should be evaluated as such. Refer to the section about decks for more information.

A balcony that is surrounded by solid walls should be drained as a low slope roof either using scuppers or floor drains. Refer to the low slope roof covering section for more information.

Construction

Common Materials The most common residential balcony structural material is wood. Iron and steel are also used. Wood that is exposed to the elements should be preservative treated or naturally durable. Wood that is not exposed can be regular dimensional lumber, I-joists, or trusses. Common balcony flooring materials include preservative treated and naturally durable wood, composite outdoor decking, roof covering materials made for regular foot traffic including some types of modified bitumen, concrete, and epoxy.

Common balcony column materials include wood posts (usually 6x6 or 4x4), boxed columns (wood posts, dimensional lumber, or steel posts surrounded by trim lumber), masonry, metal other than steel, and manufactured hollow wood columns. These columns support beams that support the balcony floor joists.

Construction Techniques Floor joist span distance for a cantilevered balcony is a function of the joist size, species, and grade, on-center spacing, and the design ground snow load. For example, a 2x10 #2 grade, southern pine joist at 16 inches on center may extend up to 53 inches from the support at the building with a ground snow load of 30 psf or less, or it may extend up to 42 inches with a ground snow load of 70 psf. This assumes a ratio of 1 inch cantilever extension for every 2 inches that the joist extends inside the home.

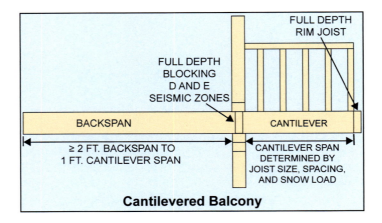

Cantilevered Balcony

Each cantilevered balcony joist is a potential water leak point where the joist penetrates the wall covering. Installation of proper flashing and a wall drainage plane at these points is essential, although these components are often concealed during a home inspection. Provisions for ventilation and inspection of balconies with concealed structural components are also essential, although these provisions are uncommon. Caulk or other sealant should also be installed at each penetration, but sealants are not a substitute for flashing. Home inspectors should examine the area around joist penetrations both inside and outside for evidence of water penetration.

Construction of balconies supported at the outside by columns and beams is similar to decks, and should be evaluated as such. Refer to the section on decks for more information.

Cantilevered Balcony.

Deck Like Balcony.

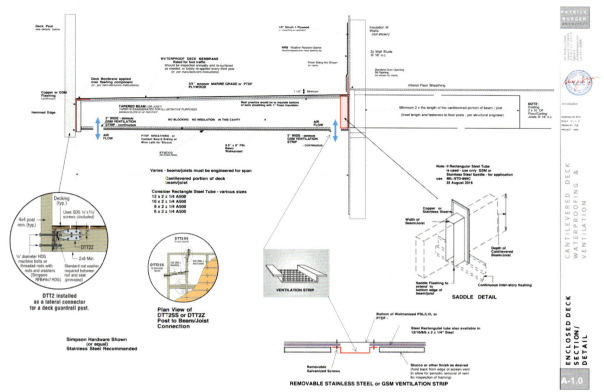

Recommended Method of Installing Flashing and Ventilation at a Balcony With Concealed Structural Components
Drawing Courtesy of Patrick Burger

Defects, Safety, Standards

Typical Defects Typical defects that inspectors should report include:

1. lack of ventilation and inspection openings where the point of attachment to the structure is concealed,
2. balcony slopes toward the house, or slopes inadequately away from the house,
3. absent or inadequate flashing at the house, especially at the door,
4. inadequate vertical offset at the door,
5. evidence of ponding water,
6. absent, inadequately sized, or improperly installed drainage components, such as scuppers and floor drains,
7. absent or inadequate flashing around guard posts and other roof covering penetrations (when balcony flooring is a roof covering),
8. absent or deteriorated sealants where joists and guards penetrate wall coverings,
9. deteriorated materials, especially flooring,
10. excessive cantilever distance,
11. loose, unstable, and damaged materials (trip hazard),

12. bowed or leaning columns,
13. deteriorated columns (especially at the base),
14. columns separating at hinge joint between different materials such as masonry and wood,
15. absent and loose guards.

Safety Issues (1) Balconies are subject to rules involving guards. Refer to the section about decks for more information. (2) Balconies with concealed structural components are vulnerable to collapse cause by deterioration of structural components.

Standards (1) IRC 2018 Table R502.3.3(2) (joist cantilever table); (2) manufacturer's instructions for composite materials and roof coverings.

DECKS

Introduction

A deck is an outdoor recreational area that is often, but not always, attached to the house. A deck can be supported on all sides by posts, in which case the deck is called a free-standing or a self-supported deck. A deck is uncovered and open-sided. A deck frequently serves as a landing for a door. Decks are often raised above surrounding grade and have steps leading to them.

Structures such as stoops, porches, and balconies that are built like a deck using common deck materials should be evaluated as a deck using the information in this section.

Construction

Common Materials The most common residential deck structural and flooring materials are preservative treated or naturally durable wood. Preservative treated wood is softwood. The wood species varies by region. Southern pine is predominant in the East. Douglas fir, hem-fir, red pine, and ponderosa pine are predominant in the West. Naturally durable wood is usually redwood or western red or white cedar. All wood deck components (ledgers, floor joists, beams, posts, handrails, guards) should be made from these materials. Deck flooring and railings made from composite materials and metal are becoming increasingly common. One familiar brand of this material is Trex. Composites are often made from wood fibers and resins. Deck flooring and railings made from aluminum and from plastics, including PVC, polypropylene, and polyethylene mixed with wood fibers are also available.

The wood treatment industry discontinued the use of the chemical CCA as of 31 December 2003. Existing stock was allowed to be sold beyond that date. Almost all wood treated before this date was treated with CCA. Replacement chemicals such as ACQ, MCQ, and CA-C have proven to be more corrosive than CCA, especially to aluminum and to a lesser extent galvanized steel. Aluminum and electroplated galvanized steel flashing, connectors, joist hangers, and fasteners should not be used on decks built since 2004. Hot-dipped galvanized steel, stainless steel, and copper are recommended instead. Dissimilar metals should be avoided because of corrosion potential. Galvanized steel fasteners should be used with galvanized steel connectors and stainless steel fasteners with stainless steel connectors.

Common deck post materials include wood (usually 6x6 or 4x4), steel, boxed columns (wood posts, dimensional lumber, or steel posts surrounded by trim lumber), and masonry (bricks and concrete masonry units). These posts support beams that support the deck floor joists.

Deck Flashing and Sealants
The deck ledger pulling away from the house is a frequent cause of catastrophic deck collapse. Water damage to the ledger and to the band board/rim joist caused by **absent or improper flashing is usually a factor when a deck collapses.** Many decks are improperly flashed. Older decks are more likely to be improperly flashed, or have no flashing at all.

Deck flashing should: (1) divert as much water as possible away from where the deck ledger is attached to the house, (2) divert water from the vulnerable area around doors that open on to the deck, and (3) allow water that is not diverted and water that enters at doors to drain and not remain in contact with wood or other building materials. To accomplish these objectives, the deck flashing should be integrated with other flashing, such as door threshold flashing, and with wall drainage plane components, such as house wrap. Much of this integration is not visible during an inspection, but some usually is and the results, water infiltration, are often visible.

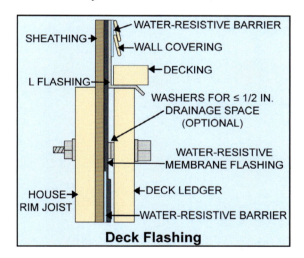

Deck Flashing

Result of Improper Flashing.

Decks, stoops, and porches should be installed so that there is a step between the landing and the door. This helps prevent water and snow from entering under or through the door. The maximum vertical step is currently 7¾ inches, measured to the top of the door threshold. The minimum vertical step depends on the house's climate. A larger step is recommended where snow accumulation and wind-driven rain may be an issue. A smaller step (1½-2 inches) is acceptable in warmer and drier climates.

Sealants such as caulk may be installed in addition to flashing. **Sealants are not a substitute for flashing**. Sealants require regular maintenance and will usually fail before the homeowner realizes it. Excessive application of sealants is often a sign of past or current water infiltration problems.

Deck Ledger Attachment The **deck ledger attachment to a house** should be designed to **resist a 3,000 pound lateral (horizontal) load** trying to pull the deck away from the house. The deck ledger attachment to a house should also resist the vertical load imposed by deck materials, deck users, and any furniture and equipment on the deck. The **prescriptive method** of attaching a deck ledger to a house is based on the following: (1) minimum ½ inch diameter lag screws or machine bolts (not carriage bolts), (2) a washer on the head end of screws, and a washer on each end of bolts, and bolts secured with a nut, (3) screws or bolts installed in a staggered pattern and at specified spacing that depends on factors such as floor joist length, (4) a 2 inch nominal thickness wood deck ledger, (5) a 2 inch nominal thickness band board, or a minimum 1 inch thick engineered rim joist, that bears directly on the foundation (**no connections to cantilevered projections** such as bay windows and framed fireplaces is allowed), (6) maximum 1 inch distance between the band board/rim joist and the deck ledger, (7) no connection through wall coverings, especially brick veneer, (8) installation of lateral load connectors.

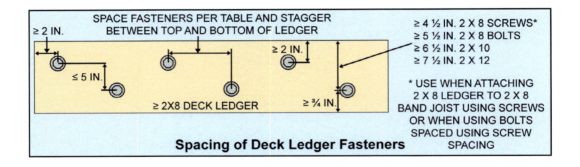

Spacing of Deck Ledger Fasteners

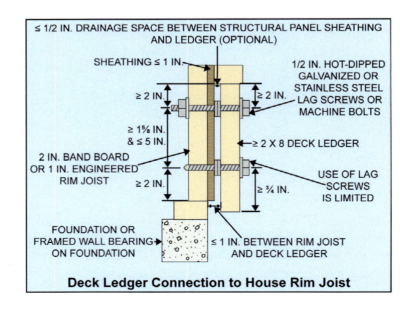

Deck Ledger Connection to House Rim Joist

Lateral load connectors are required in almost all cases when the deck ledger is attached to the house. These connectors are uncommon; however, their absence is a defect that home inspectors should report. The two most common types of lateral load connectors are the 1,500 pound connector and the 750 pound connector. Any combination of these connectors that provides at least 3,000 pounds of lateral load resistance is acceptable.

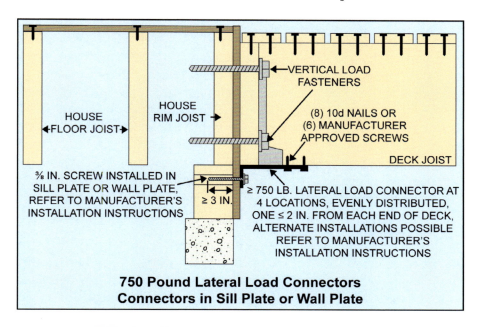

**750 Pound Lateral Load Connectors
Connectors in Sill Plate or Wall Plate**

**Example of a 1,500 Pound Lateral Load Connector.
Picture Courtesy of Welmoed Sisson**

Deck ledgers may be attached to the house using other methods and materials; however, these other methods and materials may require further evaluation to determine if they provide the required resistance to horizontal and vertical loads. Home inspectors should pay special attention to deck ledgers attached to houses that have wood I-joists and floor trusses. **Floor systems framed with wood I-joists may not have a rim joist that provides an adequate connection for the deck ledger,** and floor systems framed with floor trusses usually have no rim joist at all.

Deck ledgers should **not** be installed through wall coverings. The wall covering should be removed. Attaching deck ledgers through wall coverings increases the load on the bolts and on the band/rim joist connection. It also makes flashing more difficult. This is especially true for brick and stone veneer; however, attachment through brick and stone veneer and stucco (not EIFS) is permitted in some jurisdictions. A deck should be free-standing when removing the wall coverings is impractical, or if flashing or other considerations make attaching the deck to the house impractical.

Deck Stairs and Landings

Deck stair issues include stringers and their attachment to the deck, stair risers and treads, and stair landings. We will discuss handrails and guards later. Stringers should be attached to the deck using stringer hangers designed for this purpose; however, nails are the most common attachment method. Nails may be subject to withdrawal over time, especially toe nails. **The entire stringer plumb cut should bear on the deck rim joist** and the rim joist should be designed to bear the increased load imposed by the stairway. A single deck rim joist may deflect under the load imposed by the stairs. Cut stringers should be made using 2x12 lumber, although 2x10 stringers are common and not necessarily deficient if reinforced. Solid stringers are stronger. **Cut stringers made using 2x12 lumber should not span more than 6 feet between supports**. Home inspectors should pay special attention to stringers and their attachment.

Stringers are sometimes attached to the deck using a drop header. Drop headers are used to make installing the handrail easier. There are no authoritative prescriptive details for attaching a drop header to the deck; however, attachment using bolts is often considered acceptable. **Use of screws or nails to attach a drop header is a reportable defect** because these fasteners can withdraw and fail over time.

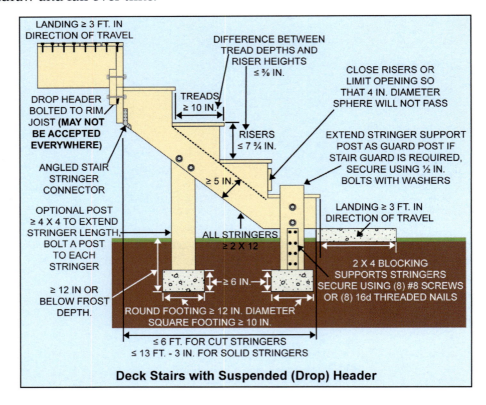

Deck Stairs with Suspended (Drop) Header

Example of an Improperly Installed (Nailed) Drop Header.

Deck stair riser and tread standards vary by jurisdiction and vary over time. The current IRC **maximum riser height is 7¾ inches** and the current **minimum tread depth is 10 inches**. Riser height and tread depth are somewhat less important than the difference in height and depth between risers and treads in a flight of stairs. A difference larger than the maximum is a fall hazard. The current **maximum height difference** between two risers and the maximum difference in depth between two treads in a flight of stairs **is ⅜ inch**.

Most deck stairs have open risers. The space at open risers should be covered so that a four inch diameter sphere cannot pass between adjacent treads.

Most stairways, including deck stairs, should have a **solid landing at the top, bottom, and at any intermediate landings**. The deck usually provides the top landing. A pad made from concrete or other solid material should provide the bottom landing. Landings should be at least as wide as the stairway (36 inches minimum width) and at least 36 inches deep in the direction of travel. A landing is not required on the exterior side of doors such as the door from the garage into the home if there are fewer than 2 risers and if the door does not swing over the risers.

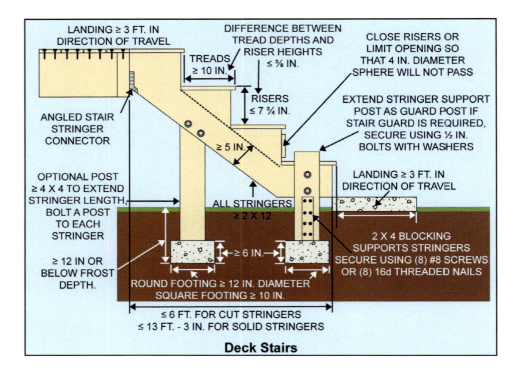

Deck Stairs

Deck Stair Handrails Handrail requirements for deck stairs are the same as for all other stairs.
Handrails should be provided for stairs with four or more risers, including the top and bottom risers. The top of the handrail should be between 34 and 38 inches above a sloped line connecting the stair treads. The handrail should begin and end with a return or a post. The grasping surface should be one of the approved handrail sizes and shapes. The commonly seen **2x4 deck handrail is not an approved handrail size and shape,** and is therefore deficient as a safety hazard. Balusters for deck stair handrails that serve as guards should be spaced so that a 4⅜ inch diameter sphere will not pass through, and should be attached such that they can resist a 50 psf load. Two ring-shank nails or two screws are recommended for attaching balusters. Note that **stair baluster spacing is different from guard baluster spacing.**

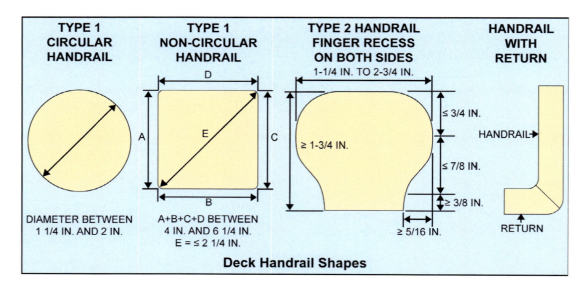

Deck Handrail Shapes

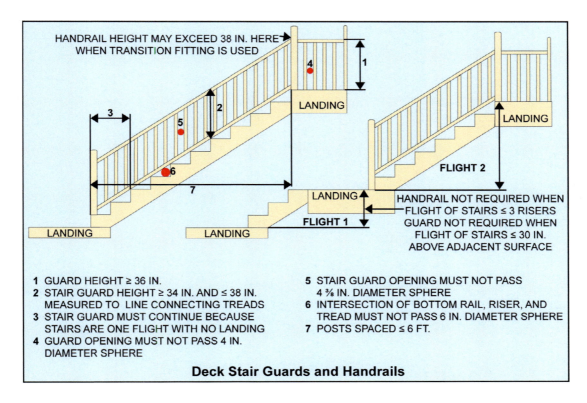

Deck Stair Guards and Handrails

Deck Guards Improperly installed and deteriorated **deck guards are a common cause of deck-related injuries**. Deck guards, and handrails that serve as guards, should not fail when a single concentrated load of 200 psf is applied in any direction at any point along the top of the guard. Home inspectors are not required to test guards for compliance with this requirement. Inspection consists of the presence of construction details as described below.

A guard is usually required when a walking surface is more than 30 inches above a surface below, measured to a point 36 inches horizontally from the walking surface. Deck guards should be at least 36 inches above the deck walking surface (42 inches in California and some other jurisdictions).

Deck **guard posts should be at least 4x4s that have not been notched**. Posts should be **spaced not more than 6 feet on center.** Guard post attachment should include a connector that is bolted to a deck floor joist or to framing that is connected to deck floor joists. This method avoids the problem of posts secured to rim joists that are in turn secured using nails that are subject to withdrawal over time. Posts that are notched, and posts secured using screws or nails, are no longer acceptable and should be reported as deficient.

Deck guard balusters should be spaced so that a 4 inch diameter sphere will not pass. Deck guards sometimes use cables, decorative metal, and other horizontal components as the guard fill-in components. Home inspectors should evaluate these **horizontal guard components** and report as a **safety hazard if they could be climbable**.

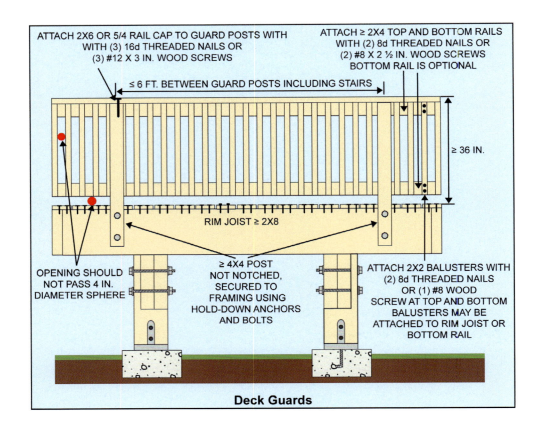

Deck Guards

Typical Cable Fill-In.

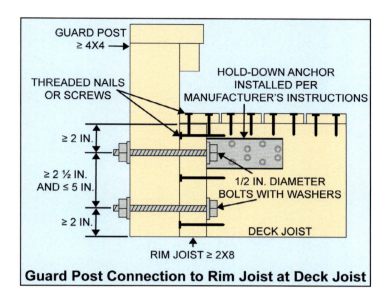

Guard Post Connection to Rim Joist at Deck Joist

Deck Framing Deck framing issues include floor joist span, joist attachment to the deck ledger and to the beam, flooring material span and attachment, and deck bracing. Determining if floor joists are over-spanned is a technically exhaustive procedure and is out of scope of a home inspection; however, home inspectors should be aware of basic joist span rules to identify joists that might be too long. Excessively long joists may deflect and stress component connections resulting in a deck collapse. Joist span tables for interior floor joists do not apply to deck floor joists because deck joists get wet and can deflect more than dry joists.

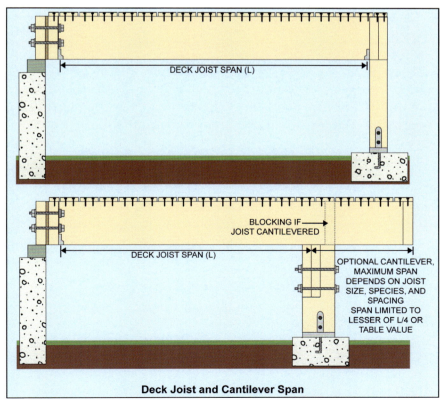

Deck Joist and Cantilever Span

Deck floor joists should be attached to the deck ledger and to the side of beams using galvanized steel or stainless steel joist hangers. Deck floor joists may be installed on the top of beams. Joist hangers should be the appropriate size. A joist hanger one size smaller than the joist is often adequate. For example, a 2x6 joist hanger may be adequate for a 2x8 joist. Refer the joist hanger manufacturer's instructions for information about appropriate joist hangers for a particular deck. Deck floor joists often bear on a 2x2 ledger strip. This was considered acceptable if 3-16d nails were installed in the ledger under each joist. Ledger strips are no longer allowed as deck floor joist support, although existing ledger strips are not necessarily deficient if they appear intact and installed according to requirements at the time of installation.

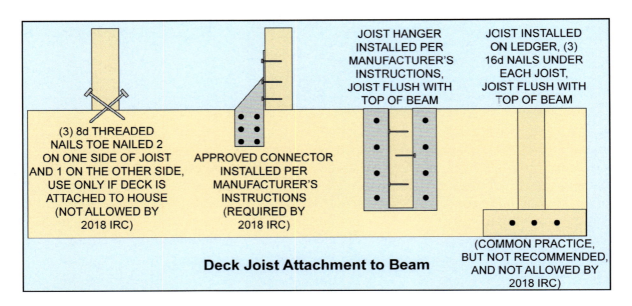

Deck Joist Attachment to Beam

Deck floor joists sometimes extend beyond the support beam and are described as being cantilevered. The maximum recommend cantilever extension for deck floor joists is the floor joist span distance before the cantilever divided by 4, or as indicated in the joist span table.

Deck wood flooring usually consists of 2x4, 2x6, 5/4x4, or 5/4x6 lumber. Wood composites, metal, and other alternative deck flooring materials are becoming increasingly common. Wood deck flooring should be attached to floor joists using screws, although ring shank nails are also acceptable. Wood deck flooring should be spaced about ⅛ inch apart between boards and where boards meet over joists to allow for expansion and for drainage. Nails and screws that are sunk into wood flooring create water traps that will hasten deterioration of the flooring. Manufacturer's instructions govern attachment of alternative deck flooring materials.

Deck flooring materials are usually installed perpendicular to the deck floor joists. In this configuration, 2 inch thick wood flooring may span floor joists spaced 24 inches on center and 5/4 wood flooring may span floor joists spaced 16 inches on center. Deck flooring materials that are installed in a 45° diagonal pattern relative to the deck floor joists may be installed beyond their recommended distance. This is true for 5/4 wood flooring, for alternative deck flooring materials, and when flooring materials are installed on deck floor joists spaced at 24 inches on center. Refer to manufacturer's instruction for the span distance of alternative deck flooring materials.

Decks are subject to wind and seismic loads that can cause decks to move. Movement of people on the deck can also cause decks to move. Movement can weaken the connections at supports and contribute to deck collapse. Bracing helps decks resist this movement. Bracing parallel to the deck support beam is required on all decks that are more than 2 feet above the ground (this height will vary by jurisdiction). Bracing is also required perpendicular to the deck support beam when the deck is not attached to the house (a free-standing deck).

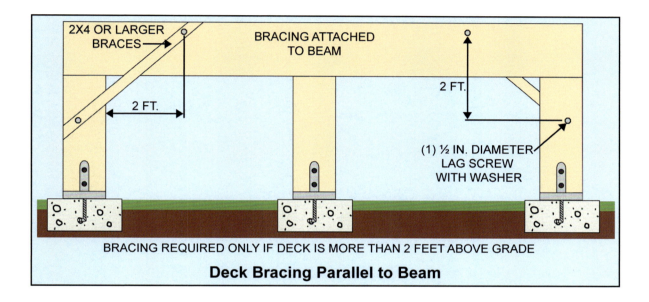

When preservative treated lumber is cut, the cut end is no longer treated. These ends are subject to rot and to insect damage. Cut ends of preservative treated lumber should be field-treated with copper naphthenate or other approved wood preservative. This is rarely done.

Deck Posts, Footings, and Beams The recommended wood deck support post is a 6x6 inch post made from preservative treated or naturally durable wood with a maximum height of 14 feet. This maximum height will vary by jurisdiction. Wood deck support posts using 4x4s are allowed with a maximum height of 8 feet. Steel deck support posts should be at least Schedule 40 thickness, at least 3 inches diameter, and painted with rust-resistant paint inside and outside. The maximum height of steel deck support posts should be determined by engineering analysis.

The unsupported span of a deck beam depends on the deck floor joist length and on the size and quantity of members that make up the beam. Deck beams are usually two or three members thick and are usually made using multiple pieces of wood. This means that a beam may have a joint at some point where two members meet. **Joints should occur over a support**. Home inspectors should look carefully at beams consisting of three members to be sure that joints in the center beam member occur at a support.

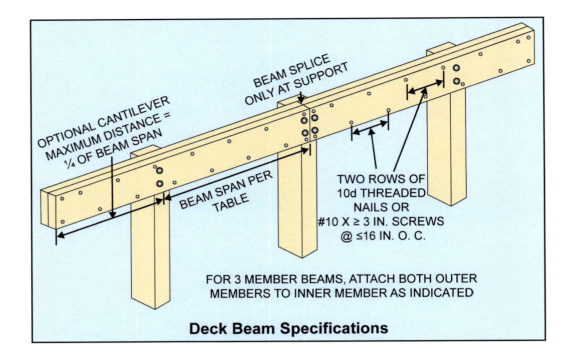

Deck Beam Specifications

Deck beams should fully bear on top of deck support posts. Attachment of beams to the sides of posts is not considered acceptable by current standards. Side attachment may be acceptable in some jurisdictions. Deck beams should be attached to the top of posts using machine bolts, or by using a manufactured post cap. Beam attachment to posts using straps is allowed in some jurisdictions and nails are allowed in some jurisdictions on decks near the ground. Note that all members of a 3-member beam will not be supported on top of a 4x4 post.

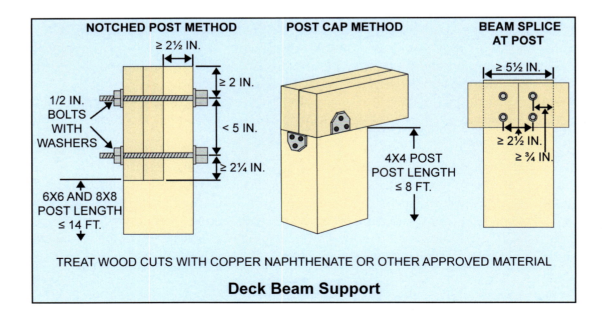

Deck Beam Support

The size and thickness of deck footings is based on the length of the deck floor joists and on the spacing of support posts. The bottom of deck footings should be below the local frost line if the deck is attached to the house. This is not required for free-standing decks, although it is a good practice. The bottom of deck footings that are closer than 5 feet to the foundation should be at the same level as the house footings to avoid placing a load on the house foundation walls. Deck support posts should be secured to the footing. Wood support posts should be secured using a post base. Embedding wood posts in concrete and burying posts in the earth is considered acceptable; however, these posts will degrade over time because of constant exposure to moisture. Home inspectors should carefully inspect posts embedded in concrete and posts buried in the earth for indications of deterioration.

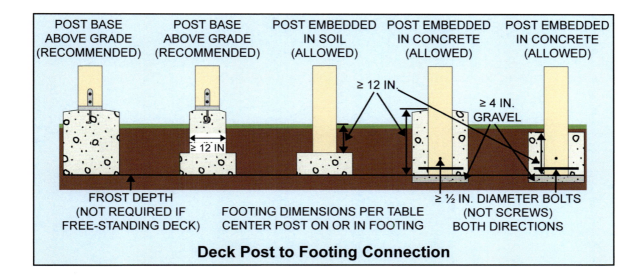

Deck Post to Footing Connection

Defects, Safety, Standards

Typical Defects, Flashing and Sealants

Typical defects that inspectors should report include:

1. absent and improperly installed flashing at the wall and at the door to the deck,
2. gaps in flashing,
3. improper and incompatible flashing materials (such as aluminum with copper based preservative treated wood),
4. absent or deteriorated sealants where joists and guards penetrate wall coverings,
5. excessive sealant (evidence of previous or current water infiltration problems),
6. evidence of water infiltration at locations including the band/rim joist, in, around, and under the deck door, and where components such as guards penetrate wall coverings (home inspectors may wish to move insulation or lift carpet to detect water infiltration),
7. step between deck and door too small.

Absent Flashing at Ledger.

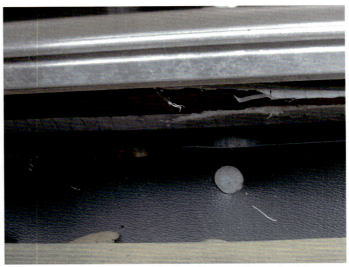
Gap in Flashing Under Door Threshold.

Water Stains Under Improperly Flashed Deck Ledger.

Severely Damaged Band Joist Behind Improperly Flashed Deck Ledger.

<u>Typical Defects, Deck Ledger Attachment</u> Typical defects that inspectors should report include:

1. ledger attached using only nails,
2. inadequate quantity or size of bolts or screws,
3. improper type of bolts or screws (e.g., not galvanized),
4. nuts not fully engaged on bolts or screws,
5. deteriorated (rusted) bolts or screws,
6. bolts or screws do not fully penetrating band/rim joist,
7. absent washers on bolts or screws,
8. bolts or screws not staggered vertically,

9. bolts or screws too close to ledger or band/rim joist edges,
10. absent, improper type or size, or deteriorated band/rim joist or ledger,
11. ledger attached through wall coverings,
12. ledger attached to cantilevered structure such as bay window or framed fireplace chase,
13. wood not preservative treated or naturally durable.

Ledger Attached Through Brick Veneer. Improper Use of Carriage Bolts. Bolts Loose. Some Joists Attached Using Only Nails.

Ledger Attached Using Only Screws. Joist Hanger Improperly Installed.

**Bolt Too Close To Bottom of Ledger, No Washer or Nut (Left).
Bolts Too Close to Top of Ledger (Right). Joist Support By Ledger Strip No Longer Allowed (Right).**

**Improper Ledger Attachment To Cantilevered Projection (Left).
Bolts Not Staggered Vertically (Right).
Joist Support By Ledger Strip No Longer Allowed (Both Pictures).**

Typical Defects, Deck Stairs and Landings

Typical defects that inspectors should report include:

1. stringers inadequately attached to deck,
2. stringers pulling away from deck,
3. stairs deflect when used,
4. cut stringer throat less than 5 inches of undisturbed wood, measured to saw kerf (saw blade cut),
5. excess stringer unsupported horizontal distance (span),
6. excess difference between riser heights or tread depths,
7. more than 4 inches open space at open risers,
8. absent solid landing at bottom of stairway,
9. landing too small,
10. excess tread unsupported horizontal distance,
11. deteriorated stringers or treads.

**Nailed Stringer Pulling Away From Deck (Left).
Inadequate Stringer Support at Deck and Stringer Split (Right).**

**Cut Stringer and Guard Post Span Too Long (Left).
Stringer Throat Excessively Cut (Right).**

<u>Typical Defects, Handrails and Guards</u> Typical defects that inspectors should report include:

1. handrail or guards absent or not continuous over all of stairway,
2. loose handrail or guards,
3. improper handrail size or shape,
4. improper handrail or guard height,

5. notched guard posts,
6. improper guard post attachment and spacing,
7. improper baluster attachment and spacing,
8. deteriorated handrails, balusters, or guard posts.

**Guard Post Improperly Notched and Nailed (Left).
Guard Posts Too Far Apart and Handrail Not Graspable (Right).**

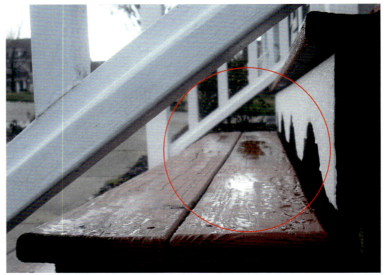

**Handrail Not Continuous and Handrail Not Graspable (Left).
Space Under Stair Guard Larger than 6 Inches (Right).**

2: Exterior Components

Typical Defects, Framing Typical defects that inspectors should report include:

1. deck slopes toward house, or inadequately slopes away from house,
2. deck joists secured to ledger or beam using only nails,
3. joist hangers or angle brackets improper size, not galvanized or stainless steel, all holes not filled with fasteners, incorrect fasteners used,
4. improper quantity or size of nails installed in ledger supporting floor joists (note: floor joist support by a ledger no longer allowed),
5. excess floor joist flooring span,
6. fasteners over-driven into flooring,
7. absent, improperly installed, improperly secured deck bracing,
8. deteriorated joists or flooring,
9. deteriorated (rusted) metal components (e. g. fasteners, joist hangers),
10. cuts in pressure treated lumber not field-treated,
11. wood not preservative treated or naturally durable.

**Joist Hanger Installed Without Fasteners in Holes (Left).
Joist Excessively Notched Joist, Measured to Saw Cut (Right).**

**Significantly Deteriorated Fasteners and Joist Hangers (Left)
Deteriorated Screw and Evidence of Water Intrusion (Right).**

**Deck Joists Attached Using Only Nails (Left)
Deck Bracing Improperly Installed (Right).**

Typical Defects, Posts, Footings, and Beams Typical defects that inspectors should report include:

1. post too tall for size and type of material,
2. post leaning or deformed,
3. post not properly attached to footing, or post not properly attached to beam,
4. post not in center third of footing,
5. post or beam deteriorated, especially at post bottom,
6. wood post split,
7. beam not properly attached to post,
8. footing too small or footing depth inadequate,
9. beam attached to side of post,
10. beam leaning, or deformed,
11. beam splice does not bear on post.

Significantly Deteriorated Deck Posts.

Footing Too Small and Too Close To Foundation (Left).
Post Base Significantly Deteriorated and Not In Center of Footing (Left).
Post Bearing on 3½ Thick Patio Slab (Right).

Beam Improperly Attached to Sides of Post (Left).
Beam Spliced and Splice Not Supported by Post (Right).

**Post Cap Bent, Improperly Installed (Left).
Improper Connector Used as Post Base (Right).**

Safety Issues Deck defects probably result in more injuries and deaths than any other system in a home. Refer to individual sections for specific information about deck safety issues.

Standards (1) IRC 2018 R507; (2) *Prescriptive Residential Wood Deck Construction Guide* (DCA6-12), American Wood Council; (3) manufacturer's instructions for alternative materials such as those used for deck flooring and deck railing.

GARAGE VEHICLE DOORS AND DOOR OPERATORS

Garage Vehicle Doors

Description **A defining feature of a garage is a door through which a vehicle may be driven.** Other vehicle storage structures, even if enclosed on all sides except the entry side, are carports. Garage vehicle doors are sometimes found in basements. Some house styles have the garage located under the house living area; this is called a drive-under or tuck-under garage. When a garage vehicle door is located under or beside a living area, the area where a vehicle could be stored should be considered a garage, and should be separated from other areas and from the story above as though it were an attached garage.

Garage vehicle doors are available in many materials, sizes, and types. Garage vehicle doors are usually made from wood, steel, or aluminum. Older doors are usually wood and most new doors are usually metal. Vinyl and fiberglass doors are also available, but are less common. Standard garage vehicle door sizes are 8 and 9 feet for single doors and 16 and 18 feet for double doors. Smaller doors, around 6 feet wide, are sometimes seen in adult communities where golf carts are popular. The standard height is 7 feet. Taller doors can be made by adding panels. Most garage vehicle doors are sectional doors that consist of 5 to 8 panels that are about 18 inches tall. Single panel doors consist of one panel that tilts up to open. These doors are more common in older garages. Roller or rollup doors consist of many small panels that roll on to a shaft when open. These doors are more common in commercial buildings.

Wood garage vehicle doors can weigh over 400 pounds. The lighter metal doors can weigh around 200 pounds, and even the lightest doors weigh around 100 pounds. Vehicle doors require springs to counterbalance the weight and to help open them.

There are two types of springs. The more common type is the **torsion spring**; this type is identified by one spring located above the door near the center. The less common type is the **extension spring**. This type is identified by two springs, one above each horizontal track. The springs are under significant tension, especially when the door is closed. Each extension spring should be equipped with a **containment cable** that is attached to the tracks and to the track supports. This cable helps keep the spring from flying loose and injuring someone if the springs breaks. **Homeowners should not attempt to adjust, repair, or replace the springs.**

<u>**Door Parts**</u> Garage vehicle doors have several parts in addition to the door itself. The following refers to sectional door parts. Each section is attached to the other using hinges. The door travels on two tracks, one on each side. The door is held in the tracks and moves on the tracks using rollers. A steel cable is attached to the bottom of each side of the door. This cable rolls on to roller drums located above each side of the door. Doors with a torsion spring have a torsion tube running through the spring and connecting the roller drums. Larger doors may have reinforcing struts installed across some panels. Additional reinforcing is usually required in high wind areas. The door should have a weather stripping at the bottom and along the sides. A weather tight seal is not expected.

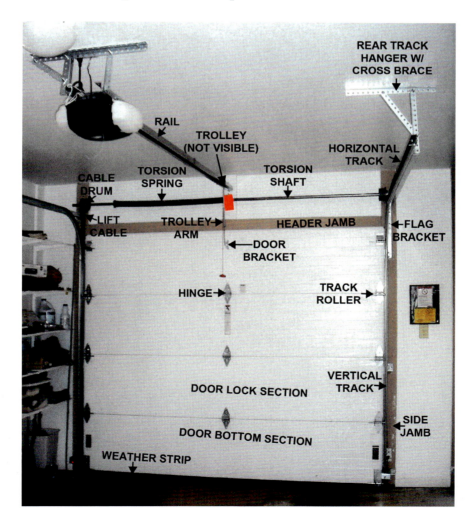

Installation Garage vehicle door tracks and torsion springs should be attached to solid framing. They should not be attached to or through a wall finish such as drywall. Wood bucks (back jambs) usually should be fastened around the door opening to serve as a place to attach the door, torsion spring, and the door operator. Bucks should not be attached to or through wall finish materials. The torsion spring and tracks should be installed using manufacturer-supplied fasteners and hardware.

Sectional door springs should be adjusted so that the door remains in position when raised about four feet above the floor. Home inspectors may check this as part of the door inspection; however, doing so requires disconnecting the door from the door operator. Worn or improperly adjusted springs are a common defect.

Back hangs (rear track hangers) are pieces of angle iron used to secure the tracks to the garage ceiling. A cross brace often should be installed to keep the tracks from moving laterally, especially if the garage has a high ceiling.

Some garage vehicle doors come with a rope that can be used to lower the door. Most come with a lock. These features should be removed or disabled when a door operator is installed. The rope can be a strangulation hazard and the lock can allow damage to the door or door operator if engaged when the operator tries to open the door.

Typical Defects Typical defects that inspectors should report include:

1. door or bucks attached through finish material (drywall) at wall,
2. damaged and deteriorated door, glazing, or weather stripping,
3. loose, deteriorated, worn, and improperly adjusted springs,
4. absent and improperly installed extension spring containment cable,
5. absent, loose, deteriorated, improper door hardware,
6. damaged and deteriorated lift cable,
7. door noisy or binds while operating,
8. evidence of significant water infiltration around or under the door (minor staining is normal),
9. unusually large gaps between the door and the opening,
10. lifting rope present when a door operator is used,
11. improper lock operation,
12. lock not disabled when door operator is used.

Safety Issues (1) even the lightest garage vehicle doors are heavy and can cause significant injury and property damage if the door closes quickly or if it falls out of its tracks; (2) home owners should not attempt to repair or adjust springs because of the risk of injury.

Standards (1) IRC 2018 R301.2.1.2 (protection of openings); (2) manufacturer's instructions; (3) Door and Access Systems Manufacturers Association (DASMA) guidelines.

2: Exterior Components

Door and Operator Improperly Attached Through Drywall.

Buck Pulling Away From Wall.

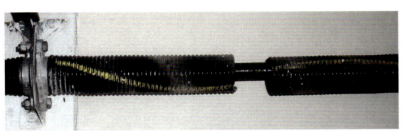

Broken Torsion Spring.

Broken Lift Cable.

**Extension Spring With Containment Cable (Top).
Extension Spring Without Containment Cable (Bottom).**

Typical Reportable Garage Door Damage.

Vehicle Door Operators

Description Vehicle door operators are more commonly called garage door openers (openers). They are electric motor-driven devices that open and close the door by radio remote control and by switches.

Openers are usually classified by the horsepower rating of the electric motor and by the drive type. The most common motor is ½ horsepower. Less common are the ⅓ and ¾ horsepower motors. One-third horsepower openers are usually appropriate only for lightweight single doors. Common drive types are the chain, belt, and screw drives. Chain drives are the least expensive, but they make more noise and require more adjustment and maintenance than belt and screw drives.

A less common drive type is the jackshaft, which may be installed where one of the common openers will not fit. Examples include when there is a low garage ceiling, and when a beam blocks the space where the opener rail must be installed. Jackshaft drive openers are mounted either above the door or on the side of the door; they turn the torsion tube instead of lifting the door.

Opener Parts Openers consist of several parts. The motor and controls are contained in the motor unit. The motor unit is attached to the rail (track) which runs to near the center of the door opening above the door. The drive mechanism (chain, belt, screw) is attached to a trolley that runs along the rail. The trolley connects to the door arm which connects to the door bracket which is attached to the door.

Installation The motor unit is suspended from pieces of angle iron. A cross brace should usually be installed to keep the unit from moving laterally, especially if the garage has a high ceiling. The rail should be attached to solid framing near the center of the door. It should not be attached to or through a wall finish such as drywall. Some lightweight doors, such as those made from fiberglass and aluminum, may need reinforcement at the door bracket. The home inspector should look for stressed connections around the door bracket.

Opener safety features are frequently improperly installed. The safety reverse sensors should be installed **not more than 6 inches** above the floor. This helps avoid crushing objects or people. The wall switch should be installed **at least 60 inches** above the floor. This makes it more difficult for children to operate the door. The manual release rope should be installed **at least 72 inches** above the floor; this is another child safety precaution. New openers have a safety label that should be installed near the wall switch. This is rarely done.

Opener Testing During Inspection

There is considerable controversy about how to test an opener during an inspection. Most standards of practice require operating the opener using normal controls; some specifically require testing the safety reversing functions. Testing the pressure reversing function involves placing a 1½ inch thick object (usually a 2x4 laid flat) at the center of the door and allowing the door to strike the object when it closes. The risk of this method is that the door or opener could easily be damaged if the opener or door is improperly adjusted or defective. Other test methods, such as stopping the door with hands, do not comply with manufacturer's instructions, and are not a valid test. The stop with hands test is commonly used, but this method can also cause door damage. Home inspectors should comply with the standard of practice. If the standard is silent about testing the pressure reverse function, the home inspector must make a business decision about how or whether to conduct this test. Reporting and disclaiming the pressure reverse function is a common business decision. Using and testing remote controls is out of scope of a home inspection, unless the opener is operated only using remote controls, and unless the remote controls are available during the inspection.

Typical Defects

Typical defects that inspectors should report include:

1. opener attachment point at door not reinforced according to door manufacturer's instructions (most common with light metal doors),
2. opener attached through finish material (drywall) at wall,
3. absent, worn, loose, and damaged parts,
4. opener does not operate using wall switch,
5. opener operates only when switch is depressed (usually a sensor problem),
6. opener unusually noisy while operating,
7. bypassed safety reverse sensors,
8. safety reverse sensors too high above the floor,
9. opener does not reverse when it strikes an object,
10. manual release cord hangs too low,
11. lights do not operate,
12. absent, damaged, not functioning wall switch.

Safety Issues

Garage vehicle doors and their openers can cause significant injury and property damage if the opener does not reverse when it should.

Standards

(1) IRC 2018 R309.4 (opener listing); (2) manufacturer's instructions; (3) Door and Access Systems Manufacturers Association (DASMA) guidelines.

**Garage Door Not Reinforced According to Manufacturer's Instructions (Left).
Damage Caused by Failure to Reinforce Garage Door (Right).**

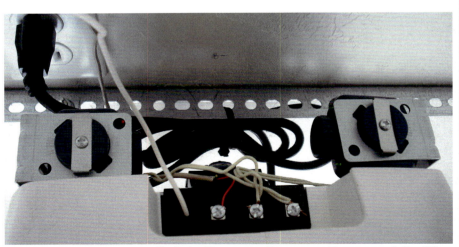

**Safety Reverse Sensors Bypassed (Left).
Safety Reverse Sensors Too High Above Floor (Right).**

Please visit https://nationalhomeinspectorexam.org/prepare-for-the-exam/ and take advantage of the practice quizzes. The questions in the practice quizzes are designed to reflect the difficulty of the questions on the actual exam. The questions on the practice quizzes are not questions on the National Home Inspectors Exam. Passing the practice quizzes does not guarantee that you will pass the National exam. You will still need to study all topics to be prepared for the National exam.

3: ROOF COMPONENTS

INSPECTION SCOPE

Roof components that are in scope of a home inspection include the visible and accessible roof coverings, such as shingles, roof drainage systems, such as gutters and downspouts, roof flashing components, such as vent flashing, and skylights.

STEEP SLOPE ROOF COVERINGS

Introduction

Steep slope roof coverings may be defined as roof coverings installed on roofs that **slope 2 inches vertically in 12 inches horizontally (2:12) or greater**. This distinguishes them from low slope roof coverings that may be installed on roofs that slope between ¼:12 and 2:12.

Most steep slope roof coverings are **water shedding** roof coverings. **A water shedding roof covering relies to some degree on a layer under the roof covering (the underlayment) to provide a water-resistive barrier system.** For example, fiberglass (asphalt) shingle roof coverings use the underlayment as a secondary water-resistive barrier. Concrete and clay tile roof coverings rely on the underlayment as the primary water-resistive barrier.

In this section, we present the steep roof coverings that home inspectors are most likely to encounter. This is not a complete list of all possible steep roof coverings.

Asbestos Cement Shingles

Description These shingles are most commonly seen as squares and rectangles, but they may also appear as polygons. They were produced in a variety of colors. Thickness is about ⅛ inch for less expensive shingles to ¼ inch for the better quality shingles. They were installed by fastening the shingles to solid-sheathed roofs, preferably over an underlayment. They were first available in the late 1900s and were most popular from 1910s to 1950s. The service life of the thinner shingles is reported to be around 50 years, and around 75 years for the thicker shingles. Asbestos was banned in most building products in 1973; however, these shingles were manufactured until the early 1990s. This roof covering is no longer available and matching replacement shingles can be difficult to find and can be expensive.

Asbestos Cement Shingles.

Typical Defects Typical defects that home inspectors should report include:

1. absent shingles,
2. cracked and damaged shingles, potentially allowing friable asbestos,
3. roof penetration located in a valley.

Safety Issues Asbestos abatement and containment protocols must be followed during cutting and removal; these procedures can be costly.

Asphalt (Fiberglass, Composition) Shingles

Description Two types of asphalt shingles are commonly available. One type, sometimes called an **organic shingle**, has a base made from felt impregnated with asphalt. Most shingles available today are fiberglass shingles that have a base made from asphalt impregnated fiberglass. Asphalt shingles are also called **composition shingles**.

Three shingle styles are commonly available. The style names and warranty length differ between manufacturers. The **three-tab strip shingle** is the least expensive style and is found on many homes. It has a flat profile and usually comes with a 20 year warranty. The next step up is the **dimensional shingle**. This shingle has a raised profile and usually has a 25 to 30 year warranty. The most expensive shingle is the **laminated shingle**. It is two shingles bonded together to present a more pronounced raised profile. The warranty on these shingles is usually 35+ years.

Three-tab Shingles.

Dimensional Shingles.

The weight per square ranges from about 200 pounds for less expensive three-tab shingles to over 400 pounds for laminated shingles. **A square is 100 square feet**. Shingles are considered a light roof covering; however, heavier shingles can create problems for roofs that are inadequately framed and when installing multiple layers of shingles. **Look for framing issues when you see laminated shingles**, especially on older homes and when there are multiple layers of shingles.

Installation Shingles should be installed on solid-sheathed roofs. The **minimum roof slope should be 2:12**, except where otherwise specified by the shingle manufacturer. Industry guidelines recommend a 4:12 minimum slope. Note that **valleys are at a lower slope than the intersecting roof planes**; therefore, valleys formed by roofs near the minimum slope may be too low slope for shingle application.

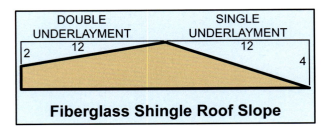

Fiberglass Shingle Roof Slope

Underlayment is specified under shingles. Underlayment should be applied horizontally with respect to the eaves and with the seams lapped. The traditional underlayment for shingle roof covering is #15 asphalt-impregnated felt. Underlayment for new shingle roof covering installations is often a synthetic material made from polyproplene or a similar material. Double underlayment is usually specified for roof slopes between 2:12 and 4:12. **Ice barrier underlayment** is specified in cold climates when required by local authorities. **Drip edge flashing is now required at eaves** (IRC 2012). Underlayment should be installed over drip edge flashing at the eaves, and under drip edge flashing at the rakes.

Felt Underlayment.

Synthetic Underlayment.

Shingles should be attached using galvanized steel or aluminum roofing **nails** that are **long enough to penetrate at least ¾ inch into the sheathing**. Manufacturers usually specify four nails per strip, except on very steep slope roofs and on roofs in high wind zones. Six nails per strip are specified in these conditions. **Nail location can be important**. Nails installed above the seal strip usually void manufacturer's warranties and may allow shingles to blow off during high wind. **Staples are a problematic shingle fastener** and are not currently permitted by the IRC. Staples may be allowed, but are not recommended, by some manufacturers.

Common shingle valley types are: open, closed-cut, and woven. Open and closed-cut valleys are usually acceptable for all shingle styles. Some manufacturers specify open valleys for laminated shingles.

Closed-cut and woven valleys should be flashed using a 36 inch wide strip of smooth roll roofing, or any open valley flashing material. Open valleys should be flashed using at least a 24 inch wide strip of aluminum or galvanized steel or two layers of roll roofing. Other valley flashing materials may be acceptable. Valley flashing should not be penetrated by plumbing vents, appliance vents, and other penetrations.

3: Roof Components 125

Typical Shingle Roof Covering Repairs Asphalt-based roofing cement is the common material used to repair and seal shingles, and as bedding cement used prior to installing flashing. **Flashing cement** usually has a thicker consistency and is intended for vertical surfaces. **Lap cement** has a thinner consistency and is intended bonding shingles together. It is difficult for home inspectors to tell these cements apart during an inspection.

Acceptable applications for lap cement include as a seal for the starter strip and when sealing other shingle tabs. When lap cement is applied to seal small holes, such as nail holes, it should be applied under the shingle tab. When applied in this manner, it is usually considered an acceptable repair.

Roofing cement is not intended as a replacement for shingles, or as a replacement for flashing. Roofing cement degrades rapidly when exposed to the elements (especially sunlight), and requires regular maintenance.

Absent and damaged shingle tabs and strips may be replaced with similar material if the new material is properly integrated into the existing material.

Clients are sometimes concerned about organic growth on shingles, such as algae and moss. Organic growth is more common in warm wet climates, and is more common on north-facing roofs that get less exposure to sunlight. Algae is usually considered a cosmetic issue, not a reportable defect. Moss can loosen granules on the shingles, causing shingle damage. Moss is a reportable defect. Many shingle manufacturers do not recommend cleaning shingles because of the risk of granule loss.

Typical Defects Typical defects that home inspectors should report include:

1. shingle deterioration such as granule loss, visible fibers at edges, curling, and a stiff/dry feel (cold shingles often feel stiff),
2. damaged and absent shingle tabs due to causes such as scraping by tree limbs, foot traffic, wind, and hail,
3. absent sealant strip at first course,
4. improper nail quantity and location,
5. exposed or withdrawing fasteners,
6. roof penetration in a valley,
7. use of dimensional or laminated shingles as cap shingles,
8. three or more shingle layers (two layers are allowed, but not recommended),
9. shingles not properly offset relative to course above, especially with dimensional and laminated shingles.

Safety Issues Shingle roof covering defects rarely present safety issues; however, older shingles often present loose granules that can make walking on the roof them more difficult and dangerous.

Standards (1) IRC 2018 R905.2; (2) National Roofing Contractors Association Guidelines; (3) manufacturer's instructions.

3: Roof Components

Significant Deterioration At End of Service Life.

Fraying at Edges and Granule Loss Near End of Service Life.

Damage, Probably Foot Traffic.

Hail Damage.

No Seal Strip and Gap at Starter Course.

Nail Above Seal Strip, No Nail at Edge.

Two Layers.

Improper Offset.

Pictures Courtesy of Welmoed Sisson

Improper Repair.

Dimensional Shingles Used as Cap Shingles.

Concrete and Clay Tiles

Description Tile roof coverings are classified by material and shape. **Concrete tiles** are made using Portland cement, water, and sand or some other aggregate. Colors are introduced by mixing pigments with the concrete, or by spraying color on the concrete during production. **Clay tiles** are made using clay, water, and other materials that add color and alter the tile's hardness and durability.

Tiles are available in many shapes. The most common shapes are the **Spanish tile** with an S shape, the **Mission (pan and cover) tile** with a C shape, and the flat (shingle) tile. **Flat tiles** may have flat sides or may have grooves that lock the tile sides together. Each shape has its own accessory tiles for ridges and rakes.

Clay Tile, Mission.

Concrete Tile, Flat.

Concrete Tile, Spanish.

The service life of the tiles of a tile roof covering can be 100 years or more depending on the quality of the tile and on the environment. The service life of the underlayment can be as little as 20 years in very hot and very cold climates. Mineral surfaced roll roofing or other durable underlayment is preferred as underlayment in these climates because #30 felt (the minimum underlayment) will probably not last as long as the tile.

Tile is considered a heavy roof covering. Weight per 100 square feet is between about 600 pounds for some clay tiles to about 1,100 pounds for some concrete tiles. Roof framing should be designed to support this weight. An engineer should evaluate the roof structure before installing tiles on a roof designed for a light roof covering.

Tiles absorb water, some more than others. The tendency of a tile to absorb water can be adjusted during the manufacturing process, or by applying a sealer to the tile. Tiles that absorb too much water may prematurely deteriorate during freeze-thaw cycles. Widespread cracking and spalling may be evidence of tile failure.

Clay tiles are usually brittle and can break easily under load and impacts. Use of clay tiles in areas where hail is likely should be carefully considered. Most home inspectors should not walk on clay tile roofs. Concrete tiles are usually sturdier than clay tiles and can usually withstand loads and impacts better than clay tiles. Home inspectors may choose to walk on concrete tile roofs when trained in proper safety procedures.

Installation Tiles may be installed on solid-sheathed roofs or on spaced structural sheathing boards. The **minimum roof slope should be 2½:12**, except where otherwise specified by the tile manufacturer. Industry guidelines recommend a 4:12 minimum slope. Note that **valleys are at a lower slope than the intersecting roof planes**; therefore, valleys formed by roofs near the minimum slope may be too low slope for tile application.

Tiles are primarily for shedding water and protecting the underlayment from solar radiation and the elements. The **underlayment is the waterproof material** that protects the roof from water entry in a tile roof covering system.

Underlayment (at least #30 felt) is specified under tiles. Underlayment should be applied horizontally with respect to the eaves and with the seams lapped. Double underlayment is usually specified for roof slopes between 2½:12 and 4:12. **Ice barrier underlayment** is specified in cold climates when required by local authorities. Drip edge flashing at the eaves is recommended, but may not be required. Underlayment should be installed over drip edge flashing at the eaves. **Underlayment should lap over rakes at least 1 inch** to protect the rake edge from water damage.

Tiles may be attached to the roof by several methods including nails, screws, wire-ties, clips, and wood battens (usually 1x2 inch boards). These methods are sometimes used in combination. The appropriate fastening method depends on the tile used, the roof slope, and local weather conditions. Manufacturer's instructions and local regulations determine the proper tile installation method.

All perimeter tiles should be fastened. The perimeter is usually defined as at least 36 inches from both sides of ridges, at the eaves, and at gable rakes. Tiles not located at the perimeter (field tiles) may not require fasteners when the tiles are supported by battens. Nails, when used, should be galvanized steel nails or aluminum nails that are long enough to penetrate at least ¾ inch into the sheathing.

Common tile valley types are open and closed. An open valley is one where the metal valley flashing is exposed. A closed (mitered) valley is one where the tiles cover the metal valley flashing. Open valleys are preferred where debris accumulation is expected and when freeze-thaw cycles are common.

Tile Roof Valley with Steel Valley Flashing and Wood Battens.

Both valley types should be flashed using a 36 inch wide strip of at least #30 felt as a base layer. An additional layer of least a 22 inch wide strip of galvanized steel with a 1 inch tall splash diverter in the center should be installed above the base layer. Valley flashing should not be penetrated by plumbing vents, appliance vents, and other penetrations.

Hip and ridge tiles are installed over a nailer, which is usually a 2x4 installed with the long side vertical. The nailer provides a place to fasten the tile. The nailer is not required to be covered with a water-resistive material. Hip and ridge tiles at the beginning and end of the hip or ridge are secured in place with mortar commonly called a **mud ball**.

Tiles should be installed with a sufficient **head lap** so that the tiles are better able to shed water. The typical head lap is 3 inches, but will vary based on tile style and manufacturer's instructions.

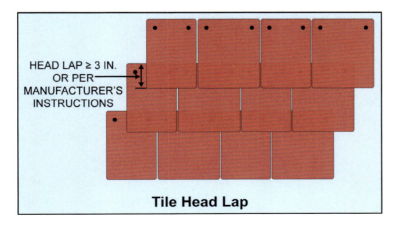

Typical Roof Covering Repairs

1. loose tiles may be repositioned and secured,
2. cracked tiles should be replaced; repair of cracked tiles with adhesive is not recommended,
3. tiles with minor chips at the corners may be left in place if the chip does not expose the underlayment,
4. damaged or deteriorated underlayment should be replaced; this is common at eaves and gable rakes,
5. a cracked mud ball should be replaced if the tiles it secures are loose.

Typical Defects Typical defects that home inspectors should report include:

1. tiles loose or not in installed position,
2. damaged or absent tiles including cracked tiles and tiles with significantly chipped edges,
3. inadequate head lap (usually at least 3 inches is recommended),
4. absent fasteners at perimeter tiles,
5. damaged or deteriorated underlayment,
6. roof penetrations located in a valley,
7. cracked or damaged mud balls,
8. over-cut tiles that expose the underlayment (usually at hips).

Safety Issues Tile roof covering defects rarely present safety issues; however, tiles can be very slippery when wet, especially tiles with a glazed surface.

Standards (1) IRC 2018 R905.3; (2) National Roofing Contractors Association Guidelines; (3) manufacturer's instructions.

Loose Tiles.

Cracked Tile.

Cracked Mud Ball.

Excessively Cut Tile Exposing Underlayment.

Fiber Cement Roofing

Description This roof covering is marketed as a **lighter weight alternative** to concrete tiles and clay tiles, slate, and wood shingles and shakes. Weight per square is reported to be between 325 and 500 pounds depending on the style. Thickness is reported to be around ¼ inch. The estimated service life is reported to be between 25 and 45 years. This product is uncommon in most market.

Some of these products are relatively new, having been introduced since about 2000. **Versions installed during the 1980s and 1990s are reported to have several significant problems,** such as cracking, deterioration, and delamination.

Installation Installation should be according to manufacturer's instructions. The following are typical installation instructions which will vary by manufacturer and by product style. This roof covering should be installed on solid-sheathed roofs. The **minimum roof slope should be 3:12** or 4:12 depending on the product style. **Note that valleys are at a lower slope than the intersecting roof planes**; therefore, valleys formed by roofs near the minimum slope may be too low slope for shingle application.

Underlayment (at least #30 felt) is specified under this roof covering. Underlayment should be applied horizontally with respect to the eaves with seams lapped. Ice barrier underlayment is specified in cold climates when required by local authorities. Drip edge flashing is not specified.

This roof covering should be attached using corrosion-resistant screw shank nails or screws as recommended by the manufacturer. Head lap varies with the product and is usually around 3 – 4 inches.

An open valley is usually recommended. An open valley is one where the metal valley flashing is exposed. Valleys should be flashed using a 36 inch wide strip of at least #30 felt as a base layer. An additional layer of least a 22 – 24 inch wide strip of galvanized steel with a 1 inch tall splash diverter in the center should be installed above the base layer. Valley flashing should not be penetrated by plumbing vents, appliance vents, and other penetrations.

Typical Roof Covering Repairs This product is too new to have a meaningful record of typical repairs.

Typical Defects Newer versions of this product are too new to have a meaningful record of typical defects. Note that older versions have experienced problems as previously discussed.

Standards Manufacturer's instructions.

Metal Shingles

Description Metal shingles are defined as being **less than 3 square feet**. This distinguishes metal shingles from metal panels which are defined as being 3 square feet or more.

Metal shingles are made from naturally weathering metals or from metals that require a protective coating. Protective coatings include zinc (galvanized steel), paint, and adhered aggregate (granules) similar to those used with fiberglass shingles. Naturally weathering metals include aluminum, copper, and stainless steel.

Some metal shingles are flat sheets or are embossed with a decorative design. Modular metal shingles are stamped to simulate roof coverings such as slate, wood shakes, and tile.

The service life of metal shingles is reported to be 50 years or more, depending on the quality of the metal, on maintenance, and on the environment.

Metal is considered a light roof covering. Weight per 100 square feet is around 100 pounds, less for some lightweight aluminum shingles, and more for shingles with an adhered aggregate coating.

Metal Shingles Simulating Tile.

Metal Shingles.

Installation Metal shingles should be installed according to manufacturer's instructions. The following are typical instructions which will vary by manufacturer. Metal shingles may be installed on solid-sheathed roofs or on closely spaced structural sheathing boards. The **minimum roof slope should be 3:12**. Industry guidelines recommend a 4:12 minimum slope. Note that **valleys are at a lower slope than the intersecting roof planes**; therefore, valleys formed by roofs near the minimum slope may be too low slope for tile application.

Underlayment is not specified under metal shingles unless required by the manufacturer. Some manufacturers may specify proprietary underlayment. Note, however, that **condensation between the metal and the roof sheathing can be an issue** if metal shingles are installed without underlayment. This condensation can present as a defect that looks like a roof covering leak. Ice barrier underlayment is specified in cold climates when required by local authorities.

Metal shingles should be attached to the roof according to manufacturer's instructions. Fasteners should be compatible with the metal shingles (e.g., no galvanized steel fasteners with copper). Installation using battens may be specified for some modular metal shingles.

Valleys should be flashed using a 36 inch wide strip of at least #30 felt as a base layer. An additional layer of least a 16 inch wide strip of metal that is compatible with the metal shingles with a ¾ inch tall splash diverter in the center should be installed above the base layer. Valley flashing should not be penetrated by plumbing vents, appliance vents, and other penetrations.

Hip and ridge shingles should be installed over a layer of underlayment wrapped over the hip or ridge. Ridges that serve as ventilation are covered by the ventilation material.

Metal shingles may be installed over existing roof coverings if the existing roof covering is not significantly deteriorated. Installing metal shingles over an existing roof covering can create problems such as sealing around penetrations, and maintaining clearance between the roof covering and wall coverings. It is usually not possible to determine the type or condition of the concealed roof covering. Home inspectors should report this limitation.

Typical Roof Covering Repairs

1. rust may be repaired by removing the rust, priming, and painting,
2. small holes may be permanently patched using the same metal and soldering the patch to the metal, then priming and painting,
3. small holes may be temporarily patched using the same metal and adhering the metal patch to the shingle using flashing cement,
4. shingles may be replaced using the same installation method as the original shingles.

Typical Defects Typical defects that home inspectors should report include:

1. deteriorated protective coatings,
2. deteriorated (rusted) shingles,
3. damaged shingles,
4. roof penetrations located in valley,
5. damaged or open seams between shingles (especially flat shingles that were soldered).

Safety Issues Metal shingle roof covering defects rarely present safety issues; however, metal shingles can be very slippery when wet and can be damaged by foot traffic.

Standards (1) IRC 2018 R905.4; (2) National Roofing Contractors Association Guidelines; (3) manufacturer's instructions.

Metal Panels

Description **Metal panels** are defined as being **3 square feet or more**. This distinguishes metal panels from metal shingles, which are defined as being less than 3 square feet.

Metal panels are made from naturally weathering metals or from metals that require a protective coating. Protective coatings include zinc (galvanized steel), paint, and adhered aggregate (granules) similar to those used with fiberglass shingles. Naturally weathering metals include aluminum, copper, and stainless steel.

Metal panels are installed in one of three ways. **Standing seam** roofs have a vertical seam between each panel that is crimped to restrict water entry. Standing seam roofs are considered a low slope roof covering with a **minimum slope of ¼:12**. **Sealed seam** roofs have seams that are lapped, fastened, and sealed with a manufacturer-approved sealant. Sealed seam roofs are considered a low slope roof covering with a **minimum slope of ½:12**. **Non-sealed (lapped) seam** roofs have seams that are lapped and fastened, usually with a screw or pop rivet. These roofs are considered a steep slope roof covering with a **minimum slope of 3:12**.

The service life of metal panels is reported to be 50 years or more, depending on the quality of the metal, on maintenance, and on the environment.

Metal is considered a light roof covering. Weight per 100 square feet is around 100 pounds, less for some lightweight panels, and more for heavier gauge steel panels.

Standing Seam Metal Roof with Seams Flattened on Arch.

Lapped Seam Metal Roof.

Installation Metal panels should be installed according to manufacturer's instructions. The following are typical instructions, which will vary by manufacturer. Metal panels may be installed on solid-sheathed roofs or on spaced structural sheathing boards. Note that **valleys are at a lower slope than the intersecting roof planes**; therefore, valleys formed by roofs near the minimum slope may be too low slope for panel application.

Underlayment is not specified under metal panels unless required by the manufacturer. Note, however, that condensation between the metal and the roof sheathing can be an issue if metal panels are installed without underlayment. This condensation can present as a defect that looks like a roof covering leak. Ice barrier underlayment is specified in cold climates when required by local authorities.

Metal panels should be attached to the roof according to manufacturer's instructions. Fasteners should be compatible with the metal panels (no galvanized steel fasteners with copper). Fasteners used with lapped seam metal panels should have a washer on the head end.

Metal panels may be installed over existing roof coverings if the existing roof covering is not significantly deteriorated. Installing metal panels over an existing roof covering can create problems, such as sealing around penetrations and clearance between the roof covering and wall coverings. It is usually not possible to determine the type or condition of the concealed roof covering. Home inspectors should report this limitation.

Typical Roof Covering Repairs See metal shingles.

Typical Visible Defects Typical defects that home inspectors should report include:

1. loose and absent fasteners (usually lapped seam roofs),
2. splayed washers at lapped seam roof fasteners,
3. deteriorated protective coating,
4. deteriorated (rusted) panels,
5. damaged panels,
6. excessive ripples in panels (sometimes called oil-canning),
7. roof penetrations located in valley,
8. damaged, opened, or improperly installed seams between panels (usually lapped seam roofs).

Safety Issues Metal panel roof covering defects rarely present safety issues; however, metal panels can be very slippery when wet and can be damaged by foot traffic.

Standards (1) IRC 2018 R905.10; (2) National Roofing Contractors Association Guidelines; (3) manufacturer's instructions.

Fastener Loose.

Fastener Not Plumb.

Absent Fasteners.

Improper Seam Lap.

Not Enough Fasteners Around Vent Boot

Slate Shingles

Description Slate shingles are stone that is quarried and shaped into shingles of various sizes and thickness. Most slate used in North America is quarried in the Northeast United States and in Eastern Canada. This is one reason why slate roofs are more common in the Northeast and are less common in other parts of North America. Some slate is imported. The color and grade of slate shingles varies depending on where it is quarried.

Standard commercial slate shingles are about ¼ inch thick; however, thicknesses up to 2 inches are available, and are used in some installations. Slate shingles are available in many standard sizes ranging from 6x10 inches to 14x24 inches. The shape is usually rectangular, but home inspectors may encounter other shapes.

The service life of slate shingles is reported to be at least 50 years, however, slate roofs over 100 years old are known to exist. The service life of soft slate shingles may be as little as 20 to 40 years, while the service life of harder slate shingles may be 200 years or more.

Slate shingles are considered a very heavy roof covering. Weight per 100 square feet is between about 700 pounds to about 1,000 pounds for standard slate shingles, and can be as much as 8,000 pounds per square for large, thick slate shingles. Roof framing should be designed to support this weight. An engineer should evaluate the roof structure before the installation of slate on a roof designed for a light roof covering.

Slate Shingle Roof Covering.

<u>Installation</u> Slate shingles should be installed on solid-sheathed roofs, although spaced sheathing may exist in older homes. The **minimum roof slope should be 4:12**. Note that val**leys are at a lower slope than the intersecting roof planes**; therefore, valleys formed by roofs near the minimum slope may be too low slope for slate application.

Underlayment is not specified under slate shingles unless required by the manufacturer. Ice barrier underlayment is specified in cold climates when required by local authorities. Drip edge flashing at the eaves is recommended, but may not be required.

Slate shingles should be attached to the roof using nails specifically designed for slate shingles, such as copper, stainless steel, bronze, or brass. The very long service life of slate shingles makes fastener selection very important. Two fasteners per slate shingle are specified. The fasteners should be driven flush with the slate shingle surface, not tight against the slate.

Common valley types are open, closed, and rounded. An open valley is one where the metal valley flashing is exposed. A closed (mitered) valley is one where the shingles cover the metal valley flashing. Closed valleys should be limited to roof slopes of 8:12 or more. A rounded valley is one where the shingles cover the metal flashing in a semicircular pattern. Rounded valleys are uncommon because of their installation cost.

All valley types should be flashed using a 36 inch wide strip of at least #30 felt as a base layer. An additional layer of a minimum 15 inch wide strip of galvanized steel (G90) or other approved corrosion-resistant metal is also required. Industry guidelines specify that the metal flashing should be at least 18 inches wide with a splash diverter. Valley flashing should not be penetrated by plumbing vents, appliance vents, and other penetrations.

Hip and ridge shingles are installed over a nailer that matches the shingle thickness. The nailer provides a place to fasten the shingles. The nailer should be covered with corrosion-resistant metal flashing. A corrosion-resistant metal ridge cap is an acceptable alternative hip and ridge cover.

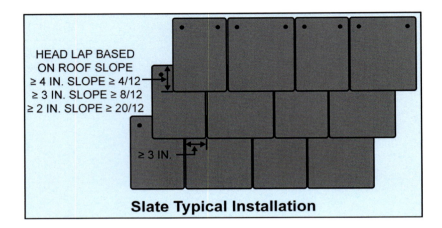

Typical Roof Covering Repairs

1. loose shingles should be repositioned and secured,
2. cracked and damaged shingles should be replaced; repair of shingles with adhesive or roofing cement is not recommended,
3. shingles with minor chips at the edges and minor delamination may be left in place.

Typical Defects Typical defects that home inspectors should report include:

1. shingles loose or not in installed position,
2. damaged, deteriorated, and absent shingles, including cracked shingles, delaminating shingles, and shingles with significantly chipped edges,
3. inadequate head lap,
4. absent, exposed, and deteriorated fasteners,
5. roof penetrations located in a valley.

Standards (1) IRC 2018 R905.6; (2) National Roofing Contractors Association Guidelines; (3) slateroofcentral.com; (4) manufacturer's instructions.

Loose Shingle. Replaced Shingles. Moderate Delamination.

Synthetic Component (Polymer) Roof Coverings

Description These roof coverings are made from polymer resins and recycled materials, like plastic and rubber. They are marketed as a more durable alternative to fiberglass shingles, wood shakes, and wood shingles. Styles that simulate concrete tiles, clay tiles, and slate also exist. Weight per square is reported to be around 275 to 350 pounds, depending on the style and on the installation method. Thickness is reported to be around ½ inch. This is a relatively new product. The first known examples of the product date to around 2000.

Polymer Roof Covering, Simulated Shakes.

Polymer Roof Covering, Simulated Slate.

Installation Installation should be according to manufacturer's instructions. Installation instructions vary widely between manufacturers and products.

Typical Roof Covering Repairs This product is too new to have a meaningful record of typical repairs.

Typical Defects This product is too new to have a meaningful record of typical defects.

Standards Manufacturer's instructions.

Wood Shingles and Shakes

Description Wood shingles and shakes are made from naturally durable wood (usually cedar) or from preservative treated wood such as southern yellow pine. Other wood species are used. Naturally durable means that the wood has some resistance to deterioration without applying a preservative; however, a field-applied preservative is often necessary. Wood shingles have a uniform butt thickness (the thick end) and a flat, smooth surface. They are usually manufactured by sawing the wood. This distinguishes wood shingles from wood shakes, which are thicker at the butt end and have a less uniform surface. Wood shakes are usually manufactured by splitting the wood.

Wood shingles are about ½ inch thick at the butt end. Shingles are ava. lengths of 16, 18, and 24 inches. Standard shapes include straight and roun several different pointed butt edges.

Wood shakes are about ⅝ to ¾ inch thick at the butt end. Shakes are available in standard lengths of 16 and 24 inches. Shakes have a straight butt edge.

Shingles and shakes are classified by grade. Premium and #1 grade are recommended for exposed shingles.

The service life of a wood roof covering is reported to be about 30 years. Factors such as environment, installation, and maintenance can significantly affect the service life.

Wood shingles and shakes are considered a light roof covering. Weight per 100 square feet is between about 250 and 350 pounds.

Wood Shakes.

Wood Shingles.

Installation Wood shingles and shakes may be installed on solid-sheathed roofs, or on spaced structural sheathing boards that are at least 1x4. Spaced sheathing has the advantage of permitting the wood to dry from both sides, which can extend its service life. Spaced sheathing for shingles and shakes should be installed using on center spacing that is equal to the weather exposure of the material.

The **minimum roof slope should be 3:12**. Industry guidelines recommend a 4:12 minimum slope. **Note that valleys are at a lower slope than the intersecting roof planes**; therefore, valleys formed by roofs near the minimum slope may be too low slope for shingle and shake application.

Underlayment is not specified under wood roof coverings unless required by the manufacturer. Industry guidelines recommend omitting underlayment under spaced sheathing to allow drying from underneath. Ice barrier underlayment is specified in cold climates when required by local authorities. Solid sheathing should be installed under ice barrier underlayment. Drip edge flashing at the eaves is recommended, but may not be required. Underlayment should be installed over drip edge flashing at the eaves.

Interlayment is specified between shake courses. The minimum interlayment is #15 felt. Industry guidelines specify #30 felt.

Shingles and shakes should be attached to the roof using galvanized steel nails or other approved corrosion-resistant nails, such as stainless steel. Staples are an acceptable method, but may not provide equivalent long term performance. The fasteners should be long enough to penetrate the sheathing at least ½ inch.

Two fasteners per shingle and shake are specified. Shingle fasteners should be placed not more than ¾ inch from each side and not more than 1 inch above the butt end above the nails. Shake fasteners should be placed not more than 1 inch from each side and not more than 2 inches above the butt end above the nails.

A space (**keyway**) should be left between shingles and shakes to allow for the wood to expand. The space between shingles should be between ¼ and ⅜ inch. The space between shingles should be offset at least 1 ½ inches between adjacent shingle courses. The space between shakes should be between ⅜ and ⅝ inch.

The length of the exposed part (exposure) of shingles and shakes varies based on the shingle length, grade, and roof pitch. Exposure for shingles varies between 5 inches and 7 ½ inches for roof slopes of 4:12 or more. Exposure for shakes is 7 ½ inches for 18 inch shakes and 10 inches for 24 inch shakes.

Common wood roof covering valley types are open, closed (mitered), and swept. An open valley is one where the metal valley flashing is exposed. A closed valley is one where the wood covers the metal valley flashing. Closed valleys are not recommended in environments with high annual rainfall amounts, and where debris can collect in the valley. A swept valley is one where the wood covers the metal flashing in a semicircular pattern. Swept valleys are uncommon because of their installation cost.

All valley types should be flashed with a minimum 20 inch wide strip of galvanized steel or other approved corrosion-resistant metal. Industry guidelines specify a minimum 24 inch width with a splash diverter and a 36 inch wide layer of at least #30 felt under the metal flashing. Valley flashing should not be penetrated by plumbing vents, appliance vents, and other penetrations.

Hip and ridge shingles and shakes should be installed over a weather-resistant membrane.

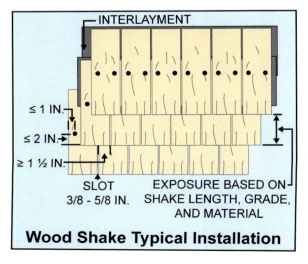

Wood Shake Typical Installation

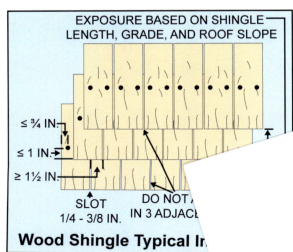

Wood Shingle Typical Installation

Typical Roof Covering Repairs

1. loose and absent shingles and shakes should be repositioned or replaced and secured,
2. split and damaged shingles should be replaced.

Clients are sometimes concerned about organic growth on wood roof coverings, such as algae and moss. Organic growth is more common in warm wet climates, and is more common on north-facing roofs that get less exposure to sunlight. Algae is usually considered a cosmetic issue, not a reportable defect; however, algae can indicate that the wood is not drying as it should. Drying is necessary for good long-term performance of wood roof coverings. Moss can damage wood roof coverings. Moss is a reportable defect. Cleaning methods, if used, should comply with the wood roof covering manufacturer's instructions.

Typical Defects
Typical defects that home inspectors should report include:

1. shingles or shakes loose or not in installed position,
2. absent or deteriorated shingles or shakes, including splits and curling,
3. improper exposure (head lap),
4. improper (too small or large) spacing (gap) between shingles or shakes,
5. biological growth such as moss,
6. roof penetrations located in a valley.

Safety Issues
Wood roof covering defects rarely present safety issues; however, wood roof coverings can be slippery when wet and should not be walked on.

Standards
(1) IRC 2018 R905.7 (shingles) and R905.8 (shakes); (2) National Roofing Contractors Association Guidelines; (3) Cedar Shake and Shingle Bureau; (4) manufacturer's instructions.

Wood Shakes Significantly Deteriorated, At End of Service Life.

Wood Shingles Absent, Loose, Typical Curling.

Ice Dams

Description An ice dam can occur in cold climates where snow remains on the roof for long periods of time. An ice dam begins when heat from the house melts snow on the roof. Water flows to the cold, unheated eaves where it freezes. A block of ice forms if enough ice accumulates from multiple melting/freezing cycles. Additional melted water can back up at the ice block, flow under the roof coverings, on to the roof sheathing, and eventually into the eaves or into the home.

Typical Visible Evidence of Ice Dams

1. ice at the eaves and icicles hanging from eaves and gutters,
2. visible water stains and damage under the eaves,
3. visible water stains and damage on exterior walls and ceilings near exterior walls.

Evidence of Ice Dams

Preventative Measures The best preventative measure is to correct the cause of ice dams. This involves reducing air leaks that allow heat to escape into the attic. Air leak sources include around openings such as around recessed lights, HVAC supply and return openings, chimney chases, HVAC duct chases, and vent chases. Other air leak sources include leaks from HVAC supply ducts run in the attic. Upgrading attic insulation and improving attic ventilation can also help correct the cause of ice dams, but these may not be as effective as reducing air leaks. Refer to the Attic Ventilation section for additional information.

Ice barrier underlayment is often required in areas where ice dams occur. These barriers consist of an impervious underlayment (often peel-and-stick flashing) that extends from the eaves at least 2 feet horizontally past the wall of the house.

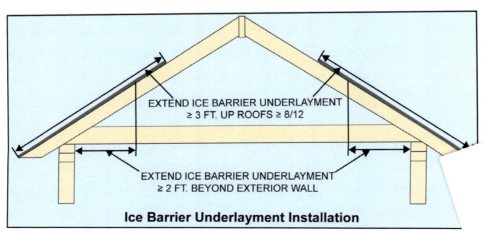

Ice Barrier Underlayment Installation

Heat strips are installed at the eaves on some roofs in an attempt to prevent ice dams. **Heat strips address the symptom, not the cause of the problem**. Heat strips are not the recommended solution for ice dams. Home inspectors should report the presence of heat strips and disclaim inspection.

LOW SLOPE ROOF COVERINGS

Introduction

Low slope roof coverings may be defined as roof coverings installed on roofs that **slope between ¼ inch vertically in 12 inches horizontally (¼:12) and 2 inches vertically in 12 inches horizontally (2:12)**. This distinguishes low slope roof coverings from steep slope roof coverings that are restricted to roofs that slope 2:12 or greater.

Low slope roof coverings are waterproof roof coverings. A waterproof roof covering relies on itself to provide a waterproof barrier system. This distinguishes it from steep slope roof coverings that are water shedding and rely on a secondary barrier (the underlayment) to create a waterproof barrier.

Low slope roof coverings are sometimes called **flat roof coverings. This is an inaccurate term. All roofs must slope toward drainage points to drain water.** Although low slope roofs do this at a much smaller slope than steep slope roofs, **low slope roofs should not be not flat roofs.**

In this section, we present the low roof coverings that home inspectors are most likely to encounter. This is not a complete list of all possible low roof coverings.

Built-Up Roof Membranes (BURS)

Description Built-up roof membranes (BURs) consist of two or more layers of roofing felt or other membranes with each layer covered with bitumen (asphalt or coal tar) or a cold-applied adhesive. A mineral-surfaced cap sheet may be applied. Ballast (gravel) is often applied. BURs are often called **tar and gravel** roofs. Note that some BURs installed in the 1960s and 1970s may contain asbestos.

BURs have been used in North America since the 1880s. Service life depends to a large extent on the number of layers installed and on proper drainage. Expected service life is reported to range from as little as 10 to 15 years to as long as 30 to 40 years.

BUR, Deteriorated.

Installation BURs should be installed according to manufacturer's instructions. The following are typical instructions which will vary by manufacturer. BURs should be installed on solid-sheathed roofs, including application over rigid insulation. The **minimum roof slope should be ¼:12**.

Typical Problem Locations Penetrations of BURs are a common leak location. Penetrations include: plumbing vents, equipment vents, exhaust caps, appliance pipes, electrical cables, interior drains, scuppers, and raised curbs for equipment and skylights. Additional BUR layers and flashing are usually installed at penetrations. **Home inspectors should carefully evaluate penetrations for defects such as loose and deteriorated materials.**

Transitions between roof coverings are a common leak location. A common example is where a steep slope roof covering meets a BUR. When a steep slope roof drains on a BUR, the steep slope roof covering should terminate a few inches above the BUR. The steep slope roof covering termination point should be installed as if it were at the eaves. Metal flashing should be installed under the BUR and run at least 18 inches up the steep slope roof, or as far as recommended by the manufacturer. Ice barrier flashing may be required at this transition in locations where ice barriers are installed.

Transition Between Tile and BUR Roof Coverings

When a BUR drains on a steep slope roof, gravel stop edge flashing should be installed at the edge of the BUR. This helps stop ballast loss. Note that gravel stop edge flashing should be installed at locations where water drains over the edge of a BUR.

Transitions between the BUR and vertical walls such as parapet walls are a ͨ location. Problems occur with both the base and counterflashing. **Home insp carefully evaluate the membrane and flashing at vertical walls** for defects such deteriorated materials.

Equipment, such as air conditioner condensers, is often mounted on wood blocks placed directly on the BUR. A term for this is **dunnage**. This method is not recommended because vibrations can cause the wood blocks to move and create wear and holes that allow moisture intrusion, and because the wood holds moisture against the roof. A raised and flashed curb is the recommended method for supporting equipment.

Typical Roof Covering Repairs This material may be repaired with a patch, using the same BUR material, that is adhered over the area requiring repair. The patching method depends on the problem being repaired and on the materials used to construct the BUR.

Typical Defects Typical defects that home inspectors should report include:

1. deteriorated membrane such as deep alligatoring (minor surface alligatoring is usually considered cosmetic),
2. damaged membrane such as holes, tears, and abrasion,
3. deformed membrane such as wrinkles, blisters, and similar surface deformities,
4. dirt, stains, or other evidence of water ponding (for more than 48 hours) due to improper drainage,
5. openings at laps and splices,
6. debris and vegetation on roof,
7. loose and deteriorated flashing around penetrations,
8. deteriorated pitch in pitch pans,
9. improper equipment supports,
10. fasteners backing out,
11. loose and deteriorated at sidewall flashing,
12. displaced ballast.

Standards (1) IRC 2018 R905.9; (2) National Roofing Contractors Association Guidelines; (3) manufacturer's instructions.

Mineral-Surfaced Roll Roofing

Description Mineral-surfaced roll roofing is available with a base made from felt impregnated with asphalt, and with a base made from asphalt impregnated fiberglass. It usually comes in a 36 inch wide roll that is about 36 feet long (about 1 square). It is sometimes called #90 roll roofing because, in the past, rolls weighed about 90 pounds. The current typical roll weight is between about 75 to 80 pounds.

This material is used as a roof covering for temporary structures, accessory structures, and sometimes for porch roofs. It is also used as an underlayment and as valley flashing. It may be used as a roof covering for permanent structures, but this use is not recommended because of this material's short service life. Service life is reported to be 10 years or less.

Do not confuse mineral-surfaced roll roofing with modified bitumen roofing. These materials appear similar. See Modified Bitumen Roofing for more information.

Installation Mineral-surfaced roll roofing should be installed according to manufacturer's instructions. The following are typical instructions which will vary by manufacturer. This material should be installed on solid-sheathed roofs. The **minimum roof slope should be 1:12**, except where otherwise specified by the manufacturer. Some manufacturers specify a 2:12 minimum slope.

Underlayment (at least #15 felt) is specified under this material. Underlayment should be applied horizontally with respect to the eaves with seams lapped. **Ice barrier underlayment is specified in cold climates** when required by local authorities; however, ice barriers are not usually required for accessory structures.

Mineral-surfaced roll roofing should be attached using galvanized steel or aluminum roofing nails that are long enough to penetrate at least ¾ inch into the sheathing. Nails should be driven into the upper edge of the first course. The lower edge of the second course should lap the upper edge of the first course 1 to 2 inches, and be sealed with lap roofing cement. This process is repeated for succeeding courses. Vertical laps (end laps) should be at least 6 inches and should be sealed with lap roofing cement. Valleys, hips, and ridges are not common with this material.

Typical Roof Covering Repairs This material may be temporarily repaired with a patch from the same material that is cemented over the area requiring repair. This material may be coated with a manufacturer-approved liquid coating to extend its service life.

Typical Visible Defects Typical defects that home inspectors should report include:

1. deteriorated membrane such as granule loss, visible fibers at edges, and curling,
2. damaged membrane,
3. deformed membrane such as wrinkles, blisters, and similar surface deformities,
4. exposed nails,
5. nails withdrawing and showing through surface,
6. openings at laps and seams,
7. roofing cement used to repair holes, exposed nails, and deteriorated areas,
8. dirt, stains, or other evidence of water ponding due to improper drainage.

Standards (1) IRC 2018 R905.5; (2) manufacturer's instructions.

Modified Bitumen Roofing

Description **Polymer modified bitumen** roof coverings are asphalt-based membrane-type roof covering systems. The systems typically consist of one or more base membranes that are covered with a cap membrane. The cap membrane may be smooth-surfaced, or surfaced, or foil-faced. Single membrane systems exist and are the most common dential construction. Residential systems are usually granule-surfaced.

Modified bitumen systems have been used in North America since the mid-1970s. Service life is reported to be in the 12 to 20 year range for the single membrane systems.

Home inspectors may confuse mineral-surfaced roll roofing with modified bitumen. Modified bitumen is thicker than roll roofing. **Modified bitumen sheets are usually around 39 inches wide** whereas roll roofing sheets are almost always around 36 inches wide; thus, the **distance between lap seams (parallel seams) should be more than 36 inches** for modified bitumen.

Modified Bitumen Roof Covering; Evidence of Poor Drainage Around Scupper.

<u>Installation</u> Modified bitumen roofing should be installed according to manufacturer's instructions. The following are typical instructions which will vary by manufacturer. This material should be installed on solid-sheathed roofs including application over rigid insulation. The **minimum roof slope should be ¼:12**, except where otherwise specified by the manufacturer.

Seams between sheets (long horizontal seams) should be lapped about 3 inches and sealed using either heat or adhesive. Fasteners, if any, should not be exposed. Laps should be installed shingle fashion such that sheets from the higher part of the roof side lap over sheets from the lower part of the roof. End laps (short vertical laps) should be lapped about 6 inches and sealed.

<u>Typical Problem Locations</u> **Penetrations of the membrane are a common leak location.** Penetrations include: plumbing vents, equipment vents, exhaust caps, appliance pipes, electrical cables, interior drains, scuppers, and raised curbs for equipment and skylights. Additional membrane layers and flashing are installed at penetrations. **Home inspectors should carefully evaluate penetrations for defects such as loose and deteriorated materials.**

Transitions between roof coverings are a common leak location. A common example is between a steep slope roof covering and a low slope roof covering. The steep slope roof covering should terminate a few inches above the low slope roof covering. The steep slope roof covering termination point should be installed as if it were at the eaves. The low slope roof covering should be installed about 18 inches up the steep slope or as instructed by the manufacturer. Ice barrier flashing may be required at this transition in locations where ice barriers are installed.

Transitions between the membrane and vertical walls such as parapet walls are a common leak location. Problems occur with both the base and counterflashing. **Home inspectors should carefully evaluate the membrane and flashing at vertical walls for defects such as loose and deteriorated materials.**

Equipment, such as air conditioner condensers, is often mounted on wood blocks placed directly on the roof covering. A term for this is **dunnage**. This method is not recommended because vibrations can cause the wood blocks to move and create wear and holes that allow moisture intrusion, and because the wood holds moisture against the roof. A raised and flashed curb is the recommended method for supporting equipment.

<u>**Typical Roof Covering Repairs**</u> This material may be repaired with a patch from the same material that is adhered over the area requiring repair. Patches should have rounded corners and should usually measure at least 16 inches in both directions. This material may be coated with a manufacturer-approved liquid coating to extend its service life.

<u>**Typical Defects**</u> Typical defects that home inspectors should report include:

1. deteriorated membrane such as deep alligatoring (minor surface alligatoring is usually considered cosmetic),
2. damaged membrane such as holes, tears, and abrasion,
3. deformed membrane such as wrinkles, blisters, and similar surface deformities,
4. dirt, stains, or other evidence of water ponding (for more than 48 hours) due to improper drainage,
5. openings at laps and splices,
6. debris and vegetation on roof,
7. loose and deteriorated flashing around penetrations,
8. deteriorated pitch in pitch pans,
9. improper equipment supports,
10. fasteners backing out,
11. loose and deteriorated flashing at sidewalls.

<u>**Standards**</u> (1) IRC 2018 R905.11; (2) National Roofing Contractors Association Guidelines; (3) manufacturer's instructions.

Deep Alligatoring.

Moderate Alligatoring.

Deteriorated Coating and Evidence of Poor Drainage.

Wrinkling and Opening at Seam.

Wrinkles and Exposed Fasteners.

Hail Damage.

Polyurethane Foam Roofing

Description Polyurethane foam roof covering is a **spray applied closed cell foam**. The foam dries hard and must be covered with an ultraviolet-resistant elastomeric top coating within 3 days after the foam is applied.

Polyurethane foam has been used as a roof covering in North America since the 1970s. Expected service life is reported to be around 30 years. Older installations are known to remain in service. The top coating must be reapplied about every 15 years. The foam will deteriorate rapidly without this coating.

Polyurethane foam is an insulating material. Unlike other roof coverings, it can provide a significant R-value.

Typical Foam Roof Covering.

Installation Polyurethane foam should be installed according to manufacturer's instructions. The following are typical instructions and will vary by manufacturer. This material should be installed on solid-sheathed roofs. It may also be applied over many common roof coverings except wood. The **minimum roof slope should be ¼:12**, except where otherwise specified by the manufacturer. Flashing at roof edges, at sidewalls, at roof penetrations (e.g., plumbing, electrical), at scuppers, at other drainage systems, and at platforms for HVAC equipment should be installed before foam application.

The **minimum foam thickness is 1 to 1½ inches thick**. The **maximum foam thickness is 4 inches**, although additional thickness may be allowed using special installation procedures. Foam should gently taper toward drainage locations. Drainage channels should not be formed.

The foam's surface should be reasonably smooth. Some texture (very coarse orange peel) is acceptable, but will require a greater amount of top coating. Texture that looks like tree bark is not considered acceptable.

Typical Problem Locations Penetrations of the foam are a common leak location; however, because the foam adheres to penetrations, leaks are less common at penetrations compared to other roof coverings. Penetrations include plumbing vents, equipment vents, exhaust caps, appliance pipes and electrical cables, interior drains, scuppers, and raised curbs for equipment and skylights. Home inspectors should evaluate penetrations for defects, such as deteriorated foam.

Equipment, such as air conditioner condensers, is often mounted on wood blocks placed directly on the roof covering. This method is not recommended because vibrations can cause the wood blocks to move and create wear and holes that allow moisture intrusion, and because the wood holds moisture against the roof. A raised and flashed curb is the recommended method for supporting equipment.

Typical Roof Covering Repairs This material may be repaired as specified by the manufacturer. The repair method depends on the problem being repaired.

Typical Defects Typical defects that home inspectors should report include:

1. surface physical damage such as significant depressions caused by hail,
2. surface blisters,
3. "tree bark" texture (improper foam application),
4. dirt, stains, or other evidence of water ponding (for more than 48 hours) due to improper drainage,
5. deteriorated top coating,
6. debris and vegetation on roof,
7. thin application,
8. improper equipment supports.

Standards (1) IRC 2018 R905.14; (2) manufacturer's instructions.

Blisters, Cracks, Ponding in Depressions. **Tree Bark Texture.**

Thin Foam Layer Over Other Roof Covering. Note Visible Seams.

Single-Ply Membrane Roofing

Description Single-ply thermoplastic membranes include those made from Polyvinyl Chloride (PVC) and Thermoplastic Olefins (TPO). These membranes are uncommon in residential constructions and will not be discussed here.

Single-ply thermoset membranes include Ethylene Propylene Diene Terpolymer (EPDM), Hypalon, and Neoprene. Thermoset membranes appear rubberlike. They can be stretched and will return to their original shape, like a rubber band. EPDM is the most commonly used thermoset membrane in residential construction, so we will restrict this section to EPDM.

EPDM membranes have been used in North America since the 1970s. Expected service life is reported to be around 30 years. Original installations are reported to remain in service.

EPDM membranes come in different thicknesses (mostly 45 and 60 mils), widths (from about 7.5 to 50 feet), and colors (mostly white and black). They are also installed in different manners, including mechanically attached using fasteners, and fully adhered using adhesives. These attributes will impact the service life and functionality of the membrane. For example, lighter color membranes are intended to reflect more solar radiation to reduce solar heat gain through the roof.

Typical EPDM Roof Covering Installations.

<u>Installation</u> EPDM membranes should be installed according to manufacturer's instructions. The following are typical instructions and will vary by manufacturer. This material should be installed on solid-sheathed roofs including application over rigid insulation. Manufacturers may have specific requirements for the roof substrate. The **minimum roof slope should be ¼:12**, except where otherwise specified by the manufacturer.

Seams between sheets and end laps should be lapped about 3 inches and sealed using the manufacturer recommended method. Laps should be installed shingle fashion such that sheets from the higher part of the roof side lap over sheets from the lower part of the roof. Aggregate may be installed over EPDM, primarily to reduce wind uplift. Coatings are not usually required on EPDM membranes, unless approved by the EPDM manufacturer.

<u>Typical Problem Locations</u> **Penetrations of the membrane are a common leak location.** Penetrations include: plumbing vents, equipment vents, exhaust caps, appliance pipes, electrical cables, interior drains, scuppers, and raised curbs for equipment and skylights. Additional membrane layers and flashing are installed at penetrations. **Home inspectors should carefully evaluate penetrations for defects such as loose and deteriorated materials.**

Transitions between roof coverings are a common leak location. A common example is between a steep slope roof covering and a low slope roof covering. The steep slope roof covering should terminate a few inches above the low slope roof covering. The steep slope roof covering termination point should be installed as if it were at the eaves. The low slope roof covering should be installed about 18 inches up the steep slope, or as instructed by the manufacturer. Ice barrier flashing may be required at this transition in locations where ice barriers are installed.

Transitions between the membrane and vertical walls such as parapet walls are a common leak location. The types of problems depend on the flashing system used, including lack of adhesion for adhesive-secured systems, and loose mechanical attachment and loose termination bars for mechanically attached systems. **Home inspectors should carefully evaluate the membrane and flashing at vertical walls for defects.**

Equipment, such as air conditioner condensers, is often mounted on wood blocks placed directly on the roof covering. This method is not recommended because vibrations can cause the wood blocks to move and create wear and holes that allow moisture intrusion, and because the wood holds moisture against the roof. A raised and flashed curb is the recommended method for supporting equipment.

Typical Roof Covering Repairs (1) this material may be repaired with a patch from the same material that is adhered over the area requiring repair. Patches should have rounded corners and should usually measure at least 8 inches in both directions, (2) this material may be repaired using manufacturer-approved tape that is adhered over the area requiring repair. The tape should have rounded corners and should usually measure at least 6 inches in both directions.

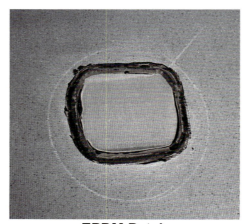

EPDM Patch

Typical Defects Typical defects that home inspectors should report include:

1. deteriorated membrane,
2. damaged membrane such as holes, tears, and abrasion,
3. deformed membrane such as wrinkles, blisters, and similar surface deformities,
4. dirt, stains, or other evidence of water ponding (for more than 48 hours) due to improper drainage,
5. openings at laps and splices,
6. debris and vegetation on roof,
7. loose and deteriorated flashing around penetrations,
8. deteriorated pitch in pitch pans,
9. improper equipment supports,
10. fasteners backing out,
11. loose and deteriorated flashing at sidewalls.

Standards (1) IRC 2018 R905.12; (2) National Roofing Contractors Association Guidelines; (3) manufacturer's instructions.

Water Ponding.

ROOF DRAINAGE SYSTEMS

Gutters (Steep Slope Roof Drainage)

Description A gutter is a horizontal trough that catches rain water from the roof, channels it to a vertical pipe, and discharges the water away from the foundation. Gutters are usually installed just below the roof at the eaves. Gutters are not required by model building codes, except in areas where unstable soils exist; however, **lack of gutters is considered a reportable defect in most markets.**

Gutters help keep the area around the foundation dry. This reduces water infiltration into basements and crawl spaces, and reduces pressure against foundations which can cause problems, such as wall cracks, bowing, rotation, and footing uplift and sinking. Wet soil around the foundation also provides an inviting environment for termites and other wood destroying organisms.

The most common gutter styles are the half-round and the L-shaped gutter called the K gutter. Metal gutters are the most common type, and are usually made from aluminum or galvanized steel. Other less common materials include copper and vinyl. Some homes have gutters made from materials such as wood. Some gutters are integrated into the eaves and lined with a roof covering material such as EPDM or metal. These integrated gutters are called Yankee gutters in some areas. Wood and integrated gutters are uncommon in most of North America.

The horizontal part of the system is called the **gutter**. It is called an **eaves trough** in some areas. The vertical part of the system is called a **downspout**. Other terms include **conductor, downpipe**, and **leader**. Downspouts should discharge on to a concrete or plastic tray called a **splash block**, or into a piece of downspout material or pipe called a **downspout extension**. Splash blocks or downspout extensions should **discharge water at least 5 feet away from the foundation**. Downspouts may be connected to an underground drainage system, but not to foundation drains.

K-type gutters are typically 5 or 6 inches wide. Downspouts are typically 2x3 inches or 3x4 inches. The gutter and downspout size should be determined by the square footage of roof draining into the gutter, the roof slope, and expected peak rainfall. Five-inch gutters are reported to drain about 5,500 square feet of roof and six-inch gutters about 8,000 square feet, assuming downspouts are spaced about every 40 feet. Installing more downspouts increases gutter capacity. Note that **determining gutter capacity is out-of-scope for a home inspection**.

Installation
One method of attaching gutters is the **spike and ferrule method**. A long nail (the spike) is driven through the top of the gutter, through a tube (the ferrule) and into the fascia. This method is more common with older galvanized steel gutters. Newer gutters are usually attached using hidden hangers or brackets. Gutters and downspouts should be securely attached so that movement is limited, especially under the weight of large amounts of rainwater.

Gutters should slope toward the downspouts at 1/16 inch per foot. Gutters with no slope or that slope away from the downspouts will not drain properly, may overflow, and may provide standing water for mosquitoes. **Improperly sloped gutters are a reportable defect**.

Typical Gutter Repairs
Gutters are usually repaired, and gutter seams are usually sealed, using silicone caulk.

Typical Defects
Typical defects that home inspectors should report include:

1. gutter not sloped toward downspout, or are holding water,
2. gutter leaks, especially at seams between sections, where downspouts connect, and at end caps,
3. debris in gutters and downspouts, and debris blocking gutter guards,
4. loose and poorly attached gutters and downspouts,
5. downspouts disconnected from gutters,
6. damaged and deteriorated gutters and downspouts,
7. absent or damaged splash blocks or downspout extensions,
8. gutter drains on to roof causing deterioration of roof covering,
9. water damage on exterior walls from built-in (integrated) gutter leakage.

Standards
(1) IRC 2018 R801.3; (2) manufacturer's instructions.

Improper Draining on Roof.

Water Directed Toward Sidewall.

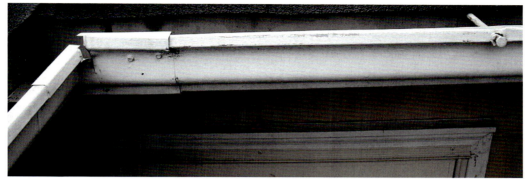
Gutter Damaged at Fitting.

Gutter Leaking (Appears Intentional).

Gutter Holding Water.

Damaged Downspout.

Downspout Directs Water Toward Foundation.

Low Slope Roof Drainage

Description Low slope roofs are drained using three methods. These methods may be used alone or in combination.

Roofs that are not surrounded by vertical sidewalls, such as **parapet walls**, usually drain over the roof edge. A gutter is sometimes installed below the roof edge to collect this water. Drip edge flashing should be installed where water drains over the roof edge to reduce water damage at the point where water leaves the roof. This drip edge flashing should be appropriate for the roof covering material. For example, gravel stop drip edge flashing should not be used at the edge of membrane roof coverings, such as modified bitumen and EPDM.

Roofs surrounded by vertical sidewalls (parapet walls) may drain through rectangular openings in the wall called **scuppers**. A small gutter and downspout may be installed to collect water from the scupper. Roof leaks at scuppers are common, so **home inspectors should carefully evaluate the flashing and roof covering installation at scuppers, and should inspect the areas around and below scuppers for evidence of water leaks. Home inspectors should also inspect scuppers for evidence of poor drainage and roof covering deterioration around scuppers.**

Scupper View From Outside

**Scupper View From Roof.
Note Evidence of Water Ponding.**

Roofs surrounded by vertical sidewalls (parapet walls) may drain through internal drain pipes. When internal drain pipes are used, the roof drains to one or more openings in the roof. The opening is connected to a pipe that channels the water outside the building. The pipe should be sized as described in the International Plumbing Code; however, it is out of scope of a home inspection to determine if the pipes are properly sized. The opening should be protected by a screen or grate that keeps debris out of the pipe. The area around internal drain openings requires regular inspection and maintenance to keep it free from blockage and to identify deterioration before leaks occur. **Home inspectors should carefully inspect the area around internal drains for issues similar to those found with scuppers.**

**Internal Drains, Absent Cover at Top of Picture.
Picture Courtesy of Welmoed Sisson**

One scupper or internal drain may not be the only roof drain. A secondary system is required. This system may be another internal drain or a scupper. The secondary system that is at least the same size as the primary system should be located 2 inches above the primary drainage system.

Typical Defects Typical defects that home inspectors should report include:

1. dirt, staining, standing water, and other evidence of water remaining on the roof for more than 48 hours,
2. leak evidence around scuppers and internal drains,
3. debris blocks scuppers and internal drains,
4. damaged, deteriorated, or absent components such as debris screens and flashing,
5. blocked internal drain pipes.

Standard IRC 2018 R903.4.

ROOF FLASHING

Roof Penetration Flashing

Description Roof penetrations such as plumbing vents and fuel-fired appliance vents should be flashed with a **boot (roof jack, thimble)** that is compatible with the penetration and with the roof covering. Other roof penetrations, such as terminations for clothes dryer, kitchen, and bathroom exhaust ducts, should terminate with a roof jack and a vent cap.

Framed chimneys covered with a wall covering other than brick should be flashed as appropriate for the wall covering. Brick chimneys, including brick veneer and solid masonry chimneys, should be flashed as brick veneer sidewalls. A chimney that is wider than 30 inches parallel to the ridge and does not run through the roof ridge should also have a **cricket (saddle)** that diverts water around the chimney.

Plumbing Vent Flashing Two types of plumbing vent flashing are available. These components are sometimes called **boots**. The lower quality type is made from materials such as **neoprene** and **thermoplastics**. The service life of these boots is between 10 and 20 years. The best quality types are made with **lead**. The service life of lead boots is 30 years or more. Boots come in various slopes to match the slope of the roof and sizes to match the pipe size. **Boots installed on a roof with a different slope, and boots that are the incorrect size may not seal the vent and may leak.**

Thermoplastic Vent Boot, Improperly Installed. **Lead Vent Boot.**

Appliance Vent Flashing Appliance vent flashing is usually made from the same material as the vent. For gas appliance vents, this material is usually galvanized steel. For oil appliance vents the material is usually stainless steel. These components are sometimes called **boots, thimbles,** or **jacks**. Appliance vent boots also come in various slopes and sizes and should be selected to match the roof slope and vent size and type. Appliance vent boots should have a metal ring installed above where the vent exits the vent boot. This metal ring is called a **storm collar** and helps reduce water entry into the vent boot.

Gas Vent With Storm Collar.

Exhaust Duct Flashing Exhaust system flashing is usually made from galvanized steel, aluminum, or plastic. These components are sometimes called **roof jacks**. These roof jacks have flanges that should be integrated into the roof covering system to create a leak-resistant seal.

Examples of Exhaust System Roof Jacks.

Sidewall and Headwall Flashing

Description Roofs and walls intersect in two ways. Vertical walls that run along the side of a roof are called **sidewalls**. Vertical walls where a roof slopes up to meet the wall are called **headwalls**. A sidewall may occur when a second story wall meets a first story gable roof, such as at a garage. A sidewall may also occur when a chimney penetrates the roof. Headwalls usually occur at shed roofs, such as porch roofs. A headwall may also occur where a chimney penetrates the roof.

Flashing between a roof and a sidewall and headwall should be installed in a **two component system** that should be integrated into the roof covering system, and into the wall drainage plane. The two flashing components are the **base flashing** and the **counterflashing**. In some situations, the base flashing may be long lengths of flashing material. In other situations, the base flashing should be smaller pieces of flashing material called **step flashing**. Counterflashing is often long strips of flashing material. Flashing installation details depend on the roof covering and on the wall covering materials.

In most cases, the roof covering underlayment should be run up the wall to provide an additional layer of protection. The base flashing should be installed on top of the underlayment. The base flashing vertical flange on the wall should be covered with counterflashing and the counterflashing covered with the water-resistive barrier. Flashing from the high side should lap over lower flashing at least 2 inches. **Base flashing should be at least 4 inches on the vertical and horizontal legs.** This multiple component system provides an effective, long term, and maintenance free barrier against water infiltration.

An especially vulnerable sidewall is one where the roof drains toward the sidewall. Water can rise above normal size flashing and counterflashing during heavy rain. The sidewall flashing should be run higher than normal up these sidewalls. Because this sidewall flashing is usually concealed, **home inspectors should carefully evaluate visible areas around these sidewalls for evidence of water infiltration.**

Sidewall flashing is usually made from galvanized steel, aluminum, or copper. Plastic and composite materials are also acceptable when approved.

Siding Flashing Sidewall base and counterflashing flashing should be installed under most siding materials including wood and wood products, fiber cement, and vinyl. This makes it difficult to determine if the flashing, especially the counterflashing, is properly installed. Long lengths of base flashing may acceptable for sidewall flashing; however, step base flashing is recommended. The base flashing should not be exposed such that water can penetrate behind the base flashing.

Brick Veneer Sidewall Flashing Flashing at brick veneer sidewalls should be installed using **stepped base flashing** and **stepped counterflashing**. The counterflashing should be installed in a **groove cut into the mortar**, secured in place, and sealed with caulk or roof flashing cement. Counterflashing that is mechanically attached (screws or nails), or that is attached using roofing cement, will require regular maintenance and is considered a deficient flashing installation.

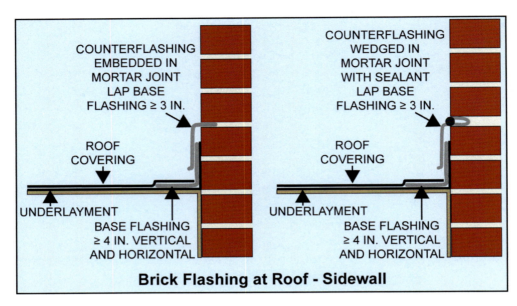

Brick Flashing at Roof - Sidewall

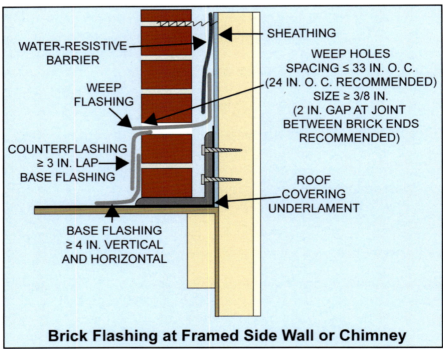

Brick Flashing at Framed Side Wall or Chimney

Stucco Flashing Sidewall base and counterflashing should be installed under stucco and adhered masonry veneer like other wall covering sidewall flashing. The weep screed should be installed above the roof covering as recommended by the wall covering manufacturer. Refer to the Wall Coverings section in the Exterior chapter for more information.

Kick Out Flashing Kick out flashing should be installed at the end of a roof when the sidewall extends past the roof. Kick out flashing turns the water away from the sidewall. Kick out flashing should turn at about a 120° angle and should be about 4 inches long and 4 inches tall. Kick out flashing is often absent, especially at older houses. **Absence of kick out flashing is a reportable defect regardless of the age of the house.**

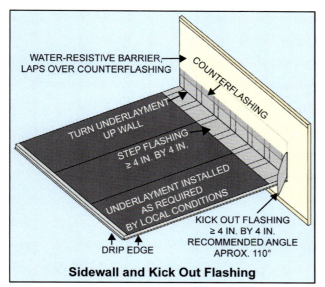
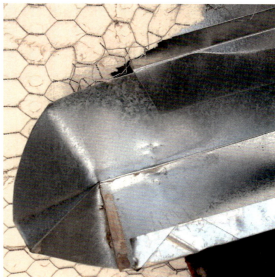

Sidewall and Kick Out Flashing

Headwall Flashing Headwall flashing should be installed using long pieces of base and counterflashing. The leg of the base flashing that extends above the roof covering is called the apron and should be at least 4 inches wide. The apron should be flush with the roof covering.

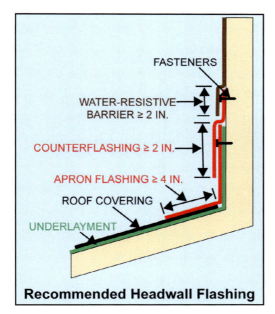

Headwall Flashing Without Counterflashing

Defects, Safety, Standards

Typical Defects Typical defects that inspectors should report include:

1. absent flashing including base flashing, counterflashing, kick out flashing, and headwall flashing,
2. counterflashing mechanically attached or attached using sealants,
3. flashing too small or not run far enough up sidewall,

4. upper flashing lapped under lower flashing,
5. absent weep holes in brick and stucco,
6. damaged, deteriorated, or loose flashing,
7. gaps between flashing and sidewall or penetration; sealants used to repair these defects,
8. absent and deteriorated sealants where sealants should be installed,
9. flashing restricting a plumbing vent opening.

Standards (1) IRC 2018 R703.8; (2) National Roofing Contractors Association Guidelines; (3) Brick Industry Association Technical Notes; (4) siding manufacturer's instructions.

Absent Kick Out Flashing.

Kick Out Flashing Too Small.

Sealant Applied Instead of Flashing.

Loose Flashing, No Counterflashing.

Absent Counterflashing.

SKYLIGHTS

Description Skylights are usually thought of as a window in a roof; however, any glazed opening that is sloped more than 15° from vertical may be considered a skylight regardless of where it is located. Skylights usually come in two shapes: (1) rectangular, and (2) round domes that use a reflective tube to transmit the light. Round dome skylights are sometimes called **tubular skylights** or **tubular daylighting devices**. Some rectangular skylights may be opened to provide ventilation, but most skylights are not operable. Most modern skylights are factory assembled units that use rigid plastic as the glazing, and usually come with manufacturer supplied flashing. Field assembled skylights and sloped glazing usually use glass as the glazing, and use field-installed flashing. **Home inspectors should carefully evaluate all skylights and especially field assembled skylights and sloped glazing.**

Glass used in skylights and sloped glazing should be laminated, tempered, wired, or heat-strengthened. A protective screen may be required under glass skylights and sloped glazing. Glass skylights and sloped glazing more than 12 feet above the walking surface and more than 16 square feet of surface area may need to be evaluated if there is no protective screen present. Screens are not usually required in greenhouses.

Skylights can increase solar heat gain in the house, especially when located on a roof that receives significant sunlight. This can place an additional load on the air conditioning system and require larger supply ducts to the rooms where skylights are located. The light from skylights can cause fading and damage to interior furnishings. Low E glazing and shade screens can help reduce this issue.

Skylight.

Tubular Skylight.

Installation Manufactured skylights should be installed and flashed according to manufacturer's instructions. Many manufacturers make skylights that are mounted on a raised curb (box) that is at least 4 inches tall. A minimum 4 inch tall curb is recommended for all rectangular skylights, and is required for skylights installed on a roof slope less than 3:12. A curb makes flashing the skylight easier and more effective.

Skylight Curb Flashing During Installation.

Round skylights come with manufacturer supplied flashing that is usually mostly concealed by the skylight cover. Rectangular skylights should be flashed like chimneys. Backer flashing and counterflashing should be installed on the up-slope side. Stepped base flashing and counterflashing should be installed down the sides. Base and apron flashing should be installed on the downslope side.

When ceiling joists and rafters must be cut to install a skylight, the load supported by the cut members must be transferred to the adjacent intact members. This may require that the adjacent members be doubled or tripled. Trusses should not be cut without an engineer-designed repair. **Improper framing is a common defect at skylights.**

Rafters Improperly Bearing on Single Header Bearing on Single Rafter. Evidence of Water Leak.

Rectangular skylights need a framed chase to channel the light into the home. This chase should be framed, insulated, and finished like an exterior wall. Improper insulation of skylight chases is a common defect.

Typical Defects Typical defects that home inspectors should report include:

1. damaged glazing including compromised hermetic seal between glazing,
2. skylight leaks,
3. water stains caused by condensation that can look like water leaks (especially common in bathrooms and kitchens),
4. improper framing of ceiling joists and rafters at skylight (especially cut trusses),
5. improper skylight chase insulation,
6. debris caught on roof at skylight upslope end,
7. ice dams and water leaks on the upslope end (usually in ice dam prone climates).

Standards (1) IRC 2018 R308.6; (2) National Roofing Contractors Association Guidelines; (3) manufacturer's instructions.

No Visible Step Flashing. Poor Counterflashing.

Obvious Skylight Leak.

Less Obvious Skylight Leak.

3: Roof Components

Please visit https://nationalhomeinspectorexam.org/prepare-for-the-exam/ and take advantage of the practice quizzes. The questions in the practice quizzes are designed to reflect the difficulty of the questions on the actual exam. The questions on the practice quizzes are not questions on the National Home Inspectors Exam. Passing the practice quizzes does not guarantee that you will pass the National exam. You will still need to study all topics to be prepared for the National exam.

4: STRUCTURAL COMPONENTS

INSPECTION SCOPE

People tend to think about house structural components in one dimensional terms. The structure of a house must do more than resist the force of gravity that tries to pull the house down. Wind applies force that tries to push the house sideways, a phenomenon called racking. Wind can also try to push the house up, especially if the windows and doors are breached. An earthquake also tries to push the house sideways. Water can also try to push or lift the house. **The structural components must reliably resist all forces over time**, the fourth dimension.

Home inspectors have two significant limitations when inspecting structural components. A home inspector is not usually an engineer. Even when the home inspector is an engineer, the home inspector is not acting in that capacity when operating under a home inspection standard of practice. **A home inspector is not required to, and should not, evaluate the adequacy of the structural components of the house**. The second limitation is that many of the structural components of the house are fully or partially concealed. This makes it difficult to directly determine the condition of many structural components. The home inspector is left to recognizing visual clues that may indicate structural defects, and to deferring to contractors and engineers to determine the nature and extent of structural defects, if any.

Structural components that are in scope of a home inspection include the visible and accessible parts of the foundation, floor structure, wall structure, ceiling structure, and roof structure.

STRUCTURAL COMPONENT TERMS

The house structure has many terms that a home inspector should know and be able to use. Here are some of the most common terms that a home inspector should know. Some of these definitions have been altered and simplified to conform to usage in residential construction.

Attic: a usually uninhabitable space above the ceiling of the highest habitable area and below the roof framing. Also called a crawl space in some markets.

Axial force (load): the vertical force acting on a structural member, such as a column or a beam, that places the member under compression at the loading point.

Basement (cellar): an area that is partially or completely below grade; often has a ceiling height of 7 feet or more, but sometimes less in older houses.

Basement (daylight, walk out): a basement that has a door to the exterior.

Beam (girder): a structural member that carries loads from other members such as joists, rafters, and other beams.

Bow (bowed): a condition where a structural member is curved along its long axis.

Braced wall: see **Shear wall**.

Ceiling joist: a horizontal structural member that forms the ceiling of a room below an attic.

Ceiling, vaulted: a ceiling that extends at an angle above the top of a full-height wall; the ceiling finish (drywall) is usually attached directly to the rafters.

Ceiling, tray (or trey): a horizontal ceiling raised above the top of a full-height wall; the ceiling is often raised in one or two risers and decorated with crown molding.

Cinder block: a concrete masonry unit made using coal ash or other residue of combustion. Cinder blocks are less common in modern residential construction. Cinder blocks may contain corrosive materials. See **Concrete masonry unit (CMU)**.

Collar tie: a horizontal member (usually a 1x4 or a 2x4) installed in the upper third of the attic between two rafters to help tie rafters together at the ridge.

Column: a generic term describing a structural member designed to support a concentrated vertical load. A column is usually a tall and relatively narrow component. Also called a post, especially when used with decks. See **Pier** and **Pile**.

Compression: The force that crushes or shortens a structural member. A beam under a vertical load is under compression on the top. See **Tension force (load)**.

Concrete masonry unit (CMU): a usually rectangular block made from concrete, aggregate, and water and intended for installation with other blocks to form walls and other structures. See **Cinder block**.

Condominium: a form of real property ownership in which the owner holds 100% ownership of a dwelling unit and shares ownership of the common elements. Condominium does not describe a type of building.

Crawl space: an accessible area within the foundation walls below the first habitable story usually having a soil floor, and a small distance between the soil and the floor joists. Also used to describe an attic in some markets.

Creep: see **Deformed**.

Crown (camber): a condition where a board or beam is curved along the long axis. See **Bow (bowed)**. Most dimensional lumber joists have a natural crown which should be installed with the high side vertical. Manufactured beams have a camber built into the beam. The crown or camber installed with the high side vertical usually becomes straight when a load is applied.

Cup (cupped): a condition where a board is curved along the face of the board.

Deflect (deflection): a condition where a structural member bends from its normal shape, such as when a joist bends under a load. Deflect implies a temporary condition wherein the member will return to its normal shape when the load is removed.

Deformed (deformation): a condition where a structural member changes shape or dimension from its normal shape or dimension. Permanent deformation occurs when the member will not return to its normal shape or dimension when the load is removed. Permanent deformation is called creep.

Dormer: a projection above a sloped roof that usually contains a window. A dormer usually has two sidewalls and a gable roof, but it may have any style roof.

Eaves: the extension of the rafters beyond the exterior wall of the building.

Footing (footer): the part of a foundation that transmits loads directly to the soil, usually made from concrete in modern houses.

Girder: see **Beam (girder)**.

Ground snow load: the estimated weight of accumulated snow on a surface; used when determining rafter span distance and fastening requirements for ceiling joists to rafters and ceiling joists to each other. Also used when determining cantilevered floor joist and deck floor joist span distance.

Grout (masonry): mortar with a high water content and a fluid-like consistency; used to fill cores of masonry such as concrete masonry units (CMUs).

Header: a beam above an opening in a wall, such as a door or window.

Joist: a horizontal structural member that supports a floor or ceiling.

Keyway: a slot or groove used to secure concrete or masonry walls that are built at different times. A keyway is cut into the footing during finishing to help keep concrete or masonry walls from sliding off the footing.

Kicker: a piece of lumber, usually a 2x4, that is connected to a rafter and to a ceiling joist to reduce rafter thrust that could move the wall on which the rafter bears. A kicker serves the same function as a rafter tie. See **Rafter tie.**

Load (dead): the downward force on a structure imposed by the building materials and by permanently attached fixtures such as HVAC equipment.

Load (live): the downward force on a structure imposed by occupants and their belongings. Live load does not include environmental loads, such as wind and earthquakes.

Pier: a column designed to support a concentrated vertical load, often installed above ground, but may be installed below ground.

Pilaster: a column that supports a concentrated vertical load. A pilaster may be on the interior or the exterior of a building, and may be taller and more decorative than a pier.

Pile: a column installed in the ground that is designed to support a concentrated vertical load. A pile is part of the foundation of a house, and is usually found where the soil has poor load-bearing capacity or is unstable.

Pitch (of a roof): the ratio of the total height of a roof to the total horizontal distance that the roof covers. For example, if the total height of the roof from the top plate to the ridge is 12 feet and the total horizontal distance between the exterior walls under the roof is 24 feet, the roof has a ½ pitch. See **Slope (of a roof)**.

Plumb: vertical.

Plumb cut: a vertical cut of a rafter at the ridge or at a hip and valley rafter; also the vertical cut of a stair stringer at its support.

Purlin: a brace installed near the midpoint of a rafter that transmits the rafter load to a load-bearing wall and allows the rafter to span a greater distance. A purlin consists of a purlin that is at least as wide as the rafter, and a purlin brace that is at least a 2x4 and bears on a load-bearing wall. Purlin braces should be installed at least every 4 feet.

Rack (racking): the distortion or movement of a structure or its components; usually caused by wind or seismic loads.

Rafter: an inclined roof structural member that supports the roof sheathing and roof covering.

Rafter (common): an inclined roof structural member that runs between the ridge and the top plate.

Rafter (fill-in): a dimensional lumber rafter used with trusses and I-joist rafters to construct parts of the roof system where trusses and I-joists are not practical.

Rafter (hip): an ascending rafter formed at the intersection of two hip roof sections. Hip rafters may need to be supported at a ridge board by a brace to a load-bearing wall.

Rafter (jack): a rafter that runs between a hip or valley rafter and the ridge, or between two rafters. Rafters that run between a hip rafter and the ridge are hip jack rafters, and rafters that run between a valley rafter and the ridge are valley jack rafters. Rafters that run between valley and hip rafters are cripple jack rafters.

Rafter (valley): a descending rafter formed by the intersection of two roofs. Valley rafters are load-bearing members. Valley rafters may need to be supported at a ridge board by a brace to a load-bearing wall.

Rafter tail: the part of a rafter that extends past the exterior wall top and forms part of the eaves.

Rafter tie: a horizontal member running between rafters on opposite sides of the roof when ceiling joists run perpendicular to the rafters. Rafter ties act like ceiling joists to keep the rafters from pushing the walls out.

Ridge: the top horizontal board or beam of a roof. Most roofs use a ridge board, which is a place to fasten rafters, and does not provide structural support. Roofs supporting vaulted ceilings should usually have a ridge beam designed to provide structural support. Ridge boards and ridge beams should be deep enough so that the entire plumb cut of the rafter bears on the ridge.

Rotate (rotation): a condition where a structural member moves laterally from its normal position relative to vertical, such as when a foundation wall moves inward due to pressure from soil.

Seat cut: the horizontal rafter cut at a wall top or a valley. Also the horizontal cut at the end of a stairway stringer.

Shear: the deformation of a structural member (such as a beam) in which parallel planes slide relative to each other.

Shear wall: a wall designed not to change shape (rack) under loads such as wind and earthquake; also called a braced wall. See **Rack (racking)**.

Sheathing: (1) the material covering the top of the rafters; (2) the material covering the top of the floor joists, also called the subfloor; (3) the material covering the exterior wall structural components.

Slope (of a roof): the number of inches that a roof increases in height (rise) for every 12 inches of horizontal distance (run). The slope is usually expressed as 4/12 or 4:12 where the first number is the rise and the second number is always 12, the run. The terms pitch and slope are sometimes used as synonyms. This is not technically correct. See **Pitch (of a roof)**.

Span: the horizontal distance between structural supports. Overspan is an informal term that refers to a joist or a rafter that is longer than allowed between structural supports. Rafter span is measured horizontally, not along the length of the rafter.

Square (squared): a condition that occurs when intersecting walls form a 90° angle. Squared walls can be determined by measuring and applying the formula A2 + B2 = C2 to the right triangle formed by the walls.

Stud: (1) a grade of lumber used in wall construction rated below #2 grade and approximately equal to #3 grade; (2) a vertical structural member in a wall.

Stud (cripple): a less than full height vertical structural member usually found under windows and in partial height walls.

Stud (jack): a less than full height vertical structural member placed under a header to provide bearing support for the header.

Stud (king): a full height vertical structural member placed on the sides of a header.

Tension force (load): The force that pulls or stretches a structural member. A beam under a vertical load is under tension on the bottom. Contrast **Compression**.

Townhouse: a single family attached dwelling with all of the following: (1) three or more dwellings in one building, (2) dwelling extends from the foundation to the roof, (3) a yard or public way on at least two sides. A townhouse is a type of building, not a form of real property ownership.

FOUNDATIONS

Forces Affecting Houses

A house can move in any direction. It can move in a single direction or it can move in multiple directions simultaneously. Movement direction depends on the forces acting on the house at a particular time. Houses should be designed and built to resist these forces.

Gravity is always trying to move the house down. Footings, or similar components such as **piles** or **piers**, must be designed not to deform, break, or subside (settle) under the load imposed by gravity, and to transmit the load to the soil or to bedrock. The materials (concrete, wood, siding, etc.) used to build the house are called the **dead load**. The load imposed by occupants, furnishings, snow, and any other variable loads are called the **live load**.

The ability of a foundation to bear the live load and the dead load depends on the material on which the foundation sits. Some materials, such as bedrock, have an excellent capacity to bear loads. Other materials, such as **organic clay** and **silt soils**, have a **poor capacity to bear loads**. In addition to load bearing capacity, materials differ in their ability to drain water and their tendency to expand or contract based on moisture content.

Soils are classified according to the **Unified Soil Classification System**. Soils such as gravel and sand are good soils because they have good load-bearing capacity, allow water to drain quickly, and do not change volume with changes in moisture. Soils such as organic clays and silt are problematic soils. These soils have low load-bearing capacity, retain water, and can change volume according to moisture levels. One way to deal with these soils is to remove them and replace with more favorable soils. Another way is to use piles that are driven or drilled down to bedrock or more favorable soils. In some cases, extra wide, deep, and steel reinforced footings will work. Still another way to deal with unstable soils is to use a drip irrigation system to maintain a consistent soil moisture level. This method is mostly found in Texas.

Home inspectors are not required to determine the soil type on which a house sits; however, home inspectors should be familiar with the soil types in their area, especially the types and typical locations of problem soils. Home inspectors should be able to recognize when a foundation problem might be the result of a soil problem, and to recommend the appropriate expert to conduct further evaluation. A **geotechnical engineer** specializes in foundation problems caused by poor soil.

Water in the soil can exert tremendous pressure on a house. Hydrostatic pressure can exert lateral (horizontal) force on foundation walls causing them to rotate, bow, and crack. Water expands when it freezes. Frozen water can exert lateral force on the foundation walls, and upward force on the footings and on horizontal foundation components such as concrete slabs. This upward force is often called **frost heave**. Water can also cause some clay soils to expand or contract. This expansion and contraction can cause lateral movement of foundation walls and upward or downward movement of footings and horizontal foundation components.

Some areas, such as many parts of Florida and land near lakes and rivers, have subsurface water that is very close to the surface. Basements are less common in these areas because they would be prone to water infiltration and to hydrostatic pressure against the foundation. Slab and crawl space foundations are more common in these areas.

Earthquakes, flowing water (during a flood), and wave action (during a hurricane) can move the house horizontally. Foundations in areas prone to these events usually need to be larger and have more and larger reinforcing steel to withstand these forces. The house framing must be adequately secured to the foundation to prevent these forces from moving the house off the foundation. Securing the framing to the foundation is the purpose of bolts and straps embedded in the foundation and attached to the sill/sole plate. Larger plate washers (at least 3 inches by 3 inches) may be required in these areas. More robust wall bracing may also be required in these areas.

Wind can move the house horizontally by exerting lateral force against the walls and roof. Wind can also move the house up. Pressure exerted by the wind can blow the roof off if the doors and windows break, and can lift the entire house off the foundation. The house walls must be adequately braced against the lateral force to prevent wall movement called **racking**. The house walls and roof must be adequately secured to the foundation to prevent wind from forcing the house or its parts up. **Securing a house against wind forces begins at the foundation and extends in an unbroken path to the rafters.** Hold-down brackets, metal straps, and threaded rods are some methods of securing the house to the foundation.

Maps are available that indicate areas subject to wind, water, and earthquakes. In addition, each building department should provide this information in International Residential Code Table R301.2(1). New houses built in wind, water, and earthquake areas have additional structural requirements. Existing houses are not required to be upgraded to current requirements; however, it may be more difficult or more expensive to obtain homeowner insurance for houses that do not comply with current requirements.

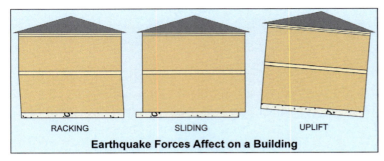
Earthquake Forces Affect on a Building

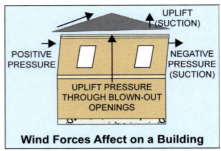
Wind Forces Affect on a Building

All houses should be built on a foundation that consists of one or more of the following components. Footings, piers, and piles transmit loads to bedrock or soil. Foundation walls bear on footings to lift the house above surrounding grade and in the case of basements to provide additional space below grade. Foundation walls should be designed to transmit the vertical loads from above to the footings, and to withstand lateral (horizontal) loads imposed by soil outside the walls. Foundation floors occur mostly in basements and garages, and provide a stable and level surface that makes the space usable. Concrete foundation floors should be at least 3 ½ inches thick and are not designed to provide structural support for loads.

Footings, Piles, Piers, and Columns

Footings The simplest footing consists of large rocks supporting large timbers raised a few inches off the ground. Footings under old houses may consist of rubble (stones) or masonry (bricks) or the house may bear directly on soil with no footing. Many of these old footings have either been replaced or the buildings have been demolished. A home inspector will usually not be able to determine if footings are present, and if present, the footing type.

A common footing for houses built during the last 100 years is the continuous **spread footing**, also called a **ribbon footing**. This footing usually consists of concrete poured into a trench lined with wood forms that have been leveled so that the top of the footing will be level. Other footing materials, such as crushed stone, solid or fully grouted concrete masonry units (CMUs), and wood are also allowed, but are uncommon. Footings in newer houses should contain reinforcing steel, although this is not required, except in seismic and high wind zones. Footings in older houses may or may not be steel-reinforced. Footings should be placed under both exterior and interior load-bearing walls. **The bottom of footings should be at least 12 inches below undisturbed ground and below the local frost line** (whichever is deeper) to reduce uplift caused by frost heave.

The minimum thickness of a modern spread footing is between 6 inches and 19 inches. The minimum width ranges between 12 inches to 49 inches. The width and thickness depends on the number of stories the footing will support, the load-bearing capacity of the soil under the footing, the snow load or roof live load, and specified construction materials, such as wood or masonry walls. Footings may be thicker, wider, and have additional reinforcing steel in order to accommodate soil with poor load-bearing capacity.

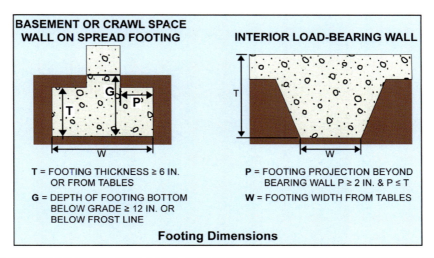

Footing Dimensions

Step Footings for a Basement.

<u>Piles and Piers</u> **Piles are used to support foundations that must be placed on soil with poor load-bearing capacity and to raise houses above the local flood level.** Pile foundations are common under newer homes located on ocean beaches and under homes in swampy areas. Piles used in residential foundations are usually wood that has a diameter between 8 inches and 14 inches or square sizes between 6x6 to 12x12 inches. Piles are often driven into the soil using a pile driver that strikes repeated blows on the pile until the pile reaches the desired depth. Piles support loads by bearing on rock or good load-bearing soil or by friction of soil surrounding the pile. Pile foundations should be designed by an engineer.

A pier is a component that supports a point (concentrated) load. A pier can be below grade and support a footing or grade beam, or it can be above grade and support a house structural beam. Piers should bear on a footing (called a pier pad or pad footing) of appropriate size. Piers may be constructed using concrete masonry units (CMUs), bricks, or poured concrete, and reinforced with steel as necessary.

Piles.

Piers in a Crawl Space.

The difference between a pile, a pier, and a column is semantic. If it is constructed using CMUs or concrete, it is often called a pier, regardless of whether it is above or below grade. If it is constructed using steel or wood and installed above grade, it is often called a column. If it is constructed using steel or wood and installed below grade, it is often called a pile. All perform the same function.

Home inspectors often find improperly installed piers and columns. Piers and columns should bear on a footing of appropriate size and thickness. Wood and steel columns should be secured against lateral movement at the bottom, except that columns 48 inches tall or less in a crawl space need not be secured at the bottom unless the house is in a D seismic zone.

Masonry piers should be built using mortar. Dry stacking is not acceptable. Masonry piers should have a solid cap at least 4 inches thick. The cap may be a solid cap block, solid bricks, or the top CMU may be filled with grout. Masonry piers should have a minimum dimension of 8 inches. The maximum height of an 8x16 inch hollow CMU pier is 32 inches and the maximum height of a an 8x16 inch solid CMU pier is 80 inches.

Columns Wood columns should be at least 4x4 inch preservative treated or decay resistant wood. Steel columns should be at least 3 inch diameter Schedule 40 pipe that is painted inside and outside with rust-inhibiting paint. **Columns in basements should be secured at the bottom**. Columns 48 inches tall or less located in crawl spaces are allowed to be unsecured at the bottom. In most jurisdictions, columns are not required to be secured at the top.

One-piece steel screw jack columns are usually acceptable as permanent columns if they are properly secured at the bottom, and if they are made from the proper materials. It does not matter which direction a screw jack column is installed (screw up or down) unless the column manufacturer specifies a direction. Some manufacturers recommend that the screw not extend more than three inches. Telescoping columns (where one section fits into another section) are usually considered temporary supports and are not considered appropriate to provide permanent support. Columns retrofitted in basements and supported by the basement floor are likely not on an appropriately thick footing.

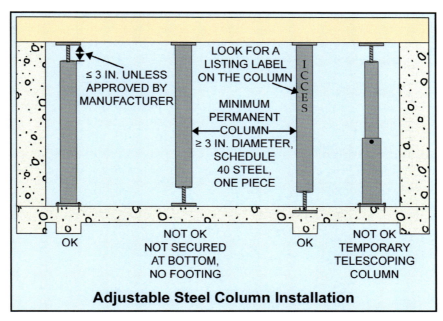

Adjustable Steel Column Installation

Acceptable Steel Screw Jack Column.

Unacceptable Telescoping Columns.

Typical Defects Typical defects that home inspectors should report include:

1. absent, deteriorated footings,
2. footings inadequate size and thickness (e. g., patio slab converted to finished space),
3. cracked, uplifted, settled footings (these defects can sometimes be inferred by the condition of the foundation wall),
4. masonry piers dry stacked, too tall for material, absent solid cap, absent or deteriorated mortar,
5. rotated masonry piers,

6. CMU hollow (core) side installed horizontally,
7. wood and steel columns not secured at bottom, bowed, rotated, wrong type or material, size too small, deteriorated especially at the bottom,
8. wood columns damaged by wood destroying organisms and fungi.

Refer to the Basement Foundation section for more information about these defects and their effects on foundations.

There is no agreed upon standard for what constitutes a reportable crack in a footing. A common guideline is that cracks exceeding ¼ inch in width or ¼ inch vertical displacement should be considered for evaluation and repair.

There is no agreed upon standard for what constitutes reportable rotation or bowing of a column or pier. A common guideline is that rotation exceeding ¾ inch in 8 feet should be considered for evaluation and action.

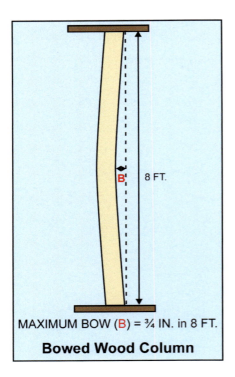
Bowed Wood Column

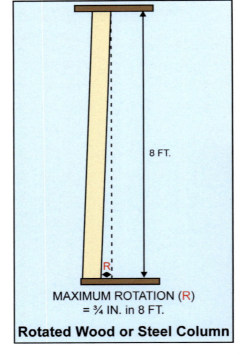
Rotated Wood or Steel Column

Column Rotated

Standards IRC 2018 R403 (footings), R404.1.9 (masonry piers), R407 (wood and steel columns) R317.1.4 (wood column decay prevention), R602.10 (anchoring braced walls).

Column Rusted and Not Secured at Bottom.

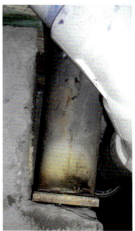
Column Not Properly Supported and Not Secured at Bottom.

Block Cores Turned Wrong Direction, Dry Stacked, No Footing.

Deck Blocks are Not Usually Adequate Footings.

Basement Foundation

<u>Description</u> A **basement is an area that is entirely or partially below grade** (has soil covering part or all of one or more sides). A basement that is entirely below grade is sometimes called a **cellar**. A basement that has a full-height door to the exterior (not a bulkhead door) is sometimes called a **walk-out or daylight basement**.

Modern basement construction begins by excavating a hole about 2 feet wider on all sides than the basement walls. This gives workers room to erect the basement walls, to install waterproofing or dampproofing, and to install foundation drains. Forms for footings are set and leveled and footings are excavated and poured. Basement walls are erected. Any plumbing and electrical components that need to be installed under the basement slab are installed, as are any radon mitigation system components. Basement wall dampproofing or waterproofing is applied and the foundation drain is installed. The foundation is backfilled and the backfill soil should be compacted. Gravel and a vapor retarder may be installed under the basement floor. Crack control wire and reinforcing steel, if any, is installed. The basement floor (and garage floor if any) is poured.

Concrete Basement Walls Modern basement walls are often concrete, either **cast-in-place** walls or **precast** walls (panels). Cast-in-place walls are made by pouring concrete into metal or wood forms set on top of previously poured footings. Vertical dowels of reinforcing steel should be placed in the footings and a U-shaped groove (called a **keyway**) should be cut into the top of the wet footing concrete to help the foundation walls resist sliding off the footings. Horizontal reinforcing steel should be installed in the walls to help the walls resist lateral load from the soil. Wall thickness and the amount and size of reinforcing steel depends on the wall height and the amount of soil on the exterior side of the wall. The wall forms are set, plumbed, squared, and braced so that the walls will not move during the concrete pour. Concrete is poured into the forms and vibrated so that the concrete will consolidate and not have areas with less concrete (called voids, honeycombing, aggregate pockets). The forms are usually removed, but some forms come with insulation as part of the system (insulating concrete forms). These forms are left in place.

Precast walls (panels) are built in a factory, shipped to the construction site, and placed in position using a crane. Precast panels usually come with sheets of foam insulation already in place. Precast concrete panels come in standard heights between 8 and 10 feet, and in lengths up to about 16 feet. An engineer should determine requirements for wall thickness, reinforcing steel, securing the walls to the footings, and securing the wall panels to each other.

**Cast-in-Place Concrete Wall.
Waterproofing Below Brick Ledge.
Dampproofing Above Brick Ledge.**

**Precast Concrete Wall.
Plumbing Being Installed Under Floor.**

Concrete Masonry Unit (CMU) Basement Walls Some modern basement walls, and many basement walls in older houses, are built using CMUs. Construction of a CMU basement wall follows similar steps to cast-in-place concrete walls. The hollow cores of modern CMU basement walls are often filled with grout or insulation and reinforced with steel. Openings that are sometimes visible in the bottom of CMU walls are for inspection to confirm that the walls were fully grouted. The cores of older CMU basement walls are often hollow and the walls are not reinforced. Note that CMUs are sometimes called **cinder blocks**. Refer to the definitions for more information.

Permanent Wood Foundations

Permanent wood foundations are used in some areas. These foundations are more commonly encountered in cold climates. An advantage of permanent wood foundations is that they can be more energy efficient compared to other foundations. Disadvantages include wood deterioration (grade and drainage is very important to avoid deterioration) and restrictions on wall height relative to backfill depth.

Footings for these foundations consist of crushed stone or gravel that is at least 8 inches deep and at least 16 inches wide. A preservative treated footing plate that is at least 2 x 8 is required, along with a preservative treated bottom plate. The basement floor should also be set on gravel with a vapor retarder installed above the gravel. Gravel or stone provide drainage that is important for preserving this type of foundation. The entire foundation system should be drained with an active sump pump system. As with other foundations, home inspectors will rarely be able to determine if these components are properly installed.

Permanent wood foundation walls are built using preservative treated plywood. The walls should be (at least) dampproofed, and a moisture barrier (at least 6 mil polyethylene) should be installed on walls below grade. Joints between panels should be sealed with caulk or other appropriate sealant. Stone or gravel fill should be placed against the wood foundation walls.

Stone Foundations

Stone foundation walls are frequently encountered in older houses (usually at least one hundred years old), although they are allowed to be built in modern construction. These walls were built by laying stones without mortar (dry-stacking), or with mortar. Stones were cut into consistent shapes and laid like masonry, or were laid as they came from the field or the river. Stone foundations may or may not have separate footings, and often do not have a separate footing in very old houses.

Current requirements for stone foundation walls include a minimum thickness of 16 inches, a maximum height of soil against the wall of 8 feet, and a maximum soil pressure against the wall of 30 pounds per square foot. New stone foundation walls may not be built in places where seismic activity is likely (the D seismic zones).

Basements with stone foundations frequently have water issues. Water can enter the basement by leaking between or through the stones, or by migrating between or through the stones as water vapor. The mortar, and occasionally the stones themselves, can deteriorate. The mortar used with old stone foundations is usually a soft lime-based mortar that is prone to deterioration when exposed to moisture. Repairing lime-based mortar with modern mortar or other cement-based can make matters worse by holding water against the lime-based mortar causing further mortar deterioration.

Stone Basement Wall, Significantly Bowed. Picture Courtesy of Welmoed Sisson

Stone Basement Wall, Water Intrusion.

Brick Foundations Brick foundation walls may be encountered in older houses in some markets. Brick foundations share most of the water issues that plague stone foundations, and can have more serious issues because brick is hygroscopic (absorbs water). Grade and drainage around brick foundations is extremely important.

Waterproofing, Dampproofing, Foundation Drains Basements that have habitable or usable space below grade should have foundation drains (except for foundations on gravel and sandy soil). All basements should be either waterproofed or dampproofed. These components are usually concealed and are not available for inspection. Older homes often do not have these components.

Waterproofing is intended to stop the flow of liquid water under hydrostatic pressure. One method of waterproofing concrete and masonry walls involves applying a tar-like substance (a bituminous coating) to the wall, and covering it with 6-mil polyethylene from the top of the footing to finish grade. Other methods and materials, including proprietary systems that may include insulation are used, especially in modern construction. Properly installed waterproofing should last for the life of the structure.

Dampproofing is intended to stop the flow of water vapor and small amounts of liquid water not under hydrostatic pressure. Masonry walls should first be parged with at least ⅜ inch of Portland cement on the exterior side. Masonry and concrete walls may then have a bituminous coating applied. Other approved methods and materials may be used. Other proprietary dampproofing systems may be used. Dampproofing has a service life in the ten to twenty year range, depending on the system used and the dampness of the soil at the foundation.

Modern foundation drains are installed using perforated plastic pipe covered with a fabric "sock" that is similar in texture to cheesecloth. The pipe is placed on and covered with gravel. Clay drain tiles are also allowed and are common in older houses if they have foundation drains. Foundation drains may consist of other materials, such as rigid plastic pipe with holes, and proprietary systems. Foundation drains may drain to daylight if possible, and if not possible should drain to a sump pump.

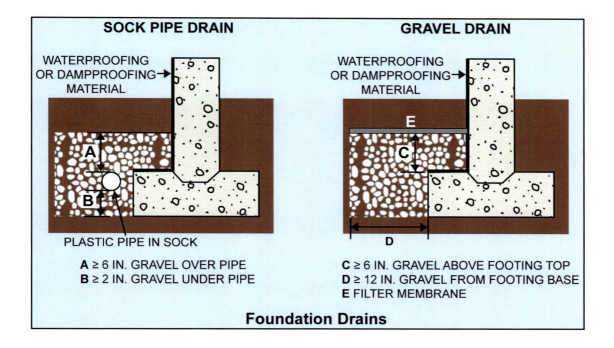

Proprietary Waterproofing System with Foundation Drain.

Cast-in-Place Concrete Wall, Waterproofing Applied, Foundation Drain Run to Daylight.

Typical Potentially Significant Basement Defects A thorough discussion of foundation defects is out of scope for this book. Analysis of a specific foundation defect depends on the foundation material (concrete, CMU, etc.), the type, location, and extent of the defect, and whether the defect may be active. The list of possible causes contains only the most common causes. Other causes are possible, including earthquake and storm damage in areas prone to these events. Foundation wall defects are not mutually exclusive. A foundation wall can have more than one defect with more than one cause. Foundation wall defects often present as cracks in brick veneer and cracks in interior wall coverings. Foundation wall problems also present as cracks and operating problems (sticking, out of square) at doors and windows.

There is no agreed upon standard for what constitutes reportable foundation defects. The possible measurement guidelines are from home builders. Home inspectors may wish to report foundation defects that present measurements that are smaller than those listed below.

1. **Wall rotating (usually leaning in from top):** possible causes: hydrostatic (water) pressure, frost heave, expansive soil, wall backfilled before wall cured, vehicles drove too close to wall, backfill too high for wall thickness, wall not secured laterally at top, wall built out of plumb. Possible measurement guideline: more than 1 inch in 8 feet.

2. **Wall bulging (part of wall protrudes in from the exterior side), and long horizontal cracks in walls:** possible causes: hydrostatic (water) pressure, frost heave, expansive soil, wall backfilled before wall cured, inadequate steel reinforcement, backfill too high for wall thickness, tree roots. Possible measurement guideline: more than 1 inch in 8 feet for bulging, more than ¼ inch wide for cracks.

3. **Vertical, diagonal, or stair step cracks wider at one end:** possible causes: settlement of soil under footing, footing not wide or deep enough, footing with no reinforcing steel, hydrostatic (water) pressure, frost heave, expansive soil. Possible measurement guideline: more than ¼ inch wide at narrowest point.

4. **Out of plane cracking (part of wall moved horizontally relative to rest of wall):** possible causes: hydrostatic (water) pressure, frost heave, expansive soil, inadequate steel reinforcement, backfill too high for wall thickness, tree roots.

5. **Out of plane cracking (part of wall moved vertically relative to rest of wall):** possible causes: settlement of soil under footing, footing not wide or deep enough, footing with no reinforcing steel, hydrostatic (water) pressure, frost heave, expansive soil.

6. **Wall sliding (entire wall moves relative to footing, wall may not be cracked):** possible causes: hydrostatic (water) pressure, frost heave, expansive soil, wall not secured to footing.

7. **Foundation settlement or rotation (entire foundation settles or rotates, can be uniform, or one side or corner can settle or rotate):** possible causes: footing settlement, expansive soil, frost heave.

8. **Building movement off of the foundation:** building walls that are not attached to the foundation can move off of the foundation; possible causes: earthquake, snow load from roof, hydrostatic (water) pressure, frost heave, expansive soil, wind storms, absent or improperly installed foundation anchors.

9. **Water stains on wall, dampness, liquid water, also owner belongings raised above floor:** possible causes: improper grading at foundation, lack of gutters, blocked gutters, downspouts discharge near foundation, irrigation system problems, plumbing drain backup or significant water supply leak, flooding, normal leaking through stone foundations, high water table.

Water Stains, Damp Left, Dry Right.

Compound Cracks, Stair Step Cracks Water Stains on Floor.

Cast-in-Place Foundation Wall Crack. Probable Footing Settlement.

Pictures Courtesy of Welmoed Sisson

Brick Foundation Wall Crack with Displacement and Water Intrusion.

Water Stains in Finished Basement.

<u>Typical Less Significant Basement Defects</u> These defects may not be structurally significant; however, cracks, voids, and honeycombing can admit water. Home inspectors should look for brown stains below the defect that indicate water possible water infiltration. Refer to the Slab-on-Stem Wall Foundation section for more about basement and garage floor slab defects.

1. **Uniform width cracks less than ⅛ inch wide:** <u>possible causes</u>: shrinkage of concrete or mortar usually due to too much water in concrete or mortar, improper concrete or mortar components mix, concrete or mortar drying too quickly.

2. **Voids, aggregate pockets, honeycombing in concrete walls:** <u>possible causes</u>: inadequate vibration of concrete during pour, aggregate too large in concrete mix.

3. **Spalling (material disintegrating; could be structural if large amounts of material are unsound):** possible causes: water in wall from grading and gutter problems, poor quality or old foundation materials.

4. **Efflorescence (white powder on walls):** possible causes: moisture migrating through the wall due to improper grading at foundation, lack of gutters, blocked gutters, downspouts discharge near foundation, irrigation system problems.

5. **Cold joint:** cause: concrete in a lower section of the wall sets before more concrete is poured above the set concrete.

Water Intrusion and Spalling.

Typical Repairs of Non-structural Cracks and Water Infiltration

These repairs assume that the causes of the problem being repaired have been identified. Repairs made before identifying and addressing the causes of the problems will likely be ineffective. These crack repair materials may be used with cracks in foundation walls and in concrete slabs when approved for use by the product manufacturer. **Home inspectors should not recommend specific repairs.** Home inspectors may be asked about repair options, and it is okay to discuss options verbally if asked.

- **Hydraulic cement:** low cost, seals well against water infiltration, prone to failure due to shrinking and cracking.

- **Polyurethane foam:** higher cost, good for larger cracks and cracks with active water leaks, forgiving of minor movement.

- **Epoxy:** higher cost, good for small cracks, provides some structural benefit, may not work if water is actively entering or if crack is active.

- **Waterproofing liquid coatings (applied to interior):** low cost, effectiveness varies based on product, wall preparation, and coating application, better at water vapor control, may be less effective at liquid water control, could allow damage (e. g., spalling) to foundation if wall cannot dry.

Foundation Repair Using Epoxy.

Typical Repairs of Structural Defects Structural repairs should be selected and designed by a qualified engineer after analysis of the causes of the problems being repaired. Repairs should be installed by a qualified contractor. These methods involve repair of the existing wall or slab. Replacement of the wall or slab is usually an option, but is expensive, disruptive, and will not fix problems associated with problem soils and problems related to water. **Home inspectors should report evidence of foundation repairs** and recommend inquiry about engineering, contractor, permits, and inspections.

- **Buttress:** usually one or more concrete masonry unit (CMU) walls installed perpendicular to a bowing or leaning wall in an attempt to prevent further movement; does not change current position of wall; usually not effective in cases of significant failure; takes usable space and is aesthetically unattractive.
- **Sister walls:** usually one or more CMU or concrete walls installed parallel to a bowing or leaning wall in an attempt to prevent further movement; does not change current position of wall; may be installed on inside or outside of problem wall; can be expensive.
- **Steel I-beams:** usually one or more beams installed in contact with a bowing or leaning wall in an attempt to prevent further movement; does not change current position of wall; may be attached to floor framing at the top, and sunk into basement floor at bottom; usually not effective in cases of significant failure, and is aesthetically unattractive.
- **Carbon fiber mats:** usually one or more mats installed in contact with a bowing wall in an attempt to prevent further movement; does not change current position of wall; usually installed in a system with epoxy crack fillers and epoxy adhesives; not effective in cases of significant failure; sold as do-it-yourself kits; evidence of installation may be covered.
- **Tieback anchors:** usually one or more rods or cables installed through a hole in a bowing or leaning wall in an attempt to prevent further movement and to change current position of wall; attached to a helical anchor placed in an excavation in the yard; evidence is plates attached to the interior wall.
- **Plate anchors:** similar to tieback anchors except anchor is a plate in the yard that does not require significant excavation to install; does not change current position of wall.

- **Push piers and helical piers:** push piers are steel rods and helical piers are like a large single thread screw; used in an attempt to raise and stabilize footings that have settled; also used to raise slabs that have settled; brackets attached to footing and pier installed down to bedrock or stable soil; evidence is one or more brackets at foundation; may be no evidence on a slab except for repaired cracks.
- **Slab jacking/foam jacking:** expanding polyurethane foam or a combination of pulverized top soil and mortar mix is forced under the concrete slab through holes drilled in the slab in an attempt to raise the slab back to original position; can work for soil that has been improperly compacted; works less well for poor soil; no evidence except for repaired cracks and injection holes; can be used on driveways and walkways; the cause of the settlement must be addressed or this repair may not be permanent.

**Tie Back Anchors (Left), Carbon Fiber Mats (Right).
Pictures Courtesy of Tarheel Basements**

**CMU Buttress Wall (Left), Steel Beams (Right).
Right Picture Courtesy of Tarheel Basements**

Standards IRC 2018 R404 (foundation walls), R405 (foundation drains), R406 (waterproofing and dampproofing).

Crawl Space Foundation

Description A **crawl space** is an unfinished area under the first story of a house and has a lower height than a basement. Crawl space clearances range from a few inches to several feet. A crawl space almost always has a soil floor. Some crawl space floors may be covered by polyethylene or a similar sheet material to reduce water vapor transmission from the soil. Some may be covered with a thin layer of concrete.

Wood floor joists that are not preservative treated should be at least 18 inches above a crawl space soil floor (whether or not covered). Wood beams that are not preservative treated should be at least 12 inches above a crawl space soil floor. Crawl spaces in some older houses may not comply with these standards.

Current minimum crawl space access opening requirements are 18x24 inches if access is through the floor, and 16x24 inches if access is through a side wall. The opening should be 22x30 inches if equipment requiring service and replacement is in the crawl space. Crawl space access openings in some older houses may not comply with comply with current requirements.

The crawl space floor should be cleared of wood, cardboard, and similar materials, including tree and plant debris and construction lumber. These materials can attract termites and other wood destroying organisms. The crawl space floor should also be cleared of construction debris including debris from repairs, replacements, and modifications to the structure or systems. Crawl space floors should usually be sloped to drain toward a low point, although this is not required unless there is a ground water or drainage problem.

Modern crawl space construction begins by excavating a level space for erecting the footings and crawl space walls. The interior of the crawl space may be partially excavated depending on the slope of the ground and the anticipated height of the crawl space walls. Forms for footings are set and leveled and footings are excavated and poured. Crawl space walls are erected. The foundation is backfilled. A vapor retarder may be installed near the end of the house construction process.

Typical Structural Defects Refer to the Footings, Piers, Piles, and Columns section and to the basement foundation section for information about crawl space structural defects.

Crawl Space Moisture Issues Refer to the Crawl Space Ventilation section.

Safety Issues Crawl spaces can present numerous dangerous and toxic animals, plants, and substances such as spiders, snakes, mold, raw sewage, and energized electrical wires.

Standards IRC 2018 R408 (crawl space), R317 (protection of wood against decay).

Slab-on-Grade Foundation

Description **Slab-on-grade** foundations are, as the name states, slabs of concrete installed on level ground. Topsoil is removed and the ground is leveled. Wood forms are installed and leveled. Plumbing pipes and any electrical cables are installed and excavations are backfilled. Gravel, a vapor retarder, reinforcing steel, and post-tensioning cables may be installed. Concrete is laid and finished in one pour. Slab-on-grade foundations are the least expensive to build.

These foundations are usually found in warmer climates because the footings (if any) are near the surface; however, monolithic slabs with deep footings can be installed in colder climates.

There are two types of slab-on-grade foundations. A **mat/floating slab** foundation is a slab of concrete that has a uniform thickness. The entire slab is essentially a footing. Mat slabs are appropriate only in climates where the frost line is shallow. A **monolithic/turned-down edge** slab foundation is a slab of concrete with footings at the perimeter and at interior load-bearing walls. The remainder of the slab should be at least 3½ inches thick. The concrete for these slabs should be laid during a single pour.

Slab-on-grade foundations, and basement floors that serve usable or habitable space, should be built on at least 4 inches of sand or gravel and at least a 6-mil polyethylene vapor retarder. This is primarily to reduce moisture entering the house from below, and it can also help reduce entry of radon and other soil gasses.

Floating Slab

Monolithic Slab

Slab-On-Stem Wall Foundation

<u>Description</u> **Slab-on-stem wall** foundations are similar to slab-on-grade foundations except that a spread footing is poured and a short wall made from CMUs or poured concrete is constructed first. The area inside the stem wall is backfilled and (should be) compacted. Plumbing pipes and any electrical cable are installed and trenches for these components are backfilled. Gravel, a vapor retarder, and reinforcing steel may be installed. Concrete is laid and finished. There are two types of slab-on-stem wall foundations. The concrete may float on the soil (a floating slab), or it may bear on the stem wall around the perimeter. Bearing on the stem wall is the better option, but is not required. The garage floor slab frequently floats.

These foundations are versatile. They are suitable for cooler climates because the footings can be placed below the frost line. They are good for flood-prone areas because the first story level can be at whatever height is necessary.

Insulation around the slab perimeter is required for both slab-on-grade and slab-on-stem wall foundations in newer houses located in cooler climate zones. Slab perimeter insulation is not required and is not recommended where termite risk is moderate to heavy because the termites can tunnel unseen behind the insulation. This is a new requirement and most older houses will not have insulated slabs.

Slab on Stem Wall.   **Insulated Slab Foundation.**

Slab Foundation Reinforcement

Slab Reinforcement Components Slab foundations (and other concrete slabs, such as in garages and basements) are sometimes reinforced with steel bars. The slab may also contain wire mesh or strands of fiberglass that are added to the concrete mix. Reinforcing bars increase the resistance of the concrete to shearing (breaking). Wire mesh and fiberglass help reduce concrete cracking. These components are less common in older homes. It is not possible to detect these components during a home inspection.

Post-Tensioned Slabs Slab foundations in areas with unstable soil may be reinforced with cables that are placed under tension after the concrete is poured. These slab foundations are called post-tensioned slabs. Steel cables are installed inside plastic tubes before the concrete is poured. The cables are placed under tension by turning bolts that pull the cables tight. Post-tensioned slabs are more resistant to cracking, settlement, and uplift because the cables help hold the slab together as a single unit.

Post-tensioned slabs should be stamped with a label that warns about the presence of the cables. This label is usually located on the garage floor near the vehicle door. Post-tensioned slabs may also be identified by regularly-spaced concrete patches around the slab perimeter. These patches cover the pockets containing the cable tails.

The cables in a post-tensioned slab are under significant tension. The cables can come out of the slab with deadly force if the cables are damaged. Only trained technicians should cut, drill, or bore into a post-tensioned slab.

Post-Tensioned Slab.

Slab Foundation Defects and Standards

Typical Defects Typical defects that home inspectors should report include:

1. cracks (often concealed by floor coverings but may be visible around the perimeter),
2. uplift and settlement,
3. uneven or not level,
4. cracking, crazing, spalling, dusting, popouts,
5. damaged perimeter insulation (newer houses),
6. efflorescence (caused by poor water management).

Refer to the Footings, Piers, Piles, and Columns section and to the Basement Foundation section for information about slab foundation structural defects.

Basement Slab Cracks with Vertical Displacement.

Slab Crack Seen From Exterior.   **Slab Crack in Garage Floor.**

Concrete Slab Surface Defects A concrete slab surface defect (e.g., crazing, dusting, spalling) is one that is **non-structural** and affects the appearance of the concrete. Almost all concrete slab surface defects occur because of one or more of the following errors: (1) improperly preparing and compacting the soil or material under the concrete, (2) using an improper concrete mix, such as too much water or inadequately air-entrained, (3) improperly placing, finishing, and curing the concrete.

Concrete cracks for many reasons, and most concrete is cracked. Smaller cracks (less than ⅛ inch wide) are often the result of concrete shrinking. Shrinkage can occur when the concrete mix contains too much water and when the concrete cures too quickly. Random shrinkage cracks can also be the result of not installing control joints or improper control joint spacing. Shrinkage cracks are usually cosmetic. Larger cracks (more than ¼ inch wide), especially cracks with vertical displacement, are often the result of the soil under the concrete settling or uplifting (e. g., frost heaving). These cracks may indicate more serious issues.

Crazing appears as many small surface cracks that may look like an irregular honeycomb. Crazing may occur because of improper finishing, or when the concrete cures too quickly. Rapid curing can occur in hot weather, when the concrete is in direct sunlight, or when there is a strong wind. Crazing does not require repair.

Spalling (scaling) is when the finished surface (about ⅛ inch deep) of the concrete separates over several square inches or more. Spalling can occur for several reasons, including freeze/thaw cycles, improper finishing, and when chemicals such as salt attack concrete that is not adequately air-entrained (lots of small bubbles in the concrete). Spalling of small areas may be repaired by surface patching; however, the patch is usually clearly visible, and the repair may not last. Further spalling may be reduced by applying a penetrating sealer.

Dusting is when a fine powder regularly appears on concrete finished surface. Dusting is often the result of improper finishing and curing. Dusting can be repaired or reduced using a surface hardening compound.

A **popout** is when a small, usually conical shaped, part of the concrete surface breaks away. Popouts are usually about 1 to 2 inches across and ½ to 1 inch deep. Popouts have many causes, but many are related to improper finishing and curing. Popouts can be repaired by surface patching; however, the patch is usually clearly visible, and the repair may not last.

<u>Standards</u> IRC 2018 R402 and R403 (concrete and footings), R404 (foundation walls).

<u>FLOOR SYSTEM</u>

<u>Introduction</u>

A floor is a horizontal surface in a house intended for occupants to walk on. A floor could be a concrete slab in a basement or in a slab foundation house. Other floors in houses are almost always framed using some type of wood, such as dimensional lumber (usually 2x10 in modern houses), I-joists, or trusses. Floor system sheathing is usually plywood or OSB in modern houses. Wood planks of various widths and thicknesses were used in houses before plywood became widely used in residential construction in the 1950s. Light gauge steel is a possible floor framing material, but it is uncommon in houses. Structural concrete floors are sometimes installed above a crawl space, but this is a limited regional technique and is uncommon.

The floor system bearing structure depends on the framing system. The most common residential framing system is **platform framing**. The first floor system in platform framing bears on the foundation, either directly on the foundation wall or on a sill plate that bears on the foundation wall. Floor systems for subsequent stories bear on top of the lower story walls. The less common residential framing system is **balloon framing**. The stud walls of a balloon framed house are erected first and bear on the foundation wall. The stud walls extend from the foundation to the ceiling joists. The first floor system bears on the sill plate and upper floors bear on wood ledger strips attached or inset into the walls.

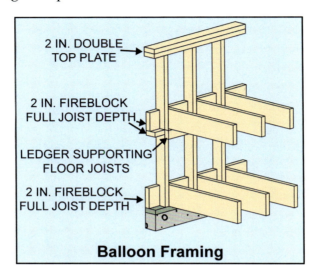

Balloon Framing

Floor systems are designed to support a specified **uniformly distributed** live load without deflecting more than a specific amount. The uniform live load is 30 psf for sleeping rooms (bedrooms) and 40 psf for all other rooms. The maximum allowed deflection under the uniform load is L/360 where L is the joist, truss, or beam span in inches. For example, a 144 inch long joist may deflect (bend) not more than about ⅜ inch under the uniform live load.

A uniformly distributed load can be different from a **point load**. An example of a point load is a person walking across a room, a water bed, or a bathtub filled with water and a bather. These loads can cause a floor system to deflect more than L/360 yet still be within the design parameters. Thus, it is possible for china to rattle in a cabinet when a person walks across the floor, yet the floor system is functioning as designed. This deflection standard may not work well for tile floor coverings. Tile industry guidelines specify a stiffer floor to reduce cracking.

Dimensional Lumber Floor Systems

Dimensional Lumber Characteristics
Dimensional lumber is wood that is cut into standard sizes. Dimensional lumber is identified by its nominal size, such as 2 inches wide by 10 inches deep (usually written as 2x10). The actual size of dimensional lumber is usually about ½ inch smaller than the nominal size; however, the actual depth of larger depth dimensional lumber is now about ¾ inches smaller than the nominal size. For example, a 2x6 is actually about 1½ inches wide by 5½ deep and a 2x10 is actually 1½ inches wide by 9¼ deep. Dimensional lumber is usually available in standard lengths from 8 feet to 24 feet in two foot increments; however, lengths over 16 feet are usually available only at framing lumber yards, and only in some lumber sizes.

Dimensional lumber is also identified by species of tree from which the lumber came and the grade (quality) of the lumber. Common species used for framing lumber include **Douglas fir**, **hem fir**, **spruce, pine, fir (SPF)**, and **Southern pine**. The availability of a lumber species can depend on the location in the country. Southern pine is more widely available in the East.

Douglas fir is more widely available in the West. Lumber grades commonly used for residential framing lumber range from the higher grade #1 to the lower grade #3. There are other lumber grades such as select structural (higher grade) and utility (lower grade), but these are less commonly used in residential construction. Number 2 grade lumber is currently the most commonly used dimensional lumber in residential floor systems. Most prescriptive tables for components such as beams and headers assume using #2 grade or better lumber. Number 3 grade lumber spans a shorter distance compared to higher grades.

Different species and grades of dimensional lumber have different properties that determine under what conditions the lumber may be used. The two most important properties are the stiffness of the lumber, and its resistance to permanent deformation (bending) under load. Higher grades are stiffer and better able to resist permanent deformation under load. Southern pine and Douglas fir are stiffer and better able to resist permanent deformation compared to hem fir and spruce, pine, fir.

Lumber Grade Stamps, #2 Southern Pine (Left), Stud Grade SPF (Right).

<u>**Floor Sheathing**</u> Plywood and OSB are the two most common products used for floor sheathing in houses built since the 1950s (OSB since the late 1970s). These products are also used as roof sheathing and as wall sheathing. Both plywood and OSB are made by layering material at 90° angles using water-resistive adhesive, heat, and pressure to achieve the desired sheet thickness. This 90° layering method increases the strength of the material. Both plywood and OSB usually come as 4 foot wide sheets in common lengths of 8, 9 and 10 feet. Plywood and OSB used as floor sheathing are usually tongue and groove style that provides support for edges between floor joists.

Both Plywood and OSB used as floor sheathing are rated for short term exposure to water use, but both can be damaged by long term water, especially exposure to standing water. Plywood will delaminate. OSB will swell and deteriorate. Both will lose structural integrity if they remain wet long enough. Delamination, swelling, and deterioration are common reasons for squeaky, soft, and uneven floors.

<u>**Typical Construction Techniques**</u> Each species and grade of dimensional lumber is allowed to span a specific distance based on factors such as the use of the room (living or sleeping) the lumber depth (usually 2x10), lumber spacing, and the assumed dead load (usually 10 psf). Dimensional lumber floor joists are usually spaced at 16 inches on center or 24 inches on center. Twelve inches on center may be used if a longer span distance is needed, or if the floor needs to be stiffer (such as when tile floor covering is specified).

Floor joists often bear on one or more beams and on headers over openings in the walls and foundation. The allowed span of beams and headers between supports is based on factors such as the number of stories and roof above, the ground snow load, and the building width.

The allowed span of floor joists, beams, and headers has changed over time. Sometimes the allowed spans increase, but more often they decrease, in part because of the decreasing quality of lumber. **Current span tables do not apply to older houses**. Home inspectors are not required to determine the allowed span of these components regardless of when the house was built. Home inspectors should use evidence-based techniques, such as excessive damage, deflection, and deformation, when evaluating dimensional lumber floor systems, beams, and headers, especially in older houses.

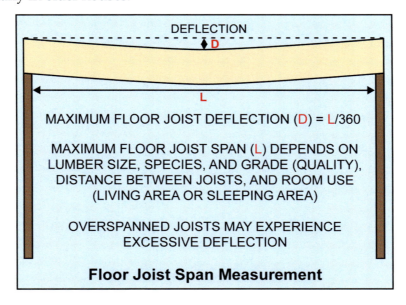

First story floor joists over basements or crawl spaces usually bear on a sill plate or directly on the concrete or masonry foundation. A floor joist or beam should have at least 1½ inches bearing on wood and at least 3 inches bearing on concrete or masonry.

Floor Joist Inadequate Bearing on Concrete.

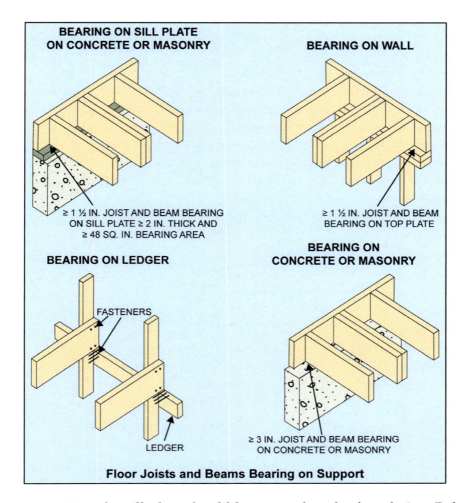

Floor Joists and Beams Bearing on Support

In modern construction, the sill plate should be secured to the foundation. Bolts at least ½ inch in diameter or straps designed for the purpose should be spaced at least every 6 feet. Bolts should have a washer and a fully tightened nut. A bolt or strap should be located not more than 1 foot from the edge of each plate section and ½ inch bolts should not be closer than 3½ inches to a plate joint. Bolts should be installed in the middle third of the plate.

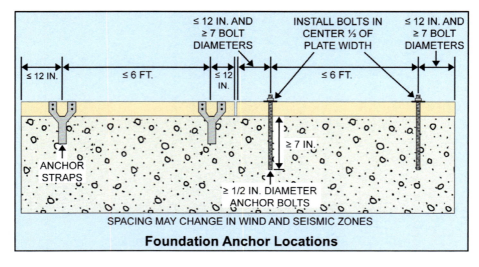

Foundation Anchor Locations

Anchor Bolts Too Close to Plate Joint.

Anchor Strap

Floor joists should be restrained against twisting by being attached to a full-depth rim joist where the joists bear on the foundation. This is called lateral restraint or **blocking**. Joists from opposite sides that meet at an interior wall or beam should lap each other at least 3 inches and should be fastened to each other. Blocking is also required at interior walls or beams if there is a load-bearing wall above.

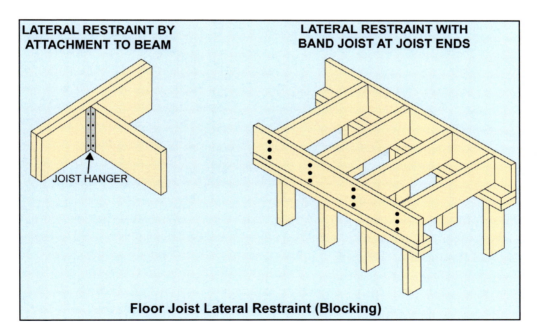

Bridging is often installed near the center of a floor joist span to help prevent twisting. Bridging can consist of full depth lumber or various types of X bridging. Bridging is not required for floor joists 2x12 and smaller; however, it is frequently installed on smaller depth joists.

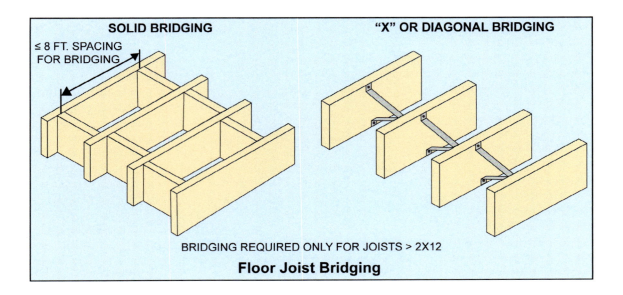

Floor Joist Bridging

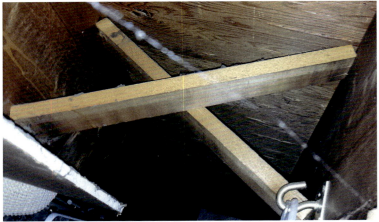

X Bridging

Floor joists sometimes extend past the supporting wall. The extension of a floor beyond a supporting wall is called a **cantilever**. The cantilevered part of the floor places an additional uplift load on the part of the floor system inside the supporting wall (the **backspan**), and places an unsupported load on the part of the floor system outside the supporting wall; thus, the cantilever distance is limited. The joist length inside the supporting wall (the backspan distance) should be at least 3 feet for every 1 foot of cantilever distance when the cantilevered floor supports an exterior bearing wall and a roof. The backspan distance should be at least 2 feet for every 1 foot of cantilever distance when the floor supports an exterior balcony. These ratios are prescriptive and an engineer may design a floor system with a different backspan ratio.

The distance a cantilevered joist may extend past the supporting wall is based on the floor joist size and spacing, the roof width (the dead load on the cantilevered joist), and the ground snow load. The IRC contains prescriptive limits for cantilever distances, which an engineer can override.

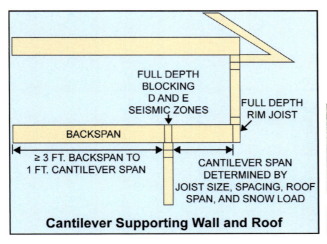

Cantilever Supporting Wall and Roof

Cantilevered Second Story.

Openings in a floor system are usually necessary to accommodate structures such as stairways and chimneys. Two (**trimmer**) joists are connected together on each side of the opening to make a beam that distributes the load imposed by the joists that are interrupted by the opening. Two (**header**) joists are installed between the trimmer joists if the opening is wider than 4 feet. Improper installation and support of floor joist openings occasionally occurs and causes settlement of the floor system around the opening. The home inspector should observe openings in floor framing when inspecting the stairway.

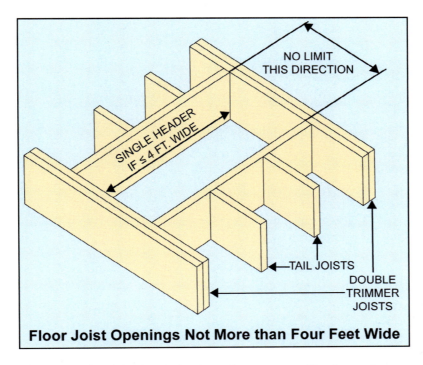

Floor Joist Openings Not More than Four Feet Wide

Additional floor joists should be installed when there are walls above that run parallel to the floor joists. At least 2 joists should be installed under non-load-bearing walls, and at least 3 joists may be necessary under some load-bearing walls.

Most dimensional lumber floor joists, especially longer joists, have a slight curve along the length dimension. This is called the **crown**. Joists and beams should be installed with the crown side facing up. The load will usually straighten the member. Joists and beams installed with the crown side down can cause floor squeaks because of the gap between the floor sheathing and the joist. Joists with excessive crowns should be discarded or cut and used for other purposes, such as blocking.

Plywood and OSB floor sheathing should be installed with the long dimension perpendicular to the floor joists and extending across at least 3 joists. No piece should be less than 24 inches wide; it will be too weak to withstand the design load. Edges between floor joists should be supported either by tongue and groove or by solid blocking. Typical plywood thickness used for floor sheathing is 15/32 (½) inch or 23/32 (¾) inch. The former is limited to floor joist spacing of 16 inches on center while the later may span up to 24 inches on center.

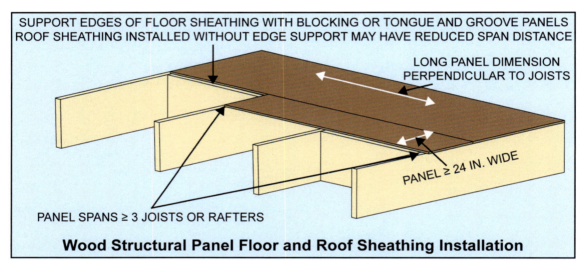

Wood Structural Panel Floor and Roof Sheathing Installation

<u>**Typical Defects**</u> Floor system defects fall into two categories. Some defects are defective per se, meaning that the condition is defective regardless of whether there is current visible evidence of an adverse impact caused by the defect. An improperly notched beam or floor joist is defective per se. The adverse impact may not have occurred, yet. Other defects are evidence-based, meaning that there is current visible evidence of an adverse impact, whether or not there is an identified reason for the defect. A deformed beam is an example of an adverse impact that may have no identified reason, yet.

- **Improperly notched joist and beam:** notches on the top and bottom of the member may not exceed ⅙ of the actual member depth except at the ends where the notch may exceed ¼ the actual depth. Notches may not be longer than ⅓ of the actual member depth; notches may not be located in the middle ⅓ of the member span.

- **Improperly bored joist and beam:** hole diameter may not exceed ⅓ of the actual member depth and may not be located within 2 inches from the edge of the member or within 2 inches of another hole or notch.

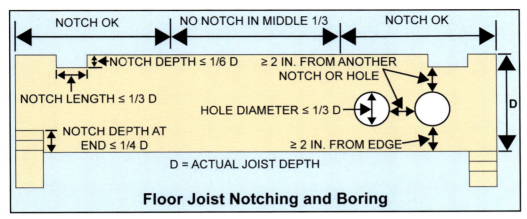
Floor Joist Notching and Boring

Floor Joists Improperly Notched.

Holes Too Close to Joist Edge and to Each Other.

Hole Too Close to Notch.

- **Inadequate joist and beam bearing on support:** joists and beams should have at least 1½ inches of wood bearing on wood and at least 3 inches of wood bearing on masonry and concrete. Joists should bear directly on top of a wall, on a sill plate or sole plate, on a beam, or on a ledger (usually a 2x2) attached to a beam; joists bearing on a ledger should have 3-16d nails installed in the ledger under each joist.

- **Inadequate beam support:** a beam supported by a wall usually should have one vertical member in the wall under each beam member (e.g., 3 studs under a 3-member beam). Beams attached on the side of a beam should be attached using an appropriately sized joist hanger, not by a ledger.

- **Improper joist hanger installation:** joist hangers should be installed according to the hanger manufacturer's instructions. Typical instructions include using the correct size hanger, filling all round and oblong holes with the correct size and type of fastener, and positioning the joist or beam within ⅛ inch of the supporting member.

Fasteners Not Installed in All Round Holes.   **Member Not Properly Seated in Hanger.**

- **Excessively long joist or beam cantilever:** joists and beams are limited as to how far they may extend beyond a vertical supporting member.
- **Damaged joist and beam:** <u>possible causes</u>: wood destroying organisms (termites, fungus), water, beam installed in pocket without air circulation, damage during shipping and installation, natural defects in wood (split, knot).

Damage From Tub Leak.   **Powder Post Beetle Damage.**
Joist Over Notched.

- **Deformed (sagging) joist and beam:** joists and beams should be reasonably straight; <u>possible causes</u>: member installed crown side down, load on member exceeds capacity, member overspanned between supports, supports removed/changed during remodel, improper drilling or notching, excessive cantilever distance, member damaged.
- **Excessively deflecting (springy) floor:** the floor system should not deflect under load more than L/360 where L = joist length in inches; <u>possible causes</u>: load on member exceeds capacity, member overspanned between supports, improper drilling or notching, member damaged.
- **Squeaky floor:** <u>possible causes:</u> improper size and type of fasteners used to attach floor sheathing, fastener missed joist, fasteners spaced too far apart, damaged or warped joist, joist installed crown down, water damaged floor sheathing, excessive deflection (loosens fasteners), failure to use adhesive.

<u>**Typical Repairs**</u> Structural repairs usually require a building permit and should be designed and installed by, at a minimum, a qualified contractor. Repairs that do not have prescriptive rules should be designed by a qualified engineer. Many procedures to repair floor joists are subject to access problems such as blockage by plumbing, HVAC, and electrical components, and insufficient access space for staging and installing materials.

- **Sister joist:** an additional joist installed next to the defective joist; <u>applicable defects</u>: most joist defects.
- **Blocking:** damaged joist is attached to blocking installed between adjacent intact joists to distribute some of the load to the intact joists; <u>applicable defects</u>: cut, notched, and damaged joists; may not work especially if the joists are carrying a significant load such as a bathtub or a wall.
- **Mending joists or plates:** joists or steel plates are attached to one or both sides of the joist to stiffen the joist at the defect; <u>applicable defects</u>: cut, notched, cracked, and damaged joists including joists with large knots; repair should be designed by an engineer.
- **Columns and piers:** columns or piers are installed to support one or more existing joists, or to support an existing beam, or to support a new beam supporting multiple joists; <u>applicable defects</u>: most joist and beam defects. Refer to the Footings, Piers, Piles, and Columns section for more about this repair.

<u>**Standards**</u> (1) IRC 2018 R502.3 (floor joist span tables), Tables R502.3.3(1) & (2) (cantilever floor joist tables), R502.4-10 (framing details, cutting and notching), Tables R602.7(1), (2), & (3) (beam and header span tables), R503.2 (floor sheathing) Tables R602.3(1) & (2) (fastener schedule); (2) manufacturer's instructions for joist hangers and other connectors.

Wood I-Joists and Engineered Wood (Floors and Roofs)

I-Joist and Engineered Wood Characteristics
Wood I-joists are engineered wood joists that are usually used as floor joists, but can be used as ceiling joists and rafters. An I-joist is made from a vertical piece of OSB (plywood before about 1990) that is usually about ⅜ inch thick and inserted in a groove cut in wood strips glued to the top and bottom of the I-joist. I-joist depths commonly used in residential construction range between 9½ inches and 16 inches. The vertical piece is called the **web** and the wood strips are called the **flanges**. Wood I-joists were

invented around 1969 and have been popular, especially among production builders, since the 1990s. Wood I-joists are sometimes called I-beams. They are also called TJIs, but this is a reference to products from one manufacturer and should not be used in inspection reports.

The primary advantages of wood I-joists compared to dimensional lumber are the ability of I-joists to span greater unsupported distances, greater strength, greater stiffness, and uniformity (no crowns). The primary disadvantage is usually higher cost. In addition, I-joists can fail more rapidly in fires compared to dimensional lumber and trusses.

One class of engineered wood used in residential construction is known broadly as structural composite lumber (SCL). This wood is used as beams, headers, rafters, studs, and for other purposes. The most common types in residential construction are laminated veneer lumber (LVL), parallel strand lumber (PSL), laminated strand lumber (LSL), and oriented strand lumber (OSL). This class of engineered wood is made from strands (thin veneers for LVLs) of wood compressed together using glue, heat, and pressure. LVL usually appears more like wood or plywood. The remaining types usually appear more like OSB. LVLs are sometimes called Microlam® beams. This is a brand name and should not be used to describe an LVL.

The other common class of engineered wood used in residential construction is called glue laminated lumber (GLL). It is used like SCL. These products are often called **Gluelams**. GLL is made from wood compressed together using glue, heat, and pressure. GLL is made with a camber (like a crown in dimensional lumber), and should be installed camber side up.

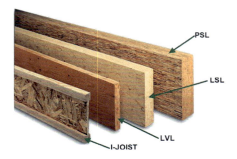

<u>Typical Construction Techniques</u> General construction techniques used when installing floor and roof systems using wood I-joists and engineered lumber are similar to those used when installing dimensional lumber. Refer to the Dimensional Lumber Floor Systems and the Dimensional Lumber Roof Systems sections for more information.

<u>Typical Defects</u> Many defects in wood I-joists are similar to those found in dimensional lumber. Refer to the Dimensional Lumber Floor Systems and the Dimensional Lumber Roof Systems sections for more information. What follows are defects unique to I-joists and engineered lumber.

Installation of wood I-joists and engineered lumber is based on manufacturer's instructions, and on the building plans. It is, therefore, **often difficult to know with certainty if these materials are improperly installed**. Home inspectors should usually recommend engineering evaluation of suspected defects in I-joists and engineered lumber; however, some I-joist manufacturers have general repair instructions for common defects and compliance with the manufacturer's general repair instructions is usually acceptable.

- **Improperly notched I-joist and beam:** the top and bottom flanges of I-joists may not be altered in any manner; at least ⅛ inch of the web should be left intact; engineered wood beams usually should not be notched.

- **Improperly bored I-joist:** the allowed location, size, and shape of holes in I-joist varies; if a home inspector attempts to evaluate a possible improper I-joist hole, the home inspector will need to know information such as the I-joist manufacturer, the joist model and depth, the joist span, the location of the hole relative to the closest support and relative to nearby holes, and the size and shape of the hole.

- **Improperly bored engineered lumber beam:** holes in engineered lumber beams, if allowed, may usually be located in a small area in the center ⅓ of the beam.

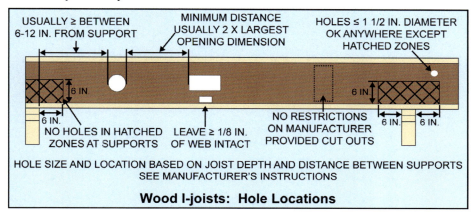

Wood I-joists: Hole Locations

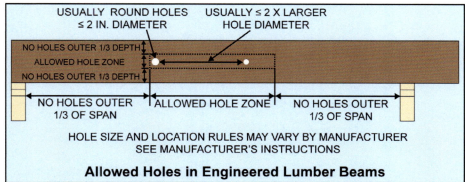

Allowed Holes in Engineered Lumber Beams

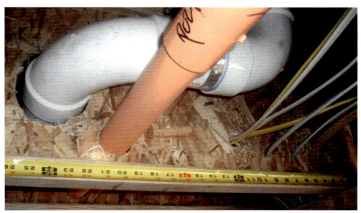

Holes Too Close to Support (Left), Too Close to Each Other and to Support (Right).

No Web Remaining at Flange. **Flanges and Web Cut Significantly.**

- **Absent/improperly installed filler blocks and backer blocks:** a backer block and a joist hanger are usually required when an I-joist provides support for another I-joist; filler blocks, a backer block, and a joist hanger are usually required when multiple I-joists provide support for another I-joist.

- **Absent/improperly installed web stiffeners or squash blocks under load-bearing walls:** web stiffeners and blocking or squash blocks are usually required to support a load-bearing wall that bears on I-joists; this usually includes cantilevered I-joists.

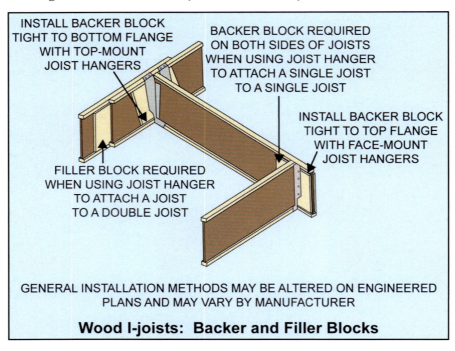

Wood I-joists: Backer and Filler Blocks

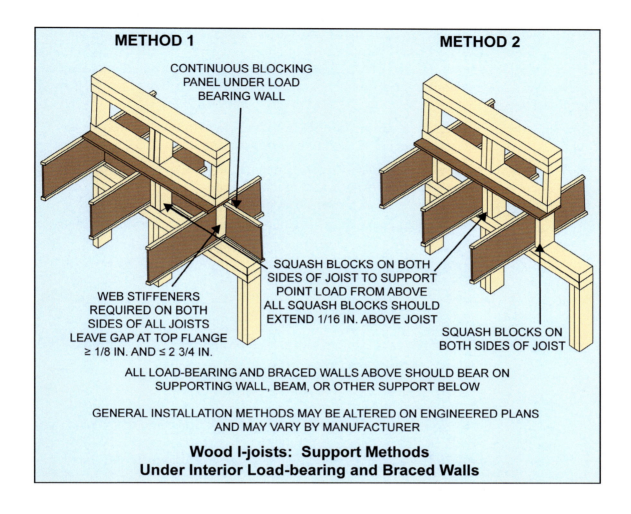

Wood I-joists: Support Methods Under Interior Load-bearing and Braced Walls

Backer Blocks Installed (Left), Backer Blocks Absent (Right).

- **Inadequate I-joist and beam bearing on support:** I-joists and beams should have at least 1½ inches (or 1¾ inches if required by the manufacturer) of the flange bearing on wood and at least 3 inches of the flange bearing on masonry and concrete; I-joist rafters should be installed so that flange bears on wood; for steep slope roofs, this may require a beveled bearing plate.
- **Absent/improperly installed support under non-load-bearing walls:** web stiffeners are usually required to support a non-load-bearing wall that bears on I-joists.
- **Dimensional lumber used in I-joist system:** dimensional lumber should not be used in an I-joist system for components such as rim joists; dimensional lumber is a different size and has different properties that make it incompatible with I-joists.

<u>Typical Repairs</u> An engineer usually should design all repairs of wood I-joists and engineered lumber and those repairs should be installed by a qualified contractor; however, some I-joist manufacturers have general repair instructions for common defects and compliance with the manufacturer's general repair instructions is usually acceptable. A wise procedure is to attach a copy of the engineer's or the manufacturer's repair instructions to the repaired members for reference by subsequent home inspectors.

<u>Standards</u> (1) manufacturer's instructions and approved building plans; (2) *APA Wood Construction Guide E30*.

Floor Trusses

<u>Description</u> Wood floor trusses are engineered components that are usually made from 2x4 dimensional lumber laid out in a rectangle with members in the center to distribute the load along the truss. The top and bottom horizontal members are called **chords** and the members in the center are called **webs**. The webs may be oriented vertically or diagonally (or both) relative to the top and bottom chords. The webs may be attached to the chords using metal plates called gusset plates, or by inserting the webs into a groove cut into the chords. Trusses using metal plates are called **metal plate connected trusses**.

Bottom Chord Bearing Trusses. **Top Chord Bearing Truss, Bearing Point Too Far From Support.**

Typical Construction Techniques General construction techniques used when installing floor systems using wood trusses are similar to those used when installing dimensional lumber. Refer to Dimensional Lumber Floor Systems for more information. This section identifies defects unique to trusses, and by implication, identifies differences in construction techniques compared to dimensional lumber.

Floor trusses are usually bottom chord bearing, meaning that the truss bottom chord bears on the sill plate or on the wall. Some floor trusses are top chord bearing, meaning that the truss bears on a vertical member connected to the top chord, or the top chord extends beyond the truss end and bears on the supporting member. The vertical member or top chord bears on the sill plate or wall. These trusses can appear modified when they are not.

Trusses usually bear on support at each end; however, they sometimes bear on support at a point within the truss span. Mid-span bearing can include cantilevered trusses. Two or more vertical members are often installed at the bearing point. The support wall should be directly under this bearing point.

Draftstopping Draftstopping is intended to slow the horizontal spread of fire in a house. It is usually required when there is usable space above and below an open area between stories that is more than 1,000 square feet. The most common areas where draftstopping may be required include the space between a basement and the first story, between the first and second story, and between the second story and any third story or habitable attic. The most common construction methods that may require draftstopping are floor trusses and suspended ceilings.

Draftstopping consists of a membrane that divides the area into approximately equal parts that are each less than 1,000 square feet. The membrane extends from the lower surface to the floor sheathing above. For example, draftstopping would be applied to one side of a truss from the top to the bottom chord. Typical draftstopping membranes include ½ inch thick drywall and ⅜ inch thick plywood or OSB. The space around penetrations of draftstopping membranes by components such as plumbing pipes and HVAC ducts should be sealed, usually by fire-resistant foam or caulk.

Typical Defects Many defects in wood floor trusses are similar to those found in dimensional lumber. Refer to that section for more information. Installation of wood floor trusses is based on manufacturer's instructions and on the engineered building plans. What follows are defects unique to floor trusses and are common to most floor truss systems.

- **Improperly modified and damaged truss:** trusses should not be damaged or modified (unless allowed by manufacturer's instructions); modifications include cut, notched, and bored members, and members that have been removed; common problem locations include around plumbing pipes and HVAC ducts and at truss ends; some trusses may be trimmed by a few inches at the ends, these trusses usually have solid wood blocks at the ends (not 2x4 vertical members).

- **Absent and damaged gusset plates:** gusset plates are installed under high pressure and may not be repaired by hammering or with fasteners; small gaps (more than $\frac{1}{64}$ inch) between the gusset plate and the wood can significantly reduce the connection strength.

End Web Removed.

Top Chord and Webs Cut.

Webs Bored.

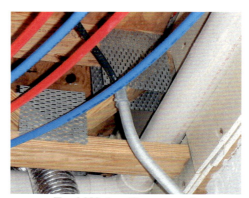
End Webs Removed.

- **Cut and damaged truss braces:** floor trusses are sometimes connected together using dimensional lumber bracing; floor trusses do not always require bracing, but if bracing is installed it should remain intact; common problem locations include around plumbing pipes and HVAC ducts.

Truss Brace Cut.

Typical Repairs An engineer should design all repairs of wood trusses and those repairs should be installed by a qualified contractor. A wise procedure is to attach a copy of the engineer's sealed repair instructions to the repaired members for reference by subsequent home inspectors.

Standards (1) manufacturer's instructions and approved building plans; (2) *Building Component Safety Information Book* 2018 Edition (current information about handling, installing, restraining and bracing of metal plate connected wood trusses).

WALL SYSTEM

Introduction

Forces Acting on Walls The wall system must perform several difficult functions simultaneously. Walls must support vertical loads from above. Walls must resist horizontal loads imposed by wind. These wind loads can simultaneously push the walls on the windward side and pull the walls on the leeward side. The wall system, including windows and doors, must remain intact during high wind conditions so that air pressure does not blow off the roof system or blow apart the walls. Walls must resist horizontal loads imposed by earthquakes. These loads move the walls from below and impose loads that are different from the other loads. The wall system must perform all these functions and retain its generally rectangular shape without excessive lateral movement along the plane of the wall (racking) and without excessive deflection perpendicular to the wall.

Wall Materials and Construction Systems Walls for houses are constructed using one or more materials. The most common residential wall framing material in North America is wood. Concrete masonry unit (CMU) walls are common in some markets and are especially common where resistance to wind loads is required. Structural brick walls were common in older houses in some markets, but are uncommon in newer homes. Insulating concrete forms are a newer wall construction material. These proprietary systems use forms that look like Legos and are made from materials such as polystyrene. Concrete is poured into the forms and the entire system remains after the concrete hardens. Structural insulated panels (SIPs) are another newer construction material that uses insulated panels built in a factory and shipped to the construction site. Other wall system materials include adobe brick, rammed earth, straw bale, cold-formed steel, stones, precast and tilt-up concrete, and logs. Houses constructed using these materials are uncommon.

Insulating Concrete Forms   **Structural Insulated Panel**

The most common residential wall framing system for wood and cold-formed steel is platform framing. In platform framing, the first floor walls bear on the first floor system which bears on the foundation. Walls for subsequent stories bear on top of the upper story floor systems that bear on the lower story walls.

Less common residential wall framing systems include balloon framing, post and beam framing, and its cousin timber framing. The walls of a balloon framed house are erected first and run up to the ceiling joists. This framing method was more common in older houses and is rarely used in newer houses. Both post and beam and timber framing rely on large horizontal wood members (beams) that transmit loads to large vertical wood members (posts) that carry the loads to the foundation. Post and beam framing uses mechanical fasteners (e.g., bolts) and steel plates to connect members together while timber framing uses mortise-and-tenon joints.

Wall systems should be designed to resist a minimum uniformly distributed live load without deflecting more than a specific amount. The maximum deflection for most walls is H/180, where H is the wall height in inches between supports. The maximum deflection for walls with a stucco wall covering is a stiffer H/360. A uniformly distributed load can be different from a point load. An example of a point load is a door closing with excessive force (slamming). A point load can cause a wall system to deflect more than H/180 yet still be within the design parameters. Thus, it is possible for a wall to shake when a door is slammed shut and the wall system is functioning as intended.

Fireblocking and Fire Separation

Description The purpose of fireblocking is to slow the spread of fire in concealed vertical spaces between stories, between the top story and the attic, and in long horizontal spaces. The fireblocking helps to reduce air flow, which in turn helps to slow the movement of hot gasses from a fire. Examples of concealed vertical spaces include wall cavities, framed columns, chases (framed shafts) for chimneys, vents, pipes, and HVAC ducts, and penetrations of fireblocking materials by pipes, ducts, and cables. Examples of concealed horizontal spaces include drop soffits in places like kitchens and bathrooms, framed arched openings, and double framed walls. Horizontal fireblocking should be installed when the concealed horizontal space exceeds 10 feet long.

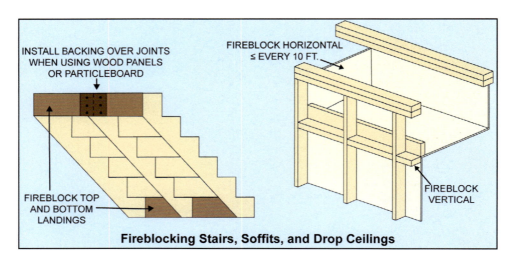

Fireblocking Stairs, Soffits, and Drop Ceilings

Fireblocking also serves an energy efficiency function. Air flow between conditioned and unconditioned spaces can significantly reduce a house's energy efficiency. Fireblocking and other air sealing steps can be as effective as adding insulation when there are many openings between conditioned and unconditioned spaces.

The purpose of fire separation is to slow the spread of fire between the garage and the house including the attic, and to slow the spread of fire between buildings. The buildings can be on the same lot or on adjacent lots, but fire separation between buildings on adjacent lots requires knowledge of lot boundaries, which is out of scope for a home inspection. Fire separation is required between townhouse units and between two-family attached dwellings. Fire separation can be accomplished using approved fire-resistant construction techniques, or it can be accomplished by distance, meaning separation between buildings.

Typical Fireblocking Materials Fireblocking materials include: nominal 2 inch lumber, 2 pieces of nominal 1 inch thick lumber, 23/32 (¾) inch thick OSB and plywood, ½ inch thick drywall, batts of mineral wool or fiberglass insulation firmly secured in place, approved fire-resistant caulk and foam.

Fire Separation Between an Attached Garage and the House An attached garage should be separated from the house by at least ½ inch thick drywall applied to the walls and ceiling installed on the garage side. A garage should be separated from habitable space above by at least ⅝ inch thick Type X drywall applied to the garage ceiling, and the structural walls supporting the habitable space above should be covered by at least ½ inch thick drywall installed on the garage side. Penetration of the garage ceiling and wall fire separation material by pet doors, flexible HVAC duct, pull-down stairs made from wood, and similar components is not allowed. HVAC systems may not have supply and return openings in a garage unless the system serves only the garage. Bedrooms should not have a door that opens into the garage. Doors between the garage and the house should be at least 1⅜ inch thick solid wood or steel and should be fire-rated for at least 20 minutes. Self-closing hinges are required in some jurisdictions.

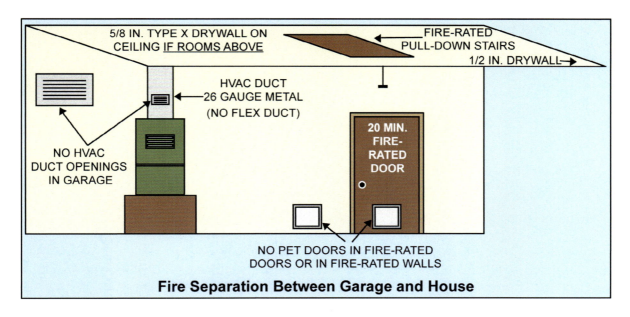

Fire Separation Between Garage and House

Fire Separation Between Buildings Buildings closer than 5 feet to the lot line should have a 1-hour rated firewall on the side near the lot line. Buildings closer than 3 feet to the lot line should have no windows or doors on the side near the lot line. Note that there are other fire separation requirements, that the requirements change if a fire sprinkler system is installed, and that the requirements change depending on local regulations.

Fire Separation Between Townhouse Units Two 1-hour rated firewalls (or one 2-hour rated firewall) running from the foundation to the roof sheathing should separate units in a townhouse building. The firewalls should **either** extend as a parapet wall at least 30 inches above the roof, **or** the roof covering should be non-combustible (e. g., fiberglass shingles) and ⅝ inch thick Type X drywall should be installed at the underside of the roof sheathing for at least 4 feet on both sides of the firewall.

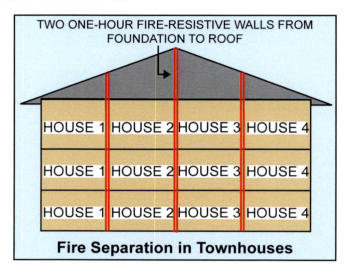

Typical Defects Typical defects that home inspectors should report include:

1. chases visible in the attic not fireblocked, especially chases around metal chimneys serving factory-built fireplaces,
2. pull-down attic stairs in the garage not fire rated (a thin plywood cover),
3. attic access openings in the garage made from wood,
4. pet doors installed in walls and doors into the garage,
5. flexible HVAC ducts penetrate the wall or ceiling,
6. bedroom opens directly into garage,
7. HVAC supply and return openings located in the garage,
8. damaged firewall in attic between townhouses and between two-family dwellings,
9. glazing in the door between the garage and the living space.

Standards (1) IRC 2018 Table R302.1 (fire separation between buildings), R302.2 (fire separation in townhouses), R302.3 (fire separation in two-family dwellings), R302.5 (fire separation in garage), R302.11 (fireblocking).

Chase Not Fireblocked.

Drop Ceiling Not Fireblocked.

Fire Separation Breach by Pull-Down Stairs.

Fire Separation Breach by Hole in Garage Wall.

Fire Separation Breach by Wood Paneling in Garage.

Fire Separation Breach by Pet Door in Door from House to Garage.

Foam Plastic Materials

Description Foam plastic materials are most often used in houses as insulation. They are also used as decorative trim; however, this use does not usually cause a fire safety issue. Foam plastic insulation comes in two broad categories: **sheet insulation** and **spray foam insulation**. Both categories of foam plastic insulation ignite easily and create toxic fumes when they burn. Because of the fire safety issues, foam plastic insulation is usually required to be covered by a **thermal barrier** or by an **ignition barrier**. This is most often an issue in attics and crawl spaces.

As compared to an ignition barrier, a thermal barrier provides increased protection against ignition and burning of foam plastic materials. A thermal barrier is usually required when foam plastic insulation is exposed in an attic or a crawl space where appliances such as a furnace, air handler, or water heater are located. Thermal barriers include at least ½ inch thick drywall or one of several other another approved materials.

An ignition barrier may be substituted for a thermal barrier in an attic or a crawl space if there are no appliances in the space. Ignition barriers include ¼ inch thick OSB and plywood, ⅜ inch thick drywall, and one of several other approved materials and coatings. The ignition barrier for foam plastic insulation often consists of an intumescent coating designed for this application. Intumescent coatings tend to darken spray foam insulation; however, it can be difficult to determine by visual inspection if a coating has been applied.

Numerous requirements and exceptions exist regarding fire protection for foam plastic materials. Some foam plastic materials are listed for installation without fire protection in some situations. Local adoption and enforcement of foam plastic fire protection varies. The home inspector should usually recommend evaluation when encountering foam plastic materials that may require fire protection.

Standards IRC 2018 R316.

Closed Cell Spray Foam in Crawl Space.

XPS Sheet Insulation

Wood-Framed Wall Systems

Description The most common residential wall system in North America is the platform-framed wall, made from dimensional lumber components including a single **sill plate** or **sole plate**, **studs**, and a double **top plate**. **Headers** provide support for spaces above openings for doors and windows. Headers are supported by **king studs** (at the sides of headers) and **jack (trimmer) studs** under the header. The horizontal wood under a window is the **sill**. Short studs under (and sometimes above) the windows are called **cripples**. Exterior walls intersect at corner posts. Interior (partition) walls intersect exterior walls at partition corner posts. Corner posts help keep walls from moving and provide a surface for fastening drywall.

Framing for Window Showing Sill Plate, Top Plate, Header, King Studs, Jack Studs, Cripples.

Double Top Plate Lapped at Corner.

Typical Construction Techniques Wood-framed wall construction techniques and requirements depend on several factors that put the house at increased risk of damage during wind and seismic events. **Wind speed risk** is one factor. Areas subject to high wind events (110+ mph) such as hurricanes need more hold-down devices and wall bracing to keep the house from lifting off the foundation, and to keep the walls from moving (racking and deflecting). These high wind areas are mostly along the Gulf and East coasts. Some interior areas, such as mountains and valleys, could be in a wind speed design area. **Wind exposure risk** is one factor. Houses in open fields, on large lakes, and on the ocean are subject to more wind load compared to houses spaced close together in the suburbs. These houses need more wall bracing to reduce racking. Seismic risk is one factor. Houses in **seismic risk** zones need more wall bracing, more robust foundations, and more robust wall attachment to the foundation to keep the house on the foundation and to reduce racking. Seismic risk zones are mostly in the West, but also around Memphis, TN and around Charleston, SC.

The following discussion of construction techniques and requirements assumes that the house is not located in an increased risk area. This discussion applies to newer houses. Updating older houses to current structural requirements is not usually required, at least, by governments. Older houses that are not updated and are located in increased risk areas may have difficulty obtaining insurance or insurance may be costly. Home inspectors may wish to alert clients about such issues, although such alerts are not required.

Wood-framed walls in newer houses are usually built using stud grade 2x4 lumber. Stud grade is a lower grade lumber similar to #3 grade. Stud grade and #3 grade lumber may be used for walls up to 10 feet tall. Taller walls should be built using #2 grade or better lumber. Studs may be solid, or they may be a form of structural composite lumber made from smaller pieces of lumber that have their ends cut in a tongue-and-groove like manner called **finger joints**. These finger joints are glued together to produce a stud that is as strong as a solid stud and usually straighter.

Size and spacing of lumber in exterior walls depends on the wall height, the number of stories above the wall, and whether the wall is load-bearing. For load-bearing exterior walls less than 10 feet tall supporting 1 story and a roof, 2x4s may be spaced up to 24 inches on center, although 16 inch on center spacing is more common. For load-bearing exterior walls less than 10 feet tall supporting 2 stories and a roof, 2x6s should be spaced not more than 16 inches on center. Walls more than 10 feet tall should usually be built using at least 2x6s.

Exterior walls should bear on at least one preservative treated sill plate made from nominal 2 inch thick material that is as wide as the stud (2x4 stud on at least a 2x4 plate). Interior walls should bear on a similar sole plate, although there are exceptions in some cases for the thickness and preservative treating requirements.

Exterior walls, interior load-bearing walls, and braced walls usually should have at least 2 top plates made from nominal 2 inch thick material that is as wide as the stud (2x6 stud under at least 2x6 plates). Top plates help the wall resist racking, so it is important that the plates are properly installed. Joints between two plates should be offset at least 24 inches. The plates should overlap at the corners so that the upper plate from one wall is attached to the lower plate from the other wall. This helps tie the walls together. Plates may be notched to allow installation of pipes and ducts. When top plates are notched more than 50%, one 16 gauge metal plate should be installed to bind the plates together.

Headers should be installed above openings in load-bearing exterior walls and above openings in interior load-bearing walls to distribute the load above around the opening. The load of the header is carried by the king studs and the jack studs, and this load should be carried through the wall and floor systems to the foundation. Deformed (sagging) ceilings and walls above windows and doors are frequently the result of headers that are undersized or that have been removed. Headers are not required above openings in interior non-load-bearing walls. Headers should be built using #2 grade lumber.

Wood members are connected to each other with fasteners, usually nails. Using the correct size, type, and quantity of fasteners is important to the structural stability of the house, and its ability to withstand imposed loads, especially high wind and seismic loads. Failure analysis of buildings subjected to high wind and seismic events has demonstrated that improper fastener installation was a major contributing factor toward the failure.

All nails are not the same, even those that have similar names. For example, a 16d common nail is longer and thicker than a 16d sinker nail, which, in turn, is longer and thicker than a 16d nail used in a nail gun. The letter "d" means penny which is a common method of describing the general size of nails. The prescriptive fastening schedules specify the type and quantity of each fastener for each connection between wood members.

Many wood-framed house walls are covered with a material called **sheathing** that provides structural stability for the wall and some resistance to air flow. Sheathing on older houses may be wood in the 1x4 to 1x8 range, or it may be an asphalt-based sheet product (black board). Sheathing in newer houses may be plywood, OSB, and various types of insulating foam sheathing made from polystyrene. Foam sheathing usually provides minimal structural stability, although some foam sheathing provides some structural support. Sheathing may not be necessary when the wall covering provides the structural stability for the wall. An example of structural wall coverings include 4x8 and 4x9 panel siding.

Wall Bracing: Exterior walls and some interior walls need to be braced to reduce racking. Bracing, like many wall system components, is usually concealed. Wall bracing is a very complex topic. Evaluating the **adequacy** of visible wall bracing is **out of scope** for a home inspection. Identifying the **presence** of visible wall bracing in exposed walls is **within the scope** of a home inspection.

Every braced wall should have at least two wall braces and longer walls may need more. Common wall bracing methods include **let-in** braces and **wood structural panel** braces. A let-in brace is usually a 1x4 that is installed in a notch cut into the studs and plates. It can also be a metal strap in newer houses. The brace should be installed at about a 45° angle from the bottom plate to the top plate and should be attached at each stud and the plates. Wood structural panel braces are usually at least ⅜ inch thick OSB or plywood, but some types of panel siding can serve as bracing. Each wall brace should begin within 12½ feet from each wall end (10 feet for new houses). There should be a wall brace at least every 25 feet. There are special bracing requirements for short length walls, such as those adjacent to garage doors.

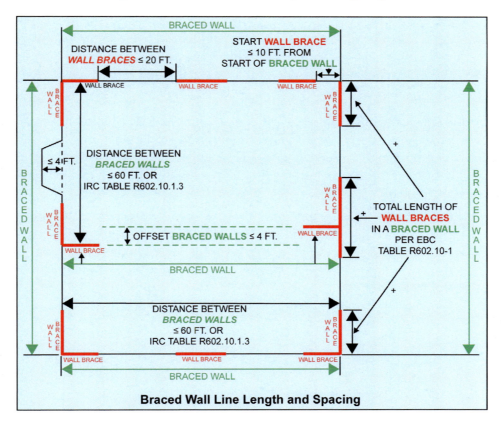

Braced Wall Line Length and Spacing

Cripple Wall Fully Braced With Wood Structural Panels (OSB).   **1x4 Let-in Brace**

Typical Defects Many wall system defects are concealed behind finish materials; however, they may be visible in unfinished basement and garages. Defects in concealed walls may or may not leave visible evidence. Note that cracks in wall coverings can occur for many reasons and are not necessarily the result of a concealed framing defect. Home inspectors should avoid speculating about the cause of a defect.

Wall system defects fall into two categories. Some defects are defective per se, meaning that the condition is defective regardless of whether there is current visible evidence of an adverse impact caused by the defect. An improperly notched stud is defective per se. The adverse impact may not have occurred, yet. Other defects are evidence-based, meaning that there is current visible evidence of an adverse impact, whether or not there is an identified reason for the defect. An excessively bowed wall is an example of an adverse impact that may have no identified reason, yet.

- **Improperly notched studs:** notches in studs in load-bearing walls may not exceed 25% of the actual stud depth; notches in studs in non-load-bearing walls may not exceed 40% of the actual stud depth. <u>Typical evidence of a concealed defect</u>: deformation and cracks around the top plate and ceiling above the defect; bowing and cracking in the wall near the defect.

- **Improperly bored studs:** holes in studs in load-bearing walls may not exceed 40% of the actual stud depth; holes in studs in non-load-bearing walls may not exceed 60% of the actual stud depth. <u>Typical evidence of a concealed defect</u>: deformation and cracks around the top plate and ceiling above the defect; bowing and cracking in the wall near the defect.

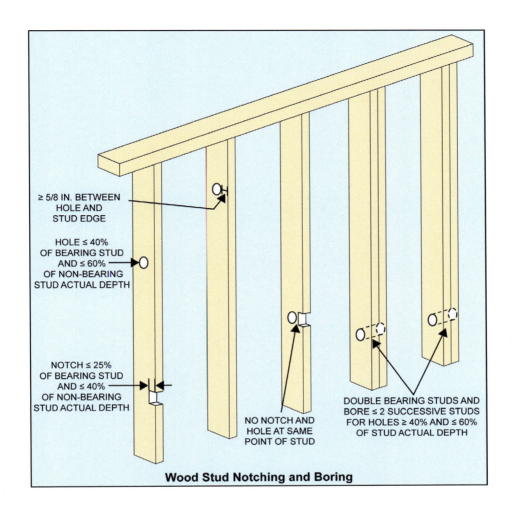

Wood Stud Notching and Boring

Hole Too Large and Too Close to Edge of Stud.

Hole Too Large.

Notch Too Large. **Notch Too Large, Stud Cut, Standpipe Too Short.**

- **Water damage:** <u>possible causes:</u> water leaks from outside, plumbing leaks, condensation of water vapor in the wall cavity. <u>Typical evidence of a concealed defect</u>: water stains that usually present above and around windows and doors, at wall ceiling intersections, at and above baseboards, and on floor sheathing and band joists.

- **Wood destroying organism damage:** <u>typical evidence of a concealed defect</u>: mud tubes, exit holes, frass (insect feces). Note that many jurisdictions restrict how home inspectors report evidence of wood destroying organisms if the home inspector does not have a pest control contractor license. Use of the term suspected wood destroying organism may be acceptable. Check with local authorities.

Water Stain at Door **Water Damage at Window**

4: Structural Components

Water Stain on Wall

Water Damaged Ceiling Without Staining

Termite Tubes

Termite Damage

- **Improper stud size, spacing, material:** studs should be the correct thickness and set at the correct spacing based on the wall height and on the load from above; studs should be the proper grade and should be dry. <u>Typical evidence of a concealed defect</u>: bowed walls; uneven walls; cracks in wall coverings such as drywall and stucco.

- **Inadequate number of studs under point loads:** as a general rule, there should be one stud under each load-bearing member above (e. g., a double roof truss should have at least two studs under the truss all the way to the foundation). <u>Typical evidence of a concealed defect:</u> bowed walls; cracks in wall coverings such as drywall and stucco.

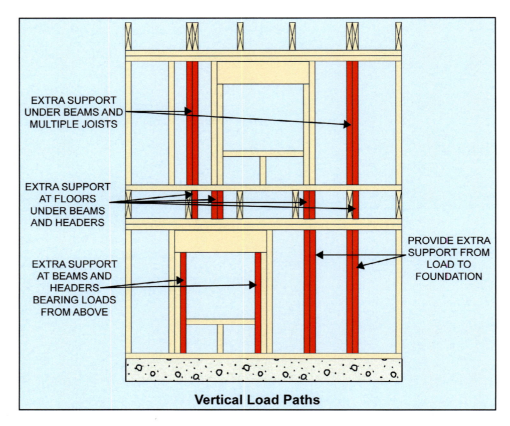

Vertical Load Paths

- **Excessively notched top plate:** top plates notched more than 50% of their depth should have at least one approved strap installed across the notch. <u>Typical evidence of a concealed defect</u>: cracks in wall coverings such as drywall and stucco, mainly at the wall/ceiling intersection.

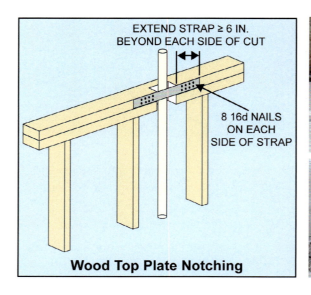

Wood Top Plate Notching

Plates Notched, Strap Needed.

- **Inadequate attachment of walls to each other:** walls should be attached to each other using a corner post; the walls should be fastened to each other over the length of the corner post and the upper top plate from one wall should overlap the lower top plate of the other wall. Typical evidence of a concealed defect: cracks in wall coverings such as drywall and stucco at wall corners.

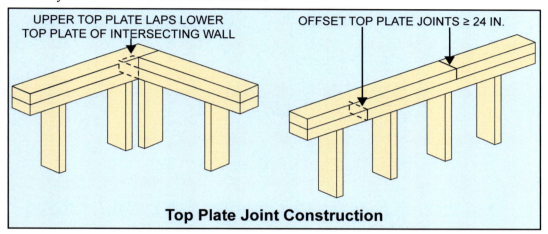

Top Plate Joint Construction

- **Improperly braced walls:** walls should be braced as required by local conditions. Typical evidence of a concealed defect: cracks in wall coverings, such as drywall and stucco, especially at windows and doors and at corners.

Typical Repairs Structural repairs usually require a building permit and should be designed and installed by, at a minimum, a qualified contractor. Repairs that do not have prescriptive rules should be designed by a qualified engineer. Many procedures to repair studs are subject to access problems such as blockage by plumbing, HVAC, and electrical components and insufficient access space for staging and installing materials.

- **Sister studs:** an additional stud is installed next to the defective stud. Applicable defects: most stud defects.
- **Stud shoes:** a manufactured metal bracket is installed around improper holes and notches in studs to strengthen the stud. Applicable defects: cut, notched, and damaged studs.
- **Blocking:** horizontal pieces of wood are attached between studs to reinforce the stud and spread some of the lateral load among adjacent studs. Applicable defects: cut, notched and damaged studs.

Standards (1) IRC 2018 Tables R602.3(1), (2), and (3) (fastener schedules), Table R602.3(5) (stud height table 10 feet or less), Table R602.3(6) (stud height table for 11 foot and 12 foot studs) R602.3 (general stud installation), R602.6 (stud drilling and notching) Tables R-602.7(1), (2), and (3) (header span table), R602.10 (wall bracing); (2) manufacturer's instructions for stud shoes, straps, and hold-down hardware.

Stud Shoe

Concrete Masonry Unit (CMU) and Structural Brick Wall Systems

Description This section addresses above-grade walls. Foundation walls below grade have different requirements and are addressed in the foundations section.

Houses in North America have been built using CMUs for over 100 years. This material remains popular in markets such as Florida, Texas, and Arizona. One reason for CMU houses in Florida and Texas is these states are subject to hurricanes and CMUs endure wind and water forces better than wood. CMU houses are less popular in other markets, mostly due to a lack of skilled labor and to the higher construction cost of CMU houses. Because of the difficulty and skill required to construct curves and angles using CMUs, these houses tend to be rectangular and boxy in appearance.

CMUs are often called cinder blocks. This term refers to a method of making CMUs that involves using fly ash and other waste products of combustion as one of the materials. Fly ash is a byproduct of burning coal. CMUs containing cinders can have corrosive properties that can damage metal pipes and wires. CMUs containing cinders are more common in older houses and are uncommon in modern construction. There is no visual means to tell if a CMU contains cinders.

Buildings have been built using structural brick since ancient times. Structural brick is more common in historic houses in some markets and is less common in newer houses. Most brick houses are really brick veneer covering wood or CMU walls.

Blocks made from glass and various forms of plastic are sometimes used as part of wall systems. These are non-load-bearing components that have more in common with windows than with structural components. Prescriptive requirements exist regarding installation procedures including lateral support for these blocks.

Typical Construction Techniques Concrete masonry unit (CMU) above-grade walls for houses are usually constructed using hollow core CMUs with nominal 8x8x16 inch dimensions. Six inch nominal dimension CMUs may be used for single story houses with a wall height of 9 feet or less. The CMU cores may be left unfilled in areas with low wind and seismic risks; however, a minimum 4 inch thick solid cap block or a fully grouted top CMU course is necessary when wood will bear on the CMUs. Reinforcing with steel rods and filling cores with grout is usually required in wind and seismic risk areas. CMUs are usually laid in a running bond pattern, meaning that vertical joints are usually offset by ½ CMU length for each course. The running bond pattern helps provide lateral support for the wall.

CMUs have good capacity to bear vertical loads but have less capacity to resist horizontal loads. Lateral support to resist horizontal loads is usually provided by the roof system and by the floor system in two-story homes. Ceiling joists may be fastened to a wood plate that is bolted to the CMU top course, or the joists may bear directly on the CMU and be fastened using metal straps. The floor system usually bears on a nominal 3 inch thick ledger that is bolted to the CMU.

Support is required over doors and windows, just as it is in wood-frame construction. Support above openings in CMU walls may be provided by steel lintels, by steel-reinforced concrete or masonry lintels, or by properly designed masonry arches.

Interior walls in houses built with CMUs may be built using wood, cold-formed steel, or CMUs. Some exterior walls may be built using wood, such as walls for bay windows and similar angled walls that are difficult to build using CMUs.

Single wythe structural brick construction is the same as for CMUs. A **wythe is a wall of bricks**, so a 1-wythe wall is one wall of bricks and a 2-wythe wall is two walls of bricks separated by no more than a few inches. The wythes of a multiple wythe structural brick wall must be bonded together by some means. Masonry headers may be used, in which case the short side of the brick will be visible at 24 to 34 inch intervals vertically. Metal wall ties may also be used, in which case there may be no visible evidence of bonding between wythes.

Both CMUs and structural bricks are **hygroscopic**, meaning they usually absorb water. CMU walls are usually covered by paint or stucco as the water-repelling material. Single wythe and fully grouted multi-wythe brick walls need a drainage plane and weep holes to drain moisture that may accumulate behind the bricks.

Typical Potentially Significant Defects
The following defects apply to both CMU and structural brick walls. Masonry refers to both CMU and structural brick walls. Wind and earthquakes could cause these defects in areas prone to these events.

- **Wall rotating (usually leaning out):** possible causes: wall not laterally supported at top; roof deflecting vertically causing the ceiling joists to move horizontally; masonry used is too thin for wall height; wall built out of plumb; outer wythe separating from inner wythe. Possible measurement guideline: more than ¼ inch rotation in 10 feet may be considered for reporting.

- **Wall bulging (part of wall protrudes out or caves in), and long horizontal cracks in walls:** possible causes: wall not laterally supported at floor level; masonry used is too thin for wall height; inadequate or no steel reinforcement; excess vertical load on wall; outer wythe separating from inner wythe.

- **Vertical, diagonal, or stair step cracks wider at one end:** possible causes: settlement of soil under footing; footing not wide enough or deep enough; footing with no reinforcing steel; frost heave; expansive soil. Possible measurement guideline: crack is more than ¼ inch wide at narrowest point.

Typical Less Significant Defects These defects may not be structurally significant; however, cracks and voids can admit water. Water infiltration can lead to more significant defects. **Home inspectors should look for brown stains,** which usually indicate possible water infiltration, inside, at, and below the defect. Note that **poor water management** such as blocked gutters, improper flashing, and absent or blocked weep holes can cause most of the following defects.

- **Uniform width cracks in mortar less than ⅛ inch wide:** possible causes: shrinkage of mortar due to too much water in mortar or mortar dried too quickly; improper mortar mix components; minor wall movement; absent movement and expansion joints.
- **Absent and deteriorating mortar:** possible causes: normal weathering and freeze/thaw cycles; mortar joint has shelf where water can collect; improper mortar mix components.
- **Loose masonry:** possible causes: normal weathering and freeze/thaw cycles; mortar joint has shelf where water can collect; improper mortar mix components.
- **Spalling:** (material disintegrating; could be structural if large amounts of material are unsound); possible causes: moisture in brick freezing; capillary water rise (wicking); defective masonry.
- **Algae:** possible causes: capillary water rise (wicking); plant growth on or near masonry.
- **Plants growing on or near masonry:** possible cause: poor landscape management.
- **Efflorescence:** (white powder on walls); possible cause: capillary water rise (wicking).

Typical Repairs Structural repairs usually require a building permit and should be designed and installed by, at a minimum, a qualified contractor. Repairs that do not have prescriptive rules should be designed by a qualified engineer.

- **Tuck pointing (repointing):** absent and damaged mortar is replaced with new mortar.
- **Anchors:** various methods are used to fasten the masonry to other structural components, such as the floor or roof systems or to other stable masonry areas; repairs may be visible as metal plates bolted to the masonry or repairs may be concealed
- **Surface sealants:** masonry and mortar can be sealed against water penetration, however, sealing then becomes a regular maintenance procedure, and sealing can prevent masonry from drying, which can lead to spalling.

Standards (1) IRC 2018 R606 (general masonry), R606.13 (multiple wythe masonry); (2) Brick Industry Association Technical Notes.

**Structural Brick on Rubble Stone Foundation.
Anchors Above First Story Windows.**

Insulating Concrete Forms Wall Systems

Description Insulating concrete forms are a wall construction material dating to the 1950s in Europe and to the 1990s in the United States. These proprietary systems use forms that look like Legos and are made from materials such as polystyrene. Concrete is poured into the forms and the entire system remains after the concrete hardens. The mass of the concrete plus the insulation on both sides of the wall creates a strong wall system that has a high R-value, is resistant to air and moisture intrusion, and can withstand wind and earthquake loads better than most other wall systems. Higher construction costs and a limited number of contractors and trades with experience using these systems are the primary disadvantages of these systems. These systems should be installed according to manufacturer's instructions, applicable industry standards, and approved building plans. HVAC systems should be designed to account for the increased wall R- value and decreased air infiltration.

Typical Construction Techniques Insulating concrete forms are often built on spread footings or on slab foundations. Above-ground forms can be installed on, or can be a continuation of, forms used for basement or crawl space foundations. The forms usually snap together to form a cavity into which reinforcing steel is placed and into which concrete is poured. Ledgers for wood floor systems and structures such as decks are usually bolted to the concrete. Exterior finishes are often stucco, adhered masonry veneer, or brick. Interior finish is usually drywall attached to ties imbedded in the forms. Electrical and plumbing are usually run through channels which are cut into the forms with a hot implement.

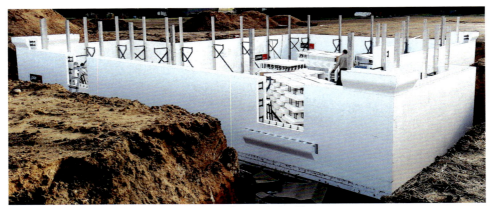
Insulating Concrete Forms

Typical Defects These systems do not have a history of significant defects related to the system itself that would be visible during a home inspection. Defects are usually related to failure of other systems such as water entry due to improper flashing or to improper fastening of wood floors or wood roof structural components to the concrete. Wood destroying organisms can tunnel in the forms, so insect damage to wood framing is possible.

Typical Modifications/Repairs Attachment of structures such as porches and decks to insulating concrete form houses should use approved connectors installed according to manufacturer's instructions.

Standards (1) Prescriptive Method for Insulating Concrete Forms in Residential Construction (HUD); (2) manufacturer's installation instructions.

Structural Insulated Panel Wall Systems (SIPS)

Description Structural insulated panels (SIPs) are constructed by gluing insulation (usually polyisocyanurate or polystyrene) between sheets of $7/16$ inch thick OSB. SIPs can be used as a wall system and as a roof system. Panels are manufactured in a factory in lengths up to 24 feet, and in several thicknesses between 4 and 12 inches, depending on the desired insulating R-value. Advantages of SIPs include high R-value, low air infiltration rates, and faster construction schedules. HVAC systems should be designed to account for the increased wall R-value and decreased air infiltration. Disadvantages include higher materials costs, a limited number of contractors and trades with experience using these systems, the need for accuracy when constructing the foundation, and panel susceptibility to water damage. It is difficult to tell if a finished house is constructed using SIPs. Houses built using this system are uncommon. SIPs are also known as stressed-skin panels.

Typical Construction Techniques Panels may be erected on slab foundations and on crawl space and basement foundation walls. The panels may be used in a platform framing system or in a post-and-beam/timber framing system. When used in a platform framing system, the panels are attached to a preservative treated sill plate. One or more studs are installed where the panels meet at corners and at window and door openings. These joints should be sealed with a caulk-like sealant made for SIPs. A double top plate is installed above the panels. All wall framing lumber should be #2 grade spruce pine fir or better.

Typical Defects These systems do not have a history of significant defects related to the system itself that would be visible during a home inspection. Defects are usually related to failure of other systems such as water entry due to improper flashing and to installation errors, such as improper fastening and sealing of the panels. OSB is very susceptible to water damage and visual detection of water damage can be difficult. Wood destroying organisms can tunnel in the forms and will eat the OSB, so insect damage to wood framing is possible.

Typical Modifications/Repairs SIPs may not be designed to provide structural support for structures such as porch roofs and decks. Modifications and additions that rely on SIPS for structural support should be designed by a qualified engineer and installed by a qualified contractor with appropriate permits.

Standards (1) IRC 2018 R610; (2) Prescriptive Method for Structural Insulated Panels Used in Residential Construction (HUD).

Uncommon Wall Materials and Systems

Description Uncommon wall materials include:

- adobe brick,
- cold-formed steel,
- logs,
- rammed earth,
- straw bales,
- structural stone.

Uncommon wall framing systems include post-and-beam and timber framing. The following are brief introductions to these materials and systems. This is not intended to provide enough information to inspect houses using these materials and systems. **Home inspectors who are unfamiliar with these systems should report their unfamiliarity and recommend evaluation by a specialist.**

Adobe Bricks and Rammed Earth
Adobe brick and rammed earth construction has been used since ancient times. Houses built using these materials share many attributes, and are most likely to be located in the Southwest.

Traditional rammed earth houses are built using soil and water that is compressed between forms into a wall. Modern rammed earth houses add Portland cement to the soil and a concrete bond beam is used to provide lateral support.

Traditional adobe bricks are made from sand, clay, and sometimes straw or grass. The bricks are formed by hand in molds and dried by the sun. Modern adobe bricks are stabilized using cement or asphalt, and are made using machines and artificial heat. A similar sand and clay mixture is used as traditional mortar because newer cement mortars move at a different rate than adobe bricks and can cause cracking of bricks and mortar. The foundation of a traditional adobe brick house may be gravel or larger stones, sea shells, clay bricks, or just soil that has been tamped and leveled. Modern adobe brick houses are usually set on modern foundations.

Traditional adobe bricks are very susceptible to water damage and must be protected against water infiltration. Mud plaster, lime stucco, and cement stucco are common methods. Modern adobe bricks are less susceptible to water damage, but may be damaged by water.

Typical defects in traditional adobe brick houses are often caused by water infiltration, inadequate foundations, and repairs and maintenance using incompatible materials. Water can cause the bricks to disintegrate and crack, especially around openings for windows and doors. Water management including grading, draining, and landscaping can reduce water damage. Regular maintenance of the water-protective coating is essential. Foundation settlement will cause cracking and should be addressed in a manner similar to foundation problems experienced by other construction materials. Adobe can be incompatible with materials such as steel, cement mortar, and latex paint. Use of these materials should usually be avoided when repairing and maintaining adobe brick houses.

Cold-Formed Steel The first houses in North America made using cold-formed steel were built in the 1930s and 1940s. Cold-formed steel houses can be found in any market.

Cold-formed steel framing is similar to wood framing. Screws are used as fasteners instead of nails. U-shaped tracks are used instead of wood plates, C-shaped steel studs are used instead of wood studs, and steel headers and beams are used in place of wood.

Many defects in cold-formed steel houses are similar to those in wood-framed houses, except that problems such as the tendency of wood to warp and change size with changes in humidity do not occur with steel. Walls can rotate, bulge, settle, and crack with steel-framed walls for many of the same reasons as wood-framed walls.

One defect that is more pronounced in steel compared to wood is **thermal bridging** because steel is a much more efficient conductor of heat compared to wood. Steel studs can conduct ten times more efficiently than a wood stove. Steel walls must be properly insulated to reduce thermal bridging, both from an energy efficiency perspective and from a condensation perspective. Thermal bridging of steel framing components can allow condensation in the wall assembly. This can corrode the steel, reduce insulation R-value, and can provide moisture for fungal growth on components such as drywall paper.

Steel Studs, Grommet Should Be Installed to Protect Cable.

4: Structural Components 237

Log Houses Log houses have been built in North America for hundreds of years. Log houses are usually found in rural areas, but this doesn't imply that log houses are necessarily of low quality or that they are inexpensive. Some luxury houses are log houses.

Modern log houses are built on the same types of foundations as other wood-framed houses, although the foundations may need to be larger to accommodate the often heavier dead load imposed by log walls. The log walls of modern log houses are usually fastened together using long spikes or machine bolts, usually spaced at intervals of 18 to 36 inches. The corners of log houses are made using one of several systems including butt-and-pass, saddle-notch, and butting into corner posts. The spaces between logs are filled with caulk or by using a process called **chinking**. This is recommended to reduce air infiltration. Modern chinking material is elastomeric.

Log house problems are similar to problems with other houses including those related to flashing, grading, drainage, gutters, and the foundation. Common log house problems include deteriorated caulking or chinking, unsealed cracks (checks) in the logs (especially on the top side), deteriorated stain or other protective coating, logs that move out of position in the log stack, and damage by wood destroying organisms. Log houses should have eaves of sufficient depth to provide some protection to the logs from the weather.

Structural Stone Above-grade structural stone wall construction has been used since ancient times. In North America, these houses are most likely located in the older parts of older cities, but can be found in other areas including those with newer custom houses. Stone is a natural material, not to be confused with manufactured stone products such as cast stone and adhered masonry veneer. Structural stone should also not be confused with natural stone veneer, which is similar to brick veneer.

Most structural stone walls are built using one of three methods. Dry stone walls are built using stones that are tightly fit together without mortar. This is the oldest method and has been used since the Pyramids. Stone masonry walls are built using stones bonded together using mortar. This is an ancient method. Slipform stone walls are walls that are assembled by stacking stones in a form and pouring concrete behind the stones. This is a modern method.

Defects in structural stone walls are similar to those found in structural brick walls. Refer to the CMU and Structural Brick Wall Systems section for more information.

Straw Bale Straw bale construction originated in the Midwest during the late 1800s. These houses are most likely to be located in the Midwest and Southwest, but can be found in other regions and in other countries. Straw bale houses dating from the 1930s exist today. Straw bale houses have walls over 20 inches thick, which provide good insulation value.

Straw bale houses are made using bales of straw. Compaction of the straw beyond normal baling is not required. Modern straw bale houses are placed on modern concrete footings. Reinforcing steel is used to provide lateral support and wires or hold-down rods are used to provide uplift resistance. Plaster (stucco) that is at least 1 inch thick is applied to the interior and exterior walls to protect against moisture intrusion and to provide lateral support. These houses are limited to 1 story.

Typical defects in straw bale houses are often caused by water infiltration, and by insects and vermin. Water can cause the straw to rot and disintegrate, especially around openings for doors and windows. Water management including grading, drainage, gutters, and landscaping can reduce water damage. Regular maintenance of the water-protective stucco coating is essential. Use of vapor retarders on the exterior is not recommended because the straw bales must have a means to dry in at least one direction. Insects and vermin will eat the straw causing the bales to lose structural integrity.

Timber and Post-and-Beam Framing Timber framing has been used since ancient times. Post-and-beam framing has been used in North America since Europeans first settled here. Both post-and-beam and timber framing rely on large horizontal wood members (beams) that transmit loads to large vertical wood members (posts) that carry the loads to the foundation. Post-and-beam framing uses mechanical fasteners (e. g., bolts) and steel plates to connect members together, while timber framing uses **mortise-and-tenon** joints. A mortise is a hole chiseled into a member and a tenon is a projection in a member designed to fit in the mortise. A wood peg secures the joint. These framing systems are usually open plans with the structural members left exposed.

Mortise-and-tennon Joint

Standards (1) ASTM E2392 (earth wall houses); (2) Local building codes; (3) IRC 2018 R603 (cold-formed steel), Appendix R (straw-clay), Appendix S (straw bale); (4) *ILBA Log Building Standards* (International Log Builders Association).

ROOF AND CEILING SYSTEM

Introduction

The rafters and ceiling joists are partners. They must be fastened together to perform three important functions. They must resist vertical live loads and dead loads pushing down from above. These loads thrust the ceiling joists horizontally and push the walls apart with them. The live load increases with the amount of snow on the roof, so more fasteners are required in snow country. They must also stay on the house during high wind events, so stronger hold-down hardware is required in high wind risk and wind exposure risk areas. Finally, the roof system must resist lateral movement in seismic areas, so more fasteners and connections are required, especially for heavy roofs such as those with concrete tiles.

The roof and ceiling system for houses is usually constructed using some form of wood. The most common system in older houses is constructed using dimensional lumber. Trusses are common in newer houses, especially in production houses, but dimensional lumber is still common in some markets. Wood I-joists are occasionally used as rafters and ceiling joists. Cold-formed steel is also used, but it is uncommon.

Rafters and ceiling joists are designed to support a specified uniformly distributed load without deflecting more than a specific amount. The uniform load for ceiling joists depends on whether the attic is designed for storage. The uniform load for rafters depends on the type of roof covering, the snow load, and whether finish material such as drywall will be attached to the rafters. The maximum allowed deflection under the uniform load for rafters with a slope greater than 3/12 is L/180 where L is the rafter length in inches between supports measured horizontally, not along the length of the rafter. The maximum allowed deflection under the uniform load for ceiling joists finished with drywall and for low slope rafters is L/240.

__Roof Styles__

Most roof systems use various combinations of four roof styles. The **gable** roof is triangle shaped with the rafters forming the legs, and the ceiling joists forming the base. The **hip** roof is one containing four roof sections that meet at the top (ridge). The **shed** roof is a usually rectangular shaped roof that usually terminates at a sidewall or a roof. Shed roofs are common on porches and on room additions. The **low slope** (flat) roof is a horizontal, usually rectangular, roof. Any roof with a slope less than 3/12 is usually considered a low slope roof, although most have a slope less than 1/12. A low slope roof should have a slope of at least ¼/12 toward the drainage points. Other less common roof styles include the **Gambrel** roof and the **Mansard** roof. These roof styles, especially the gambrel, are often associated with barns.

Each rafter forms an isosceles right triangle. Common rafter length may be estimated using the formula $A^2 + B^2 = C^2$ where C is the approximate rafter length, A is the height from the top wall plate to the ridge, and B runs from the ridge to the top wall plate. Note that the actual length of lumber needed to form a rafter is longer than the result in the formula because of cuts needed to form the rafter, and because of the rafter tail that extends past the wall. Jack rafter length may be estimated using the same formula.

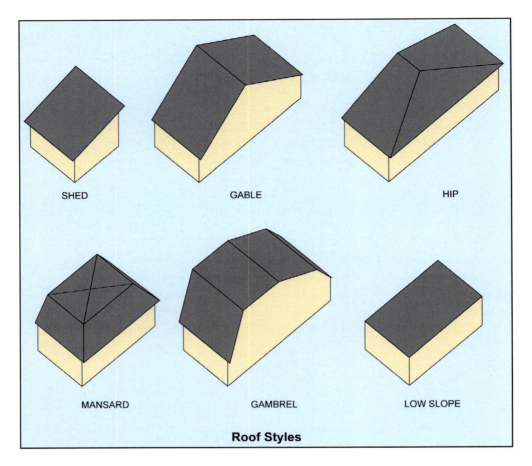

Roof Styles

Dimensional Lumber Roof Systems

Description The most common residential roof structural system in North America is the dimensional lumber (stick-framed) roof made from wood components including **ceiling joists, rafters, collar ties, rafter ties, purlins** and **sheathing**. Dimensional lumber in newer houses is often supplemented with structural composite lumber for components such as long hip and valley rafters.

Ceiling joist and rafter maximum allowed span distances are based, in part, on the species, grade, and on-center lumber spacing. See Dimensional Lumber Floor Systems for more about these characteristics. Ceiling joist spans are also based on whether the attic can be used for storage. An attic is assumed to be usable for storage if there is more than 42 inches vertical distance between the top of the ceiling joists and the bottom of the rafters. Attics that are usable for storage have a higher assumed live load compared to attics that are not usable for storage.

Rafter maximum allowed span distances are based on three additional factors: ground snow load, dead load, and whether the ceiling is attached to the rafters. Dead load depends on the roof covering. The 10 psf dead load is assumed for light roof coverings, such as fiberglass shingles and wood. The 20 psf dead load is assumed for heavy roof coverings, such as tile and slate. It is important to be aware of the situation where a heavy roof covering may be installed on rafters designed for a light roof covering. These roofs can become deformed, sometimes significantly.

The allowed span of ceiling joists and rafters has changed over time. Sometimes the allowed spans increase, but more often they decrease, in part because of the decreasing quality of lumber. Current span tables do not apply to older houses. Home inspectors are not required to determine the allowed span of these components regardless of when the house was built. In addition, requirements such as ceiling joist and rafter fastener schedules, and attic access opening size and location have changed. Home inspectors should use evidence-based techniques, such as excessive damage, deflection, and deformation, when evaluating dimensional lumber ceiling joists and rafters, especially in older houses.

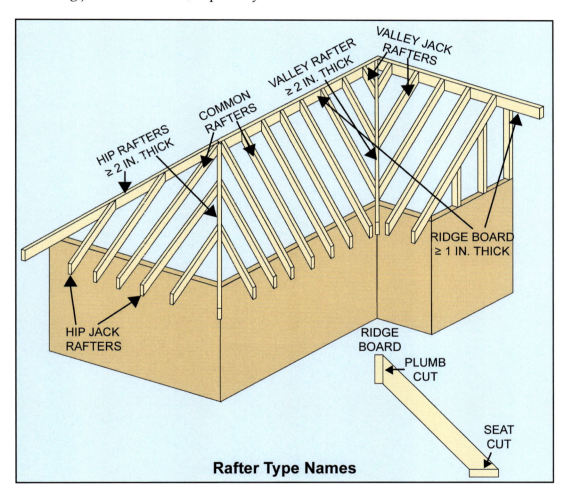

Rafter Type Names

Typical Construction Techniques

Ceiling Joists Ceiling joists are usually installed on the top of the highest story wall, although this is not required. Ceiling joists may be installed higher on the rafters to provide additional ceiling height. The allowed ceiling joist span is reduced when ceiling joists are installed higher on the rafters.

When ceiling joists are installed parallel to the rafters, each ceiling joist should be fastened to each rafter so that each ceiling joist connects the rafters on opposite sides of the house. It is unusual for one ceiling joist to extend for the entire distance between two rafters. One ceiling joist usually extends from each rafter, and the ceiling joists meet above a load-bearing wall.

The two ceiling joists should lap each other at least 3 inches. The quantity and type of fasteners at the ceiling joist lap and at each ceiling joist to rafter connection depends on the rafter slope, the rafter on center spacing, the total distance between the rafters, and the ground snow load. The quantity of fasteners is three or four in many houses, but can be much greater for lower slope roofs in high ground snow load areas.

When ceiling joists are installed perpendicular to the rafters, **rafter ties** should be installed between the rafters. Rafter ties should be installed using the same methods as ceiling joists because rafter ties perform the same function. **Kickers** may be installed instead of rafter ties.

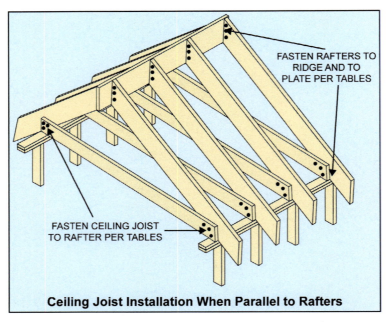

Ceiling Joist Installation When Parallel to Rafters

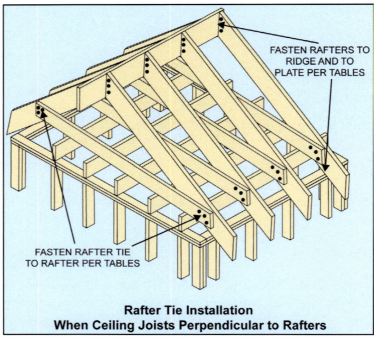

**Rafter Tie Installation
When Ceiling Joists Perpendicular to Rafters**

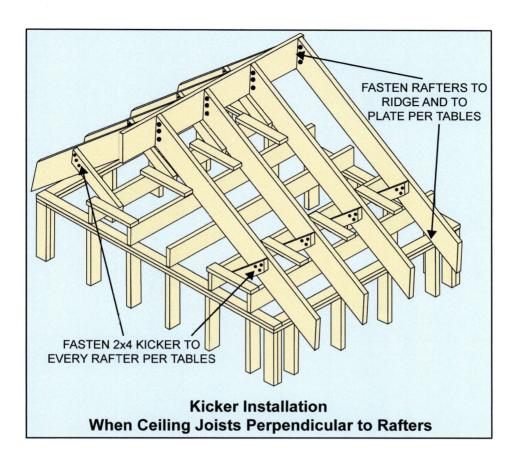

**Kicker Installation
When Ceiling Joists Perpendicular to Rafters**

Kicker

Ceiling Joist Bridging

Ceiling joists and rafters may have lateral support or bridging installed every 8 feet. This usually consists of a 2x4 fastened across the top of the ceiling joist or rafter, and may also consist of lumber fastened vertically to the horizontal member (a strongback). This lateral support is intended to keep the ceiling joists and rafters from twisting. Lateral support and bridging is usually not required except when the ceiling joists or rafters exceed 2x12 (uncommon); however, lateral support is frequently installed.

Rafters Rafters should be installed directly opposite each other at the **ridge board** or a ridge beam, if a ridge board or a ridge beam is installed. A ridge board is not required, but if used it should be at least nominal 1 inch thick and as deep as the deepest rafter plumb cut. The entire rafter plumb cut should bear on the ridge board or beam. At least 1½ inches of the rafter seat cut should bear on a wood wall plate or other wood structural support, or at least 3 inches on masonry or concrete. The seat cut should not bear only on roof sheathing.

If a ridge board or a ridge beam is not installed, rafters should be connected to each other at the ridge using a strap, gusset plate, or using collar ties. A strap or a collar tie should be installed at 4 feet on center, if this option is used. A gusset plate should be installed on every rafter pair, if this option is used. Collar ties are no longer required if rafters bear on a ridge board or a ridge beam.

Rafters and ceiling joists are often notched where the seat cut bears on the top plate. Where a rafter tail extends past the wall, this notch is sometimes called a **bird's-mouth** cut. At least 3½ inches of the rafter should be intact above the bird's-mouth cut. Where the ceiling joist is notched, not more than ¼ of the actual rafter depth may be notched.

Holes and notches in rafters and ceiling joists are subject to the same rules as dimensional lumber floor joists. Openings in rafters and ceiling joists for things such as dormers and skylights are also subject to these rules.

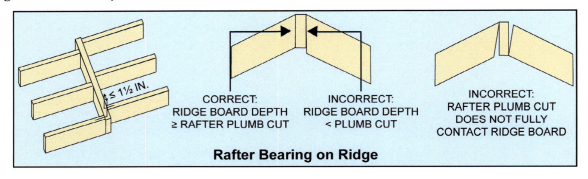

Rafter Bearing on Ridge

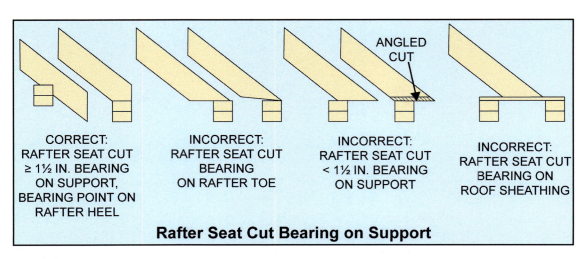

Rafter Seat Cut Bearing on Support

4: Structural Components

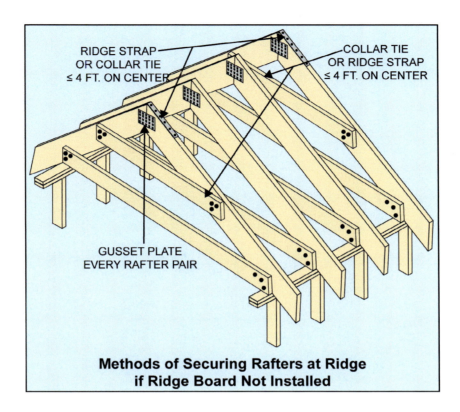

Methods of Securing Rafters at Ridge if Ridge Board Not Installed

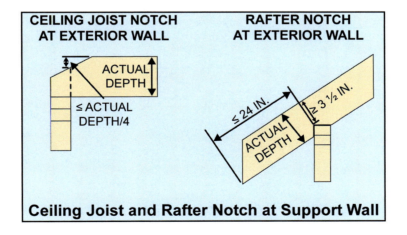

Ceiling Joist and Rafter Notch at Support Wall

Purlins A **purlin** may be used to support rafters that span too great a distance horizontally. **The purlin is the horizontal member on which the rafter bears.** It should be at least as deep as the rafter (e.g. a 2x6 purlin should support a 2x6 rafter). The **purlin brace**, also called a **strut**, should be at least a 2x4 and should be doubled if the brace length is greater than 8 feet. The purlin and brace should be installed at an angle that is **at least 45°** to horizontal; any lower angle will not provide adequate support. The braces should bear on a load-bearing wall and should not be spaced more than 4 feet apart.

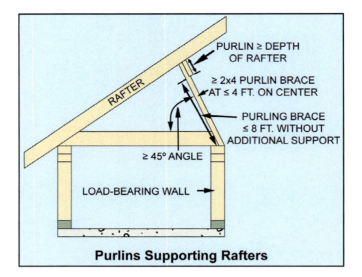

Purlins Supporting Rafters

Sheathing The rafters should be covered with some type of sheathing. Sheathing for older houses is lumber, often 1x4 to 1x8. Houses built beginning in the 1950s will often have plywood sheathing. Houses built beginning in the late 1970s will often have OSB sheathing. Lumber sheathing is usually installed closely spaced to accommodate most roof coverings. Lumber may be installed as **spaced (skip)** sheathing when wood roof coverings are used. This is recommended to help the wood roof covering dry from both directions.

Plywood and OSB roof sheathing should be installed with the long dimension perpendicular to the rafters and extending across at least 3 rafters. No piece should be less than 24 inches wide; it will be too weak to withstand the design load. The span rating for plywood and OSB is stamped on each sheet as two numbers separated by a slash, such as 24/16, 32/16, and 24-0. The first number is the maximum span between rafters when edge support is provided, and the second number is the maximum span between floor joists. Edge support for roof sheathing is usually provided by metal clips often called **H-clips**. Edge support can also be provided using wood blocking between rafters, or by using tongue-and-groove panels (uncommon).

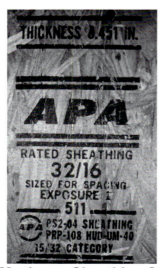

OSB Label, 32 Inches Maximum Sheathing Span with Edge Support

4: Structural Components

Typical Defects Roof system defects fall into two categories. Some defects are defective per se, meaning that the condition is defective regardless of whether there is current visible evidence of an adverse impact caused by the defect. An improperly notched rafter is defective per se. The adverse impact may not have occurred, yet. Other defects are evidence-based, meaning that there is current visible evidence of an adverse impact, whether or not there is an identified reason for the defect. An excessively bowed ceiling joist is an example of an adverse impact that may have no identified reason, yet.

- **Water staining and damage around roof penetrations such as plumbing vents, appliance vents, skylights, chimneys:** typical causes: absent, deteriorated, and improperly installed penetration flashing.

- **Water staining and damage in valleys:** typical causes: absent, deteriorated, and improperly installed valley flashing; water backing up under flashing due to debris in valley; fasteners in valley flashing; roof penetrations too close to valley.

- **Water staining and damage at sidewalls:** typical causes: absent, deteriorated, and improperly installed sidewall flashing; water running over flashing due to roof directing water toward sidewall; absent and improperly installed kick out flashing, ice damming (cold climates).

- **Water staining and damage near eaves:** typical causes: ice damming (cold climates); roof covering leaks.

- **Water staining, damage, and mold on rafters and sheathing (localized):** typical causes: roof covering leaks; moisture-laden air leaks from house condensing on sheathing (usually cold climates).

Water Damage Framed Chimney Chase (Left), Masonry Chimney (Right).

Water Stain Framed Chimney Chase.

Water Damage Around Masonry Chimney at Gable.

Water Damaged Sheathing Look for the Loose Gusset Plate.

Water Damage Near the Eaves.

Typical Minor Water Stains at Gable Ventilation Opening.

Typical Minor Water Stains at Plumbing Vent.

Water staining, damage and mold on rafters and sheathing and rust on roofing nails that penetrate the sheathing (widespread): typical causes: moisture-laden air leaks from house condensing on sheathing (usually cold climates); inadequate attic ventilation.

Widespread Water Stains Caused by Condensation.

- **Fire damage:** <u>typical causes:</u> fire. Fire weakens wood. Refer fire damage to an engineer for evaluation.

Fire Damaged Wood.

- **Improperly bored and notched ceiling joists and rafters:** see Dimensional Lumber Floor Systems for more information.

Excessive Rafter Notch. Right Picture Courtesy of Jennifer Davidson.

- **Defective purlins:** <u>typical causes</u>: purlins and braces damaged or absent; purlin too small; purlin brace too long; purlin braces improperly spaced; purlin braces not bearing on a load-bearing wall; purlin not supported at seam between purlins; purlin and brace at angle less than 45° to horizontal.

Purlins Improperly Installed. Purlin Braces Too Far Apart.

Purlin Brace Angle Less Than 45°.

- **Deformed rafters:** <u>typical causes</u>: rafter overspanned; rafter improperly cut, notched or bored; rafter damaged; excessive load on roof (heavy roof covering or a point load such as an appliance), improperly installed purlins.
- **Deformed ceiling joists:** <u>typical causes</u>: ceiling joist overspanned; ceiling joist improperly cut, notched or bored; ceiling joist damaged; excessive load on ceiling joists (purlins, appliances, storage of heavy belongings).
- **Damaged joists and rafters:** <u>typical causes</u>: damage during shipping and installation; cracking caused by heat and age; fire.

Deformed Rafters

- Wood destroying organism damage.
- **Inadequate support of hip and valley rafters:** <u>typical causes</u>: no support post for hip and valley rafter at ridge; valley jack rafters not supported on valley rafter; valley jack rafter supported on roof sheathing.
- **Inadequate bearing of rafters at ridge, hip, or valley:** <u>typical causes</u>: improper angle cut at plumb and seat cuts; rafter too short, does not make full contact at ridge, hip, or valley.

Inadequate Support at Hip Rafter Splice..

Inadequate Bearing at Hip.

Improper Offset and Inadequate Bearing at Ridge.

Inadequate Bearing at Ridge (Left). Improper Bearing on Shim (Right).

Inadequate Bearing at Seat Cut.

Inadequate Rafter Support at Skylight.

LVL Valley Rafter in Center of Picture May Need Support at Ridge.

- **Sheathing less than 24 inches wide (plywood and OSB):** <u>typical causes:</u> installation error.

Sheathing Less Than 24 Inches Wide at Ridge.

- **Inadequate attic access:** each attic area should have an access if the area exceeds 30 square feet and there is more than 30 inches between the ceiling joists and the rafters; the opening should be at least 22x30 inches. These are newer requirements and most older houses will not comply.

- **Inadequate attic ventilation:** attic ventilation may be 1 square foot net free ventilation area for every 300 square feet of attic area if a vapor retarder is installed (cold climate zones only), and between 40% and 50% of the ventilation openings are within 3 feet vertically from the ridge with the remaining ventilation in the eaves. The attic ventilation ratio should be 1:150 if these conditions are not satisfied. Net free ventilation area is the opening area minus area covered by screens and louvers. The most effective ventilation is continuous ridge vents and soffit vents.

Typical Repairs and Modifications Structural repairs and modifications usually require a building permit and should be designed and installed by, at a minimum, a qualified contractor. Repairs and modifications that do not have prescriptive rules should be designed by a qualified engineer. Many procedures to repair rafters and ceiling joists are subject to access problems such as blockage by plumbing, HVAC, and electrical components and insufficient access space for staging and installing materials.

- **Sister rafters and joists:** an additional rafter or joist is installed next to the defective rafter or joist. Applicable defects: most rafter and joist defects.
- **Spliced (scabbed) rafters and joists:** additional lumber is installed on one or both sides of a defective joist or rafter to strengthen it. Applicable defects: cut, notched, and damaged joists and rafters. This repair should be designed by an engineer.
- **Blocking:** horizontal pieces of wood are attached between a rafter or joist to reinforce the rafter or joist and spread some of the lateral load among adjacent rafters or joists. Applicable defects: cut, notched and damaged rafters or joists; sheathing with inadequate edge support and sheathing less than 24 inches wide.
- **Purlins:** purlins added to address deformed and overspanned rafters. Applicable defects: deformed and overspanned rafters. Purlins should be installed as previously described.
- **Roof for addition supported by existing rafters:** this modification should be designed by an engineer; existing rafters may not be designed to bear the additional load.

Standards IRC 2018 Tables R602.3(1), (2), and (3) (general fastener schedules), Table R802.5.2 (rafter/ceiling joist fastener schedule), Tables R802.5(1) and (2) (ceiling joist span tables), Tables R802.4.1(1 – 8) (rafter span tables), R802.2 through .9 (rafter and ceiling joist framing), Table R802.11 (rafter and truss uplift connections), Figure R301.2(6) (ground snow load).

Truss Roof Systems

Description Wood roof trusses are engineered components that are usually made from 2x4 dimensional lumber laid out in a triangle with members in the center to distribute the load along the truss. The top and bottom horizontal members are called **chords,** and the members in the center are called **webs**. The webs may be oriented vertically or diagonally (or both) relative to the top and bottom chords. The webs may be attached to the chords using metal plates called **gusset plates**, or by inserting the webs into a groove cut into the chords. Trusses using metal plates are called metal plate connected trusses.

Like rafters, trusses must stay on the house during high wind events. Stronger hold-down hardware is required in high wind risk and wind exposure risk areas.

Framing Package with Roof Trusses (Foreground) and Floor Trusses (Right Rear).

Typical Construction Techniques General construction techniques used when installing wood roof trusses are similar to those used when installing dimensional lumber rafters and ceiling joists. Refer to Dimensional Lumber Roof Systems for more information. This section identifies defects unique to trusses, and by implication, identifies differences in construction techniques compared to dimensional lumber.

Roof trusses are usually bottom chord bearing, meaning that the truss bottom chord bears on the top wall. Some roof trusses are top chord bearing. Top chord bearing trusses usually should bear within ⅛ inch of the supporting wall or beam.

Trusses usually bear on support at each end; however, they sometimes bear on support at a point within the truss span. Two or more webs are often installed at the bearing point. The support wall should be directly under this bearing point.

Trusses must be permanently braced to resist wind and seismic loads that could cause the trusses to move laterally and even collapse in a domino-like manner. Roof sheathing usually provides the top chord bracing and the ceiling finish (drywall) usually provides the bottom chord bracing. Lateral bracing between truss webs may be required for large trusses, and bracing along truss webs may be required for long truss webs. Gable-end bracing is required for most truss roof systems.

Typical Truss Permanent Bracing.

Temporary bracing of trusses is recommended to help keep the trusses from moving during installation. Temporary bracing may consist of 2x4 lumber fastened across the truss top chords. Temporary wood or metal bracing/spacing may be installed at the ridge. Temporary bracing may be removed when permanent bracing is installed, or it may be left in place. Either way is acceptable. Specific permanent and temporary bracing requirements should be provided in the truss installation instructions. General bracing guidelines may be found in the *Building Component Safety Information Book* 2018 Edition.

Typical Defects Most truss roof system defects are identical to those found with dimensional lumber roofs. Refer to Dimensional Lumber Roof Systems section for more information. This section identifies defects unique to trusses.

- **Damaged, absent, cut, modified truss chord or web:** <u>typical causes</u>: damage during shipping and installation, cuts, modification, and removal by trade contractors and homeowners to install appliances, ducts, vent, pull-down stairs, whole house fans, and other components.

Truss Web Cut for Duct.

Truss Bottom Chords Cut for Pull-Down Stairs.

Truss Web Knocked Loose, Out of Position.

Truss Webs Removed.

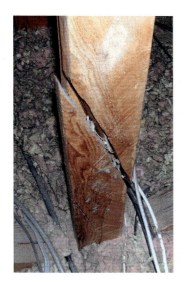 

Damaged Truss Webs.

- **Damaged, absent, loose gusset plates:** <u>typical cause</u>: damage during shipping and installation (a gap exceeding $1/64$ inch is not acceptable).

Loose Gusset Plates.

Gusset Plate in Wrong Location.

Gusset Plate Absent.

Damaged, absent, cut truss brace (including gable-end bracing): <u>typical causes</u>: installation error, cuts and removal by trade contractors and homeowners to install appliances, ducts, vent, pull-down stairs, and other components. Truss brace location should be indicated on the truss plans. The intended location of truss braces is sometimes indicated by a tag attached to the truss.

Cut Truss Braces.

- **Truss uplift:** <u>typical cause</u>: changes in temperature and humidity cause the truss bottom chord to deform; usually presents as long and possibly wide cracks and gaps between ceilings and walls; usually corrects itself when the season changes; usually considered a cosmetic issue.

- **Truss not plumb:** <u>typical cause</u>: installation error. Trusses should be installed within D/50 of plumb where D is the truss depth in inches or within 2 inches of plumb, whichever is smaller.

Trusses Not Plumb.

- **Truss chord not straight:** <u>typical cause</u>: installation error. Truss chords should be installed within L/200 of being straight where L is the truss chord length in inches or within 2 inches of straight, whichever is smaller.

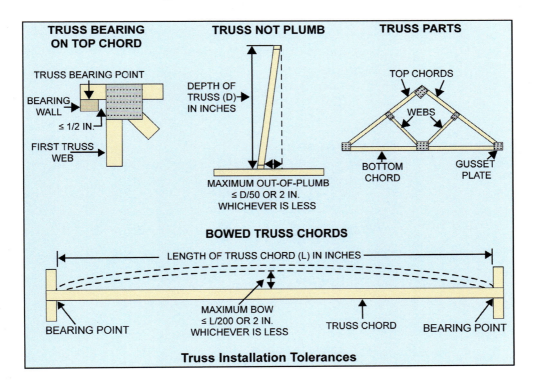

- **Piggyback truss not attached to main truss:** <u>typical cause</u>: installation error. A piggyback truss is one that bears on a truss below. Piggyback trusses may, but not always, need to be secured to the main truss. This construction detail should be on the building plans.

- **Piggyback trusses not bearing on purlins:** <u>typical cause</u>: installation error. Piggyback trusses should bear on 2x4 purlins spaces about 2 feet on center.

Piggyback Truss Bearing on Purlins. Piggyback Truss Not Connected to Main Truss.

- **Owner belongings stored on trusses or in racks hung from trusses:** trusses are often not designed to bear loads imposed by owner belongings. This can cause truss bottom chord to deform.

Typical Repairs and Modifications

An engineer should design all repairs of wood trusses and those repairs should be installed by a qualified contractor. A wise procedure is to attach a copy of the engineer's sealed repair instructions to the repaired members for reference by subsequent home inspectors.

- **Scabs on truss members:** additional lumber is installed on one or both sides of a damaged truss member. This repair usually has specific requirements for scab length and nailing pattern, and may be limited to damage near the center of the member.

Probably Improper Truss Web Repairs.

- **Gusset plate reattached using fasteners:** this repair is usually not permitted. The correct repair usually involves large pieces of OSB or plywood fastened on both sides of the joint with the damaged gusset plate.

Probably a Proper Gusset Plate Repair.

- **Roof for addition, porch, etc. supported by existing trusses:** this modification should be designed by an engineer. Existing trusses may not be designed to bear the additional load.

Standards (1) manufacturer's instructions and approved building plans; (2) *Building Component Safety Information Book* 2018 Edition (guide to good practice for handling, installing, restraining and bracing metal plate connected wood trusses); (3) IRC 2018 R802.10 (trusses), Table R802.11 (rafter and truss uplift connections).

Wood I-Joists and Engineered Wood Roof Systems

Description Wood I-joists are engineered wood joists that are usually used as floor joists, but can be used as ceiling joists and rafters. Refer to the Wood I-Joist and Engineered Wood section in the Floor Systems section for more information.

Attic Access

Introduction Attic access is required for three reasons. Access is required for inspection and maintenance, to allow firefighters to quickly access the attic, and to allow access to appliances that require maintenance and replacement.

Attic access was an afterthought until relatively recently. The attic access opening in older houses is often in a reach-in closet where it is very difficult to safely set up a ladder and climb into the attic. Owner belongings frequently block the opening. The home inspector should be cautious when attempting to enter an attic where access is difficult. **Entering is usually easier than exiting.**

Access Opening Size and Location Access should be provided to all attic spaces in which the attic floor area exceeds 30 square feet and the vertical height at some point in the attic is 30 inches or more. Note that an attic access opening may be through a wall, and that a house can have more than one attic area. The opening should be located in a hallway or another equally accessible area. Ceiling access openings are no longer allowed in small closets. The rough opening size (before finish materials are installed) should be at least 22 by 30 inches. There should be at least 30 inches of vertical clearance at some point above the opening. Note that attic access openings in older houses are not required to satisfy these newer requirements.

Access Opening Covers and Doors The current requirement for access opening covers and doors is that they be insulated and weather stripped like any other opening to the exterior if the cover or door is in conditioned space. This is a new requirement; however, the home inspector may wish to recommend insulation and weather stripping as an upgrade.

Access opening covers in an attached garage should comply with fire separation requirements. This means that the access cover in an attached garage should be at least ½ inch thick drywall. A wood cover is usually not acceptable in a garage unless it is an approved fireblocking material. Pull-down stair covers are usually very thin plywood and are a reportable fire separation breach.

Access to Attic Appliances Safe access should be provided to appliances located in the attic. The finished access opening size should be at least 20 inches by 30 inches or large enough to remove the largest appliance, whichever is larger. A solid floor and access passage should be provided. The passage should be at least 24 inches wide, 30 inches high, and not more than 20 feet from the access opening. A level service space at least 30 inches wide and 30 inches deep should be provided in front of all parts of the appliance that could require service. Note that air conditioning and heat pump evaporator coils require service. A light, with a switch near the attic access opening, and a 120 volt receptacle should be provided near the appliance.

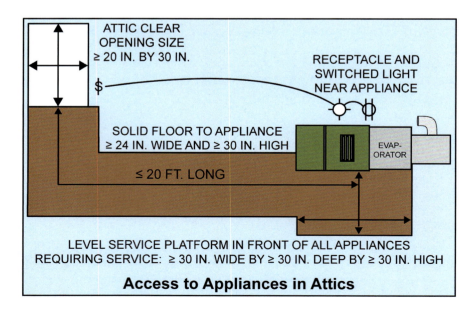

Access to Appliances in Attics

4: Structural Components

Pull-Down Stairs A pull-down stair is a folding ladder that is attached to a (usually) plywood cover. The cover is attached to springs that pull the cover shut when the stairs are not in use.

Pull-down stairs should be installed according to manufacturer's instructions. The instructions are usually contained on a label attached to newer stairs. The instructions often specify either 16d nails or ¼ inch diameter lag screws for attaching the stair frame to the ceiling framing. The stairs usually need to be trimmed so that the stair sections fold out straight. Uneven gaps between stair sections place the stairs under great stress and are unsafe. Stair hardware is sometimes absent or loose, especially at the stair section hinges and where the springs connect.

Pull-down stairs are frequently improperly installed and poorly maintained. The home inspector should exercise caution when pulling the rope on the stair cover, when unfolding the stairs, and when climbing the stairs. Some home inspectors will not climb on pull-down stairs, especially those that are not properly trimmed.

Typical Defects Typical defects that home inspectors should report include:

1. no attic access,
2. attic access too small or vertical clearance above access too low,
3. attic access located where appliance removal would require damaging permanent construction including closet shelving,
4. damaged access cover,
5. access cover type breaches fire separation in the garage,
6. access path to attic appliances too long, too narrow, or too low,
7. service area in front of appliance too narrow or not deep enough,
8. pull-down stairs do not completely close (usually weak springs),
9. stair frame improperly attached to ceiling framing,
10. truss chords cut to install pull-down stairs,
11. pull-down ladder not properly trimmed,
12. loose or absent pull-down ladder stair hardware.

Standards (1) IRC 2018 R807 (attic access), M1305.1.2 (appliance installation in attic); (2) manufacturer's instructions.

4: Structural Components

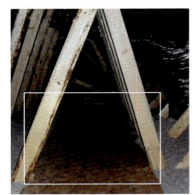
Trusses Block Path to Appliance.

Service Platform Less Than 30 Inches.

Pull-Down Stair Hinge Damaged.

Nail Not Installed Per Manufacturer's Instructions.

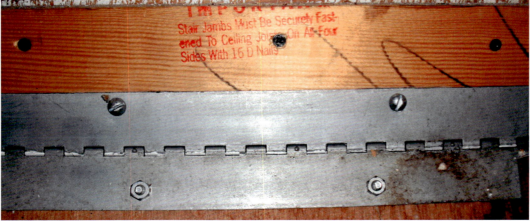
Screws Used Instead of Nails.

4: Structural Components

Please visit https://nationalhomeinspectorexam.org/prepare-for-the-exam/ and take advantage of the practice quizzes. The questions in the practice quizzes are designed to reflect the difficulty of the questions on the actual exam. The questions on the practice quizzes are not questions on the National Home Inspectors Exam. Passing the practice quizzes does not guarantee that you will pass the National exam. You will still need to study all topics to be prepared for the National exam.

5: INSULATION AND VENTILATION

INSPECTION SCOPE

The title of this section is Insulation and Ventilation, but insulation and ventilation are really just means to achieve certain objectives. Insulation is a means to maintain a comfortable interior environment, and to help make the house as energy efficient as reasonably possible. Ventilation is a means to manage moisture, remove or dilute pollutants, and maintain a supply of air for occupant health and comfort.

Insulation and ventilation components that are in scope of a home inspection include visible insulation and vapor retarders, ventilation of attics and foundation areas, and local exhaust systems, including bathroom, laundry, and clothes dryers. The condition and adequacy of exhaust components that are part of heat recovery ventilation systems (HRV) and energy recovery ventilation systems (ERV) are not in scope of a home inspection. Lack of an exhaust system where required (e.g., bathrooms without operable windows) is a reportable defect.

INTRODUCTION TO INSULATION AND VENTILATION

Insulation

People have been trying to maintain a comfortable interior environment from the beginning. The primary objective was (and still is) to do so while using as little energy as possible. Back in the day, someone had to stoke the fire to keep things warm, or wave the fan to keep things cool. Unless you were wealthy, that someone was you. Using less energy to keep yourself comfortable meant you had more energy (and time) to do other things, like feeding yourself and your family.

Various materials and methods have been used to maintain a comfortable interior environment. Thick (large thermal mass) walls work well. Thick walls slow heat movement. The problem is that thick walls are expensive to build. Cavity walls (two walls with a space between them) can work, even with nothing but air in them. The problem is that you must seal the cavity completely so the air does not move. **Stationary air is actually a good insulator. That is how most insulation achieves its R-value.** Sealing wall cavities so that air does not move is difficult, so people started stuffing material in cavity walls. Straw and other vegetable matter, animal hair, various forms of asbestos, and mineral wool (rockwool) have been used. The large tapestries found in castles were more than decoration; they helped reduce drafts. Vegetable matter and animal hair are not great insulators, and they present fire safety problems. The health effects of asbestos have been known for centuries. Mineral wool is a good insulator and is still used, although it has been supplanted by other types of insulation, such as fiberglass and cellulose.

Most people think only about insulation for maintaining a comfortable interior environment. Other, so called passive, methods have been used since the beginning and are now being rediscovered. Orienting a house in the right direction to absorb or reject solar heat is one passive method. The use of light colors to reflect heat is another. Deciduous trees are a great passive method because they provide shade in the summer and allow sunlight to pass through in the winter. Wide eaves and awnings are common in warm climates to help keep out the summer sun.

Ventilation

The primary reason to ventilate a house is to **dilute pollutants** and to **remove pollutants** that accumulate inside the house. Pollutants can include tobacco smoke, combustion products, water vapor, carbon dioxide (from breathing), and volatile organic compounds (VOC). VOC may come from any manufactured product used to build or furnish the house including plywood and OSB, cabinets, carpet and pad, paint and stain, and furniture. Long term exposure to pollutants can cause health problems for some people including exacerbating allergies and asthma. Excess water vapor can cause problems like condensation on windows and mold growth.

Ventilation in houses was not a big issue until very recently. Common wood-frame construction techniques left plenty of openings through which air could pass between the interior and exterior. **Most of these openings are small, but together they can add up to several square feet.** It is like having a door open 24/7. There was plenty of ventilation to remove and dilute pollutants, but at a large energy efficiency cost. All that outside ventilation air must be heated and cooled.

Two conditions have changed regarding ventilation. One is that builders, and sometimes homeowners, are sealing these openings, thereby reducing the amount of ventilation. Air sealing is great from an energy efficiency perspective. **Air sealing can have a greater impact on energy use than adding insulation.** The problem is that air sealing can have a negative impact on air quality in the house, and can have a negative impact on traditional methods of providing combustion air for fuel-burning appliances.

Recent building code changes mandate specific air sealing and ventilation requirements. Codes require providing outside air to houses by mechanical means if the measured rate of air changes per hour is five or fewer. **Codes also require that new houses be air sealed** so that the measured rate of air changes per hour is five or fewer (three or fewer in all but climate zone 1 and climate zone 2). This means that some form of mechanical ventilation is required in new houses and in houses that have been effectively air sealed. We discuss methods for providing mechanical ventilation later in this chapter.

The other change is that **new building materials are more complicated**, making material selection and installation more complicated. A material that is installed in the wrong location, or that is improperly installed, can trap moisture or allow moisture to flow where it can do harm. For example, a vapor retarder installed where a vapor permeable water barrier should have been installed can trap moisture in the wall cavity. At best, the trapped moisture reduces the R-value of insulation. At worst, the moisture condenses into liquid water, damaging the house and providing moisture for fungal growth.

INSULATION AND VENTILATION TERMS

The insulation and ventilation systems have many terms that a home inspector should know and be able to use. Here are some of the most common terms that a home inspector should know. Some of these definitions have been altered to conform to usage in residential construction.

Air barrier: any material or combination of materials that prevents the flow of air from unconditioned areas into the thermal envelope.

Basement wall: a wall with at least (≥) 50% of its area below grade (covered by earth on the outside) and encloses conditioned space.

Building thermal envelope: the conditioned (heated and cooled) area of the building. The envelope boundary between conditioned and unconditioned space includes walls, ceilings, floors, basement walls and slab-on-grade foundations. The thermal envelope may include the attic and the crawl space if these areas are designed and built as conditioned space.

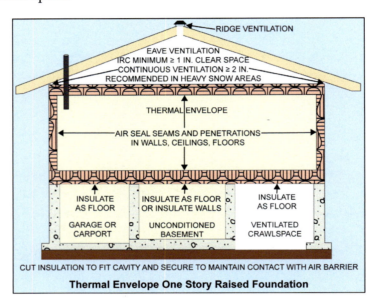

Thermal Envelope One Story Raised Foundation

Dew point (temperature): the temperature at which water vapor in the air may condense into liquid water. A higher dew point temperature indicates that the air contains more water vapor.

Fenestration: openings in the wall and roof of a house such as windows, doors, and skylights.

Humidity, relative: the amount of water vapor that is actually in the air compared to the amount of water vapor that could exist in the air at a given air temperature, expressed as a percentage. More moisture can exist in warm air than in cold air, so raising the air temperature while keeping the water vapor constant reduces relative humidity. Conversely, lowering the air temperature and keeping the water vapor content constant increases relative humidity.

Mass wall: above-grade walls made from concrete masonry units, concrete, insulated concrete forms, masonry cavity, brick (structural, not veneer), adobe, compressed earth block, rammed earth, and solid timber logs.

Permeability: the ability or property of a material to resist or allow the diffusion of water vapor through the material. Permeability (perms) is expressed as a number greater than zero. For example, glass is a very low permeability material and fiberglass batt insulation is a high permeability material.

R-value: the ability or property of a material to slow heat transfer. A higher R-value number equals a higher ability to slow heat transfer. R-value is expressed as a number greater than zero. R-value is used to compare the insulation value of materials.

Solar heat gain coefficient (SHGC): a measure of the amount of solar radiation that passes through a window. A lower SHGC means that less solar radiation passes through a window.

U-value (factor): the ability or property of a material to allow heat transfer. U-value is the inverse of R-value (R-value = 1/U-value). U-value is expressed as a number greater than zero. A larger number equals a higher rate of heat transfer and a lower R-value. U-value is primarily used in residential construction to compare the thermal performance of fenestration. For example, metal such as aluminum has a high U-value. This is why higher quality aluminum windows have a thermal break in the frame to slow heat transfer.

Vapor barrier: a technically questionable term often used when the term **vapor retarder** is intended. Class I vapor retarders are effectively vapor barriers, but the term vapor retarder is preferred.

Vapor diffusion: the process by which water vapor passes through a permeable material from an area of greater vapor pressure to an area of lower vapor pressure.

Vapor drive: a condition that occurs when heat and vapor pressure cause increased vapor diffusion. One example is when water vapor diffuses through permeable building materials from heated interior areas in the winter. Another example is when solar radiation heats wet bricks forcing water vapor through permeable building materials in the summer. Vapor drive is usually less of a factor than vapor flow by convection through openings in the building envelope.

Vapor retarder: a material that restricts the flow of water vapor. A Class I vapor retarder is rated at 0.1 perms or less. Polyethylene sheeting is an example. A Class II vapor retarder is rated at between 0.1 and 1.0 perms. Kraft paper used as the facing on some batt insulation is an example. A Class III vapor retarder is rated at between 1.0 and 10.0 perms. Latex and oil paints are examples.

Ventilation (building): the process of supplying outside air to a house or removing inside air from a house by natural or mechanical means. Ventilation can be random and uncontrolled (air leaks), or it can be designed and controlled (outside air ducts, heat recovery ventilators, energy recovery ventilators).

HOW INSULATION WORKS

To understand how insulation works, we need to recall two rules from the Cooling System and the Heating System chapters of this book.

- Heat energy transfers from some place hotter to some place colder
- Hotter air is lighter than cooler air and will rise (stack effect)

The tendency of hot air to rise and displace cooler air, which sinks, can establish convection currents that keep air moving. Moving air transfers heat more effectively than stable air. **Air moving across or through insulation reduces its resistance to heat flow (its R-value).**

We also need to recall how heat transfer works. Heat is transferred in three ways that can occur individually, but often occur together. **Conduction** occurs when heat moves through solid matter. **Convection** occurs when heat moves by circulation of a gas or a liquid. **Radiation** occurs when molecules gain heat by absorbing electromagnetic energy in the infrared part of the spectrum.

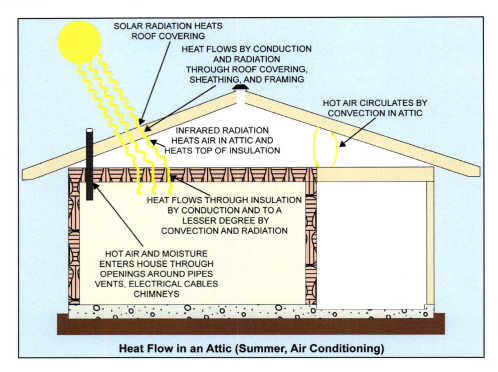

Heat Flow in an Attic (Summer, Air Conditioning)

Insulation works mostly by slowing conductive heat transfer. It does this by trapping air in the insulation material, and by keeping the air from moving. Heat does not flow easily through stable air. **Insulation that has more, but not too many air pockets, that completely fills the space in which it is installed, and that does not have air moving around or through it has a higher resistance to heat transfer (a higher R-value).**

This simple statement about how insulation works has a profound effect on how insulation should be installed, and on how a home inspector should inspect and report about visible insulation. **Insulation that is compressed, even a little, loses R-value** because it contains less air to slow heat transfer. Conversely, insulation that is "**fluffed**" also loses R-value because it is not dense enough to keep the air in the insulation stable. Fluffing is most common with blown-in insulation and occurs when the installer adds more air to the insulation during installation than is recommended by the manufacturer. Insulation that is absent or not as thick as it should be has a lower R-value for the same reason. **Wet insulation loses R-value** because heat transfers more effectively through water. Wet insulation also retains water that can provide moisture for fungal growth.

Because insulation works primarily by slowing conductive heat flow, **insulation must be in contact with an air barrier that is adjacent to conditioned space.** All conditioned spaces should have insulation installed at the surface closest to the conditioned space. The attic floor, floor sheathing above a crawl space, and the drywall or plaster at wall cavities are some obvious air barriers adjacent to conditioned spaces. Less obvious places include cantilevered floors, drop soffits such as those in kitchens and bathrooms, and framed chimney chases. Lack of insulation in these (usually) concealed spaces is difficult to detect during a visual home inspection; however, moisture stains or mold growth near these areas can be an indication of an insulation or air sealing defect. Moisture stains or mold growth around the baseboards can also be an indication of an insulation or air sealing defect.

Insulating Soffits and Drop Ceilings

Insulation Absent at Drop Ceiling for a a Closet. Closet Ceiling and Sidewalls Above Ceiling Should Be Insulated.

The ideal insulation installation has an **air barrier on all six sides of the insulation** to eliminate convection around and through the insulation, a phenomenon sometimes called wind washing. **Insulation that is not in direct contact with the air barrier at the conditioned area is practically worthless.** Air that flows between the insulation and conditioned space, and air that flows through or around the insulation, can reduce the R-value of the insulation to almost zero. House wraps and building paper are also air barriers, and if properly installed without gaps and holes and with tape applied to seams, can help reduce air flow through seams in the other air barriers.

Insulation Not In Contact With Floor Sheathing Above Crawl Space. Floor is Uninsulated.

A problem encountered when insulating framed wall, floor, and ceiling assemblies is the relatively poor R-value of wood. The R-value of a 2x4 (measured through the 3½ inch side) is about R4.4. A 2x6 is about R 6.9. The R-value of a double 2x_ header would be about the same as a 2x4. You can see this using an infrared camera; the framing material clearly shows as a different temperature (which makes infrared cameras great, if expensive, stud finders). This phenomenon is called **thermal bridging**. One effect of thermal bridging is to reduce the total R-value of the assembly. The other effect is to provide a surface on which water vapor in the assembly can condense. This tends to occur in cold climates in the winter. Strategies for reducing thermal bridging include using fewer framing members and installing insulating exterior sheathing.

HOW VAPOR RETARDERS WORK

To understand how and why vapor retarders work, we need to recall two rules from the Cooling System and the Heating System chapters of this book.

- Water vapor in the air flows (diffuses) from a place with more water vapor (higher vapor pressure) to a place with less water vapor (lower vapor pressure)
- More water vapor can exist in warm air than in cool air
- Water vapor in the air may condense into liquid water if the air temperature decreases to the dew point

It also helps to realize that each house occupant can add ½ gallon or more of water vapor to the air in the house each day by activities such as breathing, cooking, and bathing.

Water vapor can pass (diffuse) through many materials used to build houses. The ease with which this happens depends on the **permeability** of the material. Brick, wood and vinyl siding, #15 building felt, and insulation are vapor permeable, meaning they allow water vapor to pass easily. Most house wrap material is vapor permeable. Drywall, OSB and plywood sheathing, and insulation sheathing (1 inch or less thick), are moderately vapor permeable and are not considered vapor retarders. Polyethylene and foil sheeting, Kraft paper, and vinyl and foil wallpaper are vapor impermeable, meaning they do not allow water vapor to pass easily. These materials and others are considered vapor retarders, although wallpaper is not supposed to be used as a vapor retarder.

Installation of vapor retarders and water and air barriers used to be simple. **A vapor retarder was installed on the interior side of exterior framed walls in all climates.** A water and air barrier was usually, but not always, installed on the exterior side of exterior framed walls. We now know that this **one size fits all approach causes problems, especially in warm/humid climates**. Whether a vapor retarder should be installed depends on the temperature and humidity where the house is located. An intact water and air barrier (not a vapor retarder) should always be installed on the exterior side of exterior walls.

The United States and Canada are now divided into eight climate zones based on heating degree days (winter temperature). An additional division is based on humidity. The temperature zones are numbered 1 – 8. The humidity divisions are (A) moist, (B) dry, and (C) marine. Most of the continental US is in zones 2 – 7. Most of Canada is in zones 7 and 8, but some of the heavily populated areas near the US/Canada border are in zones 5 and 6. A lower climate zone number indicates a warmer climate. The moist zone is in the eastern two-thirds of the US and Canada. The dry zone is in the West. The marine zone is along the West Coast.

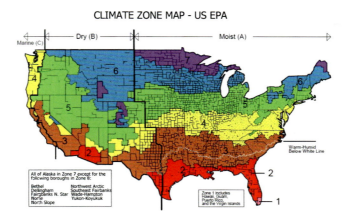

CLIMATE ZONE MAP - US EPA

Vapor Retarders in Walls A vapor retarder is not required, nor is it recommended, on either side of walls in climate zones 1 – 4 (except Marine 4). A vapor retarder is not required in these climate zones because it has been shown that water vapor condensation in wall cavities is usually not a problem. A vapor retarder is not recommended in these climate zones because lack of one allows the wall system to dry both toward the interior and the exterior if water should enter the wall cavity. **A wall cavity should be designed to dry toward at least one side**, so a vapor retarder should not be installed on both sides of a wall cavity.

A Class I or II vapor retarder is usually required on the interior side of walls in climate zones 5 – 8 and Marine 4. There are several exceptions to this requirement that allow a Class III vapor retarder. These exceptions involve using specific types of wall cladding and sheathing material.

Vapor Retarders in Attics A vapor retarder is not required in an adequately ventilated attic. Refer to the attic ventilation section for more information. A vapor retarder may be installed on the attic floor (under the insulation) in climate zones 6 - 8 as an alternative to the $1/150$ attic ventilation ratio. If a vapor retarder is installed, it should be installed in contact with the conditioned space. A vapor retarder installed above the insulation can create a moisture trap that can allow water to condense between the vapor retarder and the attic floor. Water condensation damages wood, reduces the insulation R-value, and provides moisture for fungal growth.

THE HOUSE AS A SYSTEM

In this book we discuss the systems and components in a house separately. This method is useful for organizing and explaining, but it can give the misleading impression that house systems and components are independent of each other. This is definitely not true. **House systems and components, house occupants, and the environment in which the house exists are constantly acting on each other.** This makes the house, occupants, and its environment one complex interdependent system. We introduce this systems concept here because these interdependencies are most apparent when evaluating problems involving insulation and ventilation.

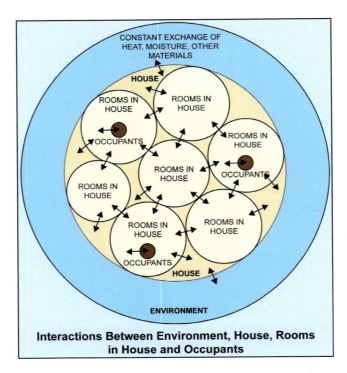

Interactions Between Environment, House, Rooms in House and Occupants

The easiest way to think about the house as a system is in terms of **pressures** and **holes**. Air and water vapor will remain motionless without pressure (a force) to move them. This is an expression of Newton's First Law of Motion. Air and water vapor will remain in the same space unless there is a hole through which they can pass.

Pressure comes in many forms. Water vapor pressure differences cause water vapor to move from higher to lower water vapor pressure. Air temperature differences cause air to rise when less dense warm air displaces denser cooler air. Imbalances in the air flow through forced-air supply and return ducts can pressurize or depressurize individual rooms or the entire house. For example, a leak in the return duct will pressurize the house because more supply air is entering the house than is being removed from the house. A room with a supply duct and no return will become pressurized and can force air into the wall cavity, the interstitial space between floors, and into the attic. Wind can create air pressure differences in a house. Wind blowing against one side of the house pressurizes that side and depressurizes the opposite side. Powered attic ventilation fans can depressurize the attic and draw conditioned air from the house, and can draw moist unconditioned air from the basement and crawl space if there are openings that connect the two.

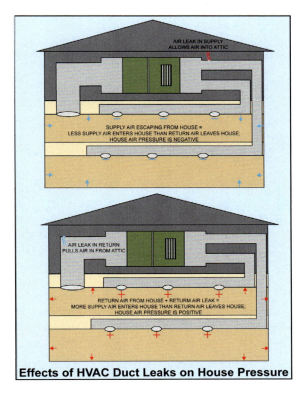

Effects of HVAC Duct Leaks on House Pressure

Holes can be visible. Examples include spaces and gaps between materials used to build the house, and the annular spaces around holes drilled for wires and pipes. Holes around electrical box and pipe penetrations of walls, floors, and ceilings that abut unconditioned space are other examples. **Holes can be microscopic.** Vapor permeable materials have holes between the molecules that allow water molecules to pass between them. We will discuss a couple practical examples of this pressure and holes approach next.

Mold and Rot in the Attic

The house is in the Midwest, climate zone 5A (cold/moist), in the winter. Bathing and cooking occurs without the use of externally exhausted fans. The attic is insulated at the current standard of R-49, which helps keep heat inside the house and keeps the attic cold. There are several older recessed light fixtures (not air sealed) in the second story ceiling. The house interior is pressurized because of a crimp in the return duct (more air flows in through the supply ducts than flows back through the return duct). The eave ventilation openings are partially blocked by the added insulation.

The problem begins when warm moist air flows through the openings in the ceiling driven by the stack effect and by positive pressure in the house with respect to the attic. The water vapor is not quickly removed from the attic because of inadequate attic ventilation. The water vapor condenses on the coldest surface, which is the attic sheathing, roofing nails, and rafters. Discoloration, mold, and rot are observed.

Several systems contribute to the situation. Repairs to only one system, such as improving attic ventilation, may or may not solve the problem. While all of the problems should be identified and repaired, the most effective repair in this situation is probably replacing the recessed light fixtures with air sealed fixtures, and sealing any other openings between the attic and the house.

Widespread Discoloration of Roof Sheathing Indicates a Possible Condensation Issue. Warm/Moist Air is Entering Attic From a Very Wet Crawl Space.

Water Stains on Attic Floor Indicate Condensation on Roof Covering Nails.

<u>**Mold and Rot in the Crawl Space**</u> The house is in the Southeast, climate zone 3A (warm/moist), in the summer. The house has a crawl space foundation. The crawl space is damp, but not unusually so. R-11 fiberglass batt insulation is installed between the floor joists with a vapor retarder toward conditioned space. The insulation is installed in an average manner with sections compressed and with some sections drooping due to lack of support. Plastic sheeting covers some of the crawl space floor. The ventilation openings are adequate quantity and open. The house is air conditioned and the occupants like to keep the temperature cool. Gutters are partially blocked and the grade is nearly flat around some of the foundation.

The problem begins when the warm moist air in the crawl space diffuses through the vapor permeable insulation and condenses in the insulation and on the floor joists. This occurs because the temperature in the insulation is reduced to the dew point temperature due to the cool temperature in the house above. The wet insulation loses additional R-value and the condensation increases as the dew point temperature in the insulation travels further down toward the crawl space floor. Discoloration, mold, and rot are observed.

Moderate Infestation of Wood-Destroying Fungi. Wood Deterioration Detected. Insulation is Poorly Installed and Only Marginally Effective.

Several factors contribute to this situation including lifestyle choices, typical lack of attention to detail in the installation of insulation and the crawl space floor vapor retarder, and inadequate maintenance of gutters and grading. Repair or replacement of damaged framing is appropriate as is replacement of wet insulation. A properly installed crawl space floor vapor retarder with seams lapped and sealed, and sealing the vapor retarder to the foundation walls will help. The most effective repair is most likely addressing the sources of the crawl space moisture. Grading, drainage, gutters, and landscape irrigation are the first line of defense against basement and crawl space moisture problems.

The other source of moisture in this situation is the crawl space ventilation openings. In warm moist climates, crawl space ventilation openings can bring in as much water vapor as they remove. **The current crawl space ventilation rules have no scientific or empirical basis and were developed before the widespread use of air conditioning.** Closed crawl spaces are now recommended by many experts to reduce crawl space moisture problems. We will discuss more about this later in this section.

Mold and rot problems can also occur in interior walls and chases that are open to the crawl space. These problems can also occur in attics if the attic is open to the crawl space, which is not unusual around chimneys and vent chases. Attic moisture problems can sometimes be traced to the crawl space. For example, a powered attic ventilation fan can depressurize the attic and draw water vapor from the crawl space through interior walls and chases. The water vapor can condense inside the walls or near where the chase or opening enters the attic.

COMMON TYPES OF INSULATION

Batt Insulation

Batt (blanket) insulation comes in rolls that are usually installed between framing members. Some batts have a vapor retarder on one side and are called **faced batts**. Some have no vapor retarder and are called **unfaced batts**. The vapor retarder is usually a heavy paper called **Kraft paper**. Aluminum foil and plastic vapor retarders are also available. Batt insulation is easily available to homeowners at a comparatively low cost, which makes do-it-yourself installation common. Poor installation of this material is common, even with professional installation.

The most common type of batt insulation is made from fiberglass. Fiberglass, as the name suggests, is made from fine glass fibers. **Mineral wool** is another less common insulation type. Mineral wool is made from natural minerals (rocks) or from waste products from steel production (slag). **Batts made from cotton** are marketed as eco-friendly insulation, but are uncommon. **Batts made from recycled plastic** are also marketed as eco-friendly, but are uncommon.

Fiberglass batts range between about **R-3 (standard) to R-4 (high density) per inch. Mineral wool batts** are about **R-3.7 per inch. Cotton batts** are about **R-3.7 per inch. Plastic batts** are about **R-4 per inch**. Note that R-values vary depending on the specific product. Unfaced batt insulation is not an air barrier nor is it a vapor retarder.

Fiberglass insulation can irritate skin and lungs, but this is not an issue for homeowners unless they are repeatedly exposed. Some claim that fiberglass insulation is a possible carcinogen; however, this claim does not appear to be substantiated.

Fiberglass Batts Improperly Installed, Not Cut to Fit Wall Cavity.

Loose Fill/Blown-In Insulation

Loose fill (also called blown-in or blown) insulation comes in bags. The material is usually poured into the hopper of a machine that uses air to blow the insulation through a hose into the space being insulated. The material can be poured directly from the bag, but this installation method may not be recommended by manufacturers because it does not provide the recommended mix of air and insulation material to provide the expected R-value.

Loose fill insulation is usually installed on the attic floor. The material can be blown into fabric suspended from the rafters in unventilated attics. Cellulose loose fill can be blown into wall cavities. This is sometimes done in new construction and when insulating older houses that do not have wall cavity insulation.

Loose Fill Cellulose Insulation Being Blown Into A Wall (Left), and Hanging From Trusses in Fabric in a Closed Attic (Right).

Most **loose fill insulation** is usually made from **fiberglass** or **cellulose**. Mineral wool and cotton are also available, but are less common. Cellulose insulation is made from recycled paper that is treated to make it fire retardant. Other loose fill insulation materials include vermiculite, perlite, and Expanded Polystyrene (EPS). We cover these materials in other sections of this book.

Loose fill fiberglass, like fiberglass batts, is available in low and high density versions. The low density version is very light and can be moved very easily by air currents in the attic. **Low density fiberglass** R-value is about **R-2.2 per inch**. High density fiberglass is heavier and is less easily moved. **High density fiberglass** R-value is about **R-2.7 per inch**. **Loose fill cellulose** insulation R-value is about **R-3.5 per inch**. **Loose fill mineral wool** R-value is about **R-3.1 per inch**. A blown-in fiberglass system called Blown-in Batts (Blankets) is also available, but is less common. Its R-value is about R-3.8 per inch. Loose fill insulation is not an air-barrier, nor is it a vapor retarder.

Cellulose insulation and mineral wool insulation are heavier than fiberglass insulation. The extra weight can be an issue when this insulation is applied in an attic framed at 24 inches on center with ½ inch thick drywall. Insulation upgrades in attics with trusses are one situation where insulation weight could create a problem.

High Density Loose Fill Fiberglass Insulation. Note Absent Insulation Shield Around Vent in Left Picture. Insulation in Right Picture is Mixed with Loose Fill Mineral Wool.

Low Density Loose Fill Fiberglass Insulation (Left). Note the Wind Wash Void Caused by Air Movement. Loose Fill Mineral Wool Insulation (Right). Pink Insulation is High Density Loose Fill Fiberglass.

Sheet/Rigid Insulation

Sheet insulation is most commonly available in 4 foot wide sheets of various lengths (8 to 10 feet are the most common). Common thicknesses are ½ and 1 inch, but thicker sheets are also available. This insulation is often applied as exterior sheathing, so it is often not visible during a home inspection. It may, however, be visible in attics and crawl spaces. Many types of **sheet and spray foam insulation may need protection from ignition because they are flammable** and because they produce toxic smoke when they burn. We discuss thermal and ignition barriers for foam plastic materials in the structural walls section in the Structure Components chapter.

Several types of sheet insulation are available. **Expanded Polystyrene (EPS)** is usually white and looks like a sheet of white beads stuck together (which is what it is). The R-value of **EPS sheets** is about **R-4 per inch**. The permeability of 1 inch of EPS is about 5.0, which makes it a Class III vapor retarder. EPS is an air barrier if the seams are sealed. EPS is also available as a loose fill material with an R-value of about R-2.5 per inch.

Extruded Polystyrene (XPS) is usually pink, blue, or green depending on the manufacturer. Its R- value is about **R-5 per inch**. The permeability of 1 inch of XPS is about 1.1, which makes it a Class III vapor retarder but very close to a Class II vapor retarder. XPS is an air barrier if the seams are sealed.

Polyisocyanurate and **polyurethane** are usually a light orange or a light yellow color. Both often have a foil vapor retarder or radiant barrier on both sides which makes them Class I vapor retarders. Both lose some R-value over time as the gas inside escapes. They may start with an R-value around R-8 per inch, but the **long term R-value is about R-6 per inch**. These sheets are air barriers if the seams are sealed.

XPS Sheet Insulation.

Spray Foam Insulation

Most spray foam insulation is either polyisocyanurate or polyurethane. These materials are available in bulk form for large jobs or in cans or kits for homeowner use. They are mixed with a blowing agent that controls how much the material expands when applied. Many types of sheet and spray foam insulation may need protection from ignition because they are flammable and because they produce toxic smoke when they burn. We discuss thermal and ignition barriers for foam plastic materials in the structural walls section in the Structure Components chapter.

Polyisocyanurate Spray Foam Insulation in a Closed Crawl Space (Left) and in a Closed Attic (Right).

Other types of foam insulation are currently available. Cementitious foam (such as Air Krete) is available, but is uncommon. Latex foam is primarily a consumer product that is sold in cans for small sealing projects. Latex foam is an open cell product and should not be used as a substitute for caulking where water sealing is required.

Spray foam insulation is used for many applications. It can be sprayed or injected into walls. It can be sprayed on roof sheathing and rafters and on crawl space walls and framing. It can be used in place of loose fill and batt insulation on attic floors, but is often not because it is more expensive. It can be sprayed on top of a roof as a roof covering.

Polyisocyanurate and polyurethane foam come in two types, **open cell** (½ pound) and **closed cell** (2 pound). Both types are effective air barriers. Open cell is not a vapor retarder and will allow passage of liquid water. Closed cell is a vapor retarder (depending on installed thickness) and will not allow passage of liquid water. Closed cell adds some structural rigidity to the framing assembly. The R-value of **open cell** is about **R-3.7 per inch**; **closed cell** is about **R-6 per inch**.

Other Insulation Types

Vermiculite and Perlite
Vermiculite is a type of volcanic rock made mostly of silicone and oxygen. It has several uses including as an insulating material. As an insulation material it is also known by the brand name Zonolite and is most commonly found in houses built before 1950; however, houses built later could have vermiculite insulation. Vermiculite insulation is usually gray/brown or silver/gold in color and looks like gravel. **Vermiculite** has an R-value of about **R-2.4 per inch**.

Vermiculite does not usually contain asbestos; however, **much of the vermiculite used in residential insulation came from a mine that also contained asbestos**. Vermiculite insulation is, therefore, a possible asbestos containing material. Most home inspectors report the presence of vermiculite with a recommendation to have a sample evaluated. Like most asbestos containing materials, vermiculite is not harmful if it is not disturbed. Also, like most asbestos containing materials, removal should be performed by a qualified abatement contractor and can be expensive.

Perlite is chemically similar to vermiculite. When used as loose fill insulation it usually presents as a coarse white gravel. Perlite is also available as a sheet insulation product. Loose fill **perlite** insulation has an R-value of about **R-2.4 per inch**. Perlite is not a possible asbestos containing material. Perlite is sometimes used to fill the cores of concrete blocks for insulation. There is some disagreement about the effectiveness of this insulation method based on the conductive heat flow through the concrete blocks. Refer to the discussion of thermal bridging.

Vermiculite Insulation.

Perlite Insulation.

Urea-Formaldehyde Foam (UFFI) This type of spray foam insulation was used as wall cavity insulation during the 1970s and early 1980s. **It is no longer used in residential applications because of formaldehyde off gassing.** This insulation will rarely be visible during a home inspection, but overflow may be visible in attics and crawl spaces. UFFI in homes was a health concern in the 1980s, but is **no longer a health concern** because the off gassing has subsided. The current concerns are that the insulation shrank somewhat after installation and that it may disintegrate over time. There is no way for a visual inspection to determine the condition of UFFI in a concealed wall.

UFFI Insulation.

Typical Defects Typical defects that home inspectors should report include:

1. **Insulation R-value is less than current standards:** this is not necessarily a deficiency unless it occurs in a newer house. The home inspector may want to recommend upgrading insulation that is significantly less than current standards. Note that measuring insulation is not required.

2. **Insulation depth is less than the normal depth for the material or less than the stated depth on the insulation card:** this is a common occurrence with loose fill insulation, especially in newer houses. Watch for installations where the insulation depth is increased near the depth markers.

**Sometimes You Measure to Find Inadequate Insulation (Left).
Sometimes They Make it Easy (Right).**

3. **Insulation is absent at conditioned space:** insulation may not have been installed or it may have fallen or been moved. This condition is common at locations, such as vertical sidewalls in attics, at skylight chases, around work performed by contractors such as electricians and cable/satellite TV installers, and between joists in crawl spaces.

Insulation Absent at Raised Wall in Attic.   **An HVAC Supply Duct Indicates Conditioned Space Below.**

Insulation Absent at Skylight Chase. **Typical, But Poor, Skylight Chase Insulation. Insulation Not Cut to Fit and Not in Full Contact With Conditioned Space.**

4. **Insulation is compressed or disturbed:** some compression by foot traffic and settlement is normal and unavoidable; however, if the compression or disturbance is widespread, the R-value is significantly reduced. This is one reason why home inspectors are not required to, and may not wish to, walk through attic insulation.

Insulation Compressed by Foot Traffic and by Debris. R-value is Minimal.

5. **Insulation is not in contact with the air barrier at conditioned space:** insulation must be in contact with the wall covering, attic floor, or floor sheathing at conditioned space to be effective. An air gap renders the insulation useless at the location of the air gap.

Insulation is Frequently Not in Contact With Air Barrier When Floor Trusses are Used for Floor Framing. This Picture is in a Crawl Space. The Floor is Uninsulated

6. **Strands of batt insulation are hanging from insulation in a crawl space:** this may indicate that the insulation is or has been damp and that the R-value may be reduced; it also may indicate crawl space moisture problems.

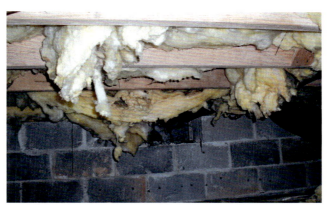

Insulation Strands and Displacement are Evidence of a Damp Crawl Space. Holes in Foundation Wall Blocks are Evidence of Termite Treatment.

7. **Insulation is blocking ventilation openings:** this often occurs at the eaves in the attic. Baffles should be installed to keep the insulation from blocking the eave ventilation openings. Baffles should allow at least 1 inch of space for air to flow; more space is better.

Adequate Baffle Installation at Eaves.

8. **Insulation is not cut to fit into the space:** insulation should be cut to fit between joists and between studs when the joists or studs are not spaced at the same width as the insulation. Insulation that is compressed loses significant R-value.

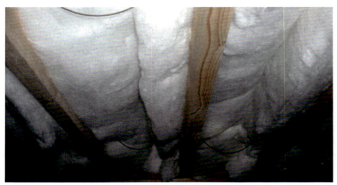 

Insulation Not Cut to Fit Between Joists. R-Value is Significantly Reduced in Left Picture and is Minimal in Right Picture.

9. **Insulation is not cut around obstructions: insulation should be cut to fit around obstructions, such as** electrical cables and boxes, plumbing pipes, and other obstructions.

10. **Chases are not fireblocked and are not insulated:** this is common for chimney and HVAC duct chases and around drop soffits such as those for cabinets and lights in kitchens and bathrooms. The chase should be fireblocked and appropriate insulation should be installed. Lack of fireblocking is a fire safety hazard and allows significant air leakage between conditioned and unconditioned spaces.

Insulation Absent at Walls Around Drop Ceiling for a Closet.

11. **Insulation is in contact with heat-generating components:** heat-generating components include appliance vents, chimneys, and recess lights that are not listed for insulation contact. Appliance vents and metal chimneys in newer houses should have an insulation shield around the vent or chimney to maintain separation from the insulation.

 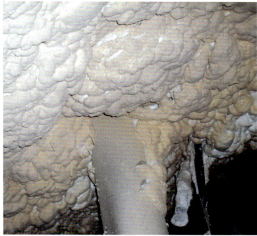

Insulation Shield Required to Separate Appliance Vent From Insulation.

12. **Vapor retarder is installed facing unconditioned space:** this creates a moisture trap that can allow condensation of water vapor between conditioned space and the vapor retarder. Exposed Kraft paper is a fire safety hazard.

Kraft Paper Vapor Retarder Should Not Be Exposed. It Says So On the Label.

13. **Multiple vapor retarders are installed:** only one vapor retarder should be installed when a vapor retarder is necessary. Multiple vapor retarders can trap moisture between the vapor retarders. Vapor retarders made from foam plastic may be a fire hazard.

Exposed Foam Plastic is Suspect Both as a Dual Vapor Retarder and as a Fire Hazard.

Standards (1) IRC 2018 R302.14 (insulation clearance to combustibles), R316 (foam plastic), Chapter 11 (energy efficiency requirements) G2426.4 (insulation shield for gas vents); (2) manufacturer's instructions.

ENERGY EFFICIENCY AND MOISTURE MANAGEMENT COMPONENTS

Water-Resistive Barriers (WRBs)

A water-resistive barrier is now required under all exterior wall cladding. These are also called **weather-resistant barriers**. A WRB has not always been required. For example, a WRB under vinyl siding is a recent requirement. Older houses may not have a WRB, or the WRB may have degraded over time. It is usually not possible to determine the presence or condition of a WRB under most wall claddings during a home inspection.

The original WRBs were asphalt saturated **Kraft paper (Grade D paper)** and **asphalt saturated felt** (usually #15). These materials work well as a WRB and provide some help as an air barrier when installed correctly. Installed correctly means horizontal seams lapped shingle fashion with upper material lapping over lower material at least 2 inches, vertical seams lapped at least 6 inches, and tears and holes repaired. **Correct installation was (and still is in many cases) uncommon.** These WRBs should not be vapor retarders in most cases.

Other WRB systems have replaced Grade D paper and #15 felt in many markets. These include **house wraps, liquid coatings,** and **wall sheathing with an integrated WRB**. House wraps have been available since the 1970s, but have become more widely used in the past fifteen to twenty years. WRB sheathing systems and liquid coatings are relatively recent products.

Installation of other WRB systems is per manufacturer's instructions. House wrap installation is usually similar to Grade D paper and #15 felt installation with horizontal seams lapped shingle fashion and vertical seams lapped. Wall sheathing with integrated WRB usually requires sealing the seams between sheets with tape supplied by the WRB manufacturer.

Modern House Wrap WRB. Improper Installation at Window. Most Manufacturers Recommend Folding House Wrap Into Opening to Integrate the House Wrap with Flashing.

Sheathing with Integrated WRB. All Joints Should Be Taped as Done in Gables.

Experience and testing indicates that liquid water and water vapor will penetrate through all wall claddings whether through holes or gaps in the cladding or by vapor drive. The problem is that many wall claddings are installed tight against the WRB leaving no air space to drain water and no air space to help reduce vapor diffusion. This is especially true of stucco and EIFS. Modern house wraps use various strategies to create a drainage channel as part of the house wrap. Strategies include grooves and dimples that give water a channel to drain. This drainage channel on the house wrap can help with draining liquid water, but it is not a complete solution. The better solution is to leave an air space between the WRB and the wall cladding, as is done with brick veneer. An air space is not currently required by model standards, but is required by some local standards for new houses.

Radiant Barriers

Radiant barriers are not insulation and provide no R-value. A radiant barrier is intended to reflect infrared radiation (heat) so that it does not enter the house. Radiant barriers are most effective in climate zones 1 and 2 (the Deep South and the Desert Southwest) in houses that are subject to significant solar heat gain. Maximum effectiveness occurs when a radiant barrier is installed in an attic that contains HVAC ducts and equipment. A properly installed radiant barrier can be quite effective at reducing attic temperature.

Radiant barriers are usually a reflective foil. In new houses, the foil can come attached to the underside of the roof sheathing. As a retrofit in older houses, the foil comes in rolls. Radiant barrier paint (interior radiation control coating) is also available; however, some of these paints may not function as a radiant barrier.

For maximum effectiveness a radiant barrier should be separated from the surface above it by an air gap. A radiant barrier may be hung from the rafters or truss top chords, or it may be installed on top of the ceiling joists or on top of truss bottom chords. Insulation should not be compressed by the radiant barrier. It is unwise to install a radiant barrier in contact with electrical cables, especially knob and tube wiring. A radiant barrier installed on top of the ceiling joists/truss bottom chords should be a perforated type that is not a vapor retarder; otherwise, moisture could be trapped under the radiant barrier and create significant mold and rot problems.

Radiant Barrier Installed on Truss Top Chords (Left), and as Part of Roof Sheathing (Right).

Perforated Radiant Barrier Installed on Ceiling Joists and Above Knob and Tube Wiring. The Knob and Tube Wiring Better Be Permanently Abandoned.

Fenestration

Houses must have windows and doors for occupant safety, convenience, health, and comfort. The problem with fenestration is that it is not possible for it to have anywhere close to the R-value of insulation. A typical **single pane wood window** has an R-value around **R-1**. A typical **double pane wood window** has an R-value around **R-1.8**. The best (very expensive) **triple pane inert gas filled windows** are only about **R-4.5**. A typical **wood door** is about **R-2**. Windows and doors with metal frames often have lower R-values unless the frame has a thermal break to reduce conductive heat flow through the metal.

Current standards require flashing and air sealing around fenestration to reduce water and air infiltration around these vulnerable openings. Current standards also require that fenestration be more energy efficient. Improved energy efficiency is achieved by building windows with a higher R-value (lower U-factor) and by installing coatings that reflect infrared radiation. Minimum fenestration R-values range from about R-2.5 in warm climates to about R-3.1 in cold climates. Determining fenestration R-value and proper installation of reflective coatings is out of scope for a home inspection.

Fenestration R-value improvements in windows include reducing air flow between the window and frame and reducing thermal bridging through the frame. Solar heat gain improvements in windows are achieved by installing low emissivity coatings on the glass. Refer to the exterior windows section in the Exterior Components chapter for more information about low emissivity coatings.

Clients sometimes ask home inspectors about replacing old windows with more energy efficient windows. The consensus appears to be that the time required to recover the investment in new windows is usually measured in decades, making replacement windows a questionable financial investment. The financial aspect does not account for the risk of improper flashing and other installation problems that could cause damage to the house.

Recommended Energy Efficiency Values

The following table presents current (2018) minimum R-values and U-factors for residential building insulation and fenestration. Interpretation and enforcement of these values will vary among jurisdictions. There are multiple methods of complying with energy efficiency requirements, so failure of a component or assembly to comply with these values is not necessarily a defect, even in new construction. Existing construction is not required to comply with current requirements; however, replacement windows and doors may be required to do so.

Options are provided to achieve some recommended R-values. For example, the wood-framed wall R-value in the climate zone 3 row means that the R-value may be achieved by using continuous insulation (usually spray foam or sheet insulation) at R-20 or framing cavity insulation at R-13 plus sheet insulation at R-5. For example, the crawl space walls R-value in climate zone 6 may be achieved by using continuous insulation R-15 or framing cavity insulation at R-19.

Insulation and Fenestration Minimum Requirements

Climate zone	Fenestration U-factor (max.)	Skylight U-factor (max.)	Glazed fenestration and skylight SHGC (max.)	Ceiling R-value (max.)	Wood-framed wall R-value (min.)	Mass wall R-value (min.)	Floor R-value (min.)	Basement wall R-value (min.)	Slab R-value/depth (min.)	Crawl space walls R-value (min.)
1	none	0.75	0.25	30	13	3/4	13	0	0	0
2	0.40	0.65	0.25	38	13	4/6	13	0	0	0
3	0.32	0.55	0.25	38	20 or 13 + 5	8/13	19	5/13	0	5/13
4 except marine	0.32	0.55	0.40	49	20 or 13 + 5	8/13	19	10/13	10/ 2 ft.	10/13
5 and marine 4	0.30	0.55	none	49	20 or 13 + 5	13/17	30	15/19	10/ 2 ft.	15/19
6	0.30	0.55	none	49	20 + 5 or 13 + 10	15/20	30	15/19	10/ 4 ft.	15/19
7 and 8	0.30	0.55	none	49	20 + 5 or 13 + 10	19/21	38	15/19	10/ 4 ft.	15/19

Standards (1) IRC 2018 R703.2 (water-resistive barriers), Table R703.3(1) (wall cladding installation), R703.1.1 (flashing), Table N1102.1.2 (energy efficiency requirements); (2) manufacturer's instructions.

MECHANICAL VENTILATION AND EXHAUST

Mechanical Ventilation Systems

Introduction Ventilation involves **bringing (fresh) outside air inside the house** and **removing (polluted) inside air to outside the house**. Both are usually required. Refer to the beginning of this chapter for more about ventilation requirements.

Current standards allow intermittent or continuous ventilation when whole house mechanical ventilation is required. With new air sealing standards, whole house mechanical ventilation is often required in new houses. Intermittent whole house mechanical ventilation may involve connecting an outside air duct to the HVAC return. Outside air is drawn by the return suction when the system is running. Local exhaust systems, such as for bathrooms and the kitchen, provide inside air removal in this system. Continuous or intermittent mechanical ventilation may be provided by a whole house ventilation system such as a Heat Recovery Ventilation System (HRV) or an Energy Recovery Ventilation System (ERV).

Adding Outside Air by Duct Connected HVAC System The HVAC connected outside air duct method is inexpensive to install, and can provide the recommended outside ventilation air. This method is common in some markets. An **automatic damper** that closes when the system is not active should be installed in the duct system.

There are several possible problems with this method. The first problem is that this method is unbalanced, meaning that more air may enter the house through the outside air duct than leaves the house through other openings and through local exhaust systems. The air entering the house through the outside air duct may increase the air pressure in the house and can force air out of the house. If this air is moist and collects in the wall cavities or in the attic or crawl space, it can create moisture and mold problems. Another problem is that the homeowner must pay to heat and cool this outside air, which can add to the energy bills. Some people discover this problem and block off the outside air duct. Still another problem is that cold outside air can cause water to condense in the HVAC system and create mold problems. This condensation problem mostly occurs in cold climates in the winter. Finally, this method relies on occupants to use the local exhaust systems to remove pollutants, which is something they often do not do. These and other problems make the outside air duct a less than ideal solution for providing ventilation air.

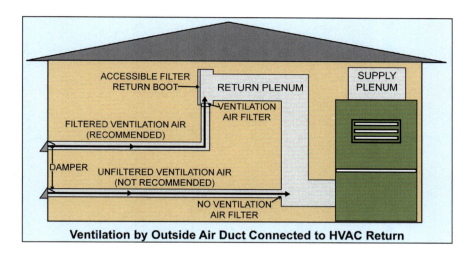

Ventilation by Outside Air Duct Connected to HVAC Return

Outside Air Duct (Right Side of Picture) is Properly Connected to Filter. Unfortunately Sellers Did Not Know About the Filter, So It Had Not Been Replaced in Years.

Ventilation by Heat Recovery Ventilation Systems (HRVs) and Energy Recovery Ventilation Systems (ERVs)
HRVs and ERVs may provide ventilation by operating continuously or intermittently. They rely less on occupant intervention to provide the recommended amount of ventilation air and to remove pollutants compared to the HVAC connected duct method; however, HRVs and ERVs rely more on occupant intervention to clean the equipment, replace filters, and maintain the system. Because these systems are new in many areas, occupants are frequently unaware of the need to clean and maintain them. HRVs and ERVs are more expensive to install and to operate compared to the HVAC connected duct method.

During heating season, both HRVs and ERVs absorb some of the heat from the exhaust air leaving the home and transfer it to the ventilation air entering the home. During cooling season, they absorb heat from the ventilation air entering the home and transfer to the exhaust air leaving the home. This reduces the energy efficiency penalty when the unconditioned supply air is brought into the house.

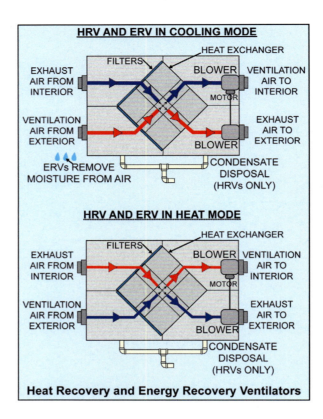

The difference between an HRV and an ERV is that **HRVs transfer only heat** between the incoming supply and outgoing exhaust air, while **ERVs transfer heat and some moisture**. Absorbing some of the moisture from the incoming supply air reduces the latent load on the air conditioning system, which improves air conditioning efficiency and reduces air conditioning costs.

HRVs and ERVs are installed in one of three duct configurations. The **fully ducted** configuration uses exhaust ducts connected to grilles in bathrooms, the kitchen, and laundry to remove pollutants and uses supply ducts to provide outside ventilation air to the living areas. The fully ducted configuration operates independently from the HVAC system and is the only suitable configuration for houses without ducted heating and cooling. The **partially ducted** configuration uses exhaust ducts connected to grilles in bathrooms, the kitchen, and utility rooms to remove pollutants and provides outside ventilation air to living areas through the HVAC return duct. The **simplified duct** configuration draws some pollutants from the HVAC return duct, and provides outside ventilation air through the HVAC return duct by connecting the outside ventilation air further downstream from where the exhaust air duct connects to the return duct. The simplified duct configuration relies on the local exhaust fans to remove most pollutants and on the HVAC system fan to circulate outside ventilation the air. The HVAC system fan must either be set to run continuously or the fan must be linked to the HRV or ERV controls and set to run on a timed basis. The fully ducted configuration relies on the HRV or ERV internal fans to remove pollutants and circulate ventilation air.

5: Insulation and Ventilation

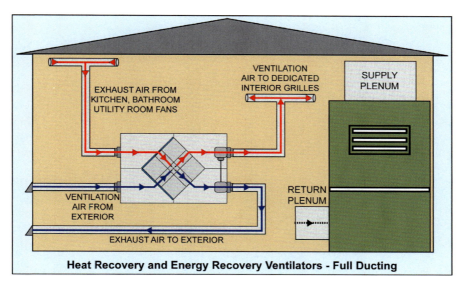
Heat Recovery and Energy Recovery Ventilators - Full Ducting

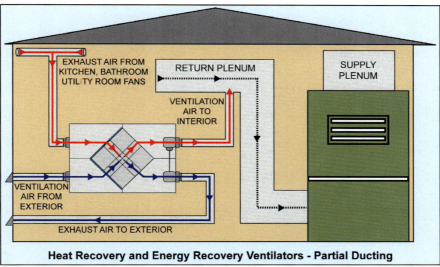
Heat Recovery and Energy Recovery Ventilators - Partial Ducting

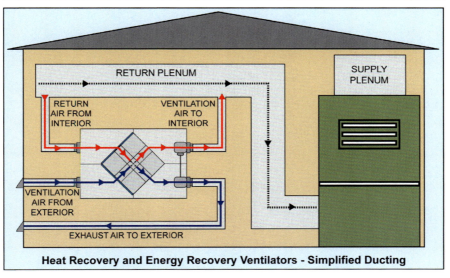
Heat Recovery and Energy Recovery Ventilators - Simplified Ducting

Heat Recovery Ventilator.

Installation of HRVs and ERVs should be according to manufacturer's instructions. **HRVs may be installed in any climate** and are **recommended for cold climates**. **ERVs are recommended for mild climates** and are **not recommended for cold climates**. Installation in conditioned space is usually recommended for more reliable operation and for ease of cleaning and maintenance. Exhaust ducts should not be installed in a room with a combustion appliance, including a fireplace. Some manufacturers recommend installing a washable filter in an exhaust grille terminating in the kitchen. Exterior supply and exhaust termination hoods usually should be installed at least 18 inches above grade or above the anticipated snow accumulation depth. There should be at least 6 feet horizontal separation between the two hoods. The exterior terminations should be covered with a screen. HRVs produce condensate during the defrost cycle and need a condensate drainage system. Pipes or tubes may be used per manufacturer's instructions. An auxiliary condensate management system may be required by local jurisdictions.

Exhaust and supply air flow through HRVs and ERVs should be balanced during installation and balancing should be verified periodically. Balancing is usually accomplished by adjusting dampers that are installed in the exhaust intake and ventilation outlet ducts.

It is not possible to determine if HRVs and ERVs are properly balanced and operating as intended during a home inspection. Home inspectors should consider disclaiming a system functional inspection and recommending evaluation by a qualified contractor.

<u>**Typical Defects**</u> Typical defects that home inspectors should report include:

1. **Air intake exterior opening too close to a vent or exhaust:** a mechanical air intake opening should be at least 10 feet horizontally or 3 feet below a chimney, fuel-burning appliance vent, a plumbing vent, or an exhaust termination. The air intake opening should also be at least 6 feet from the HRV/ERV exhaust termination.

2. **Exhaust exterior opening too close to a building opening:** an exhaust opening should be at least 3 feet from a door, operable window, or the property line. The opening should be at least 10 feet horizontally or at least 3 feet above a mechanical air intake opening.

5: Insulation and Ventilation

3. **No screen or protection at air intake or exhaust exterior opening:** exterior openings should be protected by a screen, louvers, or grille.

4. **Blocked exterior openings:** openings are sometimes blocked because of poor installation or by animal nests.

5. **No filter on air intake:** a filter is not required on HVAC duct connected systems; however, lack of a filter can allow dust and debris to block the evaporator coil.

6. **Crimped or damaged ducts:** ducts serving these systems should be installed using the same guidelines as HVAC ducts.

7. **Lack of recommended maintenance:** HRVs and ERVs need regular cleaning of filters and heat exchanger cores; discovering this may require removal of an access panel.

Standards: (1) IRC 2018 R303.4 (mechanical ventilation requirements), R303.5 and 6 (opening location and protection), N1103.6 (dampers for openings), Chapter 11 (energy efficiency requirements), M1505 (mechanical ventilation requirements); (2) ANSI/ASHRAE 62.2-2016 (residential ventilation); (3) manufacturer's instructions.

Whole-house Fans

Description A traditional whole-house fan is a large (usually 24 to 36 inch diameter) fan that is installed in the ceiling, usually in a central hallway. When a traditional whole-house fan is activated, louvers in the ceiling open and the fan pulls air from open windows through the house and exhausts the air into the attic. A newer style fan exhausts the air through an opening in the roof or a gable wall and connects the fan using ducts to an opening in the ceiling. Both fan styles work by making occupants feel cooler because of evaporation of moisture from their skin caused by the air movement.

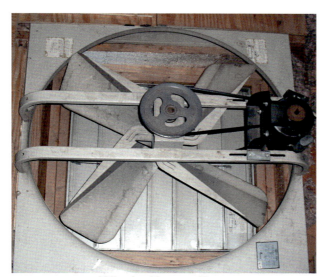

Whole-House Fan.

A whole-house fan can reduce the need to run air conditioning. These fans use only a small fraction of the electricity used by an air conditioner. Fans are most cost-effective in cooler and dryer climates where air conditioning is used for fewer months during the year. They are less effective in warm/humid climates and in hot climates.

Whole-house fans can create several problems. The primary occupant complaint about whole-house fans is **noise**, especially traditional models. Another problem is that **they allow large amounts of conditioned air to escape into the attic during the winter**. This problem can be mitigated by building an insulated box that is placed around the fan during the winter. Fans that rely on exhausting the air into the attic should have sufficient attic ventilation openings to allow the air to escape and not be forced back into the house through openings between the attic and the house. A ratio of 1 square foot of net free ventilation openings per 750 cubic feet per minute of fan air flow is a common recommendation.

There are at least two situations when a whole-house fan is not recommended. **A fan should not be used when a combustion appliance draws combustion air from inside the house.** This applies mostly to gas water heaters and gas clothes dryers because furnaces and other heating appliances are usually not running at the same time as the fan. **A fan should not be used when the attic has possible asbestos containing substances such as vermiculite insulation, or any other potentially toxic substance.** This material could be blown back into the house.

<u>**Typical Defects**</u> Typical defects that home inspectors should report include:

1. fan does not operate using normal controls,
2. damaged louvers, some or all do not operate,
3. loose or worn fan drive belt,
4. winter cover damaged or not available,
5. attic ventilation openings inadequate in area or blocked.

Local Exhaust Systems

<u>**Introduction**</u> Local exhaust systems include those for the **kitchen, bathrooms, laundry,** and the **clothes dryer**. These systems are often called vents, as in kitchen vent or bathroom vent. The **preferred term is exhaust** because it more accurately describes the function of these systems, and it distinguishes them from other systems, such as appliance vents and plumbing vents.

Some requirements apply to all air intake and exhaust systems, except for the clothes dryer exhaust (no screen allowed). Install a **screen on the outdoor air intake and exhaust openings** to restrict vermin entry. The screen should have openings between ¼ and ½ inch. Install a **damper in the air intake and exhaust system that automatically closes** when the system is not operating. Install an accessible filter in the HVAC connected air intake system to remove some of the dust in the outside air (recommended but not required).

<u>**Clothes Dryer Exhaust**</u> Proper installation of the clothes dryer exhaust system is important for safety and for efficient clothes dryer operation. Lint can collect in properly installed ducts, and is more likely to collect in improperly installed ducts. **Lint is flammable and if ignited can cause a fire.** Fires in clothes dryer exhaust ducts number in the thousands; many of these are caused by lack of cleaning. Blockage of the duct by lint will reduce air flow and cause the clothes dryer to take longer to dry clothes.

The clothes dryer exhaust duct should be **4 inches in diameter**, minimum 28 gauge, **smooth wall metal** (usually galvanized steel). PVC ducts encased in concrete may be allowed in some jurisdictions. A smaller diameter may not allow sufficient air flow for the dryer to function properly. A larger diameter may not allow the air to flow at sufficient velocity to carry the lint through the duct. Duct sections should be connected such that the smaller end fits into the larger end in the direction of air flow. The sections should be mechanically fastened using pop rivets or sheet metal screws not longer than 1/8 inch. These rules help avoid projections that could trap lint. The duct should be supported at least every 12 feet (4 feet for gas clothes dryers).

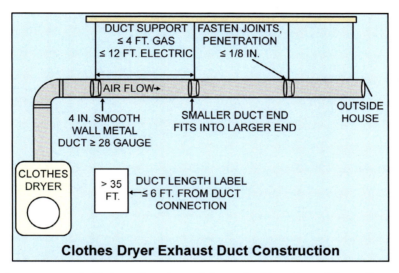

Clothes Dryer Exhaust Duct Construction

The duct should not exceed 35 feet developed length. Developed length means the straight length of the duct plus additional length to account for the reduction in air flow caused by fittings that change duct direction. Add 5 feet for most 90° bend fittings and 2½ feet for most 45° bend fittings. Long (smooth) radius bend fittings are available. These fittings have a smaller developed length. Refer to the fitting manufacturer's instructions or the IRC for developed length of these fittings. **Duct developed length does not include the transition duct.** It is acceptable for the duct developed length to exceed 35 feet if the clothes dryer manufacturer's instructions permit, which many do.

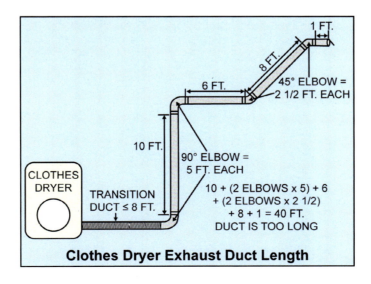

Clothes Dryer Exhaust Duct Length

The **transition duct** is the (usually) flexible duct between the clothes dryer and the exhaust duct. The transition duct should **not be more than 8 feet long. It may not be run through walls, floors, or ceilings and may not be concealed.** The transition duct should be made from a metallic material that conforms to UL2158A. The transition duct should be cut as short as possible and should not be crimped or constricted. Improperly installed transition ducts reduce air flow, cause the clothes dryer to work longer, and could cause additional lint accumulation in the exhaust duct. Clothes dryers and the transition duct are out of scope of a home inspection; however, some home inspectors comment about the transition duct.

Not Much Air Will Flow Through This Crimped Transition Duct.

Condensing clothes dryers are available. These appliances condense the moisture from the dryer exhaust and discharge it into the plumbing waste pipes. These appliances do not require an external exhaust duct. These appliances are uncommon in the United States.

Clothes dryers exhaust a lot of air. This air must come from somewhere. When a clothes dryer is located in a closet and the doors are shut, there is probably not enough makeup air to allow effective dryer operation. This could cause the dryer to operate for longer periods and could allow lint to collect in the exhaust duct. **An opening of at least 100 square inches should be provided for gas dryers located in a closet.** The opening may be in the door or as an opening in the wall. This requirement is specific to gas-fired dryers located in closets; however, it is a good idea for any dryer located in a closet or small laundry room.

Typical Defects, Clothes Dryer Exhaust
Typical defects that home inspectors should report include:

1. **Duct too large or too small:** the duct should be 4 inches diameter unless the manufacturer's instructions for the installed dryer allow another size; this exception is uncommon.

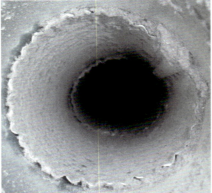

Three Inch Diameter Corrugated Duct. Note Lint Accumulation in Duct.

2. **Duct terminates inside an enclosed space including the attic or crawl space:** the duct should terminate to the exterior. Excess moisture accumulating in enclosed space can damage materials and provide moisture for fungal growth. Lint accumulation can be a fire hazard.
3. **Duct disconnected before the exterior termination hood:** this is a moisture damage hazard and a fire hazard.

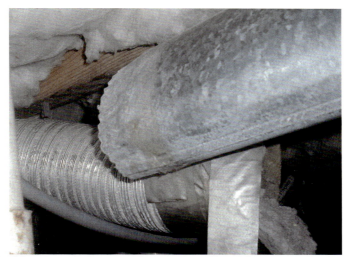

Duct Disconnected in Crawl Space. Transition Duct Improperly Run in Crawl Space.

4. **Duct terminates within 3 feet from a door, window, mechanical air intake, or crawl space ventilation opening:** this may allow the dryer exhaust to return into the house.
5. **Duct terminates within 3 feet from a condenser:** hot and moist dryer exhaust can reduce condenser efficiency and damage the condenser.

Termination Too Close to Door.   **Termination Too Close to Condenser.**

6. **Duct terminates into a bucket:** these indoor lint trap buckets are not an approved method of exhausting a clothes dryer.
7. **Duct blocked by lint:** lint reduces air flow in the duct and is a fire hazard. Eucts sometimes need cleaning, especially if occupants do not clean the dryer lint filter.

8. **Excessive lint behind the dryer or at the termination hood:** this may indicate that the duct is blocked by lint.
9. **Screen installed at the termination hood:** a screen will trap lint and block the opening.

Wonder What the Duct Interior Looks Like?

A Screen Will Trap Lint.　　　　**Panty Hose Are Also Unacceptable.**

10. **Exterior damper stuck open or shut:** dampers are often blocked by wall coverings or by the screen at the terminal.
11. **Damaged or absent exterior damper:** the damper may not operate. An open damper provides a path for air to enter the house. An open damper allows vermin to enter the duct.
12. **Transition duct penetrates a floor, wall, or ceiling:** this is a fire hazard.
13. **Constricted or damaged transition duct:** this restricts air flow into the duct.

Maximum Transition Duct Length is 8 Feet.

Transition Ducts May Not Penetrate Floors.

Standards Clothes Dryer Exhaust (1) IRC 2018 M1502 (electric clothes dryer exhaust), G24394 (gas clothes dryer makup air and exhaust); (2) manufacturer's instructions.

Kitchen Exhaust An exhaust fan is not required in a kitchen. If installed, the fan is not required to be ducted to the outdoors if mechanical or natural ventilation is provided. Mechanical ventilation means a forced-air HVAC system or one of the whole-house ventilation systems described in this section. Natural ventilation means an operable window in the kitchen area. If installed, the fan should operate at a rate of at least 100 cubic feet per minute.

Higher exhaust rate fans are sometimes installed in houses, especially when with commercial-type cooking appliances are installed. These higher rate exhaust fans can draw air from other fuel-burning appliances, especially if combustion air is drawn from inside the house. Makeup air should be provided for fans with an exhaust rate exceeding 400 cubic feet per minute. Makeup air is required only if there is a gas, liquid, or solid fuel-burning appliance within the house air barrier. An exception exists for direct vent and mechanical draft appliances. The makeup air system should be equipped with a damper.

Kitchen exhaust fans are available in two general types. The most common is a **hood or a microwave oven** with an exhaust fan installed above the cooktop. These exhaust fans can usually be installed as an externally exhausted fans with an exhaust duct, or as a recirculating fan. The less common type is the **downdraft,** in which a fan and duct are installed under the cooktop. Downdraft exhausts are often used when the cooktop is located in an island.

Kitchen exhaust ducts installed above ground should be constructed using single wall metal with a **smooth interior surface.** Galvanized steel is the most common material. Stainless steel and copper are also allowed. Kitchen exhaust ducts may be installed under a concrete slab. The duct material for under-slab ducts may be Schedule 40 PVC.

Kitchen exhaust fan ducts should terminate outside the house. **Outside does not include the attic or the crawl space.**

Duct size and length are per the fan manufacturer's instructions. Round ducts are usually at least 6 inches diameter. Rectangular ducts are usually at least 3¼ x 10 inches. The duct should be air tight from the fan to the termination hood. A backdraft damper should be installed. The damper may be installed at the termination hood or at the fan.

Standards, Kitchen Exhaust (1) IRC 2018 M1503 (kitchen exhaust); (2) manufacturer's instructions.

Typical Defects, Kitchen Exhaust Typical defects that home inspectors should report include:

1. **Duct constructed using non-metallic materials, or materials without a smooth interior wall:** kitchen exhaust ducts run above ground may not be constructed using materials other than smooth wall galvanized steel, stainless steel, or copper.

Unacceptable Kitchen Exhaust Duct Materials.

2. **Duct not air tight:** a common installation technique is to blow the fan exhaust into the cabinet space above the hood or microwave without connecting the fan to the duct. This allows some of the grease in the exhaust air to collect in the wood cabinet and could result in a grease fire.

3. **Absent or damaged screen or protection at exterior opening:** exterior openings should be protected by a screen, louvers, grille, or exterior damper to keep vermin out and to keep them from blocking the duct.

4. **Blocked exterior opening:** openings are sometimes blocked because of poor installation or by vermin nests.

5. **Exterior damper is stuck open or shut:** dampers are often blocked by wall coverings or by the screen at the terminal.

6. **Small duct or exterior terminal:** this will restrict air flow, the exhaust will not function properly and grease could collect in the duct.

Exhaust Opening Size Restricted by Stucco.

7. **Absent or blocked grease filters:** the fan will not function properly without these filters. Grease could collect in the duct creating a fire hazard.
8. **Duct terminates inside the building:** exhaust ducts should terminate outside the building. **Attics and crawl spaces are considered inside the building.**

Termination at a Gable Ventilation Opening is Inside the Building.

<u>**Bathroom Exhaust**</u> **A local exhaust fan is not required in a bathroom if mechanical or natural ventilation is provided.** Mechanical ventilation means one of the whole-house ventilation methods described in this chapter. Mechanical ventilation does not include a forced-air HVAC system. Natural ventilation means an operable window in the bathroom. Bathroom exhaust fans were often not installed in older houses where an operable window was located in the bathroom. **Current best practice is to install an exhaust fan in all bathrooms including those with an operable window.** Failure to follow best practice is not a deficiency; however, the presence of moisture related problems in a bathroom without an exhaust fan is a reportable deficiency. If installed, the fan should exhaust at a rate of at least 50 cubic feet per minute when operation is controlled by a switch.

Bathroom exhaust fans should be exhausted to the exterior. The exterior does not include the attic, crawl space, or soffit. Exhausting bathroom fans into these areas was common practice until recently. Some home inspectors report bathroom fans that are not exhausted to the exterior in older homes as a deficiency and some recommend outdoor exhausting as an upgrade.

Duct size and length are per the fan manufacturer's instructions; however the 2018 IRC effectively eliminates the use of 3 inch diameter flexible duct. Typical duct material is flexible foil covered 3 or 4 inch diameter. Insulated flexible HVAC duct is sometimes necessary when running bathroom ducts though uninsulated spaces in cold climates to reduce condensation on the duct.

Typical Defects, Bathroom Exhaust Typical defects that home inspectors should report include:

1. fan exhausted into the attic, crawl space, soffit or other location that is not to the exterior,
2. damaged, kinked, or crushed duct,
3. duct connected to another system such as a plumbing vent or the clothes dryer exhaust duct,
4. absent, damaged, stuck shut or stuck open damper at exterior termination hood,
5. fan does not function,
6. unusually noisy fan,
7. grille blocked by dust,
8. water staining near fan or duct, sometimes caused by condensation.

Standards, Bathroom Exhaust (1) IRC 2018 R303.3 (bathroom exhaust), M1505 (local exhaust); (2) manufacturer's instructions.

Duct Terminates in Attic. This Material and Duct Diameter is No Longer Allowed.

Duct Not Extended Through Wall. Probably Pushed in During Wall Covering Installation.

Damaged Duct.

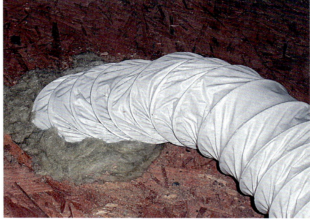
Crushed Duct.

Damper Will Not Open.

Absent Hoods and Dampers.

ATTIC VENTILATION

Ventilated Attics

Introduction If an attic is to be ventilated, it is important that the ventilation openings and ventilation devices be properly planned and installed. **Attic ventilation includes roof structures where there is no accessible attic**, including when finish materials such as drywall are applied to the bottom of the rafters (vaulted ceilings), and **including low slope roofs that preclude an accessible attic**. Attic ventilation also **includes attics above unconditioned spaces**, such as an attached garage.

The alternative to a ventilated attic is to completely seal the attic from the outdoors and turn the attic into conditioned space. This alternative is attractive in high wind zones because it reduces opportunities for water intrusion and for wind-caused attic pressurization that can lift the roof off of the house. This alternative is also attractive when HVAC equipment is installed in the attic because it places the equipment in conditioned space and improves its operating efficiency and effectiveness.

The benefits of attic ventilation change with the seasons and vary based on climate zone. Attic ventilation helps keep the roof deck cold in the winter so that ice dams are less likely to form and helps remove water vapor that leaks into the attic from the house. This benefit is most important in cold climates. Attic ventilation helps reduce the attic temperature in the summer, both to reduce air conditioning costs, and to protect roof coverings from overheating and reducing their service life. This benefit is most important in warm climates. It is important to note, however, that roof covering color (lighter and more reflective) and radiant barriers can have a greater impact on reducing attic temperature than can attic ventilation.

Attic ventilation that functions properly involves more than just installing the required ventilation area. The goal is uniform air flow throughout the entire attic, with air entering from the eave openings and exiting through the ridge openings. The types of ventilation openings and their locations are important to achieving this goal. The stack effect is one engine driving attic air flow. Cooler air enters through the eave openings and warmer air leaves through the ridge openings. Wind is another engine driving attic air flow. Wind flowing across the roof creates negative pressure at the ridge that can help pull air through the ridge openings. This is one reason why it is important to locate ridge ventilation openings at the ridge.

Equally important to good attic ventilation is avoiding ventilation openings and devices that compete with each other, and potentially disrupt the air flow. For example, a powered attic ventilator fan installed with ridge ventilation openings will compete with each other. The fan will draw air from the nearest air source, the ridge ventilation opening. Air circulation will occur mostly high in the attic. This situation makes the powered attic ventilator ineffective and potentially harmful because air flow from the eave ventilation may be reduced. This can create hot areas in the lower attic.

Another example of potentially competing attic ventilation openings involves using different types of openings high in the attic, such as ridge ventilation and gable ventilation. This situation frequently occurs when new roof coverings are installed and continuous ridge ventilation is installed in a house originally equipped with gable ventilation. Depending on the wind speed and direction, the ridge ventilation may draw most or all air from the gable ventilation creating dead air zones lower in the attic. Gable ventilation openings should be blocked when ridge ventilation is installed.

The traditional focus of attic ventilation was installing the prescribed amount of ventilation openings. As discussed earlier, a house is a system. **An important part of achieving the benefits of attic ventilation is addressing the entire attic system.** Sealing openings between the attic and the house is important. Sealing leaks from HVAC systems located in the attic is important. Avoiding recessed lights or using models that are air sealed and insulation contact rated is important. Reducing the moisture and temperature problems caused by these other systems can mitigate problems created by less than ideal attic ventilation.

<u>**Ventilation Area**</u> The **default attic ventilation area** requirement is **1 square foot of net free area for every 150 square feet of attic floor area** or other ventilated space. This default ventilation area requirement is **almost always reduced to 1 square foot of net free area for every 300 square feet of ventilated space** by installing the prescribed ratio of openings near the ridge and at the eaves. Net free ventilation area is the ventilation opening area reduced by the insect screen that usually covers the opening, and by any grilles or louvers that cover the opening. Screens should have a maximum opening of ¼ inch.

Calculating the net free attic ventilation area is out of scope of a home inspection; however, a home inspector should be able to make an educated estimate of attic ventilation area to determine if further evaluation may be appropriate. The net free area of a ventilation opening should be stated by the manufacturer. This information is almost never available to a home inspector. A reasonable assumption is that screens reduce the gross opening area by at least 25% and screens combined with louvers or grilles reduce the gross opening area by at least 50%.

Ventilation Installation The ideal locations for attic ventilation openings are continuous ventilation at the ridge and continuous ventilation in the eaves. At least 40% and not more than 50% of the opening area should be at the ridge with the remainder in the eaves. The ridge openings should be at the ridge, but are allowed to be located not more than 3 feet below the ridge. Eave openings were allowed to be installed above the eaves; however, installation at the eaves is required by current standards.

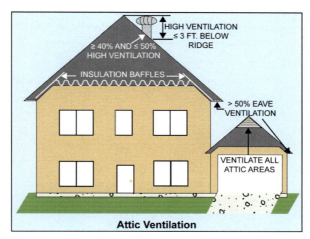

Attic Ventilation

These percentages and locations are important. An equal or smaller percentage of ridge ventilation to eave ventilation will create a neutral or slightly pressurized attic. This helps reduce leakage of air from the house into the attic. A larger percentage of ridge ventilation to eave ventilation will create a depressurized attic which can increase house to attic air leakage. Balanced opening percentages and locations are also important for achieving uniform air flow and attic temperature, especially in warm climate zones.

Ventilation openings should be protected from water intrusion. Ridge ventilation devices should have end caps or similar protection to prevent water intrusion. Gable ventilation should be protected by louvers, wide eaves, or other devices to reduce wind-blown rain. Ventilation covers, such as louvers and turbines, should be installed with the openings in the intended direction, be properly flashed, and be integrated into the roof covering.

The ventilation path should be continuous and unobstructed from the eaves to the ridge. The most common obstruction is insulation. The most common location where insulation obstructs the ventilation path is at the eaves. Baffles should be installed at the eaves to keep insulation from blocking the eave openings. Baffles are usually made from cardboard or foam plastic. The baffles should provide at least 1 inch of free area for air flow, although there is disagreement about this. Two inches is recommended by some experts and ½ inch is considered adequate by others. Baffles are often poorly installed, especially in retrofit situations when it is difficult to reach the area at the eaves from inside the attic.

Properly ventilating vaulted ceilings where the finish material (drywall) is installed directly on the rafters is a common problem. Insulation often blocks ventilation unless baffles are installed. Baffles should be continuous from the eaves to the ridge. Skylights are another obstruction that block continuous ventilation in vaulted ceilings. Installing ventilation openings above and below the skylight is one method of providing continuous ventilation. Notching the trimmer rafters on each side of the skylight is another method, but care must be taken not to impair the structural integrity of the rafters. Recessed lights in vaulted ceilings can also be a problem, especially the older models that are not air sealed. The home inspector should look for moisture staining on vaulted ceilings, especially around skylights and recessed lights. This staining could be caused by condensation, not by roof leaks, so evaluation by a **roofing contractor and an insulation contractor** may be prudent in this situation.

Ventilation Devices and Opening Covers
Attic ventilation openings consist of intakes at and near the eaves and exhausts at and near the ridge. Boxed eaves that are enclosed using wood products usually have individual openings cut between the rafter and covered by a rectangular or round louvered cover. Rectangular louvers are often 8x16 inches or 4x16 inches. Round louvers are available in various diameters. Continuous opening covers are usually between about 2 and 4 inches wide. Boxed eaves covered using vinyl and aluminum usually have perforated panels as the ventilation covers. Opening covers in open eaves are usually screen-covered holes in wood panels installed between the rafters or by the ventilated drip edge.

Ventilation opening covers and ventilation devices are available in several styles. A ridge ventilation opening cover covers an opening cut in the roof sheathing at the ridge. Some styles are simple aluminum covers with downward-facing perforations. More sophisticated styles may be a fiber or plastic mesh material that is covered by the roof covering cap, or may be metal or plastic with various configurations of perforations or baffles.

Various styles of ventilation opening covers are used to cover openings cut into the roof sheathing. The passive or static types include rectangular and round covers that are often called louvers or turtlebacks. These covers are used with most roof coverings including low slope roof coverings. Dormer covers are raised above the roof with louvered openings that are mostly vertical with respect to the roof; they get their name by looking like dormers projecting from the roof. O'Hagin covers are flat or rounded covers. Dormer and O'Hagin covers are popular with tile roof coverings. The turbine (or whirlybird) cover is an active type cover that rotates when blown by the wind. The rotating louvers create a slight suction that pulls air from the attic.

Gable ventilation openings are installed in gable end walls. They can be triangular, rectangular, or round. Gable ventilation openings are allowed; however, they are not ideal. They are subject to water intrusion, especially during high wind events. Water stains and water-compressed insulation are often found near gable ventilation openings. Gable ventilation openings do not ventilate well, especially if only one opening is installed in an area. Wind blowing against a single gable opening can drive air back into the attic. If there are two gable openings across the attic from each other, and if the wind is blowing against one of them, then cross circulation can take place. The problem is that the gable openings are acting as both the intake and exhaust. This can disrupt the air flow leaving the hot air near the roof deck. Gable openings also tend to act as both the intake and exhaust when the wind blows perpendicular to the gable openings. Ventilation occurs mostly near the gable openings leaving the remainder of the attic poorly ventilated.

5: Insulation and Ventilation

**Typical Rectangular Eave Ventilation Opening Cover.
Opening in Soffit is Much Smaller Than the Cover, a Common Defect.**

Modern Continuous Ridge Ventilation Opening Cover.

Turbine Ventilator. Note Lack of Cap Shingles on Ridge.

Turtleback Ventilation Opening Cover.

O'Hagin Ventilation Opening Covers.

Gable Ventilation Opening.

Typical Defects Typical defects that home inspectors should report include:

1. eave openings blocked, usually by insulation or poorly installed baffles,
2. ventilation opening covers (usually at the eaves) blocked, usually by paint,
3. damaged or absent ventilation opening covers,
4. ventilation opening covers, such as ridge covers, installed where no opening has been cut, or the covers are not installed directly over the opening, or openings are too small,
5. turbine ventilator does not turn,
6. powered attic ventilation fan does not function (service life can be as short as five years),
7. evidence of water infiltration near ventilation openings (usually at gable openings),
8. inadequate total ventilation opening area,
9. improper ventilation opening area distribution between eave and ridge openings,
10. improper ventilation opening location.

Standards (1) IRC 2018 R806 (roof ventilation); (2) manufacturer's instructions.

Poorly Installed Baffles.

Turbine Ventilator Cap Not Secured to Base.

Unventilated (Closed) Attic

Introduction **A closed attic is conditioned space** even if it has no HVAC supply or return duct openings. **Insulation and vapor retarders should be installed** above or below the roof sheathing, and at gable walls **in a similar manner to walls and ceilings in other conditioned parts of the house.**

Three methods exist for installing closed attic insulation and vapor retarders. **Attention to details is essential for effective installation of all closed attic methods.** Essential details are usually not visible during a home inspection, and the results of improper installation may not be visible during the inspection. **The home inspector should report this limitation to the client and recommend evaluation if the client wants more information about the installation details and the condition of the closed attic system.** Warning that hidden defects could exist is prudent.

Installing some roof coverings above a closed attic presents challenges. Current standards require a ventilated air space between wood roof coverings and the insulated attic assembly. Asphalt shingle manufacturers' warranties require a ventilated air space between the sheathing to which shingles are attached, and the insulated attic assembly. A home inspector should verify that some method of ventilation under these roof coverings exists or report that ventilation could not be confirmed and explain the consequences, including that the deficiency may void any manufacturer's warranty.

All closed attic methods share some common requirements. A Class I vapor retarder (such as polyethylene sheeting) should not be installed on the attic floor or at the ceiling above the closed attic space. Doing so would mean that vapor retarders are installed on both sides of the assembly and would trap any moisture entering the assembly. Air-impermeable insulation board installed between rafters or trusses should be sealed at the rafters or trusses and between sheets to form a continuous vapor retarding layer. **Sealing the joints is necessary to form a complete vapor retarder.** In cold climates, air-impermeable insulation should be a Class II vapor retarder, or should have a Class III vapor retarder applied to the attic ceiling side of the insulation.

A vapor diffusion port is required in closed attics located in climate zones 1, 2, and 3 when air-permeable insulation is installed. A vapor diffusion port allows movement of water vapor out of the attic, but does not allow air movement into or out of the attic. Refer to the IRC for additional information. The vapor diffusion port is a new requirement, so even recently built houses may not have one. Lack of a vapor diffusion port where currently required is, however, a reportable defect because lack of one can result in long term condensation problems in the attic.

Air-Impermeable Insulation Method Air-impermeable insulation may be installed either above or below the roof sheathing. Insulation board or closed-cell spray foam insulation may be installed below the sheathing, or insulation board may be installed above the sheathing. When asphalt shingles are used, a ventilation space can be constructed between the roof sheathing and insulation installed below the roof sheathing. This would involve installing a lower layer of roof sheathing to which insulation is applied, then installing spacers below a second layer of roof sheathing to which the roof covering is attached.

Air-Permeable Insulation Method Air-impermeable insulation is installed above the roof sheathing, and air-permeable insulation is installed below the roof sheathing. Air-impermeable insulation should also be installed below the roof sheathing in cold climates. The air permeable insulation can be batts, cellulose hung in fabric, or open-cell spray foam. The air-impermeable insulation can be insulation board above or below the roof sheathing, or the closed-cell spray foam below the roof sheathing. This method would be difficult to use with wood roof coverings and asphalt shingles and provide the required roof covering ventilation space.

Combination Method - Air-Permeable and Air-Impermeable Insulation Air-impermeable insulation is installed below the roof sheathing and air-permeable insulation is installed below the air-impermeable insulation. A ventilation space can be constructed between the roof sheathing and the air-impermeable insulation using this method.

Typical Defects Typical defects that home inspectors should report include:

1. openings to the exterior not sealed,
2. vapor retarder installed in the wrong location or not installed,
3. ventilation not provided for roof coverings when required,
4. thermal barrier or ignition barrier not installed to protect foam insulation,
5. damaged insulation,
6. absent or improperly installed vapor diffusion port where required.

Standards (1) IRC 2012 R316 (foam plastic fire protection), R806 (roof ventilation), Table N1102.1.2 (insulation amount requirements); (2) manufacturer's instructions.

CRAWL SPACE VENTILATION

Ventilated Crawl Spaces

Introduction The current majority opinion is that **passive crawl space ventilation as specified by current standards is not a good idea in most areas.** Places where ventilated crawl spaces can perform acceptably include hot dry climates, cool dry climates, and cool damp climates. Warm humid climates present problems such as condensation for crawl spaces in the summer. Cold climates present problems such as freezing pipes for crawl spaces in the winter.

Passive ventilation can bring more warm and humid air into a crawl space during the summer than is removed by the passive ventilation. The moisture is more likely to condense into liquid water because the air temperature in the crawl space is closer to the dew point temperature and because the temperature near the floor sheathing is cool because of air conditioning. Moisture often condenses on HVAC ducts located in the crawl space and sometimes condenses inside the ducts. Condensation can deteriorate the ducts. Moisture can condense on framing members and in insulation installed between floor joists. This can cause wood rot and fungal growth. Wet insulation has a significantly reduced R-value. Refer to the house as a system section in this chapter for an example of this problem.

Bringing cold air into a crawl space during the winter can cause water pipes to freeze and can increase heating costs by lowering the temperature in the crawl space. Occupants often close crawl space ventilation openings during the winter in cold climates. Sometimes they forget to open them in the spring.

Current standards require that a crawl space be either ventilated or closed, so the home inspector should determine if the crawl space is adequately ventilated or adequately closed. If the crawl space is ventilated (the vast majority are) the home inspector may wish to briefly advise the client about the problems associated with a ventilated crawl space.

It is important to remember that many crawl space (and basement) moisture problems are really grading, drainage, gutter and downspout, and landscape irrigation problems. **Attempts to correct crawl space moisture problems using sump pumps, interior foundation drains, and dehumidifiers often address the symptoms instead of providing a cure.** Discharging water away from the foundation and not applying water near the foundation (landscape irrigation) will often solve crawl space (and basement) moisture problems.

<u>**Ventilation Area**</u> The **default crawl space ventilation area requirement** is **1 square foot** of net free area for every **150 square feet** of crawl space floor area. This default ventilation area requirement **may be reduced to 1 square foot** of net free area for every **1,500 square feet** of crawl space floor area by installing a Class I vapor retarder (usually 6 mil polyethylene sheeting) on the crawl space floor. **The crawl space vapor retarder is frequently poorly installed.** While not required in a ventilated crawl space, the vapor retarder seams should be sealed and the edges should be sealed to walls and piers for maximum effectiveness. The home inspector should evaluate the installation to determine if the vapor retarder may function properly as installed.

Calculating the crawl space ventilation area is out of scope of a home inspection; however, a home inspector should be able to make an educated estimate of crawl space net free ventilation area to determine if further evaluation may be appropriate. Net free ventilation area of an opening is the ventilation opening area reduced by the insect screen that usually covers the opening, and by any grilles or louvers that cover the opening. Screens should have an opening of not less than ¼ inch. The net free area of a ventilation opening should be stated by the manufacturer. This information is almost never available to a home inspector. A reasonable assumption is that screens reduce the gross opening area by at least 25% and screens combined with louvers or grilles reduce the gross opening area by at least 50%.

Ventilation Installation Ventilation openings should be located so that cross ventilation of the crawl space is possible. At least one opening should be located within 3 feet from each corner of the house.

Plenty of Ventilation Openings for This Crawl Space.

Typical Defects Typical defects that home inspectors should report include:

1. ventilation openings blocked or are stuck shut,
2. damaged or absent ventilation opening covers,
3. inadequate total ventilation opening area,
4. improper ventilation opening location,
5. vapor retarder poorly installed and may not function properly,
6. dark areas or efflorescence on crawl space walls indicate water infiltration,
7. evidence of active water infiltration such as liquid water and wet soil,
8. damp insulation or strings of insulation hang down from the insulation,
9. significant fungal growth on framing materials,
10. evidence of past or current attempts to correct water infiltration are observed, such as waterproofing material on the crawl space walls, interior foundation drains, and dehumidifiers.

Standards (1) IRC 2018 R408 (crawl spaces); (2) manufacturer's instructions.

Damaged Opening Cover. Screen Absent.

Examples of Significant Wood Destroying Fungal Growth.

Examples of Excessively Damp Crawl Spaces.

Crawl Space Still Damp After Interior Foundation Drain Installed.

Unventilated (Closed) Crawl Spaces

Introduction The current majority opinion is that **most crawl spaces should be closed.** The exception is crawl spaces in flood-prone areas.

Vapor Retarder Installation The minimum vapor retarder thickness is usually 6 mil, but this material will not last long if the crawl space has much traffic. Ten to 12 mil (or better) reinforced material is more realistic, especially if there are appliances that require service in the crawl space. Seams between sheets should be lapped at least 6 inches and should be taped or sealed. The vapor retarder should be turned up the crawl space walls and piers and sealed. Radon mitigation components should be installed before installing the vapor retarder.

Ventilation Installation Ventilation air should be provided to the crawl space. The rate should be 1 cubic foot per minute for every 50 square feet of crawl space floor. It is important that the actual rate not be significantly above or below the required rate because a different rate could pressurize or depressurize the crawl space.

Ventilation may be accomplished by a continuously operating fan that exhausts to the exterior. The alternative method is to provide conditioned air to the crawl space. A pressure relief duct to the house interior or an opening to the interior covered by a grille should be provided to equalize pressures. The duct or opening should not be connected to the HVAC return duct.

Crawl Space Wall Insulation Crawl space walls, including framed walls and the band joist or rim board, should be insulated. Insulation may be installed on the interior or the exterior side of the walls. Crawl space access doors should be weather stripped and insulated like other doors to the exterior. Typical insulation types include closed-cell foam, sheet insulation, and batt insulation in any framed wall cavities. A small gap in the insulation (2 to 3 inches) is usually required in areas where termites are a problem, so that termite tubes can be seen.

Closed Crawl Space Walls Insulated With Closed Cell Spray Foam.

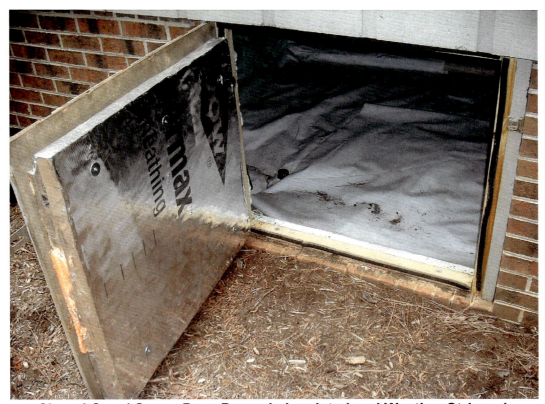
Closed Crawl Space Door Properly Insulated and Weather Stripped.

Typical Defects Typical defects that home inspectors should report include:

1. openings to the exterior not sealed,
2. damaged vapor retarder or seams not sealed,
3. thermal barrier or ignition barrier not installed to protect foam insulation,
4. damaged insulation,
5. insulation or vapor retarder not adequately fastened to foundation walls,
6. access door not insulated and weather stripped.

Standards (1) IRC 2018 R316 (foam plastic fire protection), R408 (crawl spaces), Table N1102.1.2 (insulation amount requirements); N1102.2.11 (unventilated crawl space insulation); (2) manufacturer's instructions.

BASEMENT WALL INSULATION

Introduction Insulating a full-height framed basement wall is relatively easy. The wall should be insulated like any other framed exterior wall. Insulating a concrete and masonry basement foundation wall is more difficult, and potentially more dangerous. The danger comes from liquid water and from water vapor that can diffuse through the wall and condense. Considerable damage and fungal growth can occur before the problem is discovered.

Fiberglass Batt Insulation A common method of insulating and finishing basement foundation walls **was** to build a stud wall inside the basement foundation wall and insulate the framed wall using fiberglass batts. This method is still used by some contractors. **This method can work if two conditions are satisfied; however, both conditions have significant practical limitations.** One condition is that the foundation wall is dry; meaning no liquid water flows and little or no water vapor diffuses through the wall. Dry foundation walls are an unusual situation in some areas. The other condition is that water vapor entering the framed wall cavity can dry toward conditioned space. This means not installing a vapor retarder on the interior side of the wall. Not installing a vapor retarder on the warm in winter side of the wall works if the wall temperature remains above the dew point. This method of insulating a wall is more likely to work in warm climates, but is less likely to work in cold climates and in wet climates.

A variant of the foundation wall fiberglass batt insulation method involves installing a Class I vapor retarder between the foundation wall and the batt insulation. The vapor retarder method can work if there is limited vapor diffusion through the foundation wall, and if the foundation wall temperature remains above the dew point so that liquid water does not form behind the vapor retarder and flow out from under it. The vapor retarder method also requires not installing a vapor retarder on the finished side of the framed wall. This avoids the dual vapor retarder problem and allows the framed wall to dry toward the interior.

Another variant includes leaving an air space between the foundation wall and the insulation. Leaving an air space between the fiberglass batt insulation and the foundation wall does not work because insulation must be in contact with an air barrier on all sides to be effective. **All fiberglass batt insulation methods are no longer recommended in any climate as a way to insulate concrete and masonry foundation walls.**

Sheet and Foam Insulation The current recommended methods for insulating basement foundation walls involve installing vapor impermeable insulation either on the interior or the exterior of the foundation wall. Installing insulation on the wall exterior is cost-effective only for new construction. The primary advantage of exterior insulation is that the insulation can be integrated with the waterproofing system to provide a more secure barrier against entry of liquid water and water vapor. Exterior insulation also slightly improves the R-value of the entire foundation wall assembly by taking better advantage of the thermal mass of the foundation wall. Exterior foundation wall insulation is usually installed using sheet insulation. Interior insulation can be installed using sheet insulation or closed-cell foam insulation. Foam is usually the better alternative because it avoids the problem of sealing seams in the insulation.

Basement Water Intrusion **A basement should not be insulated and finished until there is reasonable certainty that all liquid water intrusion has been stopped**. Most basement and crawl space liquid water intrusion problems are really grading, drainage, gutter, and landscape irrigation problems, so addressing these issues is the first step. Verifying the condition (and presence) of the exterior foundation drain is another step. A camera can be used if the drain is accessible. An interior foundation drain and sump pump is another way to deal with liquid water intrusion into existing basements, but this method is disruptive and expensive.

Inspecting Finished Basements A home inspector who is inspecting a finished basement should pay special attention to evidence of moisture problems behind the wall and in the basement. Evidence of finished basement moisture problems includes:

- water stains and fungal growth, especially near the floor,
- rust on drywall and trim nails and rust on exposed metal columns,
- musty smells,
- presence of a dehumidifier, especially if it appears to be constantly running,
- stained or loose floor coverings (lifting carpeting at a corner to observe the tack strip can provide good evidence).

The home inspector should disclaim inspection of concealed components, such as framing and the foundation walls, and recommend evaluation if the client wants more information about the condition of concealed components. Destructive testing may be required to obtain more information. This testing is out of scope for a home inspection. Some home inspectors advise the client that basements will eventually leak. An analogy is that a basement is a concrete boat in a sea of soil moisture.

Standards (1) IRC 2018 R406 (foundation waterproofing and foundation drains), Table N1102.1.1 (insulation amount requirements); (2) manufacturer's instructions.

Wall Spalling, Peeling Paint, and Damp Floor All Indicate Active Water Intrusion.

Stains on Wall Covering and Floor Covering All Indicate Active Water Intrusion.

Stains Indicate Water Intrusion, Current Activity Unknown.

Please visit https://nationalhomeinspectorexam.org/prepare-for-the-exam/ and take advantage of the practice quizzes. The questions in the practice quizzes are designed to reflect the difficulty of the questions on the actual exam. The questions on the practice quizzes are not questions on the National Home Inspectors Exam. Passing the practice quizzes does not guarantee that you will pass the National exam. You will still need to study all topics to be prepared for the National exam.

6: THE HOUSE INTERIOR

INSPECTION SCOPE

A house is a system in which many components interact, and in which many components are parts of different systems. For example, walls consist of exterior wall coverings, structural framing, insulation, and interior wall coverings. Walls may contain components from other systems, such as electrical cables, plumbing pipes, and HVAC ducts. Walls are connected to systems such as the foundation, floor, roof, and roof covering. **Defects in any of these systems may present as defects on interior components**. While the home inspector is not obligated to determine which system or component is causing the defect, it is important to identify defects that present on interior components, and be able to guide the client about who might best be able to evaluate the defect and determine its cause.

House interior components that are within the scope of a home inspection are wall and ceiling finishes such as drywall, interior doors and their locks and hardware, interior stairways, handrails and guards, and countertops and cabinets. Kitchen appliances may be in scope depending on the standard of practice. We will discuss these in another chapter. Exterior windows are often inspected during the exterior inspection and during the interior inspection; refer to the Exterior Windows section in the Exterior Components chapter for more about inspecting windows. Fireplaces and similar systems are also in scope and will be discussed in another chapter.

It is important to distinguish between floor coverings, such as carpet, tile, and wood, and the structural floor system. Defects in floor coverings may be out of scope depending on the standard of practice; however, **defects in floor coverings caused by defects in other systems such as the foundation or floor systems are in scope**, at least insofar as they present clues about the structural system defects.

Inspecting the interior presents a special challenge of identifying cosmetic defects. Cosmetic defects occur in other systems, but are more likely to be an issue inside because this is where clients live and are more likely to notice them. **A cosmetic defect is defined as one that does not significantly affect the ability of a component to perform its intended function**. An additional definition of a cosmetic defect is a defect that a reasonable client could see and understand while conducting the recommended pre-closing inspection of the property. **Cosmetic defects are out of scope of a home inspection**. Whether a home inspector elects to report a cosmetic defect is a business decision. Some clients expect reporting of cosmetic defects. Referring parties, such as real estate agents, are sometimes reluctant to refer home inspectors who report too many cosmetic defects.

The installation and use of computer and communication (internet) technology in buildings is increasing at a rapid rate. This technology goes by names such as **smart homes** and the **internet of things. At this time, there is no broadly accepted definition of these terms**, so it is difficult for a home inspector to know how to identify and how to inspect this new technology.

Most standards of practice are clear, however, that **all devices and wiring that are not part of the house high voltage (120/240 volt) electrical system are out of scope of a home inspection**. Home inspectors should disclaim inspection of such devices and wiring and recommend evaluation by a qualified specialist if the client wishes information about the condition and functionality of installed devices and wiring.

INTERIOR WALL AND CEILING FINISHES

Drywall Drywall is the most common interior wall and ceiling finish in newer houses. This material has many names including **gypsum board**, **plasterboard**, and the brand name **Sheetrock**. It has been available since the 1910s but was not widely used until the late 1940s. It is made from the mineral gypsum, which is placed between two sheets of paper. The edges of drywall are usually slightly thinner than the nominal board thickness to allow for a smooth finished surface after application of tape and joint compound during finishing.

Drywall is available in many sizes and types. Drywall sheets are usually 4 feet wide and are usually available in lengths between 8 and 16 feet. Longer lengths are usually stocked only at drywall supply companies, and are very heavy. Standard thicknesses are ½ inch and ⅝ inch; ¼ and ⅜ inch thicknesses are also available but are usually not recommended for uses other than application over other interior finish surfaces. Three-eighths inch drywall is sometimes used to cover radius walls where thicker drywall will not bend. **Type X drywall** is made with additional fire-resistant materials and is **part of fire-rated wall and ceiling assemblies**. **Green drywall (green board)** is made with paper that has some water-resistant properties. Green board was allowed as a backing for wall tile in showers and bathtubs with a shower, but this is no longer allowed.

Drywall is fastened to wood framing using drywall nails or screws. Adhesive may also be applied to help secure the drywall; this is especially recommended for ceilings. There are specific fastening schedules for securing drywall to framing, and there are specific schedules for where certain types and thickness of drywall should be installed. Once the drywall is finished, it is usually not possible to determine if the drywall was installed according to these schedules. Some drywall defects may be caused by failure to follow standard installation schedules.

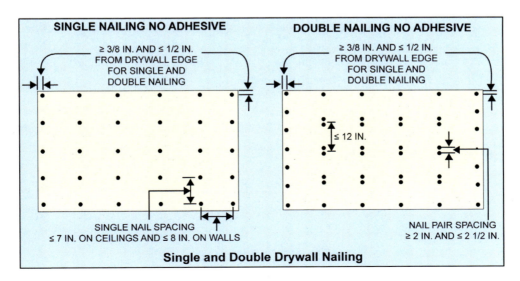

Single and Double Drywall Nailing

Drywall is finished by first applying drywall tape and joint compound (mud) to the seams between sheets and to inside wall and ceiling corners; only joint compound is applied to the fastener indentations. The tape is usually paper but may be fiberglass mesh if extra strength is desired. Outside wall corners are reinforced using **corner bead**, which is usually metal, but may be plastic. This first finishing process is called **taping and bedding**. A skim coat of joint compound is applied to the seams and corners to provide a smooth surface. This is called **skimming**. The joint compound will be sanded if a smooth finish is specified. Sanding is not necessary if a spray-applied texture coat is specified.

The two most common drywall finish types are **smooth** (slick) and **textured**. A smooth finish presents a uniform appearance. A textured finish presents a rough appearance. A smooth finish requires more time and skill in applying and sanding the joint compound, and, as such, is more expensive. A textured finish is applied using a machine that sprays a damp texture material on the drywall. The texture may be left as sprayed, such as in a popcorn pattern, or the texture may be troweled by hand into one of many finish patterns. These hand-troweled finishes are sometimes called **knock-down** finishes because the finisher knocks down the spray finish with the trowel. Textured finishes require less time and skill, and as, such are, less expensive and may be found in lower-priced houses in some markets.

The choice of finish is aesthetic. One is not necessarily better than the other. Smooth finishes tend to show more surface defects, especially in bright light. Textured finishes are more difficult to repair because matching the texture pattern requires some skill and experience.

Some texture material applied before the 1970s may contain asbestos. This is especially true of popcorn ceilings. Home inspectors may wish to advise clients of this fact, and recommend testing to determine if asbestos is present.

<u>**Plaster**</u> Plaster is the most common interior wall and ceiling finish in houses built before the 1950s. The basic formulas and techniques have been used since ancient times. Plaster is rarely used today as an interior wall finish, except to repair existing plaster.

Plaster is a combination of solid materials mixed with water to form a workable substance that can be applied to surfaces, shaped, and left to dry to a rigid state. The solid materials include either lime, gypsum, or cement. An aggregate is added to the mix. The aggregate is usually sand, but may be vermiculite or perlite. A binder may be added to help the plaster resist cracking. Animal hair was the original binder; fiberglass is the modern substitute. Lime and cement plaster may be used inside or outside. Gypsum plaster is appropriate only for interior work. Lime plaster was the commonly used interior plaster before the 1900s. Gypsum plaster was also used from the 1900s until drywall was widely adopted in the 1950s.

Interior plaster was usually applied over wood lath, which were closely space wood boards. Later installations may be applied over gypsum lath, called **rock lath**. Lath provides structural support and stability. The **plaster application process is identical to 3-coat exterior stucco** and included a **scratch, brown,** and **finish coat**. The total thickness of all three layers is approximately ⅞ inch.

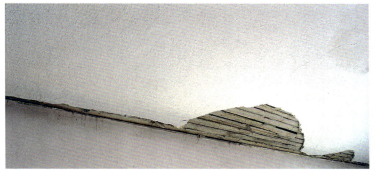

**Plaster on Wood Lath.
Picture Courtesy of Don Lovering.**

Plaster dries hard. The combination of plaster and wood or rock lath adds structural stability and is less prone to cracking than drywall. Plaster will crack given sufficient movement of the structure or given physical damage; however, a more common reason for plaster cracks is separation of the lath from the framing.

<u>**Wood**</u> Wood is a wall finish that can be found in houses of any age, but is more common in older houses. Wood is sometimes used as a ceiling finish, but this is uncommon in houses. Wood has been used as an interior finish since ancient times.

Wood can be installed in many different ways to create different finish effects. Wood may be applied to the entire wall, or it may be applied only to the lower part of the wall. Wood applied to the lower part of the wall is called **wainscoting**. Wood finishes may consist of wood planks of various sizes and species. Wood panels are sometimes seen in houses built during certain eras and in finished basements. Wood panels are usually between ⅛ and ¼ inch thick and are much easier to install than other finish materials. Wood may not be used as a wall or ceiling finish in a garage because it does not provide fire separation.

Wood May Not Be Used as Wall Covering in an Attached Garage.

<u>**Suspended Ceilings**</u> Suspended ceilings in houses are most often found in basements where they conceal the framing and other components, and may provide some sound control. These ceilings are also called **drop ceilings** and sometimes **acoustic ceilings**. The concept of suspended ceilings has been around for hundreds of years, but the modern version was developed in the early 1960s. The system consists of a metal grid suspended by (usually) metal wire hangers. Tiles are inserted into the suspended grid. Some fibrous ceiling tiles manufactured in the 1950s to 1970s may contain asbestos.

Suspended ceilings present a challenge for home inspectors because they conceal important components, and because they can be moved to provide some visibility. The **home inspector is not required to move suspended ceiling tiles**; however, some do. Moving suspended ceiling tiles is a business decision. Note, however, that **older ceiling tiles can be brittle and can break when moved**. Tiles can be difficult to reseat in the grid once moved, and it can be difficult to find matching replacements.

Interior Trim

Interior trim has a practical and an aesthetic function. The practical function is to conceal the gap between different components such as wall coverings and windows and doors. The aesthetic function is to improve the appearance of rooms. The home inspector should be able to identify common trim types, if for no other reason than to provide direction about where defects are located.

Interior trim is usually made from wood. The wood is usually solid lumber, but in newer houses trim may be pieces of wood glued together in a process called **finger jointing**. Trim may also be made from composite materials such as plastics and medium density fiberboard (MDF).

Trim is sometimes called **molding** and that term is sometimes added to the description of some types of trim. For example, trim at the floor that runs along the wall is called **base, baseboard**, or **base molding**. **Quarter round** or **shoe molding** is used to cover the gap between the base and floor coverings, such as wood, tile, and vinyl. Quarter round is slightly larger than shoe molding. Trim that is sometimes installed near the middle of the wall is called **chair rail**. Chair rail is frequently found in dining rooms and similar formal rooms. Trim that is installed at the ceiling/wall intersection is called **crown** or **crown molding**. Trim around the perimeter of windows and doors is called **casing**.

Trim sometimes appears as though it is separated from the wall, floor, or ceiling. Most of the time, this condition is just deteriorated caulk. Sometimes the trim is improperly installed, such as being fastened into the wall covering instead of to the framing. Occasionally this separation indicates a structural problem such as a foundation problem or a deformation of framing material.

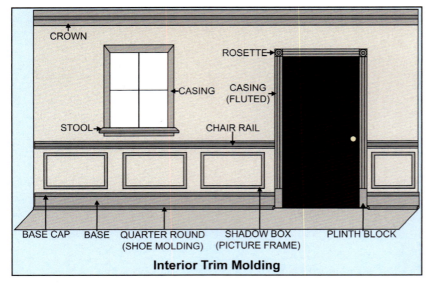

Interior Trim Molding

Typical Window Trim Molding.

Interior Trim Molding.

Cracks, Nail Pops, and Water Stains Cracks, nail pops, and water stains in wall and ceiling finish materials are a frequent source of client concern and questions for home inspectors. **Distinguishing between cosmetic cracks and cracks that can indicate more serious issues can be challenging.** Most home inspectors do not want to make an issue of cosmetic cracks; however, home inspectors should report cracks that could indicate more serious and expensive problems. Learning how to report cracks in finish materials requires knowledge and experience.

Most cracks and almost all nail pops are cosmetic and result from issues such as minor framing settlement, minor framing movement caused by wind or seismic activity (racking), wood expansion and contraction caused by humidity and temperature changes, and poor material fastening and finishing. Cosmetic cracks are usually thin and often occur along seams, especially seams at wall and ceiling corners.

Cracks that occur at the corners of doors and windows may also be caused by minor framing movement; however, **cracks at these locations in combination with other defects,** such as door and window operation problems (sticking, rubbing, difficult to operate), visible unevenness in floors, walls, or ceilings, or openings that are out-of-square **may indicate more serious problems, such as foundation settlement**. Cracks that run through material such as drywall, not just along the seams, may also indicate more serious problems. Wide cracks (more than about ¼ inch) and cracks that increase in width often indicate more serious problems.

Water stains are both very simple and very complex. **The simple aspect is reporting. The home inspector should report all visible water stains and water deterioration**, and recommend evaluation to determine the source and the method of repair. The complicated aspect can be determining the water source. Sometimes the source seems obvious, such as a stain located directly under a roof penetration or a plumbing fixture. Many times the source is not obvious. In both cases the recommendation is the same, evaluation by a qualified contractor. Even water stains with what appears to be an obvious source can sometimes have other concealed sources. **Repair of the obvious source may not solve the problem.**

Typical Defects Typical defects that home inspectors should report include:

1. cracked finish materials,
2. water stained or water deteriorated finish materials,
3. significantly damaged finished materials,
4. significant wall rotation, bowing, or unevenness,
5. uneven ceiling,
6. finish shows evidence of recent repair or painting (could be an attempt to conceal a problem),
7. trim separated from the wall, floor, or ceiling.

Standards IRC 2018 R702.2 (interior plaster), R702.3 (drywall).

Cosmetic Nail Pop. Popcorn Ceiling. Smooth Wall.

Crack Indicating Structural Issues. Textured Knock-Down Drywall Finish. Picture Courtesy of Bryck Guibor.

Cracks and Cabinet Settlement Indicating Structural Issues.

Condition of Floor Framing Below Cracks and Settlement in Previous Pictures.

INTERIOR DOORS

Cased Openings

Description A cased opening is a trimmed opening between rooms that does not have a door. Cased openings are usually found in the public areas of the house. A framed rough opening for a door is installed during framing. Trim lumber is installed at the header and jambs and casing is installed around the perimeter. A cased opening is usually rectangular but may be framed and trimmed as an arched opening. Openings between rooms may be cased using drywall; this is common in some markets.

Typical Defects opening is physically damaged.

Hinged Swinging Doors

Door Types, Styles, Materials Interior hinged swinging doors usually open in one direction, swing on two or three side-mounted hinges, and usually open at least 90°. A single door consists of one door (leaf) mounted in a frame. A double door consists of two doors (leaves) mounted in one frame. One side of a double door is usually held in place with surface bolts or with bolts built into the door stile. Hinged swinging doors are made in standard sizes. Height is usually 80 inches. Widths are usually from 12 to 36 inches in 2 inch increments.

Hinged swinging doors are usually constructed using natural or engineered wood. Doors constructed using fiberglass, vinyl, and composite materials are also available. Doors may be solid, or may be hollow core with only the perimeter made from solid material. Solid wood doors are common in older houses. Hollow core doors are common in newer houses.

Many common hinged door styles exist including the flush (single) panel door, the raised-panel door (often six or eight panels), and doors containing various sizes and styles of glazing. A French door (casement door) is a hinged door that consists mostly of fixed glazing, usually divided into several (often nine or twelve) small pieces.

Hinged Door and Frame Parts Solid wood hinged swinging doors consist of parts including a top and a bottom rail, a stile along each side, a vertical mullion (between panels, if any), and a lock rail near the center. Hinged doors made from other materials may be molded or routed to simulate stile and rail construction.

Hinged swinging door frame parts consist of a header at the top, a hinge jamb on one side where the hinges are mounted, a strike jamb on the other side where the lock strike plate is mounted, and a stop around near the center of the header and jambs that stops the door when it closes. An astragal (T-astragal) is attached to one side of a double door to seal the gap where the doors meet.

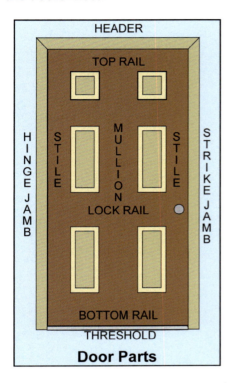

Door Parts

Framed Rough Opening For a Sliding Door.

Installation Hinged swinging doors are usually installed in a framed rough opening appropriate for the door size. The rough opening size is specified by the door manufacturer. The rough opening is larger than the door on the top and sides to provide room for the door frame and to allow the door to be installed plumb and square in the opening. The door frame is installed in the rough opening, checked for plumb and square, shimmed as necessary, and fastened to the frame. There should be an even reveal (gap) between the door and the frame of about ⅛ inch on all sides. The door should remain in place when partially open. Doors that move when partially open are improperly installed, or the framed opening may have shifted position.

Doors are usually attached to wood framing using 16d casing nails driven through the shims and elsewhere through the header and jambs as required for secure attachment. Extra nails may be installed around the hinges and the lock strike plate for additional support at those vulnerable points. When doors come with pre-installed casing, nails are also driven through the casing.

Locks, Hardware, Accessories A **hinge plate** is mounted on the door and on the frame jamb, usually in a recessed mortise. A pin connects the two plates and allows the door to swing.

A **privacy lock** restricts entry through the door from the exterior by requiring a key. The key is usually nothing more than a small piece of metal. A small straight blade screwdriver will often open the lock. A **passage lock** is operated using a knob or handle and provides no impediment to entry. Privacy locks are usually installed on bedroom and bathroom doors. Passage locks are usually installed on other interior doors.

Typical Defects Typical defects that home inspectors should report include:

1. improper lock operation (e.g., does not latch),
2. door rubs on frame,
3. warped door,
4. loose hinges,
5. absent, loose, damaged, improperly operating bolts on the fixed side of double doors,
6. physically damaged door and glazing,
7. door not painted/sealed on all sides,
8. door does not remain open,
9. interior door used as exterior door.

Standards manufacturer's instructions (for door installation and maintenance).

Sliding Doors, Pocket Doors, and Bifold Doors

Description Sliding doors and bifold doors are usually closet doors. A sliding door moves on rollers inside a track that is installed on the header. One door slides past the other. Some sliding doors have mirrors installed. The mirrors are not required to be made using safety glazing if they have solid material or another approved as a backing such as a rubber-like material. Bifold doors consist of two or four leaves that open to the side of the jambs. Bifold doors also move on a track that is installed on the header. The outer leaf door pivots on pins at the jambs and inner leaf pivots on a hinge. Most sliding and bifold doors are made using hinged swinging doors and installing rollers and other hardware. Refer to Hinged Swinging Doors.

A pocket door is a type of sliding door that slides into an opening in the wall. Pocket doors are used when there is no room for swinging door, or when a swinging door would strike or interfere with another door. Pocket doors are sometimes not properly adjusted, and their privacy lock, if any, sometimes does not latch.

Bifold Doors (Left).   Bifold Door Upper Track (Center).   Pocket Doors (Right).

<u>Installation</u> Sliding doors and bifold doors are installed in a cased opening. The track is attached to the header. Brackets are attached at the jambs to accept the pins installed in the bifold door outer leaves. These brackets are adjustable so that the doors can be adjusted to close evenly and plumb. Sliding doors usually have a bracket at the bottom near the center to keep the doors from moving perpendicular to the opening.

<u>Typical Defects</u> Typical defects that home inspectors should report include:

1. doors significantly out of plumb,
2. doors difficult to operate,
3. physically damaged door and glazing,
4. wood door not painted/sealed on all sides,
5. absent bottom guide on a sliding door,
6. improper lock operation (e. g., does not latch),
7. warped doors.

<u>Standards</u> manufacturer's instructions (for door installation and maintenance).

FLOOR COVERINGS

Introduction

Floor coverings cover the subfloor; their function is strictly aesthetic. **Reporting the condition of floor coverings is out of scope of a home inspection because their condition is a cosmetic issue.** Many clients, however, expect reporting of floor covering defects, especially those involving expensive floor coverings such as wood and tile. Some floor covering defects, such as cracks that run through tiles, may indicate structural issues that warrant further evaluation, or may just indicate that someone dropped a heavy object on the tile.

Carpet

Description Carpet is usually defined as a natural or synthetic yarn that is attached to a backing system. Most carpet comes in 12 foot wide rolls; a few styles may be available in widths such as 13½ and 15 feet. Carpet can also be purchased as peel and stick squares which can be installed similar to vinyl squares. Carpet is usually installed from wall to wall, as distinguished from rugs, which are similar, but cover only part of the floor area in a room.

Carpet is usually made from synthetic yarn, such as nylon, acrylic, and polyester. Wool and cotton yarns are used, but comprise a very small market share due to price. Carpet should be installed over a pad, which helps extend the life of the carpet and provides a better feel for those who walk on it.

Carpet problems are usually the result of improper installation. The temperature and humidity in the house should be at normal state when carpet is installed. Significant changes in temperature and humidity after installation can cause shrinking and swelling. Carpet should be power-stretched during installation to help avoid shrinking and swelling.

The service life of carpet varies significantly based on carpet and pad quality, use, and maintenance. Low quality carpets that are poorly maintained can show significant wear in a few years. High quality carpets that are well maintained can last for fifteen to twenty-five years. A ten year service life is a reasonable estimate.

Installation Carpet can be installed over almost any subfloor, although installation over very damp subfloors or in areas subject to wetting is not recommended. Carpet seams are joined using seam tape, which is a heat-activated adhesive on a heavy fiberglass or plastic material. Carpets are secured in place at the perimeter by tack strips, which are wood strips with small spikes that are secured to the floor using nails.

Typical Defects Typical defects that home inspectors should report include:

1. dirty, stained, worn, faded, or damaged floor covering,
2. floor covering has shrunk or expanded causing it to pull away from the wall or to ripple,
3. loose floor covering,
4. unusually visible seams (some types of carpet tend to show seams more than others),
5. floor covering installed in a damp area causing odor and mold issues,
6. odors detected immediately after installation (usually short term),
7. absent, improper type, improperly installed transition piece between different floor coverings.

Standards manufacturer's instructions.

Good Transition, Carpet to Laminate.

Good Transition, Vinyl to Laminate.

Laminate and Engineered Wood

Description Laminate floor coverings provide the appearance of other floor coverings, but usually at a lower cost. They are usually seen as imitating wood, but are also made to imitate floor coverings, such as brick and stone. They usually consist of multiple layers, including the design layer, which is a photographic image of the imitated floor covering. Laminate floor coverings are available in different thicknesses which correspond roughly to quality and price. While laminate floor coverings can look like wood floor covering, laminates are different and should not be described as wood floor covering.

Most manufacturers do not recommend installing laminate floor covering on floors that are subject to moisture from the subfloor. Subfloor moisture is most likely to occur at below-grade floors (basements), but can occur at on-grade concrete floors, especially new ones, and at framed floors above damp crawl spaces.

Most laminate floor covering problems are a combination of installation and moisture problems. Problems such as buckling are usually the result of too much moisture. Problems such as gapping (spaces opening up between boards) are usually the result of too little moisture, but this is uncommon. Failure to allow the laminate to acclimate before installation, failure to check the moisture condition of the subfloor, and failure to install a vapor retarder and padding are common installation errors that can contribute to problems.

Unlike natural wood floor coverings, laminate floor coverings cannot be refinished. Minor scratches and damage can sometimes be repaired with available repair kits. The service life of laminate varies based on quality, installation, use, and maintenance. Low quality materials that are poorly maintained can show significant wear in a few years. High quality materials that are well maintained can last for fifteen to twenty-five years.

Engineered wood floor coverings are similar to laminate floor coverings in that both are made from layers of materials. The difference is in the materials. Engineered wood is made from layers of wood arranged at 90° angles to each other in a manner similar to plywood. The top layer of engineered wood is natural wood, as opposed to the picture of wood used in laminates. The better grades of engineered wood can be sanded and refinished a couple of times.

Engineered wood floor coverings are reported to be more dimensionally stable and less prone to moisture-related problems compared to laminates and to natural wood floor coverings. The service life of engineered wood floor coverings varies based on quality, installation, use, and maintenance. Low quality materials that are poorly maintained can show significant wear in a few years. High quality materials that are well maintained can last for fifteen to thirty years.

Installation Laminate and engineered wood floor coverings should be installed according to manufacturer's instructions. These floor coverings should be allowed to acclimate to the temperature and humidity conditions of the house before installation. These floor coverings should be installed over a water barrier, such as #15 roofing felt, and over a pad designed for these floors. Many laminate floors are floating floors that require no adhesives or fasteners; some may be attached using adhesives.

Typical Defects Typical defects that home inspectors should report include:

1. dirty, stained, worn, faded, buckled, loose, or damaged floor covering,
2. gaps between pieces of floor covering, or between floor covering and wall (gaps may open and close with changes in humidity),
3. absent, improper type, improperly installed transition piece between different floor coverings.

Standards manufacturer's instructions.

Water Damaged Laminate.

Linoleum and Vinyl

Description Linoleum and vinyl are often used as synonyms. These products, called **sheet goods**, are different. Linoleum is made from linseed oil, wood, resins, and other materials bonded to a jute backing. Vinyl is made from petrochemicals and is usually bonded to a fiberglass backing. Linoleum and vinyl come in 12 foot wide sheets. Both products are available in peel and stick squares and vinyl is available in peel and stick strips.

Both products are very sensitive to anomalies in the floor over which they are installed. Seams and unevenness in the subfloor can show through these products soon after installation. This is usually a cosmetic issue, but some anomalies such as nail pops can protrude through the products causing tears. A smooth plywood subfloor underlayment is often recommended under these products.

Linoleum and vinyl are vapor retarders. Most manufacturers do not recommend installing these materials on floors that are subject to moisture from the subfloor. Subfloor moisture is most likely to occur at below-grade floors (basements), and can occur at floors over moist crawl spaces. Stains on these materials in areas where there is no visible water source can be an indication of condensation and fungal growth between the floor and the material.

The service life of linoleum and vinyl varies significantly based on quality, use, and maintenance. There are conflicting opinions about the expected service life of these materials. Low quality materials that are poorly maintained can show significant wear in a few years. High quality materials that are well maintained can last for twenty-five to fifty years. A twenty-five year service life is a reasonable estimate, but they can appear faded and worn well before that.

Linoleum and vinyl manufactured before the 1970s may contain asbestos. Home inspectors may wish to advise clients about this, especially if there is damaged or deteriorated linoleum or vinyl in the house.

Installation These products should be installed according to manufacturer's instructions. Some products are adhered using adhesive over the entire installation and some are adhered only at the perimeter. The material should be rolled using a tool designed for this purpose to remove air pockets and other anomalies.

Typical Defects Typical defects that home inspectors should report include:

1. dirty, stained, worn, faded, buckled, loose, or damaged floor covering,
2. gaps at seams, or between floor covering and wall,
3. unusually visible seams,
4. absent, improper type, improperly installed transition piece between different floor coverings.
5. color changes or efflorescence at floor covering,
6. floor covering torn where the laundry washer and dryer have been removed. If a professional moving company tore the floor covering during the move, they will usually replace the floor covering if the seller files a claim.

Standards manufacturer's instructions.

Damaged Vinyl Tiles, Pre-1970s, Possible Friable Asbestos. Picture Courtesy of Welmoed Sisson.

Vinyl Tiles Poorly Adhered and Loose.

Water-damaged Vinyl. Picture Courtesy of Mike Casey.

Tile and Stone

Description Tile is a generic term that is used to describe many products with different properties. The most commonly used tile is ceramic tile. A subcategory of ceramic tile is porcelain tile. Saltillo tile is a terra-cotta clay tile from Mexico; its use is mostly in the West. Other tiles are made from stone such as granite, marble, limestone, travertine (a type of limestone), and slate. Stone tiles are better described as stone and by the type of stone, if known.

Tile and stone are rigid materials and are unforgiving of movement. They are vulnerable to deflection and unevenness in the floor over which they are installed. Larger sizes are especially vulnerable. These anomalies can cause cracking in the grout, tile, or stone soon after installation. Cracks in the grout are often a cosmetic issue. Cracks that run through the tile or stone may be more difficult to repair, and can sometimes indicate structural issues.

Floor framing materials and deflection that are permitted by building standards are usually not permitted for tile and stone. Cracks caused by excessive deflection may require structural modifications that provide additional support. Cracks caused by subfloor unevenness can sometimes be repaired by replacing the tile and grinding or filling the uneven subfloor. Cracks caused by foundation movement should not be repaired until the cause of the foundation movement has been identified and repaired.

Tile and stone floor covering should last for the life of the house if properly installed and maintained. Replacement, if any, is usually a decorating selection.

Installation These products should be installed according to manufacturer's and tile industry instructions. Common defects can often be reduced by installing a cement layer or cement board before installing the tile or stone, but this adds to the installation cost and is often not done.

Typical Defects Typical defects that home inspectors should report include:

1. damaged or loose tile or stone,
2. cracked grout, tile, or stone,
3. tile edges at different heights,
4. hollow sounds heard under tile or stone,
5. transition piece between different floor coverings is absent, improper type, improperly installed.

Standards (1) manufacturer's instructions; (2) *Tile Council of North America Handbook*.

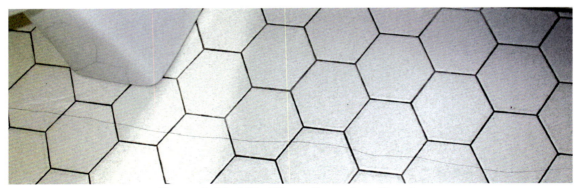

Reportable Tile Floor Covering Crack.

Reportable Tile Floor Covering Cracks.

Wood

Description Wood floor covering is often called hardwood because it was often made using oak and using wood from other deciduous trees. Wood floor covering is available using pine and wood from other conifers which are known softwoods. It is also available in materials such as cork, which is tree bark, and bamboo, which is grass. Laminate floor covering can look like wood floor covering, but laminates are different and should not be described as wood floor covering. Looking at the edge of the floor can help you tell if the floor covering is wood or laminate. Wood will be one solid piece. Laminate and engineered wood will have multiple layers.

Most manufacturers do not recommend installing wood floor covering on floors that are subject to moisture from the subfloor. Subfloor moisture is most likely to occur at below-grade floors (basements), but can occur at on-grade concrete floors, especially new ones, and at framed floors over damp crawl spaces.

Most wood floor covering problems are a combination of installation and moisture problems. Problems such as buckling and cupping are usually the result of too much moisture. Problems such as splitting and gapping (spaces opening up between boards) are usually the result of too little moisture. Failure to allow the wood to acclimate before installation, failure to check the moisture condition of the subfloor, and failure to install water barriers are common installation errors that can contribute to moisture problems.

Wood floor coverings can usually be refinished if not significantly damaged. They should last for the life of the house.

Installation Wood floor coverings should be installed according to manufacturer's instructions. Wood should be allowed to acclimate to the temperature and humidity conditions of the house before installation. Wood floor coverings should be installed over a water barrier, such as #15 felt. Blind stapling or nailing is the common fastening method, but this method may not be advisable over subfloors such as particleboard. Some wood floor coverings may be attached using adhesives.

Typical Defects Typical defects that home inspectors should report include:

1. dirty, stained, worn, faded, cupped, split, buckled, loose, or damaged floor covering,
2. gaps between pieces or between floor covering and wall (gaps may open and close with changes in humidity),
3. absent, improper type, improperly installed transition piece between different floor coverings.

Standards (1) manufacturer's instructions; (2) *Installing Hardwood Flooring* (NOFMA installation manual).

Wood Floor Covering Finish Deteriorated.

Wood Floor Covering Possible Water Stain.

Wood Floor Covering Split/Damaged.

Wood Floor Covering Protruding Nails.

STAIRWAYS AND LANDINGS

Introduction

A stairway, also called a **staircase**, is a passageway between floors that are on different vertical levels. A stairway consists of a series of **risers** (vertical), **treads** (horizontal), and **landings** (horizontal). The risers and treads are supported by **stringers**.

Every stairway has at least two landings, one at the **top** and one at the **bottom**. Intermediate landings may exist between the top and bottom landings. **A flight of stairs is a series of risers and treads between two landings** A stairway consists of one or more flights of stairs.

Most stairways have one or more **handrails**. Stairs that do not have a wall on one or both sides should have a **guard** on the open sides to protect against falls. The guard and handrail are usually combined on open-sided stairs. This combination is sometimes called a guardrail.

Standards for stairways, handrails, and guards vary over time and between jurisdictions. A component is not necessarily deficient because it does not comply with current national standards. The home inspector should learn the standards that apply where he/she practices. The home inspector should use good judgment regarding whether and how to report stairway, handrail, and guard defects; safety is the paramount issue. **If the home inspector believes that the component is unsafe, reporting the unsafe condition may be required, and is certainly recommended.**

Standards for stairways, handrails, and guards are the same regardless of whether the components are located inside or outside the house. Refer to the Decks section in the Site Conditions chapter for additional information about exterior stairs.

Stairways

Description The most common stairway consists of generally rectangular treads connecting generally rectangular landings. Some treads and landings may be curved or triangular shaped. These curved or triangular shaped treads and landings are sometimes called **winder treads** and are used to change the direction of travel on the stairway. Some stairways consist solely of triangular shaped treads that connect to a central pole and run in a spiral pattern between landings. These stairways are called **spiral stairways**; they have **different requirements from other stairways.**

Stairway Components A stairway consists of several components. The primary supports for the stairway are **stringers**. The horizontal surfaces are **treads** (often called **steps**). Treads sometimes have a projection beyond the face of the risers; this projection is a **nosing**. The vertical parts are **risers**. A **skirt board** is a piece of trim (usually wood) that is installed beside exposed risers and treads for a decorative appearance.

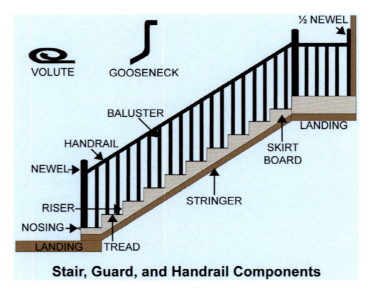

Stair, Guard, and Handrail Components

Stairway Construction Interior stairway construction is often concealed by finish materials. Stairways in unfinished areas are sometimes visible, and the home inspector should observe construction of the stairway and of the opening in the floor system around the stairway. Refer to the Floor System section in the Structural Components chapter for more about openings in the floor system at stairways.

Stairways were, and often still are, built using dimensional lumber stringers, usually 2x10 or 2x12. Stairways in newer houses, especially production houses, may be built in a factory and installed on site. Stairways in newer houses may be site-built using engineered lumber. Stairways built and installed using alternate methods and materials should comply with manufacturer's instructions. Note that there are no prescriptive standards about how to build an interior stairway. The following are **conservative recommendations** for stairways built using dimensional lumber and based on recommendations from authoritative sources. Other methods and materials may be acceptable.

The stairway should feel firm when used. A little deflection is expected, but more could indicate that the stringers are too weak, or that attachment of the stringers to the landings is inadequate. **Dimensional lumber cut stringers should have at least 5 inches of solid wood below the riser/tread cuts** or the wood below the riser/tread cuts should be reinforced with additional wood. Measurement is to the deepest saw cut (kerf), not to the intersection of the riser/tread cut.

The entire stringer plumb (vertical) cut should bear on support at the top landing. The stringer should be firmly attached to the top landing support; fastening by toe nailing is common, and while not ideal, is acceptable if there is no visible withdrawal of the fasteners. Plumb cut attachment using brackets or hangers is recommended, but is not required. Most of **the stringer seat (horizontal) cut should bear on the bottom landing.** Look for stringer splitting at the bottom landing if less than the full seat cut bears on the landing.

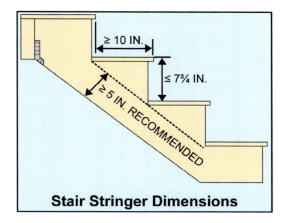

Stair Stringer Dimensions

Poor Stringer Bearing on Support. Picture Courtesy of Don Lovering.

Stairways in most houses are built using two or three stringers. Stairways much wider than 36 inches should be built using at least three stringers. Stairway treads made from nominal 2 (1½ actual) inch wood (#2 grade or better) should not clear span more than about 36 inches. Stairway treads made from nominal 5/4 inch wood (#2 grade or better) should not clear span more than about 18 inches. Thinner lumber for treads may not provide adequate deflection resistance. The treads should be adequately secured to the stringers; fasteners and adhesive are recommended, but are not required. Squeaky stairs are usually caused by loose treads rubbing against the stringers or tight treads rubbing against other stair parts.

<u>Risers</u> **The current IRC maximum riser height is 7¾ inches.** Riser height is measured at the leading edge of adjacent treads. Maximum riser heights in the 8 to 9 inch range were considered acceptable in the past. There is no minimum riser height.

The difference between any two riser heights in a flight of stairs should be not more than ⅜ inch. Riser height difference may be more important than riser height because a person expects to feel consistent riser heights. Inconsistency can cause the person to trip and fall. Riser height differences are most likely to occur at landings, especially where there is a different floor covering on the stairway than on the landing. Some jurisdictions allow more riser height difference at landings.

Most risers on interior stairways are closed with a trim board; but some are open, especially at basement stairs and in stairs not made using wood. **Open stair risers should not allow passage of a 4 inch diameter sphere.**

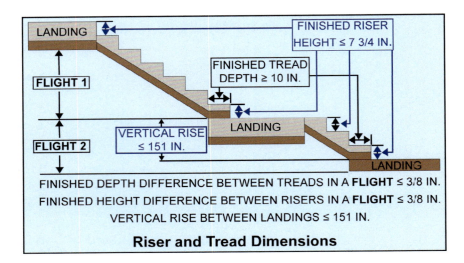

Riser and Tread Dimensions

Rectangular Treads The current IRC minimum tread depth is 10 inches. Tread depth is measured between the leading edge of adjacent treads. Minimum tread depths in the 9 inch range were considered acceptable in the past. There is no maximum tread depth.

The difference between any two tread depths in a flight of stairs should be not more than ⅜ inch. Tread depth consistency is important for the same reason as riser height consistency. All treads and landings may not slope from horizontal in any direction more than 2 percent. That is about ¼ inch for a tread measured perpendicular to a riser, and about ¾ inch for a tread measured parallel to a riser for a 36 inch wide stairway.

The minimum tread depth includes a tread nosing. A tread nosing is a projection of the tread beyond a closed riser. A tread nosing is not required; however, the minimum tread depth should be 11 inches if there is no nosing. The nosing, if installed, should project at least ¾ inch and not more than 1¼ inches beyond the closed riser. The difference between any 2 tread nosing depths should be not more than ⅜ inch in a stairway, not in a flight of stairs. Tread nosing depth and consistency is important for safety.

Uneven Tread Depth.

Tread Depth Too Narrow Measured From Tread Nosing Above.

6: The House Interior 347

Tread Nosing Too Deep.

Winder Treads The current IRC **minimum winder tread depth is 10 inches measured 12 inches from the narrow side of the tread**. The current IRC **minimum winder tread depth at any point on the tread is 6 inches**. Tread depth is between the leading edge of adjacent treads. There is no maximum tread depth. The difference between any two tread depths in a flight of stairs should be not more than ⅜ inch, measured at the same location on consistently shaped treads.

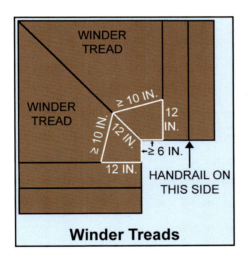 

Winder Treads.

Winder Treads Too Narrow.

Stairway Width and Headroom Height The current IRC minimum stairway width is 36 inches measured above the handrail. The current IRC minimum stairway headroom height is 80 inches measured from a line connecting the treads. Stairway width is an emergency egress issue. It is less important in houses because fewer people use the stairs in an emergency. Smaller stairways can be a major problem for moving furniture. Stairway headroom height is a safety issue. People could lose their balance and fall if they bump their heads while traversing stairs.

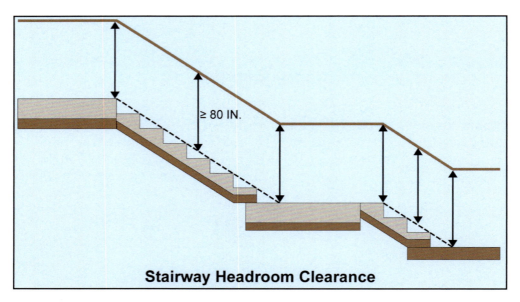

Stairway Headroom Clearance

Low Headroom at Left Side of Landing.

Low Headroom Where Ceiling Projects Above Treads.

Spiral Stairway.

Spiral Stairways Spiral stairways should have identical treads. The current IRC minimum spiral stairway tread depth is 7½ inches, measured 12 inches from the narrow side. The maximum spiral stairway riser height is 9½ inches. The minimum spiral stairway width is 26 inches at and below the handrail.

Landings All landings, including the top, bottom, and any intermediate landings, should be at least as wide as the stairs. For example, a 36 inch wide stairway should have landings at least 36 inches wide. All landings should be at least 36 inches deep measured in the direction of travel. A flight of stairs should not rise more than 151 vertical inches without a landing. Landing width is a safety issue. People could trip and lose their balance on a landing that is narrower than the stairway. Landing depth is less important, but it can cause a major problem for moving furniture.

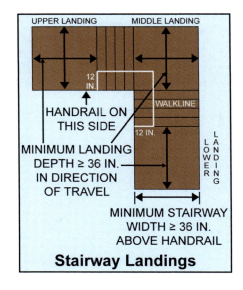
Stairway Landings

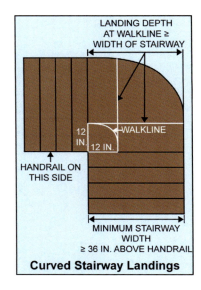
Curved Stairway Landings

Ramps Ramps are installed to provide access for people who cannot traverse stairs, such as those in wheelchairs. Ramps are uncommon, so the home inspector may wish to disclaim inspection of ramps and recommend evaluation by someone qualified in accessible construction.

A ramp serving the egress door (usually the front door) should have a maximum slope of one unit in 12 units (8.3%). Ramps serving other doors should have a maximum slope of one unit in eight units (12.5%). Landings and handrails are required on ramps; requirements are similar to those for stairs.

Typical Defects, Stairs and Landings Typical defects that home inspectors should report include:

1. stringers inadequately attached to support or pulling away from support,
2. damaged components,
3. stringers deflect when used,
4. treads squeak when used,
5. inadequate undisturbed wood at cut stringers,
6. riser height too tall,
7. tread depth too small,
8. difference between riser heights or tread depths too large,
9. space between open risers more than 4 inches,

10. headroom height too low,
11. landing too small,
12. stairway too narrow,
13. carpet or other floor covering loose on treads,
14. stairway inadequately illuminated,
15. stairway lights are not switched at top and bottom landings when the stairway has six or more risers.

Standards: IRC 2018 R311.7 (stairways and landings), R311.8 (ramps).

Stairway Too Narrow. Open Risers. Improper Handrail Shape.

HANDRAILS AND GUARDS

Handrails

Description **A handrail is required on stairways with four or more risers.** A handrail is recommended on other stairways for safety and for the convenience of people with reduced mobility. The handrail should be continuous from above the top riser to above the lowest riser of a flight of stairs. A person should not need to release the handrail and grasp another handrail while traversing the stairs. A handrail is not required at a level intermediate landing.

A handrail should be securely attached to structural support. This is usually accomplished with bracket designed to support handrails. The handrail should be securely attached to the support bracket. **Loose handrails are a common defect**.

A handrail should be between 34 and 38 inches above the stairway, measured from a sloped line connecting the treads. This is a safety issue. A handrail that is too low or too high may not provide a graspable support for some people.

A handrail should have one of the grip patterns shown in the following illustration. This is a safety issue. A handrail that is too large or too small may not provide a graspable surface for some people. A handrail should terminate with a return toward the wall or to a newel post. A return is piece of handrail that turns at an angle to the handrail to provide a graspable surface at the end of the handrail, and prevents something, such as clothing, from catching between the handrail end and the wall. **Handrail problems are common defects.**

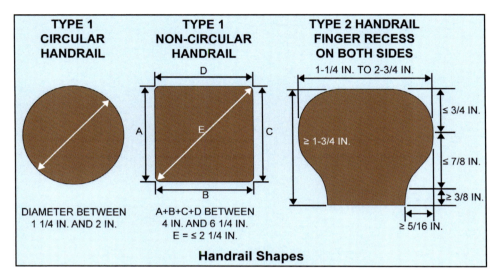
Handrail Shapes

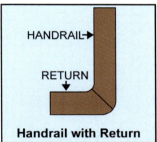
Handrail with Return

No Handrail At a Flight of Stairs.

**Handrails Not Continuous.
Right Picture Courtesy of Welmoed Sisson.**

Handrails Not Graspable and Do Not Terminate in a Return.

<u>Guards</u>

<u>**Description**</u> A **guard** is sometimes called a **guardrail**, **balustrade**, or **banister**. A guard is often made from components used for handrails, and is often found on the open side of stairways. A guard need not be made from handrail components. A guard is sometimes a full or partial-height solid wall. It may be a wall that contains (safety) glazing. It may be any structure that satisfies the guard specifications.

Guards may be made from several components and many different materials. The most common material is wood. Other materials include metal, safety glazing, plastic, and composites. The top component is the **top rail**; this is the **handrail**. The bottom component may be a **bottom rail**, or it may be the floor or stairway tread. Fill-in components fill the space between the top rail and the bottom rail or floor. **Vertical fill-in components** are called **balusters** or **pickets**. **Newels** are posts that are usually installed at stairway landings, at the beginning and end of guardrails, and at points within long guardrails to provide the necessary support to resist rotation. A **volute** is a handrail in a spiral shape that may be installed at the bottom tread as a decorative feature. A **gooseneck** is a curved handrail that makes a vertical continuous connection between a landing newel and a stairway handrail. An **easing** is a curved handrail that helps make a continuous connection between handrails that run in different directions.

Specifications **A guard is required at any walking surface located more than 30 inches vertically above any surface within 36 inches horizontally.** This usually includes stairways, hallways, balconies, stoops, decks, ramps, and landings.

The current minimum **IRC guard height at a level surface is 36 inches above the finished floor** or walking surface (42 inches in some jurisdictions and in commercial buildings). Guards that serve as handrails for a stairway (stair guards) may be at handrail height.

Guard fill-in components should not allow a 4 inch diameter sphere to pass. Stair guard fill-in components should not allow a 4⅜ inch diameter sphere to pass. The space under a stair guard bottom rail and a stairway riser and tread should **not allow a 6 inch diameter sphere to pass.** This does not mean that the space between fill-in components must be 4, 4⅜, or 6 inches or less at all points. The space may be wider if the space is less at enough points to block the sphere.

Guards, and handrails that serve as guards, should not fail when a single concentrated load of 200 psf is applied in any direction at any point along the top of the guard. Fill-in components should not fail when a single concentrated load of 50 psf is applied. Home inspectors are not required to test guards for compliance with these requirements; however, most home inspectors push on guards to determine if they seem unusually loose (this is by no means an accurate test).

Typical Defects, Handrails and Guards Typical defects that home inspectors should report include:

1. handrail or guards absent or not continuous over all of stairway,
2. loose handrail or guards,
3. improper handrail size or shape,
4. improper height handrail or guards,
5. absent handrail or guard where required,
6. handrail does not terminate in a return,
7. guard posts spaced too far apart,
8. balusters spaced too far apart,
9. damaged or deteriorated handrails, balusters, or guard posts.

Standards: IRC 2018 R311.7.8 (handrails), R312.1 (guards).

Guards Not Present Where Required.

Opening Between Guard Bottom Rail, Riser, and Tread Larger than 6 Inches.

Guard Height Less than 36 Inches.

CABINETS AND COUNTERTOPS

Cabinets

Description A cabinet is a box-shaped component that is intended for storage. It may have shelves and drawers. Cabinets are usually found in the kitchen and in bathrooms and may be found in other areas such as the laundry and the garage. Installed cabinets are within scope of a home inspection. Installed means permanently attached such that removal requires tools.

Most cabinets are made from wood or wood-based products, such as plywood, particleboard, and medium density fiberboard (MDF). Other materials include metal and composites. Wood cabinet doors, drawer fronts, and face frames that are intended for a stain finish are made from wood such as oak, maple, cherry, ash, and pine. Cabinets intended for painting may be made from wood-based products, such as MDF.

Home inspectors should know some basic cabinet nomenclature to be able to describe where defects are located. Cabinets that are installed on the wall above the countertop are **wall cabinets.** Cabinets that are installed on the floor are **base cabinets**. Cabinets are often referred to by their function. A cabinet intended for use at the sink is a **sink base**. A sink base may also be used under a cook top. A cabinet with only drawers is a **drawer base**. An oven cabinet has a large opening for ovens and usually has drawers below. Cabinets are usually installed next to each other, but when cabinets meet at an interior corner a **filler strip** is often required. A filler strip keeps cabinet doors and drawers along one wall from interfering with the doors and drawers along the other wall. When drawers hit other drawers or hit appliances, the cause is often lack of a proper size filler strip.

Each part of a cabinet has a name. The doors and drawer fronts are the most visible parts. The frame around the front of the cabinet is the **face frame** (some cabinets do not have a face frame). The panels that comprise the box are the bottom, sides, and back panels. The recessed area at the bottom of a base cabinet is the toe kick (toe strip). The doors open on hinges. The drawers slide on **drawer glides** (slides).

Cabinet dimensions depend on where and how they are intended to be used. Kitchen base cabinets are usually 24 inches deep and installed so that the countertop is about 36 inches above the finished floor. Wall cabinets are usually 12 inches deep and installed so they are about 18 inches above the countertop. Bathroom vanity cabinets vary between 18 and 22 inches deep. The traditional bathroom vanity cabinet height is about 31 inches but some modern bathroom cabinets are closer to 36 inches. The opening for the refrigerator should be at least 36 inches wide and preferably wider. A small opening will not accommodate many modern refrigerators.

Installation Cabinets should be installed so they are secure. Better quality cabinets will have back rails of solid wood through which the fasteners should be installed. Lower quality cabinets may be fastened through the rear panel. Cabinets should be fastened into solid framing using #8 x 2½ inch or larger screws. **The screws should have an enlarged head or be installed with a button cap or washer to distribute the load**. Cabinets should be installed level and plumb. Shims are often required to compensate for floors that are not level and walls that are not plumb. Home inspectors are not required to check cabinets for level and plumb, but home inspectors should report obvious visual indications of poor cabinet installation.

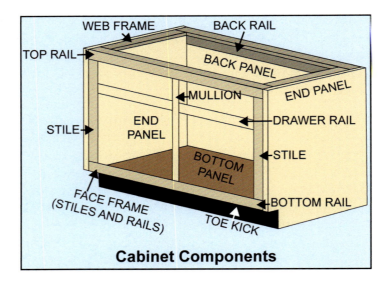

Cabinet Components

Typical Defects Typical defects that home inspectors should report include:

1. worn or damaged cabinets, especially sink cabinet bottom panels,
2. improper fasteners (e. g., no washer or button cap),
3. loose cabinets,
4. cabinets not level or plumb,
5. drawers or doors strike other drawers, doors, or appliances,
6. absent or loose handles or pulls (not all cabinets have these),
7. loose doors or drawer fronts,
8. drawers do not open and close easily,
9. wall cabinets are hung too low,
10. shelves sag.

Standards manufacturer's instructions.

No Washer on Fastener.

End Panel Separating.

Water-Damaged Cabinet Bottom Panel.

Loose Wall Cabinets.

Drawer Strikes Range Handle.

Countertops

Description One of the most common countertop materials is the **laminate countertop** which consists of a thin plastic layer adhered to plywood or particleboard. Laminate countertops are easy to cut and burn and are difficult to repair if damaged. Laminate countertops sometimes lift from the substrate at seams and edges if the adhesive was not properly applied or allowed to cure. These countertops are sometimes referred to by the brand name Formica; there are many other manufacturers.

Ceramic tile is a common countertop material. These countertops are more difficult to cut or burn compared to laminate countertops, but can be damaged by dropping heavy objects on them. They are reasonably easy to repair if matching tile is available. Keeping the grout clean is a major problem, grout sealing can help, but does not eliminate staining. Tile countertops are less common today because of maintenance problems.

Natural stone countertops such as granite and marble are popular and common. Granite is reasonably resistant to cutting and burning; marble is softer and more fragile. Both are susceptible to staining, especially if poorly sealed. Both require sealing at installation and periodically thereafter to maintain appearance and to resist staining. Minor pitting and scratches can be repaired. Major scratching, pitting, and staining may not be repairable.

Engineered quartz countertops are newer and are becoming more popular. Engineered quartz countertops are made mostly from quartz dust and resins. They are reasonably resistant to cutting and staining but not to burning. They do not require sealing or other maintenance other than normal cleaning. Minor repairs can be made.

Solid-surface countertops are manufactured using acrylic or polyester resins. They are easy to cut and burn, but minor damage can be repaired. They are reasonably resistant to staining. These countertops are sometimes referred to by the brand name Corian; there are many other manufacturers.

Less common countertop materials include concrete, soapstone, stainless steel, wood, and various recycled materials such as glass and paper. These materials have their own advantages, disadvantages, and repairability.

Most of the kitchen countertop materials are also used as bathroom vanity countertop material. A popular bathroom countertop that is not used in the kitchen is **cultured marble**. Cultured marble starts as a liquid polymer mixed with marble dust and other ingredients. It is poured in a mold where it hardens. Cultured marble is fairly soft and is very easy to scratch and burn. Minor scratches can be repaired, but less so for burns and major cuts and damage. It tends to look worn over time, especially if poorly maintained. Cultured marble can have a service life up to twenty years, but it tends to look worn before then.

The **backsplash** is the area between the countertop and the wall cabinets. It may be covered using the countertop material or using a different material. It may be left uncovered. Cultured marble countertops usually have a side splash on any perpendicular wall. A side splash hides the gap between the wall and the countertop and helps keep water from entering the gap.

Installation Countertops should be secured to the base cabinets so that the countertop does not move. Any seams in the countertop should be located well away from the sink. Countertops should be installed level in both directions. Very heavy countertops, such as granite and marble, may need extra support especially if the top is cantilevered to form a breakfast bar or similar surface. Countertops usually should not be cantilevered more than about 12 inches without support under the countertop.

Typical Defects Typical defects that home inspectors should report include:

1. worn or damaged countertops or substrate, especially particleboard under laminate,
2. loose countertops,
3. countertops not level,
4. laminate loose at seams or edges,
5. countertop seams near sink,
6. unsealed gap between countertop and backsplash or side splash,

7. worn or absent at tile countertops grout,
8. improperly supported cantilevered countertops,
9. countertops have sharp edges.

Standards manufacturer's instructions.

SMART HOME TECHNOLOGY

Description At this time, there is no broadly accepted definition of what constitutes a smart home. The following is one definition put forward by the real estate firm Coldwell Banker and CNET, a website that reviews technology products.

> A smart home is one that is equipped with network-connected products (i.e., "smart products," connected via Wifi, Bluetooth, or similar protocols) for controlling, automating, and optimizing functions such as temperature, lighting, security, safety, or entertainment either remotely by a phone, tablet, computer or a separate system within the home itself.
>
> The home must have a smart security feature or a smart temperature feature in addition to a reliable internet connection. It then must include at least two features from a list of smart options, including appliances, entertainment, lighting, outdoor sensors, and safety detectors.

A reliable internet connection for purposes of a smart home is usually defined as a high-speed (broadband) connection. High-speed is usually defined to mean download speed of at least 25 megabits per second.

Various delivery technologies can provide a high-speed internet connection to the house. Two of the most common wired technologies are coaxial cable and fiber optics. Digital subscriber line (DSL) is an older technology that can provide a high-speed connection, but DSL speed is usually slower compared to other technologies. Various types of wireless and satellite technologies are emerging that can provide speeds comparable to cable and fiber optics. The soon-to-be-available 5G wireless technology is reported to provide these high-speed connections.

Communication between smart products within the house is usually some version of wireless technology. Connection speeds are often higher, and service is usually more reliable, when devices are connected by cables. Connection by cables is often called **structured wiring** or hard-wiring.

Structured wiring is often prewired in new houses built since about 2010. Structured wiring can be retrofitted into existing houses, but as with most retrofits this is more expensive. Prewired structured wiring usually consists of multiple cables that are run to a box located in a closet, laundry room, or a similar area. The box usually contains a 120 volt electrical receptacle to provide power for routers and modems.

Structured wiring, especially the interface wiring between a wire-connected service provider and the house communication hub (wireless router), should be high-speed wiring. Examples include coaxial cable (preferably RG-6) or Cat 5e (or higher) cable. Category 3 (old-style twisted-pair telephone cable) can be used, but network speed will be slower.

Examples of smart products include:

- **Security systems** that can include sensors at openings, motion sensors, fire and carbon monoxide sensors, and cameras with either local or cloud-based storage of recordings. Manufacturers include Nest and SimpliSafe.
- **Smart thermostats** that are programmable at the device and remotely using an internet-connected device. Manufacturers include Ecobee and Nest.
- **Smart speakers** that respond to voice commands to play music, control devices, and provide information. Products include Amazon Alexa and Echo, Apple Home, and Google Home.
- **Internet-connected entertainment devices** that provide streaming of audio and video from internet sources such as Amazon, Facebook, Hulu, Netflix, and Sling.
- **Smart lighting** that can be programmed or remotely controlled to activate and deactivate based on time of day or on the presence of someone in the area. Smart lighting can be indoor and outdoor lighting. Manufacturers include Lifx and Belkin.
- **Smart receptacles and switches** that can be programmed or remotely controlled to activate and deactivate electrical devices such as lights and fans. Recent electrical code changes require that a grounded (neutral) conductor be available in many switch boxes to provide power to smart switches. Manufacturers include Apple, Belkin, and Lutron.
- **Smart leak detectors** that can detect water leaks and freezing temperatures that could cause pipes to burst.
- **Smart window treatments** that can be programmed or remotely controlled to raise and lower based on time of day. These devices can improve energy efficiency.
- **Smart appliances** can be programmed or remotely controlled to begin and end food preparation and other operations. These appliances can also be programmed to track the stock of household food and cleaning supplies and automatically order when supplies run low.

Some smart devices or products are controlled by a technology called IFTTT (if this, then that). This technology allows users to create simple conditional programs called applets that provide control of smart devices based on rules programmed by the user. If a condition occurs (**if this occurs**) then the smart device will perform an action (**then that occurs**). A this condition could be receiving a text or email with a certain word or phrase. A that occurs action could be activating a light or an appliance.

Installation All smart home technology should be installed according to manufacturer's instructions. Instructions and communication protocols are often not uniform and compatible between manufacturers, so a device from one manufacturer may not work with a device from another manufacturer.

Inspection Inspection of smart home devices and wiring is out of scope of a home inspection. Home inspectors should report the presence of smart home devices and wiring, disclaim inspection, and recommend evaluation by a qualified specialist if the client wishes information about the condition and functionality of installed devices and wiring.

Some smart home devices, such as entertainment systems and speakers, are likely to be personal property that is not installed and does not convey with the house. Other devices, such as thermostats and switches, may be installed and may convey with the house. Either way, inspection of these devices is out of scope.

The home inspector who attempts to inspect or to operate smart devices faces challenges and assumes risks. Some smart devices cannot be operated, or cannot be fully operated, without knowing access codes or wake-up words or without a specific control device, such as the occupant's phone. Each device and system has its own unique method of operation, which can make inspecting and operating the device or system difficult or impossible without specific knowledge. The risk of damaging a smart device or system by attempting to operate it is relatively low; however, the risk of interfering with the operation of the smart device or system, and the risk of interfering with the operation of or damaging connected devices or systems is higher. It may be difficult to know which devices or systems may be affected by operating a smart device, and it may be difficult to know how to reset the devices or systems to the occupant's original setting.

Please visit https://nationalhomeinspectorexam.org/prepare-for-the-exam/ and take advantage of the practice quizzes. The questions in the practice quizzes are designed to reflect the difficulty of the questions on the actual exam. The questions on the practice quizzes are not questions on the National Home Inspectors Exam. Passing the practice quizzes does not guarantee that you will pass the National exam. You will still need to study all topics to be prepared for the National exam.

7: ANALYSIS AND REPORTING

INSPECTION SCOPE AND LIMITATIONS
Inspection Scope

A home inspection is an observation of certain systems and components in, on, and around the inspected property. **The objective is to provide the client with information about the condition of the observed systems and components at the time of the inspection.** There are several important concepts in these two sentences. We will discuss these in general terms next and in more detail later.

Observation implies that the home inspector relies on senses to gather information. Sight is the primary sense, but home inspectors often use hearing, smell, and touch to gather information. The home inspector does not rely solely on the use of senses to gather information. The home inspector operates certain components, such as the HVAC systems and plumbing fixtures, to gather information about their condition. Most home inspectors use simple instruments, such as receptacle testers and thermometers, to gather information about the condition of certain components.

Some home inspectors use more complex instruments such as electrical circuit analyzers, combustible gas detectors, carbon monoxide detectors, and infrared cameras. Use of these more complex instruments is out of scope for a home inspection. **While using more complex instruments can locate additional deficiencies, it can subject the home inspector to additional risk by moving the inspection beyond the visual inspection as stated in the Standard of Practice (SOP).**

Only those systems and components listed in the SOP used by the home inspector are included in a home inspection. Most SOPs list the same systems and components, but there are differences between SOPs. The home inspector must inspect all required systems and components. The home inspector may inspect systems and components that are not required, but doing so increases the home inspector's risk. Home inspectors who report about out-of-scope systems, components, or conditions should include limitation statements in the report clarifying that doing so does not expand the scope of the inspection, and that other deficiencies could exist in the out-of-scope systems and components.

An inspection report provides information about the condition of inspected systems and components, but what information is required about what conditions? The answer to this question is essential to providing a report that complies with the SOP used by the home inspector. Different SOPs have different requirements that are expressed in different terms. One SOP requires that the home inspector report when a system or component is:

- not functioning properly
- significantly, deficient
- unsafe
- near the end of its service life

We will discuss these conditions in more detail in another section.

A home inspection is a report about the conditions during the inspection. Conditions change, sometimes within minutes after the inspection is complete. This is an important inspection limitation that the home inspector should communicate to the client, verbally and in the report, and to all others with an interest in the property.

Inspection Limitations

Most SOPs contain a long list of limitations and exclusions that help define what is not included in a home inspection. We will not discuss each limitation and exclusion. The following are important general limitations and exclusions that home inspectors should know and that they should communicate to clients. We will discuss limitation statements in more detail in another section.

A home inspection is **not technically exhaustive**. This is a made-up term recognizing the fact that a home inspector should know something about all of the systems and components of the house, but usually is not an expert about any of them. **The home inspector is a generalist**. Even if a home inspector is trained and licensed in another trade or profession, such as an engineer, contractor, electrician, or HVAC technician, the home inspector is not acting in that capacity when performing a home inspection. **The home inspector is not required to, and usually should not, attempt to determine the cause of a deficiency**, use tools, take measurements, or make calculations that are within the scope of another trade or profession's services.

A home inspection cannot report on concealed and latent deficiencies. Concealed includes within walls, floors, and ceilings, under floor coverings, behind insulation, and underground. Concealed also includes behind occupant belongings. It is important that the client be made aware of this important limitation in the inspection agreement, at the inspection, and in the report. A latent deficiency is one that exists during the inspection, but presents no visible evidence of being present or active.

A home inspection cannot report on deficiencies located in areas that are **not readily accessible**. A readily accessible area is one that the home inspector can see without moving occupant belongings, snow, or other obstructions. A readily accessible area is one that is safe for the home inspector to enter without harming the home inspector or others, and without risking damage to the property. Except for electrical panel dead front covers, a home inspector is **not required to dismantle** (take apart) or remove components to make an area readily accessible, **unless the component is intended to be taken apart or removed by the occupant during normal maintenance.**

A home inspection is **not intended to report cosmetic deficiencies**. A cosmetic deficiency is one that does not have a significant impact on the ability of a component to perform its intended function. What constitutes a cosmetic deficiency can be difficult to determine. Deteriorated interior paint is a cosmetic deficiency if it does not significantly impact the ability of the wall covering to perform its intended function. Deteriorated exterior paint could be a reportable deficiency if the deterioration were so severe that it could allow damage to exterior wall coverings. A worn floor covering is usually a cosmetic deficiency, but a torn floor covering could be a reportable deficiency if it constitutes a trip and fall safety hazard.

STANDARDS OF PRACTICE (SOP)

A SOP defines what should occur during an inspection and what should be reported in the inspection report. The SOP is an essential part of every inspection. **The home inspector should not perform an inspection (or any other service) without specifying the SOP that the home inspector will use.** The home inspector should, at a minimum, identify one SOP in the inspection agreement and in the inspection report.

Many SOPs exist. Some are published by professional associations such as ASHI, CAPHI, CREIA, and InterNACHI. Some are published by government licensing authorities. Which SOP the home inspector should use depends on where the home inspector practices and to which professional association(s) the home inspector belongs. In some cases, a home inspector might be subject to more than one SOP; however, **the home inspector should use only one SOP during an inspection**. Home inspectors who practice in multiple jurisdictions where home inspectors are licensed should use the SOP required by the jurisdiction where the building is located.

The appropriate SOP for an inspection depends on the situation. When a home inspector performs an inspection under a government license, **the home inspector should use the SOP designated by the licensing authority** (if any). Some licensing authorities allow the home inspector to select a SOP from a list of approved SOPs. If the home inspector is not performing under a government license, **the home inspector should use the SOP published by the professional association to which the home inspector belongs** (if any). If the home inspector is not performing under a government license, belongs to more than one professional association, or belongs to no professional association, the home inspector should select one SOP and use that for every inspection.

A home inspector should ask three important questions during a home inspection. A SOP answers one of these questions and partially answers the others.

1. **What should I look at?** This question identifies the specific systems and components that the home inspector should inspect. A SOP identifies these systems and components, such as structural components, wall coverings, and roof coverings.
2. **What should I look for?** This question identifies the deficiencies that the home inspector should report. A SOP identifies these deficiencies in general terms, such as not functioning properly and unsafe, but the home inspector must rely on knowledge and experience to identify specific deficiencies.
3. **Why is something deficient?** This question involves knowing the possible causes and implications of a deficiency. The SOP tells the home inspector to advise the client about the implications of a deficiency if the implications are not self-evident to the ordinary client. This knowledge is gained through education and experience, which is one reason why continuing education is essential for success in the inspection profession.

The following example demonstrates this three-question approach. The SOP answers the **what should I inspect** question by telling the home inspector to inspect the **exterior wall coverings**. The SOP answers the **what should I look for** question by telling the home inspector to report conditions that are **not functioning properly, significantly deficient, unsafe, and near the end of service life**. The condition of paint is an exterior wall covering deficiency that the home inspector should look for. Paint that is worn, faded, blistering, or peeling is a reportable deficiency because the condition could be classified as not functioning properly, significantly deficient, and near the end of its service life. The SOP tells the home inspector to explain to the client in the report why the paint is deficient. The implications of deficient paint include the expense of repainting and the potential for damage to wall coverings if the paint is not maintained.

REPORT WRITING

Communication

A home inspection consists of two tasks. The home inspector must **gather information about the condition of systems and components** that are required to be inspected according to the applicable SOP. The home inspector must **communicate the information in terms that the client can understand and use to make decisions**. Both tasks are important. It is not possible to produce a complete and accurate report based on incomplete or inaccurate information. It is possible, however, to produce an incomplete or inaccurate report based on complete and accurate information. In other words, **a good report will not make up for a poor inspection, but a poor report will make a good inspection useless**.

Home inspectors are in the communication business. This important fact cannot be over-emphasized. Clients need and expect that the home inspector will provide them with information they can understand and use to make decisions about one of the most important purchases they will make. All communications with the client, verbal and written, should be in service of the client's need for useful information.

All communications should be consistent. The home inspector should not make verbal statements that are contradicted in the written report. The home inspector should not make verbal statements that are omitted in the report. The home inspector's verbal tone, facial expressions, and body language should remain businesslike and consistent throughout the inspection and during all communication with all parties.

All communications should be understandable by an ordinary and reasonable person. Communication should be in simple terms. Technical terms, abbreviations, and acronyms should be avoided or at least defined.

Report Formats

A report format is a method of organizing and producing a written report that communicates the information gathered during the inspection. The first inspection report formats were hand-written lists of defects. These report formats evolved into two basic report formats that are still used today.

One format lists common defects on pre-printed forms. Additional space is provided for home inspector comments and for defects not contained on the form. This report format is often called a checklist report. Some home inspectors continue to use these pre-printed checklist reports with handwritten home inspector comments. Some of these checklist reports are computer generated and may contain canned comments that, when properly written, can comply with SOP reporting requirements. Some of these checklist reports with canned comments have evolved into a hybrid report format using checklist and narrative components.

The other format involves using a library of canned narratives that, when properly written, can comply with SOP reporting requirements. This report format is often called a narrative report. These reports are computer generated using word processing software (such as Microsoft Word) or using software designed to produce inspection reports. The home inspector selects which narratives to include in the report based on the information gathered during the inspection.

Each report format has its advantages and disadvantages. Checklist reports are often faster to produce. The inspector may be able to enter findings and pictures during the inspection and can deliver the report on site in many cases. This makes checklist reports popular with some home inspectors, clients, and real estate agents. Checklist reports may not fully comply with SOP reporting requirements, especially the requirement to report deficiency implications. Failure to comply with SOP reporting requirements does not serve clients, and increases home inspector risk.

Narrative reports often take longer to produce, resulting in next day or later report delivery. This reduces home inspector productivity and can cause distress for clients and real estate agents, who are under deadlines for submitting repair requests and for obtaining evaluations by specialists. Narrative reports, when properly written, are more likely to fully comply with SOP reporting requirements.

Inspection report software available from vendors usually comes with a library of canned comments (narratives). These comments can be a useful starting point for producing inspection reports, but the home inspector should not rely exclusively on these comments. Some comments may not apply to defects that are common in the home inspector's practice area. Some comments may not fully comply with licensing authority SOP requirements. The home inspector, not the software vendor, is responsible for inspection reports produced using vendor supplied comments. The home inspector may need to modify existing vendor supplied comments and add comments to fully comply with SOP requirements.

Deficiency Statements

Introduction
Deficiency statements are probably the most important part of an inspection report. Clients usually focus on these statements to the exclusion of all else in spite of exhortations urging them to read the entire inspection report. Deficiency statements must comply with the SOP used by the home inspector and with state regulations. The following are common elements of a deficiency statement. Each element is usually required unless otherwise indicated. The form or wording of each element may change depending on the report format used and on the deficiency, but the information provided should be similar regardless of the report format and the deficiency.

Identify or Describe the Deficiency
The deficiency statement should provide enough information to help the client understand the type or nature of the deficiency. The deficiency description should be accurate and precise. Inaccurate and imprecise statements can cause confusion and the home inspector may be held accountable for damages caused by any confusion.

For example, the home inspector sees a thin crack in the mortar of the brick veneer wall covering. An example of a potentially confusing description statement is: "We observed a crack in the bricks on the front of the house." This statement can be interpreted many ways. The client could assume that the bricks are structural bricks, not brick veneer. The client could assume that the crack runs through the bricks. This is a potentially more serious condition than a crack in the mortar. The client has no information to determine the width or length of the crack. Thin cracks are common and are usually not serious, but wide cracks are often more serious. A better description statement is: "We observed a thin crack in the brick veneer mortar on the front of the house." This statement accurately describes the crack as running through the mortar of brick veneer, and precisely describes the crack as thin which is a term the ordinary client can understand.

Explain the Implication of the Deficiency

The deficiency statement should provide enough information to help the client understand why the deficiency is important or what could occur if the deficiency is not addressed. In other words, why should the client care about the deficiency? **The implication statement is important and is often excluded or poorly explained** in inspection reports. Without this statement, the client may not have enough information to make an informed decision about how to address the deficiency with the seller or other party. Dissatisfied clients often use the lack of an implication explanation as a reason to hold the home inspector responsible for repairs and damages.

The implication statement need not be long; in fact, too much information can be as confusing as too little information. For example, the home inspector sees an electrical cable splice that is not contained in a box. A good implication statement is: "This is an electrical shock and a fire ignition hazard." A simple statement such as this explains the risks if the deficiency is not corrected in terms that the ordinary client can understand.

The implication statement should **strike a balance between helping the client understand the implications of the deficiency, and not being unduly alarming.** This balance can be difficult, especially when the deficiency involves subjects that the client may not understand. The implications of structural deficiencies are often difficult for clients to understand. For example, the home inspector sees a beam that has been notched in the center to install a garage vehicle door operator. The home inspector does not see any deformation or other damage. The implication statement might acknowledge the current lack of observed deformation or damage to reduce unnecessary client apprehension, yet also explain the implication of the deficiency. The implication statement might read: "We did not observe current deformation of the beam; however, deformation or failure could occur under certain conditions. We cannot predict whether deformation may occur in the future."

Advise the Client About How to Address the Deficiency

The deficiency statement should provide the client with the home inspector's recommendation about how to proceed. **This does not mean that the home inspector should specify or design a repair.** The home inspector should not do this even if qualified to do so. The home inspector is not hired or paid to assume this risk.

Most SOPs provide three options that the home inspector may use to advise the client:

- repair/replace the system or component
- have a qualified specialist evaluate the system or component
- monitor the system or component for possible future action

The home inspector should select one of the options provided by the SOP that the home inspector uses.

Repair/replace is the default option for deficiencies reported using not functioning properly and unsafe. The home inspector should recommend this option unless there is a valid reason for using another option. The decision to repair or replace should be based on the recommendation of the specialist that the client hires. A repair/replace recommendation might read: "We recommend repair or replacement as recommended by a qualified specialist."

Further evaluation by a qualified specialist is the appropriate recommendation when:

1. evidence of a deficiency exists but the cause or current state of the deficiency cannot be determined,
2. evidence of a deficiency exists, but confirmation requires analysis or procedures that are out of scope of a home inspection,
3. the system, component, or deficiency is beyond the home inspector's expertise.

Moisture stains on interior surfaces are an example of the first situation. Further evaluation is usually required to determine the source of the moisture and whether the moisture source is active. Malfunctioning HVAC systems (such as a low temperature drop across the evaporator coil) are an example of the second situation. Further evaluation is usually required to determine if there is a malfunction, why it occurs, and what repair might be appropriate. Home inspectors cannot know everything about every system and component that might be installed in a house. It is far better for the client and the home inspector when the home inspector acknowledges ignorance and recommends evaluation by a specialist. A further evaluation recommendation might read: "We recommend further evaluation by a qualified specialist and action as recommended by the specialist."

Monitoring for possible future action is the most difficult action recommendation, in part because it has the highest potential for improper use. Monitoring is most appropriate for systems and components that are still functioning properly but are near the end of their service life. These systems and components may need more frequent service and will need replacement at some future time. Monitoring may be appropriate when the home inspector wants to alert the client to a condition that the home inspector believes is not deficient at the time of the inspection, but may become deficient at some future time.

A monitoring recommendation should include advice about what conditions the client should look for and what the client should do if the conditions occur. For example, the home inspector sees a long thin crack in the mortar joint of a concrete block foundation wall. The wall presents no evidence of deformation or water infiltration. An appropriate monitoring recommendation might read: "We recommend that you monitor the crack on a regular basis. We recommend evaluation by a qualified foundation contractor if the crack becomes wider, presents horizontal displacement, or admits water."

Evaluate and monitor are frequently misused in inspection reports. They should rarely, if ever, be used when a system or component is not functioning properly, significantly deficient, or unsafe and when repair/replace is the clearly appropriate recommendation. They should not be used to avoid upsetting a real estate agent in an attempt to downplay a deficiency. **Evaluate should not be used to transfer risk back to the client by recommending evaluation of everything.** This diminishes the importance of the inspection and the reputation of the home inspector.

Recommend the Appropriate Contractor

Recommending the appropriate contractor to repair/replace or evaluate a deficiency is not specifically required by most SOPs; however, most home inspectors do so. This is part of providing the client with information necessary to make decisions. Recommending the appropriate contractor does not mean recommending a specific contractor. If the home inspector elects to recommend a specific contractor, the home inspector may not accept any compensation or consideration for the recommendation. Doing so could be an ethical violation or, at best, create the appearance of a conflict of interest.

Recommending the appropriate contractor is often easy. Plumbers handle plumbing deficiencies, electricians handle electrical deficiencies, etc. One difficult situation is when the cause or source of a deficiency is not apparent. Moisture stains are an example. Sometimes moisture stains are caused by a roofing deficiency, sometimes they are caused by a plumbing deficiency, and sometimes they are caused by an insulation or vapor retarder deficiency. In these situations, the home inspector may either use his/her best judgment about which contractor is most likely to be appropriate, or the home inspector may make a generic recommendation about using an appropriate specialist.

Another difficult situation involves structural deficiencies. Should the home inspector recommend a contractor or an engineer? Recommending a contractor is appropriate when there is a common or prescriptive action to address the deficiency. An example of such a deficiency is an improperly drilled or notched dimensional lumber floor joist. This deficiency can usually be addressed by installing blocking or by installing a sister joist. Refer to the Structural Components chapter for more about typical repairs of structural deficiencies. If after evaluating the deficiency, the contractor believes that the situation is beyond the contractor's expertise, the contractor should engage an engineer.

Recommending an engineer is appropriate when there is no common or prescriptive action to address the deficiency. An example of such a deficiency is an altered truss. An engineer must design and approve truss repairs. Many foundation-related deficiencies are also examples of deficiencies that require an engineer-designed repair.

Describe the Location of the Deficiency

Describing the location of the deficiency is not required by SOPs; however, many home inspectors do so. This serves all users of the report and reduces unnecessary and unproductive communication by helping people find the deficiency. Home inspectors often define directions used in the report by specifying that left and right are based on looking at the house from the street.

Include a Picture of the Deficiency Pictures are not required by SOPs; however, many home inspectors include them in reports. A picture helps identify and describe the deficiency, helps people locate the deficiency, and documents the condition of the system or component at the time of the inspection. A picture of each room can document the conditions during the inspection. Pictures can be very useful if questions about the inspection arise later.

Deficient Conditions

Introduction SOPs identify general conditions that the home inspector should identify and report. Most SOPs use similar terms; however, some use other terms, the meaning of which can be unclear. The home inspector must have a clear understanding of what constitutes a reportable deficiency both to serve the client and to avoid liability for failure to report a deficiency. The following are common terms used in SOPs to identify reportable deficiencies, and definitions of those terms. These definitions may vary by jurisdiction based on interpretations by regulators and by courts.

Reporting deficient conditions is often easy and obvious, but it can be difficult. The home inspector must decide for each potential deficiency whether to report it and what words to use when reporting it.

Not Functioning Properly (Not Functioning as Intended) A system or component that is not functioning properly is failing to perform an important function during the inspection, or evidence is visible that the system or component has failed. Examples are numerous and range from major deficiencies to minor adjustments or repairs. Specific examples include evidence of active water leaks, deformation of structural components, doors that stick or rub on the frame, and dripping faucets.

Significantly Deficient A system or component that is significantly deficient may, or may not, function properly during the inspection; however, **it presents a deficit that is likely to cause improper functioning under certain conditions or at some future time.** Conditions that can cause significant deficiencies include failure to comply with manufacturer's installation instructions or other standards, damage (intentional or unintentional), and deterioration. Examples include evidence of water leaks (current activity cannot be determined), structural components that are damaged, deteriorated, or improperly installed (e.g., over-spanned joists), clearance to combustible materials issues, and many electrical issues (e.g., double-tapped circuit breakers and wire splices that are not in covered boxes).

One difficult aspect of significant deficiencies is deciding whether and how to report significant deficiencies that have existed for years or decades without failing. Many systems and components are over engineered such that failure will occur only under unusual conditions. A significantly deficient system or component may not have been, and may never be, subjected to conditions that can cause failure. **Just because a significantly deficient system or component has not failed does not mean it will never fail.**

One example of a significant deficiency that can take years or decades to cause failure is the clearance between heat source and combustible materials. Pyrolysis can cause a reduction of the ignition temperature of wood, and this process can take many years depending on the temperature and frequency of exposure. Failure (ignition) can occur without visible evidence and without warning.

Unsafe Whether or not a condition is unsafe is based on the judgment of the home inspector, as is the decision when and how to report an unsafe condition. A condition is unsafe if it satisfies **all** of these criteria:

- **serious** injury could occur
- the injury **risk** is **significant**
- the injury could occur during **normal use** of the system or component

A serious injury may be defined as one that requires the injured person to be treated by a doctor. Significant injury risk means that the risk is fairly large or that the probability of injury is fairly high. What constitutes a fairly large risk or fairly high probability is difficult to quantify. This is a judgment call for the home inspector. Normal use means using the system or component in the intended manner for the intended purpose.

The definition of an unsafe condition varies over time and usually becomes broader. This can make it difficult to decide whether and how to report conditions that may have been considered safe in the past but are currently considered unsafe. The decision is simple, **there is no grandfathering of safety conditions**. A condition that satisfies all of the criteria is unsafe regardless of whether it may have been considered safe in the past, and regardless of whether it complied with regulations in effect when the system or component was installed.

If the home inspector believes that an unsafe condition exists, the more difficult decision is how to report the condition. The home inspector has **two options**. The home inspector can report the unsafe condition as a **deficiency and recommend that it be repaired/replaced**. This option is most appropriate for unsafe conditions in newer houses and for conditions that constitute a very high injury risk. The other option is to report the unsafe condition as **information and recommend that care be exercised** when using the system or component. This option is most appropriate for unsafe conditions in older houses, and for conditions that constitute a lower injury risk.

There are many examples of potentially unsafe conditions that have been accepted in the past. Stairs present many possible safety issues. Risers with more than ⅜ inch height difference are now considered unsafe because of the fall hazard potential. Handrails that are not graspable are now considered unsafe because of the fall hazard potential. Balusters that allow passage of a 4⅜ inch diameter sphere are now considered unsafe because of the child strangulation hazard.

End of Service Life Some SOPs require that the home inspector report systems and components that are near the end of their expected service lives. This is frequently (and incorrectly) interpreted as requiring that home inspectors report the age of components such as water heaters, HVAC equipment, and roof coverings. **Component age is usually an important factor when estimating whether a component may be near the end of its service life, but it is not the only factor.** Damage, deterioration, and improper installation are other factors that can reduce the service life of a component. Lower quality components often have a shorter service life compared to higher quality components. For example, an average quality air conditioning condenser usually has an expected service life of fifteen years in many areas. Condensers near the ocean can have an expected service life of five years because of deterioration by salt spray. For example, a three-tab fiberglass shingle presenting granule loss, stiffness or breaking when bent, or visible fiberglass strands at the edges may be near the end its expected service life even if it has not yet reached its twenty year warranty, and even if it presents no evidence of leaking.

A system or component that is near the end of its service life is not necessarily deficient. **Being near the end of service life is a condition, not necessarily a deficiency.** The home inspector should report the near end of life condition. A typical report statement might include setting client expectations for increased maintenance costs and for replacement at some future date.

A system or component that is at or beyond the end of its expected service life could be deficient because the system or component has a higher probability of imminent failure. The home inspector should report this condition and may consider recommending evaluation of the system or component so that the client might gain a better understanding about the system or component's condition. The home inspector should also set client expectations for increased maintenance costs and replacement at a date that could occur in the near future. **In no case should the home inspector make any statement that could be interpreted as an estimate of the remaining service life of a system or component.**

Several published lists of system and component expected service lives are available. One is the *Residential Rehabilitation Guide* published by the United States Department of Housing and Urban Development. It is free and can be downloaded from the publisher's websites.

Habitability

A few SOPs use the phrase "adversely affect habitability" as a deficiency that home inspectors must report. A definition of habitability is: "The condition of a building in which inhabitants can live free of serious defects that might harm health and safety." (*Black's Law Dictionary*, Seventh Edition) This definition has the potential to expand the definition of unsafe that is commonly used by home inspectors, and has the potential to introduce environmental and health issues that are typically excluded from a home inspection. Home inspectors who use a SOP that contains the term habitability should review their inspection agreement with a local attorney to reduce the chance that the term habitability could be interpreted in a detrimental manner.

Imminent Threats to People and to Property

One general inspection rule is that the home inspector may **not discuss findings and recommendations with anyone except the client** without the client's permission. Another general inspection rule is that the home inspector should **leave the property as it was before the inspection** and should not turn on or off any system or component that does not function using normal operating controls. The exception to these rules involves situations that present an imminent threat to occupant health and safety or an imminent threat of property damage. These imminent threat situations are uncommon; however, the home inspector should be prepared to respond appropriately when they occur. **A home inspector might be held responsible for damages if the home inspector fails to respond appropriately, even if the home inspector did not cause the situation.**

Imminent threats include, but are not limited to, significant fuel (gas or oil) leaks, water distribution pipe leaks, significant drainage pipe leaks, chimneys and vents that are blocked, disconnected, leaking, or significantly damaged, exposed and energized electrical components, probable fire hazards (e.g., fuel stored near an ignition source), the presence of dangerous amounts of carbon monoxide (if the home inspector tests for the presence of carbon monoxide), and houses where drugs such as methamphetamines may have been prepared (meth houses).

The appropriate response depends on the threat level and on conditions during the inspection. The home inspector should leave the house with all other parties during imminent life safety threats such as significant fuel leaks inside the house, dangerous carbon monoxide levels, and meth houses. The home inspector should call, or ensure that someone calls, the appropriate emergency service. The home inspector should attempt to turn off the water supply if a water distribution pipe leak is observed, and turn off the branch circuit serving exposed and energized electrical components. The home inspector should attempt to turn off the fuel supply if a significant fuel leak is observed inside the house if the home inspector believes it is safe and prudent to do so. Fuel leaks outside of the house, such as at the gas meter, are usually less dangerous because the flammable vapors are have more space in which to disperse.

The home inspector should notify, attempt to notify, or witness someone notify the property owner or the owner's representative if an imminent threat is observed. The owner's representative is usually a real estate agent, preferably the listing (seller's) agent. The home inspector should carefully and completely document notification attempts including the names and telephone numbers of people spoken to, the times of the calls, and a summary of the conversations. This includes leaving voice or text messages when people cannot be reached immediately. The home inspector should carefully and completely document all actions taken by the home inspector and other parties present to prevent or mitigate damage. The home inspector should take pictures if it is safe to do so. The home inspector should report that attempts were made to notify responsible parties about an imminent threat and should make appropriate recommendations not to use affected systems or components until repairs are made.

System and Component Descriptions

Introduction SOPs usually require that the home inspector describe certain systems and components in the inspection report. One reason for descriptions is to inform the client about the nature of important systems and components. Another reason is to demonstrate that the home inspector observed the systems and components.

The home inspector must accurately describe systems and components. In almost all cases, clients do not care about descriptions. If questions arise about the inspection, all aspects of the inspection and report can come under intense scrutiny. **Description errors can be used against the home inspector.**

Many houses have more than one type of system or component that the home inspector is required to describe. The home inspector should describe each type of system or component that are present at the property.

Definition of Describe All required system and component descriptions should be in the inspection report. Descriptions need not be long, but they should be **accurate and in sufficient detail so that the reader can distinguish the system or component from similar systems and components**. For example, describing hardboard lap siding as wood siding is not an acceptable description. There are many types and styles of wood-based siding.

Some components can be difficult to distinguish from similar components. Some components are often fully or partially concealed, such as wall structural components and floor structural components at the second story of a two-story house. The home inspector may speculate about the likely structural component type and material, but the home inspector should report that the components were concealed and that the nature and condition of the concealed components could not be confirmed. The home inspector should report any uncertainty about the type of component. The home inspector should recommend inquiry and evaluation if the client wants additional information about the nature and condition of concealed components, and about the nature and type of components about which the home inspector is uncertain.

Structural Component Description SOPs usually require that the home inspector describe the structural components of the house including the foundation, and the floor, wall, ceiling and roof structure. Refer to the Structural Components chapter for more about structural components.

The foundation description includes the foundation type and materials. Typical foundation types include slab on grade, slab on stem wall, crawl space, and basement. Typical foundation materials include concrete masonry units, concrete, bricks, stone, and wood.

The floor, ceiling and roof system descriptions include materials used. Typical materials include dimensional lumber, wood I-joists, and wood trusses. Typical floor and roof sheathing materials include wood, plywood, and oriented strand board (OSB). Some home inspectors describe the size of materials used, such as 2x10 floor joists, 2x8 ceiling joists, and 2x6 rafters. Describing floor, ceiling, and roof material size is optional.

The wall system description applies to above grade walls. Below grade walls and walls that are partially below grade are described with the foundation. Typical wall system materials include dimensional lumber, concrete masonry units, and bricks. Wall system components are usually concealed. Describing wall material size is optional.

Exterior Wall Covering Description SOPs usually require that the home inspector describe the exterior wall coverings of the house. Refer to the Wall Coverings and Related Trim section in the Exterior Components chapter for more about typical wall coverings.

The home inspector should accurately describe wall covering materials. Some houses do not have a wall covering material, such as houses made using structural brick and concrete masonry units. These houses may be painted. Paint is a coating, not a wall covering material. Some wall coverings can be difficult to distinguish from other wall coverings. EIFS versus stucco is a common example. Adhered artificial stone veneer versus adhered natural stone veneer is a less common example. The home inspector may wish to recommend evaluation of EIFS for moisture intrusion, especially for houses built before 2000.

Roof Covering Description SOPs usually require that the home inspector describe the roof coverings of the house. Refer to the Roof Components chapter for more about typical roof coverings.

The home inspector should accurately describe roof coverings. Some roof coverings can be difficult to distinguish from other roof coverings. Modified bitumen versus roll mineral is a common example.

Plumbing Descriptions SOPs usually require that the home inspector describe the interior water distribution pipes and DWV pipes of the house, domestic hot water equipment, including the energy source of the equipment, and the location of the main water supply and fuel supply shut off valves. The water service pipe and the building sewer pipe are almost always buried, so describing them is not required. Refer to the Plumbing System chapter for more about plumbing components.

Descriptions should be accurate and in sufficient detail to distinguish between similar materials and equipment. Plastic plumbing pipe should be described by the specific type such as PVC, ABS, CPVC, polybutylene, and PEX. Domestic hot water equipment should be described by the specific type such as storage tank, demand (often called tankless), and tankless coil. Energy source is usually electric, gas, or oil. Distinguishing between natural and propane gas is a good idea, but this is not specifically required.

The location of the main water shutoff valves and fuel shutoff valves should be in sufficient detail so the client can find them without unreasonable difficulty. Some home inspectors attach tags to these valves. This is a good idea, but it is not required and does not change the requirement to report the location of these valves. General directions such as left, right, center, front, and rear of the house combined with general locations such as crawl space, basement, and exterior are usually sufficient. The appropriate level of detail will vary by common practices in the home inspector's area. For example, if the main water shutoff valve is often located in an interior closet, the home inspector should identify the location and general purpose of the closet (foyer coat closet, kitchen pantry, etc.).

Water shutoff valves and fuel shutoff valves are sometimes concealed by plants, occupant belongings, and other materials. The home inspector should report if a shutoff valve was not located and recommend inquiry about the location. **Home inspectors are not required to, and usually should not, operate shutoff valves.** They could leak or become stuck in one position.

Electrical System Descriptions SOPs usually require that the home inspector describe the electrical service current of the house, the predominant branch circuit wiring method, the presence or absence of smoke alarms and carbon monoxide alarms, the location of the main electrical service disconnect equipment (the service equipment), and the location of all subpanels. Refer to the Electrical System chapter for more about electrical components.

Determining the service current can be difficult if there is no one labeled main service disconnect. A split bus panelboard is an example of when there is no single main service disconnect. The home inspector can sometimes estimate the service current rating by determining the lowest rated component among the service entrance conductors, the electric meter, or the service equipment panelboard. Situations exist when the service entrance conductors are not visible or the label has been removed from the service equipment panelboard cabinet. The home inspector should report if he/she estimates the service current, and if he/she cannot determine the service current. The home inspector should recommend evaluation if the client wants assurance about the service current.

Branch circuit wiring method descriptions should be accurate and in sufficient detail to distinguish between similar wiring methods. Typical branch circuit wiring methods include nonmetallic sheathed cable (NM), armored cable (AC), underground feeder cable (UF), intermediate metallic conduit (IMC), and liquidtight flexible conduit (LFC). The home inspector should not use brand names (such as Romex and BX) to describe wiring methods.

Most SOPs require only that the home inspector report whether or not a smoke alarm and a carbon monoxide alarm are installed in the house. The home inspector usually is not usually required to inspect the alarms to determine if the alarms are functional, properly installed, and installed where currently recommended. The home inspector is not required to determine the smoke alarm type and the smoke alarm and carbon monoxide alarm age. Some home inspectors perform some of these out-of-scope services.

The location of the main electrical service disconnect equipment and subpanels should be in sufficient detail so the client can find them without unreasonable difficulty. The location descriptions are the same as for the water shutoff valves and fuel shutoff valves.

Heating and Cooling System Descriptions SOPs usually require that the home inspector describe the heating and cooling systems of the house, including their energy source. Refer to the Heating System chapter and the Cooling System chapter for more about these components.

Heating systems should be described by the specific type such as gas-fired or oil-fired forced-air furnace, gas-fired or oil-fired hot water boiler, gas-fired or oil-fired steam boiler, and electric baseboard heater. Most cooling systems and heat pumps should be described as split systems with an air-source condenser outside and an evaporator coil inside. Package heating and cooling systems are usually described as gas packs, if gas-fired, or as package heat pumps. The home inspector should report if package systems supply both heating and cooling (they usually do). Through-wall units may provide heating, cooling, or both. The home inspector should report which functions the through-wall unit performs.

Insulation and Vapor Retarder Descriptions SOPs usually require that the home inspector describe the visible insulation and vapor retarders in unfinished areas, and report the absence of insulation at conditioned spaces. The requirement to describe insulation, vapor retarders, and to report the absence of insulation includes unfinished attics, crawl spaces, and basements. This also includes slab foundations; however, the requirement to insulate slab foundations is recent and has not been adopted in all jurisdictions. The home inspector should use good judgment when reporting the absence of insulation around slab foundations at older houses and in jurisdictions where this requirement has not been adopted. Refer to the Insulation and Ventilation chapter for more about these components. Most SOPs do not require that the home inspector disturb insulation to observe the vapor retarder and to observe components concealed by the insulation.

Insulation should be described by the general type, such as loose-fill fiberglass, loose-fill cellulose, spray foam insulation, sheet insulation, and fiberglass batts. Measuring the insulation or estimating its R-value is not required; however, many home inspectors perform this service. The vapor retarder should be described by the general type such as Kraft paper, foil, and polyethylene sheeting.

Fireplace and Fuel-Burning Appliance Descriptions SOPs usually require that the home inspector describe masonry and prefabricated fireplaces, fuel-burning appliances and accessories installed in fireplaces, and installed fuel-burning appliances such as decorative gas fireplaces and wood-burning stoves. Some SOPs require that the home inspector describe chimneys. Refer to the Heating System chapter and Fireplaces and Chimneys chapter for information about these components.

A fireplace should be described as a masonry or prefabricated fireplace that is designed to burn wood. A masonry and prefabricated fireplace that was designed to burn wood, but has been converted to use vented or unvented gas logs, should be described using these terms. The home inspector should report if a gas log lighter has been installed.

A fireplace insert or a wood-burning stove should be described using these terms and by its fuel type. Typical fuel types include gas, wood logs, and wood pellets.

A vented fireplace that is designed to burn only gas or oil should be described as a decorative gas (or oil) fireplace or as a decorative gas (or oil) appliance. Describing the vent system is a good idea because these appliances have several different types of vent systems, but a vent system description is not required. An unvented gas or oil "fireplace" should be described as being unvented or vent-free.

A chimney should be described as a masonry chimney or a prefabricated metal chimney. The home inspector should report if the chimney has been converted to allow only gas-burning appliances, or if the chimney may still accommodate a wood fire.

Attic, Crawl Space, and Roof Inspection Method Description SOPs usually require that the home inspector describe the methods used to inspect the attic, crawl space, and roof coverings. This is probably **the most important description because it informs the client about inspection limitations that are often encountered when inspecting these areas**.

Attic inspections usually consist of one or more of the following methods. Some roof systems (such as low slope roofs and vaulted ceilings) have no accessible attic, so there is no attic to inspect. The home inspector should report this fact even though it seems obvious. Some home inspectors perform a head-and-shoulders attic inspection in which the home inspector views the attic from the access opening without entering the attic. This is a limited inspection that will not allow observation of most attic areas. Some home inspectors inspect the attic from the equipment service platform (if any) or from the access opening by entering the attic and standing above the access opening. This is a limited inspection that will not allow observation of many attic areas. Some home inspectors inspect the attic by traversing as much of the attic as they believe is safe. This is a full attic inspection, but even full inspections usually have limitations. Home inspectors are not required to traverse attic structural members that are obscured by insulation or other materials.

Almost all attic inspections have some limitations regarding the areas that are accessible. Access is usually restricted by low headroom height, especially near the eaves. Obstructions, such as HVAC ducts, truss webs, and ceiling height changes can limit access. The home inspector should report to the client about which attic areas were inaccessible or that were inspected from a distance. The home inspector should be as specific as possible in describing the inaccessible areas and the reasons that they were inaccessible.

Crawl space inspections are similar to attic inspections. Some crawl spaces are inaccessible. Some are inspected using the head-and-shoulders technique and some are entered partially or fully depending on whether the home inspector believes it is safe to do so. Most SOPs do not require that home inspectors enter crawl space areas that have an opening smaller than 16x24 inches or that have a vertical distance between the crawl space floor and an obstruction of less than 24 inches.

Many home inspectors enter crawl space areas that do not comply with the minimum accessibility guidelines; however, the home inspector should be aware that crawl spaces can be dangerous areas and that home inspectors are not required to enter areas that the home inspector believes are not safe to enter because of the risk of personal injury or property damage. Crawl space dangers include toxic or poisonous plants and animals, raw sewage, energized and exposed electrical wires, and fall and entrapment hazards such as wells and cisterns. The home inspector should assess the risks of entering a crawl space and report to the client about specific crawl space areas that were not inspected, and the reasons they were not inspected.

Roof covering inspections usually consist of one or more of the following methods. The best roof covering inspection is performed by walking on the roof. This is the best way to observe deficiencies and the only way to observe some deficiencies. Some home inspectors perform roof covering inspections from a ladder placed against the eaves at several accessible locations around the house. This is a good way to inspect roof coverings if walking on the roof is not safe or prudent. Some home inspectors perform roof coverings from the ground using binoculars. This is a limited inspection that may not allow observation of many deficiencies.

Many home inspectors walk on roofs if the roof is accessible and if the home inspector believes it is safe and prudent to do so; however, walking on the roof is not required. Some roofs, especially second story roofs, are too high to safely reach with ladders carried by many home inspectors. Some home inspectors reach second story roofs by setting up the ladder on a low slope roof below the second story roof; this is not required. Some roofs are too steep to safely walk on. What constitutes too steep is a decision that the home inspector must make at each inspection. Roofs that are wet should not be walked on. Some roof coverings, such as clay tiles and slate, are too fragile to safely walk on. Some roof coverings, such as metal and glazed concrete tiles, are often too slippery to walk on.

It is common to use multiple inspection methods when inspecting roof coverings. Some roof areas may be accessible and other roof areas may be inaccessible. The home inspector should be specific when reporting which roof areas were accessible and inaccessible, and should be specific when reporting roof areas, if any, that were not inspected using any methods.

Inspection Limitation Statements

Introduction Most SOPs require the home inspector to **report when a system or component that is required to be inspected is not inspected**, and to **report the reasons why it was not inspected**. In addition to reporting each system and component not inspected and the reasons why, the home inspector **should include in all limitation statements a recommendation that the client have the system or component inspected, and a warning that the uninspected system or component may possess costly deficiencies**. This additional recommendation and warning are not required; however, situations have occurred when the home inspector was held responsible for the condition of an uninspected system or component in spite of reporting the inspection limitation.

Most SOPs contain a long list of out-of-scope systems and components, general limitations, and specific conditions and tasks that are excluded from a home inspection. In theory, the home inspector should be able to rely on the limitations and exclusions of the SOP. In practice, home inspectors have found that it is prudent to report and document inspection limitations that apply to each inspection. The home inspector should take pictures to document limitations such as locked doors, unusual obstructions, and concealment by occupant belongings. The pictures are not required to appear in the report.

Access and Visibility Limitations It is common practice not to inspect certain components because of restricted access and visibility. Examples include the heat exchangers of modern furnaces, the combustion chambers of modern water heaters, and the interiors of chimneys. A statement about the limitations of inspecting fully or partially concealed parts of each such component is sufficient. A typical limitation statement about a furnace that has sealed access covers might read: "We did not observe the internal components in the furnace including the automatic safety controls and the heat exchanger. We did not observe the internal components of the evaporator coil and those parts of the condenser behind sealed access panels. The access panels were not readily openable or were sealed shut. Some parts of the HVAC system components including, but not limited to, vents, ducts, coolant tubes, and control cables are concealed or are otherwise not visible for inspection."

It is often not practical to fully inspect known problem components, such as Federal Pacific electrical panels, or to list the potential problems with these components. The home inspector should include a statement about such known problem components along with an evaluation recommendation. A typical statement might read: "The main electrical panelboard appears to be manufactured by Federal Pacific, also known as Federal Electric and Challenger. These panelboards and circuit breakers present various potential electrical and fire safety hazards. These panelboards and circuit breakers are usually past their expected service life. We recommend that a qualified electrical contractor who is familiar with this type of panelboard thoroughly examine it and provide a written evaluation of its current condition and cost of replacement, if recommended."

Many components are frequently concealed within walls and ceilings, behind and under soil, behind plants, and behind or under other construction materials. These components include structural components such as studs and joists, plumbing pipes, electrical cables, HVAC ducts, appliance vents, and exterior wall coverings. A general limitation statement about components that are usually concealed is often sufficient. A typical statement might read: "We were not able to observe the wall, ceiling, and second story floor structural components because they were concealed by finish materials and by insulation."

Attics, crawl spaces, and roofs are frequently not accessible for a full inspection. This is discussed in the System and Component Descriptions section in this chapter. Reasons why these areas are not accessible include safety, low clearances, height above ground, locks, and concealment by snow, soil, and occupant belongings. The home inspector should include specific limitation statements about which areas were not fully inspected and about the reasons why they were not inspected. A typical statement might read: "We entered the crawl space and observed the accessible areas. Some areas were not accessible due to low clearances under framing, HVAC ducts, and similar obstructions. The following areas were not accessible: approximately 400 square feet in the left crawl space area."

Shutdown Limitations Plumbing, electrical, and HVAC systems and components are sometimes shut down. Shutdown can affect part of the system such as a plumbing fixture or an electrical branch circuit. In this case the home inspector should report the specific component that was shut down and the cause of the shutdown. Typical causes of partial shutdowns include tripped or blown overcurrent protection devices and closed valves. Shutdown can affect the entire system. System shutdown is usually caused by the utility service being turned off. The home inspector should report the utility shutdown and disclaim inspection of all affected components. A typical statement might read: "The water was turned off during the inspection. We were not able to fully inspect or test water supply and drain pipes and fixtures, water heaters, and any appliances or systems that require water to operate such as dishwashers."

The home inspector should not activate systems or components that have been shut down. Experienced home inspectors ask about the status of utilities when scheduling the inspection; however, real estate agents and clients are sometimes not aware about the status of utilities.

Out-of-Scope Component Limitations The home inspector should not rely on a SOP to identify components that were present on the property and were not inspected or were only partially inspected. Examples of out-of-scope components include: accessory buildings and structures, fences, swimming pools and spas, recreational equipment, water features, outdoor cooking equipment, outdoor fireplaces and fire pits, radon mitigation systems, and large decorative accessories such as planters.

Some types of systems and components are in-scope while similar components are out of scope. Examples of out-of-scope systems include heat and energy recovery ventilation systems and ground-source and water-source heat pumps.

The home inspector should specifically disclaim inspection of out-of-scope components that are not inspected. If the home inspector elects to inspect any of these components, the home inspector should report what aspects of the component were inspected and disclaim inspection of the remaining aspects.

Inspection of and comments about out-of-scope components could be interpreted as expanding the scope of the inspection. The home inspector should include a limitation statement that any inspection of or comment about out-of-scope components is performed as a courtesy and that the inspection does not change the agreed-upon inspection scope. A typical statement might read: "We observed a barn-like structure on the property. ASHI standards do not require that we inspect such structures. Our inspection of such structures consists of a limited safety inspection, the objective of which is to determine if the structure presents an immediate and significant hazard to health and safety. While conducting this limited safety inspection we may observe and report visible deficiencies. Reporting deficiencies does not expand the scope of the inspection. The structure does not appear to present an immediate and significant hazard to health and safety unless otherwise specified in this report."

Incomplete Work Limitations Inspection of new construction and houses undergoing remodeling sometimes have systems or components that are not complete and ready for inspection. The home inspector should report that these systems or components were not ready for inspection and were not inspected.

Environmental Hazards Limitations Environmental hazards include, but are not limited to: air and water quality, fungi (mold), lead, asbestos, and dangerous, damaging, and annoying animals including their feces. These hazards are out of scope of a home inspection; however, it is common practice to report visible significant environmental hazards and recommend evaluation. The home inspector should include a limitation statement advising the client that reporting visible environmental hazards does not alter or expand inspection scope, and that additional environmental hazards could be present. A typical statement might read: "Determining the presence or absence of environmental hazards is specifically excluded from home inspections by ASHI standards. Environmental hazards include, but are not limited to, fungi (mold and related organisms), radon, asbestos, animals (including their nests and droppings), plants, noise, and other conditions that may be harmful or inconvenient. This exclusion applies whether the hazards are visible or concealed. We do not express a finding about the presence or absence of environmental hazards whether visible or concealed. We may report about environmental hazards, but doing so does not mean that we report all hazards and doing so does not remove or change the environmental hazards exclusion."

Fungal growth is common in some parts of a house, such as the crawl space, and is common in some locations, such as warm/humid climates. Home inspectors in locations where fungal growth is common should include a limitation statement advising the client that fungal growth is common, and that reporting the presence of fungus is not within the scope of a home inspection. A typical statement might read: "Almost all homes in this area have some level of fungal infestation, especially homes on crawl space foundations. Fungi are almost always present on materials in the crawl space and inside HVAC ducts and equipment. Most people tolerate fungal infestations without significant adverse effects; however, some people are allergic or sensitive to fungi. We do not express a finding about the presence or absence of fungi whether visible or concealed. We recommend evaluation of the home by a qualified industrial hygienist if you wish assurance about the presence or absence of fungi in the home."

Other Report Contents

Introduction Experienced home inspectors have found that certain information is useful in inspection reports. Most of the following information becomes useful only if questions arise later about the inspection.

Recommended Report Information Some jurisdictions have specific language that is required to appear in reports. The home inspector should include any such language exactly as specified by the jurisdiction and in all documents as specified by the jurisdiction.

The full legal name of the inspection company should appear in all reports. This includes designations, such as Inc. and LLC, indicating that the inspection company is a separate legal entity from the home inspector. Contact information such as the company address, telephone number, and email address may also be included. Some of these may be required items in jurisdictions where home inspectors are regulated.

The name of the home inspector who performed the inspection and the home inspector's license number, if any, should appear in all reports. This is especially important for multi-inspector companies. This may be a required item in jurisdictions where home inspectors are regulated. Some jurisdictions require that the home inspector sign the report.

The names of all known clients should appear in all reports. The home inspector should ask about the identity of all parties that will have an interest in the property being inspected; however, only one client name is on many reports. This is acceptable.

The full mailing address of the inspected property should appear in all reports. A legal description is unnecessary. This is usually a required item in jurisdictions where home inspectors are regulated. Many home inspectors publish a picture of the front of the house to help identify the property. This is a good idea but is not required.

The inspection date and beginning and ending times of the inspection should appear in all reports. This helps establish the conditions under which the inspection occurred. The inspection date may be a required item in jurisdictions where home inspectors are regulated.

A means to identify the parties present during the inspection should appear in all reports. This helps identify witnesses to what occurred during the inspection in case questions arise later. Names are better, but titles such as client, seller, buyer's agent, and seller's agent are acceptable.

A statement identifying the SOP under which the inspection was conducted should appear in all reports. Only one SOP should be identified. The SOP in the report should be consistent with the SOP in the inspection agreement. This may be a required item in jurisdictions where home inspectors are regulated. Some home inspectors include a copy of or a link to the SOP with the report. This is a good idea but is not required.

A section that establishes the reader's expectations regarding the inspection and report should appear in all reports. This information should include subjects such as the inspection objective and scope; these should be consistent with the inspection agreement. This may be a required item in jurisdictions where home inspectors are regulated. Terms that have a particular meaning as used in the report should be defined. An example is terms such as *satisfactory* or *acceptable*, that are used to describe system or component condition.

A statement establishing the ownership of the report by the home inspection company should appear in all reports. This statement should, among other topics, define the appropriate uses of the report and restrict distribution of the report to parties that are not involved in the transaction or that otherwise should not receive the report. A common example is restricting distribution of the report to subsequent purchasers of the property.

A statement advising the client to read and act upon all recommendations in the report should appear in all reports. This statement should recommend that repair work be performed by a licensed and qualified specialist, and that all necessary inspections and consultations with specialists occur during the inspection (due diligence) period. This is an important statement because clients often delay taking action under the normal time pressures in real estate transactions. The home inspector may wish to advise the client that issues not addressed before the sale closes become their issues. Even if the client is not concerned about an issue, the next purchaser might be concerned and the client may be required to pay for repairs to facilitate their sale of the house.

Optional Report Information Home inspectors include many different types of information in reports. The criterion for evaluating whether information should be included in a report is whether the information serves the client's interest by helping make the report easier to understand and use.

Many home inspectors include the weather conditions during the inspection such as temperature, whether precipitation occurred recently before or during the inspection, and whether there was snow on the ground or on the roof. This can be useful information establishing inspection conditions; however, this information can be obtained after the fact from available sources. Weather conditions often change during the inspection. The home inspector should report the conditions that fairly represent the average conditions during the inspection.

Some home inspectors include general statements about conditions that are common to houses in the home inspector's service area. These statements may be based on the house type and the era during which the house was built. Common statements include information about asbestos in houses built before about 1980 and about lead paint in houses built before about 1978.

INSPECTION TOOLS

Introduction Home inspections are primarily visual inspections; however, many home inspectors use tools during the normal inspection process to confirm or verify visual information, and to conduct further analysis of defects. The following is a discussion about some of the commonly used tools. Inclusion of a tool in this discussion does not mean that the tool is required, and exclusion does not mean that the tool has no value. Each home inspector should make a business decision about which tool to purchase, when to use them, and whether to charge additional fees for their use.

Home inspectors who use more advanced (and costly) tool often do so under a separate inspection agreement and charge additional fees for the services. Some jurisdictions that license home inspectors specify certain minimum tool and specify when they must be used. Some jurisdictions prohibit home inspectors from performing certain services or require additional licenses or certifications to perform the services.

Three-Light Receptacle Tester A three-light receptacle tester is intended to determine if a receptacle is wired correctly. Some also have a button that allows testing of the GFCI function of GFCI receptacles and circuit breakers. Refer to the Electrical System chapter for more about using these testers to test GFCI operation. These testers can detect common receptacle wiring errors, such as reverse polarity (hot/neutral reverse), disconnected neutral, and disconnected ground. Most home inspectors use these testers, and their use (or use of a more Sophisticated instrument) is required by some SOPs.

These testers can produce inaccurate results. They cannot detect multiple wiring errors. They may provide inaccurate results caused by problems with equipment connected to the receptacle branch circuit. They will produce an inaccurate result if a bootleg ground has been installed. This is when the receptacle grounding terminal is connected to the receptacle neutral terminal.

The home inspector should not report that a receptacle is incorrectly wired based on the results from a three-light tester. The incorrectly wired receptacle should be reported as having tested as incorrectly wired and should be referred for further evaluation. Similarly, the home inspector should not report that receptacles are correctly wired based on results from a three-light tester. The correct finding is that no wiring errors were detected.

More sophisticated instruments, usually called **circuit analyzers,** are available. These devices are more accurate than three-light testers and can detect more defects. They can cost a few hundred dollars compared to around ten dollars for a three-light tester. Circuit analyzers are not required by SOPs and are used by relatively few home inspectors as compared to three-light testers.

Voltage Sniffer This tool is also known as a voltage detector, voltage tester, and a tick tracer. A voltage sniffer detects voltage at wires, receptacles, switches, and other locations where electricity is present. It does so without touching the energized component by detecting the magnetic field emitted by electricity. It emits a beeping or ticking sound when voltage is present. This tool is a good safety device for home inspectors, especially when encountering potentially energized wires in attics and crawl spaces. It is also useful for determining if electricity is present at receptacles and switches.

Use of a voltage sniffer is not required by SOPs. Their use by home inspectors is common in most markets.

Multimeter This tool is also known as a clamp-on ammeter, which describes one of its most commonly used functions. A multimeter is most commonly used by home inspectors to measure current drawn by appliances such as condensers, electric water heaters, and electric heating elements. The home inspector opens the jaws of the multimeter and clamps them around one of the energized wires serving the appliance. Probes can be used to measure voltage and resistance in a circuit.

Use of a multimeter is not required by SOPs. Their use by home inspectors is varies between markets.

Moisture Meter A moisture meter detects and measures water within materials. There are two types of moisture meters. The pin-type measures the resistance between pins inserted into the material being tested. Resistance decreases as the moisture content of the material increases. The pinless-type uses radio frequency to measure the moisture in the material. Some moisture meters combine both types. Each meter type has advantages and disadvantages.

Pin-type meters are limited to measuring about as deep as the pins are long (about 5/16 inch). Some pin-type meters have long pins that can be inserted deep into the material. These meters are often used for EIFS moisture intrusion inspections. Pin-type meters leave holes in the material where the pins are inserted. This can be a problem when measuring finish materials.

Pinless meters measure moisture to a depth of between ½ and 1 inch. Moisture deeper than this may not be detected. Pinless meters are best when measuring moisture under hard materials that cannot be penetrated by pins, and under finish materials where damage by the pins would be objectionable.

Most moisture meters are calibrated to measure moisture in wood. Some have adjustments that can recalibrate for measuring other materials. **Both types of meters can produce inaccurate results if not properly calibrated and used.**

Moisture meters should not be used as an inspection tool, meaning that they should not be routinely used where water infiltration is not suspected. Use of moisture meters as an inspection tool takes the inspection beyond a visual inspection. The home inspector might be held responsible for water intrusion problems that were not detected.

Moisture meters are better used as a confirming tool, meaning that they may be used to confirm or deny the presence of water where evidence is observed, for example, stains, and where water intrusion is suspected. They are good when used to measure differences in moisture between different areas.

Use of a moisture meter is not required by SOPs. Their use by home inspectors is common in most markets.

<u>Infrared (Laser) Thermometer and Infrared Camera</u> An infrared thermometer and an infrared camera measure the infrared radiation emitted from the surface of the object being measured. **They cannot see though objects and cannot determine the condition inside the object** unless the condition affects the infrared radiation emitted from the surface of the object.

An infrared thermometer and infrared camera convert the infrared radiation measurement into a temperature readout. A camera provides an image of the object, the colors of which correspond to the temperature of the object. Typical uses of an infrared thermometer involve determining the temperature of air around HVAC supply registers and return grilles, circuit breaker temperature, and hot water temperature. Typical uses of an infrared camera involve detecting moisture intrusion, absent or improperly installed insulation, circuit breaker temperature, and air leaks.

Temperature measurements using an infrared thermometer and an infrared camera are subject to error. The error can be significant. Infrared thermometers display the average temperature over an area. The size of the area increases with the distance from the thermometer, so the **temperature measurement error is usually larger when the thermometer is further away from the object.** The size of the area is usually a function of the price of the infrared thermometer. Less expensive models measure a larger area compared to more expensive models.

Infrared thermometer and infrared camera temperature readings are affected by the emissivity of the object being measured. Emissivity may be simply defined as the ability of the object to emit infrared radiation. Lower emissivity means a greater chance that the measured temperature will be incorrect. Shiny metal usually has a lower emissivity than oxidized or dull metal, but most metal has a relatively low emissivity unless it has been covered with a dark, dull material. Most non-metal objects usually have a relatively high emissivity.

Use of infrared thermometers is not required by SOPs. Their use by home inspectors is common in most markets. They may be used as an inspection tool when used properly. A probe-type thermometer is usually more accurate and should be used instead of an infrared thermometer when possible.

Use of infrared cameras is not required by SOPs. An infrared camera should not be used as an inspection tool for the same reason as a moisture meter. It may be used as a confirming tool or as an added inspection service using an inspection agreement written for an infrared camera inspection.

Probe Thermometer A probe thermometer is a temperature measurement device that has a thin metal probe about six inches long that may be inserted into the object being measured. Typical uses of a probe thermometer involve determining the temperature drop across the air conditioning evaporator coil and hot water temperature.

Use of a probe thermometer is not required by SOPs. Their use by home inspectors is common in most markets.

Combustible Gas Detector A combustible gas detector detects gas such as methane (natural gas) and propane. Typical use involves testing gas fittings for leaks. All but the least expensive models will detect other combustible gasses, but these gasses are uncommon in houses. Less expensive models provide an audible tone that varies with the amount of gas detected. More expensive models also provide a visual indication of the gas amount detected.

Use of a combustible gas detector is not required by SOPs. Their use by home inspectors is uncommon in many markets. Their use is common practice in some markets and their use may be prudent in markets where using a combustible gas detector is the local standard of care. In most markets, a combustible gas detector may be used as a confirming tool but should not be used as an inspection tool. The home inspector should not report the use of a combustible gas detector unless a leak is confirmed. In this case, the home inspector should recommend evaluation of the fuel gas supply system as recommended by a qualified specialist.

A few home inspectors attempt to detect a cracked heat exchanger by using a combustible gas detector or a carbon monoxide detector to test the heated air leaving a fuel-fired furnace. These instruments are not designed for this use and the results are unreliable. This is not a recommended procedure.

Carbon Monoxide (CO) Detector A carbon monoxide gas detector detects the presence of carbon monoxide. Typical uses involve testing for the presence of CO in the house, around fuel-burning appliances, and in vents and chimneys. Less expensive models provide an audible tone that varies with the amount of gas detected. More expensive models provide a digital display of the CO amount detected.

Use of a CO detector is not required by SOPs. Their use by home inspectors is uncommon in many markets. In most markets, a CO detector may be used as a confirming tool, but should not be used as an inspection tool. The home inspector should not report the use of a CO detector unless CO is confirmed. In this case, the home inspector should recommend evaluation of fuel-fired appliances as recommended by a qualified specialist.

Infrared Thermometer, Multimeter, Moisture Meter.

Three-Light Tester, Probe Thermometer, Voltage Sniffer.

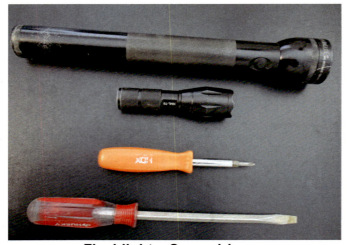
Flashlights, Screwdrivers.

Infrared Camera.

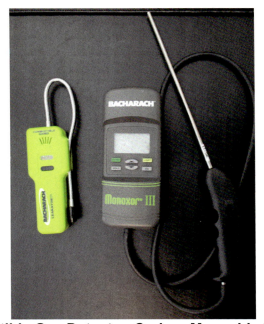

Combustible Gas Detector, Carbon Monoxide Detector.

THE INSPECTION PROCESS

Introduction Each home inspector develops a routine for conducting an inspection. There is no correct routine. The important thing is to develop a routine and use it consistently on every inspection. Consistency is the best method of inspecting all required systems and components.

The following is one inspection routine. Typical systems and components that are usually inspected in each will be identified. The list of typical components is not intended to be complete and will vary by region, type of house, and age of house. The order of steps may vary depending on events such as when the client and the real estate agent arrive.

The material in this section is not included in the National Home Inspector Examination content outline. It is unlikely that exam questions will be based on this material. This material is presented to help home inspectors.

Arrival at the Inspection Experienced home inspectors usually take note of the neighborhood while driving to the property. They note the general condition of the neighborhood, types of houses, and any significant differences between the houses in the neighborhood and the property to be inspected. This observation can provide clues about components that may need special attention. For example, if there is snow on the roof of other houses but none on the house to be inspected, this could indicate poor insulation or air leakage into the attic. The home inspector should inspect the attic for lack of insulation, lack of fireblocking, indications of ice damming, and moisture problems such as rust on nails and staining and deterioration of wood.

Some home inspectors arrive early and begin the inspection prior to the appointment time. Use caution because the client may feel slighted if he/she wanted to be present for the entire inspection. Also, an early arrival may annoy the occupant.

Meet and Greet The home inspector should take charge of the inspection. After appropriate introductions and pleasantries, the home inspector should take the client and agent aside for the pre-inspection conference. Typical conference events include discussing the inspection agreement and signing the agreement if this has not already occurred, discussing inspection objectives, scope, and limitations, and discussing any client concerns about the house or the inspection. The home inspector should invite the client to accompany the home inspector and establish the guidelines for client activities, such as not accompanying the home inspector on the roof, into the attic, and into the crawl space.

Walkabout Some home inspectors like to get an overall impression of the property by conducting an initial walkabout on the outside and on the inside. During the walkabout, the home inspector notes the location of things like attic and crawl space access points, electrical panels, water heaters, heating equipment, cooling equipment, fuel storage and supply components, shutoff valves, and accessory structures. Experienced home inspectors will get a feel for the overall condition of the property and for systems and components that may require special attention.

Exterior Inspection Many home inspectors like to begin the inspection at the exterior of the house. The exterior inspection includes site conditions and the exterior components. The home inspector can also gain clues about the type and condition of some structural components.

Typical components inspected during the exterior inspection include grade and drainage, vegetation, retaining walls, driveways and walkways, stoops, stairs, guards, handrails, decks, patios, wall coverings, eaves, windows, doors, sidewall and penetration flashing, roof coverings and roof penetrations, gutters and downspouts, and chimneys. Electrical components inspected during the exterior inspection include the service drop, electric meter, service equipment, panelboards, receptacles, and lights. HVAC components inspected during the exterior inspection include condensers and their service cutoff boxes, package HVAC equipment such as gas packs, and vents serving fuel-burning appliances. Plumbing components often inspected during the exterior inspection include the presence of a building sewer cleanout (not always present outside), hose bibbs, and plumbing vents.

The home inspector should note the condition of grade, drainage, gutters, and downspouts. Water directed toward the foundation alerts the home inspector to look for water infiltration and foundation defects. This can provide clues to the location of possible water infiltration issues in the basement or crawl space.

The home inspector should note the condition of attic and crawl space ventilation components. This will help with the subsequent attic and crawl space ventilation inspections.

The home inspector should note cracks in the foundation and wall coverings, especially rigid wall coverings such as brick, stone, and stucco. The location, length, direction, width, and width increase can provide clues to the location of possible foundation and framing issues that might be visible in the basement or crawl space.

Some home inspectors like to inspect the roof coverings, roof penetrations, and flashing from the outside then inspect the attic afterwards. They also like to inspect for roofs that drain into small areas and roofs that drain toward sidewalls. They believe this inspection sequence provides better clues about where to look in the attic for water leaks. Other home inspectors like to enter the attic first to determine if there are deteriorated sheathing areas that may fail if walked upon from the roof surface. Either order is fine.

Garage Inspection
Some home inspectors inspect the attached garage before beginning the exterior inspection and some do so upon completing the exterior inspection. Either order is fine. A detached garage and carport are usually inspected during the exterior inspection.

Typical components inspected during the garage inspection include the vehicle door, the door operator (if any), the service door (if any), the door into the house, windows (if any), fire separation between the garage and the house, and the garage walls, floor, and ceiling. Electrical components include panelboards (if any), receptacles, and lights. Plumbing components may include a water heater and vent, a sink, water and fuel supply pipes, and water and fuel shut-off valves. HVAC components may include a furnace or air handler, ducts, and vents.

Inspection access is often restricted in garages by occupant belongings. The home inspector should report unusual access restriction and document with a picture.

Attic Inspection
Some home inspectors inspect the attic before beginning the interior inspection and some do so upon completing the interior inspection. Either order is fine; however, it is better in the summer to get into the attic as early as possible during the inspection while it is still relatively cool. It can be dangerous to spend too much time in a very hot attic.

Typical components inspected during the attic inspection include the visible framing and sheathing, fireblocking, insulation, ventilation, chimney, and pull-down stairs (if any) or other attic access opening. Plumbing components may include a water heater, water and fuel supply pipes, and plumbing vent pipes. HVAC components may include a furnace or air handler including service access, ducts, condensate disposal components, and vents. Electrical components may include subpanels, wiring, receptacles, and lights.

Interior Inspection
The home inspector should select a place to start the interior inspection and start at that place each time. The home inspector should move from the start point in the same direction each time, such as always turn left or always turn right. Some home inspectors like to start on the second story and work down. This can help identify plumbing

leaks from second story bathrooms that may appear on first story ceilings. Home inspectors who inspect kitchen appliances should start the dishwasher at or before the beginning of the interior inspection because a full cycle can take more than an hour.

Typical components inspected during the interior inspection include the walls, ceilings, and floors, stairs, guards, and handrails, windows, doors fireplaces and other fuel-burning appliances, cabinets and countertops, and kitchen appliances (if inspected). Plumbing components may include a water heater, water and fuel supply pipes, bathroom and kitchen plumbing fixtures, and bathtubs and showers. HVAC components may include a furnace or an air handler including service access, ducts, condensate disposal components, vents, and grilles and registers. Electrical components may include panelboards and subpanels, wiring, receptacles, and lights. The home inspector should report the presence or absence of smoke alarms and carbon monoxide alarms. Remember that testing of the alarms themselves is out of scope.

The home inspector should note cracks at the walls, floors, and ceilings, especially at the corners of windows and doors. The location, length, direction, width, and the width increase can provide clues to the location of possible foundation and framing issues that might be visible in the basement or crawl space. Difficult window and door operation can provide similar clues, especially when combined with cracks.

The home inspector should note floors that are significantly uneven or sloping, especially around openings in the floor system such as for chimneys and stairways. These can also provide clues to possible foundation and framing issues.

Inspection access is often restricted inside by occupant belongings and occasionally by locked doors. The home inspector should report unusual access restrictions and document with pictures.

Basement/Crawl Space Inspection Many home inspectors perform the basement/crawl space inspection at the end of the inspection. When performing a crawl space inspection, some home inspectors chose to wear a protective suit. This is especially true for the crawl space inspection because it often is dirty and difficult. The home inspector should avoid tracking crawl space contents back through the house. Plumbing leaks can be easier to detect near the end of the inspection because the home inspector should have run plenty of water in all plumbing fixtures.

Typical components inspected during the basement/crawl space inspection include the foundation walls, floor framing, stairs, guards, and handrails, windows, doors, fireplaces and other fuel-burning appliances, insulation, ventilation, and vapor retarders. Plumbing components may include a water heater, water and fuel supply pipes and shutoff valves, drainage pipes, bathroom plumbing fixtures, bathtubs and showers, sump pumps and sewage ejectors. HVAC components may include a furnace, boiler, or air handler including service access, ducts and pipes, condensate disposal components, vents and chimneys, and grilles and registers. Electrical components may include panelboards and subpanels, wiring, receptacles, and lights. The home inspector should report the presence or absence of smoke alarms and carbon monoxide alarms in the basement. Remember that testing of the alarms themselves is out of scope.

Crawl spaces, attics, and some basements are places people seldom go. They are the places where deficiencies are most likely to be found. The home inspector should plan to spend a significant part of the inspection in these places.

Inspection Wrap Up The home inspector should strongly encourage client attendance at the inspection, at least at the wrap up. There is no substitute for discussing inspection findings with the client and showing the client important deficiencies when practical. The home inspector should schedule time to answer client questions without being rushed to conduct the next inspection.

Most home inspectors expect payment at the end of the inspection. This is the appropriate time to ask for payment. Delaying payment until closing involves increased paperwork and involves the risk of not receiving payment if the sale does not close. Delaying payment could also be perceived as a conflict of interest in that the report may have been written to facilitate the sale.

The home inspector should walk around the house to ensure that appliances are off, water is off, thermostats have been set to the same temperature as when the home inspector arrived, windows and doors are closed and locked, lights are on or off as when the home inspector arrived, and that the house is in the same condition as when the home inspector arrived.

Please visit https://nationalhomeinspectorexam.org/prepare-for-the-exam/ and take advantage of the practice quizzes. The questions in the practice quizzes are designed to reflect the difficulty of the questions on the actual exam. The questions on the practice quizzes are not questions on the National Home Inspectors Exam. Passing the practice quizzes does not guarantee that you will pass the National exam. You will still need to study all topics to be prepared for the National exam.

8: PROFESSIONAL RESPONSIBILITIES

BUSINESS LAW

Introduction

Business owners need to know about the legal environment in which they operate. In order to protect themselves and to serve their clients, home inspectors should understand the basics of business law. The following is a very brief discussion of basic legal concepts and procedures as they relate to operating a business. Business schools spend at least one semester teaching these concepts, so a few paragraphs are only to introduce the concepts.

Laws dealing with the conduct of business, including conducting business with consumers, are governed mostly by **state laws**. These laws vary significantly between states. The following discussion of business law is based on **general principles**. When dealing with laws, the devil is very much in the details. **The details could make a substantial difference in how home inspection agreements and home inspection reports should be written.**

Dealing with Dissatisfied Clients

Introduction Operating any business comes with risk. This is true for home inspection as well. A claim against a home inspector begins with a dissatisfied client. The client may have legitimate reasons for being dissatisfied; however, many claims are without merit. These meritless claims often result from the client's misunderstanding about the scope and objective of a home inspection. From a practical perspective, however, it does not matter whether the claim has merit. The home inspector must defend both legitimate and meritless claims and the cost to do so can be similar. The difference occurs at the end. The home inspector may have to pay a judgment in addition to legal costs for a legitimate claim, or no judgment for a meritless claim.

While uncommon, the first notice the home inspector may receive about a dissatisfied client is a monetary demand letter from an attorney. Home inspectors who carry Errors and Omissions (E&O) insurance should notify their E&O insurance company immediately and turn the matter over to the company to defend. Home inspectors who do not carry E&O insurance should turn the matter over to their attorney immediately to defend. **Home inspectors should not attempt to deal with claims themselves after attorneys become involved.**

Resolving an Incident The more common first notice of a dissatisfied client is when the client contacts the home inspector to discuss the client's concerns. **Home inspectors who carry E&O insurance should report this contact to their insurance company.** Doing so is called reporting an incident, and is usually required by the terms of the insurance policy. **Failure to report an incident could result in denial of coverage if the incident escalates into a claim.** Reporting an incident usually does not affect policy cost or renewal.

Attempting to resolve an incident with the client involves a risk that the home inspector could do or say something that makes the situation worse. If the home inspector elects to risk attempting to resolve the issue, the following tactics have proven useful. **Listen** to the client without getting defensive. Gather as much information as possible about the client's perspective, and about the client's issues. **Take pictures** to document the issues. **Do not admit fault or apologize.** An apology could be construed as admitting fault. Attempt to reach a settlement, even if you may not be at fault. Consider the settlement a cost of doing business. If you reach a settlement, **obtain a full release from all claims** regarding the home inspection. A release is a legal document that your attorney should draft. Your E&O insurance company may have a model release form for you to use.

The E&O Claim Process

Each E&O insurance company has its own claims process. The following process is a summary of a typical claim. When a claim is received, a claim file is opened. At this time the home inspector's policy deductible is usually payable. Any part of the deductible that is not spent processing and investigating the claim should be refunded to the home inspector; however, do not expect a refund.

The claim may be assigned to an investigator who investigates the claim in order to determine if the insurance policy covers the claim, and if home inspector complied with the applicable standard of care. This investigation may involve reviewing the claim and any supporting documentation provided by the claimant (usually the home inspector's client), interviewing the home inspector, reviewing the home inspection report, and conducting an on-site investigation. The investigator issues an opinion to the insurance company regarding whether the home inspector complied with the applicable standard of care.

The insurance company will, in many cases, attempt to settle the claim regardless of whether the home inspector appears to be at fault. This is a business decision to avoid the expense and uncertainty of litigation. If a settlement is reached, the insurance company obtains on behalf of the company and the home inspector a full release regarding all claims that may result from the home inspection. If a settlement is not reached, the company turns the claim over to a local attorney to defend the claim. The company pays all costs to investigate, defend, and pay any settlement or judgment above the home inspector's deductible.

The Litigation Process

Civil litigation involves a dispute between two or more parties. Most civil litigation is handled in state courts. **Each state has its own rules and procedures for dealing with civil litigation.** Litigation involving a home inspector would rarely, if ever, be tried in federal court. The amount involved in home inspector litigation is usually below the $75,000 threshold to qualify for federal court jurisdiction, and the dispute usually does not involve a matter that falls within federal court jurisdiction.

The following is a brief summary of the civil litigation process. It assumes that the home inspector (defendant) and the client (plaintiff) are the only parties. In reality, there may be other defendants, such as the seller and the real estate agents.

Parties in litigation may file additional claims against each other. The defendants may file **cross-claims** against each other. A cross-claim is litigation between defendants (or plaintiffs) that relates to and is carried on within the litigation between the defendant and the plaintiff. One common purpose of a cross-claim is to shift any potential liability among the defendants.

The defendant may file a **counterclaim** against the plaintiff. A counterclaim may or may not relate to the underlying action. A counterclaim is litigation initiated by a defendant carried on within the original litigation. Purposes of a counterclaim may include to help mitigate the client's claims, and to litigate any claims the defendant might have against the plaintiff. Clearly, counterclaims and cross-claims can add significant complexity.

Civil litigation begins with a **complaint** filed with the court. The complaint is the beginning of a process called the **pleadings**. Complaints in Federal Court and many state courts identify the parties and contain a short and plain statement of the claim that will give the defendant fair notice of what the plaintiff's claim is and the grounds upon which it rests. Complaints in other states identify the parties, describe the basic facts of the case, describe the legal reasons supporting the plaintiff's case, and request the relief (damages) sought by the plaintiff.

Upon receipt of a properly filed complaint, the court issues a **summons** to the defendant notifying the defendant of the complaint and requiring the defendant to provide an **answer**. Failure to provide an answer or a motion to dismiss can result in a default judgment against the defendant. **A summons, therefore, should never be ignored.**

The defendant should file an answer to the complaint with the court within the time stated in the summons. **Timely filing of all pleadings and motions is essential.** Failure to make timely filings can be used against the failing party. The answer will usually admit, deny, or plead insufficient information to admit or deny the plaintiff's alleged facts. The answer may contain **affirmative defenses** that deny the defendant's liability. The answer may also contain a **motion to dismiss** the complaint.

Discovery is the next step. Discovery is the compulsory disclosure of information relevant to the litigation. The purpose of discovery is to make each side aware of information held by the other side so that there are no surprises at trial. **Interrogatories** are written questions from one party that are answered in writing by the other party. **Document production** is the request for documents that are relevant to the case. Documents can be paper and electronic and can include emails and text messages. **Depositions** are verbal answers to questions posed by the opposing attorney. Depositions are conducted under oath, are recorded by a court reporter, and may be recorded using audio or video.

Litigation often ends in one of several ways before a trial. The parties may reach a **settlement**. The parties may voluntarily enter **arbitration** or **mediation**, or the court may order mediation before trial. The court may grant a motion by the defendant to dismiss the case. **Dismissal** may occur when the plaintiff's complaint is legally defective. A defective complaint would be one in which the plaintiff failed to plead facts, law, or both that would support the plaintiff's request for relief, or one in which the complaint was defective in form. The court may grant a motion by either side for **summary judgment**. Summary judgment occurs when there is no significant disagreement about the facts and when the moving party is entitled to win as a matter of law.

A trial may be a **bench trial** or a **jury trial**. A judge hears the case in a bench trial, decides which facts seem to be most accurate, applies the law, and renders a decision. A jury performs these functions in a jury trial under the direction of a judge. The judge or the jury are said to be the **trier of fact**.

Prevailing in a civil trial does not mean that the judgment you receive will be paid. A judgment is an opportunity to collect money from the defendant. Defendants can make it difficult and costly to collect a judgment, up to and including bankruptcy, which can make the judgment worthless. For this and many other reasons, **civil litigation should be avoided**.

Small Claims Court Most jurisdictions have a court system that deals with civil disputes in which there is not enough money in dispute to warrant hiring (and paying) a lawyer. Typical disputes include breach of contract, return of personal property, and tenant evictions. The maximum amount in dispute varies between jurisdictions and is usually between $5,000 and $10,000.

The procedures in small claims court are less formal than in other courts. Lawyers are not required, and may not be allowed in some jurisdictions. A judge hears from both sides and renders a decision. The losing party may appeal to the next higher court in that jurisdiction. The losing party may attempt to avoid collection of the judgment as previously described.

If you sue or are sued in small claims court it is important to find out about all forms and filing requirements. It is also important to prepare a brief (a written summary of your case), and provide a copy to the clerk of the court when you arrive, for the judge or commissioner to read. Most of the time they do read it.

Types of Home Inspector Liability

Introduction Many home inspectors perform ancillary services in addition to home inspections. Examples of ancillary services include radon measurement, mold sampling, water quality sampling, pool and spa inspections, wood destroying organisms inspections, and new construction inspections. Each ancillary service subjects the home inspector to potential liability similar to a home inspection. The following liability discussion focuses on home inspections. Liability types are the same for ancillary services.

Breach of Contract A breach of contract occurs when a party to the contract fails to perform the party's promises. Consider the following situation. The home inspection contract cites the ASHI Standard of Practice (SOP) as the standard under which the home inspection will be performed. The home inspector's promise is, therefore, to perform the home inspection using the ASHI SOP. The client alleges that the home inspector failed to properly report a defect that should have been reported using the SOP. The home inspector may be liable for breach of contract if the client can prove the allegation, and if the client can prove damages as a result of the breach.

The usual remedy for a breach of contract is monetary damages, the amount of which the party alleging the breach must prove. There are many types of damages. Actual (compensatory) damages usually include the cost to repair or replace the improperly reported system or component, but should not include the cost of upgrades or improvements. Actual damages may include other damages such as loss of use of the house during the repairs. "Benefit of the bargain" damages attempt to compensate for the reduction in the value of the property due to the alleged defects, which the plaintiff did not know about when making the deal to purchase. **Nearly every claim against a home inspector will include: "I would not have bought the house had I known about the alleged defects."**

Most claims against home inspectors involve monetary damages; therefore, breach of contract should be the typical basis of a complaint against a home inspector. **Compensation for personal injury is usually not recoverable under breach of contract**; personal injury claims are usually brought as a negligence claim.

Negligence Negligence, as usually alleged against home inspectors, is divided into two classes. The most common is **ordinary/simple negligence**. Ordinary negligence is the failure to exercise the standard of care that a reasonably prudent person (home inspector) would have exercised in a similar situation. Less common is **gross negligence**, which some define as the failure to exercise slight care and others define as a conscious act or omission in reckless disregard of a legal duty.

The classic elements of negligence are: (1) the defendant (home inspector) had a **duty** toward the plaintiff (usually the client), (2) the home inspector **breached the duty** (failed to perform a competent home inspection), (3) the home inspector's **breach was the cause of the plaintiff's damages**, and (4) the **plaintiff suffered physical injury**. The plaintiff is usually responsible for proving these elements by a preponderance of the evidence.

The duty of the home inspector toward the client is derived from two concepts. One concept is the **fiduciary relationship** between the home inspector and the client. A fiduciary relationship arises when someone has a duty to act for the benefit of another on matters that are relevant to the relationship. **The home inspector has a duty provide accurate information for the client's benefit.** The other concept is the home inspector's **duty to exercise due diligence** when conducting the home inspection and reporting the results. Diligence is the attention and care required from a person in a given situation. Due diligence is the diligence that a reasonable person would undertake to satisfy a legally required duty.

It is interesting to note that **all parties on the purchase side of a real estate transaction have a duty to exercise due diligence. This includes the real estate agents and the buyer.** The extent of the due diligence varies as does the knowledge that the party is expected to bring to bear on the situation. It is possible that a client's failure to exercise due diligence could reduce or even bar recovery from a home inspector if the client alleges negligence.

The definition of negligence contains the potentially troubling concept of the **standard of care (SoC). The SOC for a home inspection is usually the applicable SOP that should be stated in the home inspection contract**; however, exceptions are possible. If the plaintiff can establish that a different SOC is practiced by home inspectors in the area, then it is possible that the home inspector could be held to that SOC regardless of whether the SOP sets a different standard. For example, the SOC in some markets is to use a combustible gas detector to detect gas leaks. Use of a combustible gas detector is considered a technically exhaustive procedure in most SOPs and would not usually be required. If the plaintiff can establish that the SOC is to use a combustible gas detector, then the plaintiff might prevail if the client suffered damage as a result of the home inspector's failure to properly use a combustible gas detector.

The tort of negligence was originally developed as a means for the plaintiff to recover damages for personal injury, not for damages that are solely monetary in nature. The Economic Loss Rule may bar negligence claims for which damages are solely monetary, as are many claims against home inspectors. This rule may not apply in all jurisdictions, and may be interpreted differently depending on the facts of a case.

The typical remedy awarded in negligence claims is actual damages incurred by the plaintiff, the amount of which the plaintiff must prove. Punitive damages and attorney's fees may be awarded in gross negligence cases.

Fraud There are many types of fraud. The two types most likely to be alleged against a home inspector are **common law (tort) fraud** and what might be called **statutory fraud**. Common law fraud is the knowing misrepresentation of the truth or the concealment of a material fact to induce another to act to his/her detriment. Statutory fraud is defined by legislation, often as part of a consumer protection law.

Statutory fraud may have different elements, different remedies, and may have other differences compared to common law fraud. While many states have consumer protection laws, their applicability to home inspectors varies by state.

Common law fraud has similar elements in many jurisdictions. The usual elements of common law fraud are: (1) a past or present **material fact was not accurate**, (2) the defendant **knew the fact was not accurate or stated the fact with a reckless disregard for accuracy**, (3) the defendant **intended** for the plaintiff to act on the inaccurate fact, (4) the **plaintiff did not know** the fact was not accurate, (5) the plaintiff **reasonably relied** upon and acted upon the inaccurate fact, (6) the plaintiff suffered **damage** that was caused by the inaccurate fact.

Common law fraud is different from other civil litigation in at least two respects. Courts usually require pleadings that describe the specific fraudulent conduct. Many jurisdictions require a **clear and convincing evidence burden of proof** rather than the preponderance of evidence burden of proof applicable in most civil litigation. These differences make common law fraud more difficult to allege and to prove.

The typical remedy awarded in fraud claims is monetary damages incurred by the plaintiff, the amount of which the plaintiff must prove. Punitive damages and attorney's fees may be awarded. Rescission of the real estate purchase contract is possible, though unlikely, if the fraud induced the buyer to purchase the property.

Negligent Misrepresentation Negligent misrepresentation is a relatively new tort. It attempts to bridge the gap between negligence and fraud by creating a **duty among those in the business of providing information to take reasonable care to provide accurate information**. As stated in the Restatement (Second) of Torts §522: "One who, in the course of his business, profession or employment or in any other transaction in which he has a pecuniary interest, supplies false information for the guidance of others in their business transactions, is subject to liability for pecuniary loss caused to them by their justifiable reliance upon the information, if he fails to exercise reasonable care or competence in obtaining or communicating the information."

The elements of negligent misrepresentation are identical to those of fraud with one important **exception**. The **defendant may have believed the inaccurate information to be true**, but had no reasonable basis for believing that it was true. There is little case law applying negligent misrepresentation to home inspectors; however, this tort would seem to apply directly to home inspectors. Home inspectors should, therefore, take care when making statements and reporting about the lack of defects in a system or component. Such statements should be made based on reasonable information to support the statements.

The typical remedy awarded in negligent misrepresentation claims is monetary damages incurred by the plaintiff, the amount of which the plaintiff must prove. Punitive damages and attorney's fees are usually not awarded.

PRE-INSPECTION AGREEMENTS (CONTRACTS)

Introduction

No inspection service should be performed without first having a signed pre-inspection agreement (contract). Getting a signed contract before every inspection has been difficult in practice, but with modern communications (email, the internet) and modern methods to obtain signatures on documents, it should not be too difficult to obtain a signed contract before beginning each inspection. Some states that regulate home inspections, and many insurance companies that write errors and omissions insurance for home inspectors, require obtaining a signed contract prior to the start of the inspection.

Contracts are governed by state laws (statutory law) and by court decisions (case law). **The rules governing contracts are different in every state.** Some contract provisions, such as limitations of remedies (liability), are allowed in some states and not in others. The following discussion covers information about contracts that is common among most states; however, this is not intended to offer legal advice. The home inspector should review all contracts with a local attorney, ideally one that is knowledgeable about home inspections or one with some experience in real estate law.

Many home inspectors perform ancillary services in addition to home inspections. Examples of ancillary services include radon measurement, mold sampling, water quality sampling, pool and spa inspections, wood destroying organisms inspections, and new construction inspections. **Each ancillary service is different** with different objectives, scope, and limitations. Each service should be performed using a separate inspection agreement that is written to address the unique nature of the ancillary service. The following discussion of contracts applies to home inspection contracts and to contracts for ancillary services.

Contract Basics

Definition of a Contract A **contract is an agreement** between two or more parties that creates obligations that may be enforceable at law. The operative word in this definition is agreement. There must be an agreement between the parties that a contract exists, and an agreement about the terms of the contract, otherwise there is no contract. This agreement (mutual assent) was sometimes called a meeting of the minds.

Most contracts need not be in writing; in fact, **the written document is not the contract. The agreement between the parties is the contract**. The written document is just the vehicle for documenting the agreement. In practice, unwritten (oral) contracts are extremely difficult to enforce because it is difficult to objectively establish the terms of the agreement. All contracts should, therefore, be in writing. Once a written agreement has been reached between the parties, oral testimony is usually not allowed to alter the terms. All contract terms should, therefore, be within the four corners of the final written document.

Elements of a Contract Four elements must exist before there is an enforceable contract. **All four elements are required.** The elements are offer, acceptance, consideration, and mutual assent. There are, of course, other elements, rules, and exceptions involved when dealing with contracts. These are out-of-scope for this book, and beyond what most home inspectors need to know.

There must be an **offer**. An offer is a promise to do something, or to refrain from doing something at a future time under certain conditions. For example, a home inspector's website lists a fee of $350 to inspect a house up to 2,000 square feet; this constitutes an offer.

There must be **acceptance** of the offer as offered. Acceptance may be an act, or may be inferred by conduct. An attempt to accept an offer that changes the terms of the offer is not acceptance; it is a **counteroffer**. For example, a prospective client calls the home inspector and schedules a home inspection of a 1,999 square foot house; this would constitute acceptance. Scheduling a home inspection of a 2,001 square foot house for $350 would constitute a counteroffer, which the home inspector would need to accept before an agreement is reached.

There must be an exchange of **consideration**. Consideration is something of value. Consideration may be money, property, or a promise to do or not to do something. Continuing the example, the home inspector's consideration is the promise to perform a home inspection for $350, and the client's consideration is the promise to pay the home inspector $350.

There must be mutual assent (**agreement**) to enter into a contractual relationship. The best way to establish mutual assent is by both parties signing the written contract; however, mutual assent may be established by the actions of the parties. Electronic signatures are usually valid.

Agency As a general rule, the contracting parties, **the principals, should agree to the terms of the contract**. For home inspection contracts, the principals are usually the home inspector and the clients, usually the buyers. Internet-based methods of delivering and signing contracts make it easier to get client signatures on inspection contracts. There are times, however, when it is not practical to have all principals, or any principals, sign the inspection contract. This raises the question about **who, other than the principals, may sign an inspection contract**. The answer is based in the concept of agency.

Agency is a fiduciary relationship in which one party (**the agent**) may **act on behalf** of another party (**the principal**) and, among other actions, enter into an agreement (contract) that binds the principal. A real estate agent is only one type of agent; there are many others.

Whether an agent (real estate or otherwise) may sign an inspection contract and bind the client (buyers) depends on whether the agent is acting **within the scope of the agent's authority**. In other words, did the clients authorize the agent to act on their behalf and sign the inspection contract? This can be a complicated question. It is uncommon for the home inspector to have actual knowledge of the scope of an agent's authority. As a general rule, home inspectors should have their client's sign the contract because a real estate agent's signature may not bind the client(s) to the terms and conditions of the contract. The home inspector should consult with a local attorney to determine how the state laws impact whether agents can sign home inspection contracts on behalf of clients.

Adhesion Contracts An adhesion contract (also known as a contract of adhesion), in colloquial terms, is an **offer he can't refuse**. The conditions for an adhesion contract can occur when there is no opportunity to negotiate the contract terms, especially when a court finds that one party has more power or knowledge compared to the other. When dealing with clients, the home inspector is considered to have more power or knowledge than the client. A finding that an inspection contract is an adhesion contract can cause the contract itself or clauses, such as a limitation of remedies to be severed from the contract and deemed unenforceable.

A common reason why an inspection contract may be deemed an adhesion contract is that the contract was presented to the client at the inspection, or worse, after the inspection. An inspection is often considered essential to proceeding with a real estate purchase contract, and the inspection (due diligence) period is often short. Any delay in the inspection process, such as to find and schedule another inspection, may be impractical and the client may believe there is no alternative other than to agree to the home inspector's terms contained in the home inspector's contract.

The home inspector should provide the inspection contract to the client before the inspection. The ideal time would be within a day after the inspection is scheduled. The minimum is the day before the inspection, but even this could be challenged in some circumstances. Providing a copy of the inspection contract on the home inspector's website is helpful, but it is **not a substitute for sending the contract to the client before the inspection**. Anything other than a signed contract may not be enforceable. Delivery of the inspection contract to the client should include an offer to discuss the contract with the client before the inspection.

Pre-Inspection Agreement (Contract) Contents (Required)

Introduction Contract contents, like all other aspects of a contract, are governed by state law. The following are contents usually required in inspection contracts. Some of these contents may be required by state home inspector regulations.

Inspection Company Name The inspection contract should state the full **legal name of the home inspection company**. This is extremely important when the home inspection company is operating as a corporation or LLC. **Failure to use the company name could subject the home inspector to personal liability for damages**. Some states require the name and license number of the home inspector performing the inspection be on the inspection contract.

Client Names The inspection contract should state the names of all parties who are purchasing the property, or who will have a financial interest in the property. This is to ensure that another party is less able to claim after the fact that the party was not bound by the contract. In practice, inspection contracts often contain only the name of the party scheduling the inspection. This is acceptable, if not ideal. Adding a clause stating that the signature of one party binds all parties might help in cases where all parties are not known.

Inspection Location The inspection contract should state the full address of the property to be inspected. The legal description is not necessary.

Inspection Date The inspection contract should state the inspection date. Some jurisdictions require including the inspection time.

Inspection Fee The inspection contract should state the inspection fee. If the fee consists of multiple services (for example a radon test and a water quality test) then the fee for each service should be listed separately.

Inspection Objective/Purpose The inspection contract should contain a statement of the inspection objective/purpose. An objective/purpose statement might read: "The objective of this inspection is to identify major deficiencies requiring immediate major repair that may exist on the property at the time of the inspection." The inspection contract may contain statements that define terms such as major deficiency and immediate major repair. Doing so helps remove uncertainty about how these important terms could be defined.

Standard of Practice (SOP) The inspection contract should identify one SOP under which the inspection will be performed. The SOP should be incorporated by reference into the contract. This makes the SOP part of the contract as though it were actually printed in full in the contract.

Exclusions and Limitations The inspection contract should contain a comprehensive list of the important exclusions and limitations of the inspection. The list can be a summary of the exclusions and limitations in the SOP identified in the contract.

Signatures The inspection contract should contain the signatures of all parties named in the contract. **Home inspectors operating as a corporation or LLC should sign the contract as a representative of the company** by placing their title after their name. For example, John Smith, Member (for a LLC), or John Smith, President (for a corporation). This is extremely important when the home inspection company is operating as a corporation or LLC. Failure to sign as a company representative could subject the home inspector to personal liability for damages.

Pre-Inspection Agreement (Contract) Contents (Optional)

Introduction The following are terms that may be contained in an inspection contract. Some of these terms may not be allowed or may be restricted by state law.

Client Responsibilities Making the client contractually responsible for certain tasks may help reduce the client's ability to substantiate some common claims against home inspectors. Client responsibilities might include: (1) making the home inspector aware of concerns contained in the seller's disclosure, (2) reading the full inspection report and acting on all recommendations during the due diligence period, (3) initiating a telephone call with the home inspector if the client does not attend the inspection, (4) conducting a walkthrough of the property after the seller's belongings have been removed, (5) ensuring that permission has been secured for the home inspector to enter and inspect the house.

Disclosure of Inspection Findings Home inspectors are restricted by codes of ethics and sometimes by state home inspector regulations from distributing the inspection report and discussing inspection findings with anyone except the client. This includes real estate agents. Including a release from this restriction in the inspection contract allows the home inspector to use good judgment about report distribution and discussing findings with other parties who have a legitimate need for the information. The client should be able to delete the release if he/she wishes.

Report Redistribution It is common for inspection reports to be used by subsequent purchasers when the home inspector's clients do not purchase the property. Reports are also used by third parties. The inspection contract should contain a clause that prohibits transfer of the report to third parties. A similar statement should be placed in the inspection report. The inspection contract may contain an indemnification clause that obligates the client to defend the home inspector against third party claims and to pay judgments against the home inspector that result from third party claims.

Recovery of Legal Fees and Expenses As a general rule, each party in a dispute is responsible for its own costs incurred during the dispute. The inspection contract may contain a clause that allows the prevailing party to recover costs from the losing party. The clause should apply equally to both parties. This clause can help discourage frivolous claims; however, this can be a double edge sword because the home inspector could be responsible for the client's costs if the home inspector loses.

Right to Observe Claims The inspection contract should contain a clause that gives the home inspector the right to observe alleged errors and omissions before the alleged errors and omissions are repaired. The clause should bar claims based on alleged errors and omissions that the home inspector was not allowed to observe prior to repair. The clause should allow emergency repairs.

Time Limitation on Filing Claims The inspection contract should contain a clause that limits the time during which a client can file a claim based on alleged errors and omissions. The time limitation should be reasonable. One year is a common limit. Time limitation may be set by law in some jurisdictions. The time should begin on the inspection date regardless of when the alleged error or omission is discovered, if allowed by state law. This prevents the home inspector from being liable, perhaps in perpetuity, for errors and omissions discovered long after the inspection.

Inspection Scope Expansion Home inspectors often report about out-of-scope deficiencies and out-of-scope systems and components. Doing so could be interpreted as expanding the inspection scope to include other out-of-scope deficiencies, systems, and components. The inspection contract may contain a clause stating that reporting out-of-scope deficiencies does not change the inspection scope.

Alternative Dispute Resolution Disputes processed through the courts are often very costly and time consuming. Alternative dispute resolution venues, such as arbitration and mediation, can be a more cost-effective way to resolve disputes involving the relatively small amounts that are typical in home inspection related claims.

Mediation and arbitration share some similarities, but the results are different. Both are voluntary, although mediation can be court-ordered prior to litigation. Mediation is a facilitated negotiation between the parties. The mediator attempts to help the parties reach a voluntary settlement. Mediation ends if the parties cannot reach a settlement. Arbitration is a quasi-judicial process in which the arbitrator considers the evidence presented by both parties and renders a decision. The arbitrator's decision is binding and can be enforced by court order.

It is important to note that an agreement to use alternative dispute resolution, especially arbitration, restricts or eliminates the right to litigate disputes. Enforcing an alternative dispute resolution clause on a client may be more difficult in some situations, including adhesion contracts. The following procedures may not be necessary, but they may help in some situations. Make the clause conspicuous by means such as a larger type font or placing the clause inside a box. Have the client initial the clause.

It is important to note that **alternative dispute resolution**, while less expensive than litigation, **is not free**. The client may be required to pay a fee up front to begin the process. This fee may be greater than the limitation of remedies recovery potential. It is important that the combination of an alternative dispute resolution clause and a limitation of remedies clause not work together to effectively limit the client's alternatives for pursuing claims against the home inspector. This combination could cause both the alternative dispute resolution and the limitation of remedies to be severed as unconscionable and deemed unenforceable.

Most states have laws regarding alternative dispute resolution such as the Uniform Arbitration Act. The home inspector should consult with a local attorney about how to craft an enforceable alternative dispute resolution clause. Some insurance companies offer a reduction in the premium paid for errors and omissions insurance for specifying a specific arbitration company they desire in the pre-inspection agreement.

Limitation of Remedies (Liability) Home inspection is a risky business. For a fee of a few hundred dollars, **home inspectors assume thousands of dollars of potential liability**. This potential liability exists even when the home inspector performs the service exactly as specified by the SOP. Many home inspectors attempt to limit this liability by including a limitation of remedies clause in the inspection contract. A limitation of remedies clause attempts to limit the amount that the client can collect for a claim against the home inspector. A limitation of remedies clause does not prevent a client from initiating a claim or action against the home inspector. **A limitation of remedies clause does not limit the remedies of parties who are not named in the contract.** An example of such a party is the real estate agent who is sued along with the home inspector and everyone else involved in a house sale gone bad.

Enforcing a limitation of remedies clause against a client may be difficult, and may not be allowed in some jurisdictions. The following may improve the likelihood of successful clause enforcement.

- Make the clause conspicuous.
- Have the client initial the clause.
- Make the limitation amount more than the inspection fee. This might help convince the court that the clause is fair.
- Provide the client with an opportunity to negotiate the limitation clause by including an offer to negotiate within the clause, or by offering to remove the clause for an additional fee.
- Explain the reason for the clause in terms of allocating risk between the home inspector and the client so that the inspection may be performed for the agreed-upon fee.
- Include all legal causes of action in the clause such as negligence.

A limitation of remedies clause definitely needs to be reviewed by a local attorney to determine if one is allowed and enforceable in a particular state.

Disclaimer of Warranties **Some clients believe, or at least try to allege, that a home inspection creates or provides a guarantee or insurance policy** against problems that may occur in the home. This may be caused in part because some home inspectors offer limited warranties as part of their inspection service, and because some home inspectors use the term "insurance" in their marketing materials. Home inspectors should refrain from using terms such as guarantee and insurance in their marketing materials unless they provide such services.

Limited home warranties are available from third parties. The home inspector may elect to purchase such a warranty, and to provide it to the client as part of the inspection service. The home inspector may, as an alternative to purchasing a third-party warranty, provide a self-insured limited warranty. The home inspector who elects to provide a warranty as part of the inspection service should take great care to define the terms of the warranty in an agreement that is separate from the inspection agreement.

The inspection contract of a home inspector who does not provide a warranty should contain a clause that disclaims all warranties regarding the condition of the property, and disclaims that the inspection provides insurance coverage against problems that may exist or may occur at the property.

INSURANCE

Introduction

The risks involved in conducting a business are different from and usually greater than the risks covered by common individual insurance policies such as homeowner's insurance and vehicle insurance. The home inspector should properly insure against these risks. Some types of insurance may be required before obtaining government licenses or permits.

Bond

In the context of the home inspection profession, **a bond is a promise by a third party to pay a judgment against the bonded home inspector** if the home inspector fails to pay the judgment. The issuer of the bond (the surety) would probably attempt to collect the amount paid by the surety from the home inspector. **A bond is, therefore, not insurance.** To collect on a bond, a client would need to file suit against the home inspector and win a judgment. The home inspector would need to refuse to pay the judgment. The client would need to apply to the surety for payment. Some jurisdictions require that the home inspector post a bond as a condition for a home inspector license.

Errors and Omissions Insurance (E&O)

Home inspector E&O insurance is a promise by an insurance company to pay the home inspector's client if the home inspector fails to properly report about a defect in the home and the client suffers damage as a result. This insurance is sometimes called **professional liability insurance**. Failure to properly report about a defect is usually determined by comparing the home inspector's report and other actions against the Standard of Practice (SOP) applicable to the home inspection, and possibly to the local Standard of Care.

E&O insurance also pays to defend claims made against the home inspector even if the claim has no merit. The maximum exposure of the insured home inspector is the policy limit and the deductible. The home inspector should be aware, however, that the deductible is usually payable when the claim is filed, and is usually used to help defray the cost of processing and investigating the claim. **The deductible is often not refunded**.

There are two common types of E&O policies. The **claims made** policy is more common and usually less expensive. A claims made policy covers claims filed while the policy is in effect. A claims made policy does not cover claims that originated while the policy was in effect but were filed after the policy lapsed. The **occurrence policy** covers claims that occurred while the policy is in effect regardless of when the claim is filed. Coverage for prior acts (home inspections occurring before the policy is in effect) and coverage for claims filed after the policy lapses can sometimes be purchased.

An E&O policy may not cover common ancillary services that some home inspectors provide without additional endorsements. Examples of ancillary services include radon, mold and air quality, wood destroying organism, pool and spa, and construction inspections. Home inspectors who offer ancillary services should verify coverage for those services.

Some jurisdictions require that the home inspector purchase E&O insurance as a condition for a home inspector license.

General Liability Insurance (GL)

Home inspector GL insurance is a promise by an insurance company to pay for **damage or personal injury that the home inspector causes while performing the home inspection**. Other risks, such as libel and slander, may also be covered. GL insurance also pays to defend claims made against the home inspector even if the claim has no merit

It is important to understand that **E&O and GL insurance cover different risks**. For example, E&O would cover the home inspector for failing to report a hole in the ceiling. GL would cover the home inspector for making a hole in the ceiling. GL would cover the expenses if someone else were injured when the home inspector made a hole in the ceiling, but it would not cover the home inspector's injuries. GL is required by some builders before they will permit a home inspector to perform construction inspections. Some jurisdictions require that the home inspector purchase GL insurance as a condition for a home inspector license.

Worker's Compensation Insurance

Worker's compensation insurance is a **government-run insurance program** that provides medical care, lost wages, and death benefits for employees injured or killed while working for an employer that is enrolled in the program. The employee must be injured or killed while on the job to be covered. Worker's compensation insurance is a **no fault system**. Benefits are paid regardless of whether the employee, employer, or someone else was at fault. The trade-off for this no-fault system is that the worker relinquishes the right to sue the employer regarding the workplace injury.

Most employers are required to carry worker's compensation insurance; there are exemptions for very small businesses. Exemptions and regulations vary by state. Sole proprietors, partners, and LLC members are usually not considered employees and are usually not required to be covered by worker's compensation insurance. Most businesses that are not required to carry worker's compensation insurance do not because it is usually quite expensive.

Homeowner's Insurance

Homeowner's insurance may provide **little or no coverage for home inspector tools and equipment**. Coverage may also be limited for injuries suffered by clients conducting business at the home inspector's home; this situation is uncommon. Endorsements may be available for specific business related property. Home inspectors with expensive tools and equipment (such as computers, infrared cameras, radon monitors, and blower doors) may wish to check coverage with their insurance carrier.

Vehicle Insurance

Home inspectors who use their **personal vehicle for business may not be covered** for losses incurred while using the vehicle for business. A business use endorsement is usually required to ensure coverage for business-use losses.

HOME INSPECTION ETHICS

Introduction

The term ethics is easy to define. **Ethics are the rules or standards governing the conduct** of a person or members of a profession. **What is not at all easy to define is what those rules and standards should be, and how to put them into practice.** Different people, professional associations, and states have different opinions and interpretations about the definition of ethical behavior in the home inspection profession. The following is a common, but not universal, perspective.

In order to be successful, both as an individual and as a profession, **home inspectors must be, and must be perceived as, an honest source of information** about the condition of the inspected property. In order to accomplish this goal of honest information source, the home inspector must act ethically in three areas. The home inspector must:

- avoid actual and perceived conflicts of interest,
- accurately, completely, and fairly report the condition of the inspected property,
- conduct business activities to avoid actual or perceived fraud, deceit, or misleading activities.

We discuss each of these areas in more detail next.

Conflicts of Interest

Home Inspector Financial Interest in the Property
The home inspector should not inspect any property in which the home inspector has or may have a financial interest. This does not preclude the home inspector from inspecting his/her personal home; however, many home inspectors hire another home inspector to perform the inspection to avoid the appearance of a conflict of interest.

Home Inspector Financial Interest in the Sale
The home inspector should not inspect any property on a contingent basis whereby the home inspector may derive compensation based on the results of the inspection. The home inspector should not inspect any property whereby the home inspector may derive compensation based on the sale of the property. This could preclude, for example, a home inspector performing an inspection on a house for which the home inspector's spouse is a real estate agent involved in the transaction. The spouse's commission is contingent on the sale; therefore, the home inspector has a financial interest in the sale.

Pay to Play
Pay to play refers to the practice by some real estate companies and other referral sources to demand compensation for inclusion in preferred provider and recommended home inspector lists. Other referral sources may include real estate attorneys, mortgage companies, banks, and title insurance companies. This also refers to direct payments to referral sources in return for referrals.

This is a difficult ethical area. Activities such as nominal cost gifts to referral sources are usually acceptable. Sponsorship of legitimate referral source company events is usually acceptable. Advertising in a referral source company publications may be acceptable on a case by case basis. Some jurisdictions that license home inspectors have interpretations of what is and is not acceptable this area.

Paid to Play
Paid to play refers to the practice of a home inspector accepting compensation from vendors for directly or indirectly recommending the vendor. This is often interpreted to include accepting compensation for scheduling free inspections of systems such as security systems and accepting compensation for referring a pest inspection company. It may not include accepting compensation for scheduling and billing the pest inspection with the home inspection because the home inspector is performing a service for the pest inspection company. Some jurisdictions that license home inspectors have interpretations of what is and is not acceptable in this area.

Repairing Inspected Property
The perception of the home inspector as an honest information source could easily be damaged if the home inspector were perceived as finding problems that the home inspector could turn around and charge the client or the seller to repair. **The home inspector may not, for compensation, perform any construction or repair work on an inspected property for one year after the inspection.**

This is another difficult ethical area. This restriction is not included in all home inspector codes of ethics. It may not apply if the company that performs the work is owned by the home inspector's relative, not by the home inspector. Some jurisdictions that license home inspectors have interpretations of what is and is not acceptable in this area.

Ethical Reporting

Reporting Within the Scope of Expertise Even the very best and most experienced home inspectors do not know everything about every system and component that could exist in a house. What these experienced home inspectors know is when to say: "**I don't know,**" and recommend inspection or further evaluation by someone who does know. This is not only ethical behavior, **it is smart business.**

Just the Facts, Ma'am There can be great temptation to write a deficiency comment in a manner that understates or overstates the actual condition of the system or component, or that overstates or understates the significance of the deficiency. Reporting only the facts, as the home inspector understands them, is not only ethical behavior, in the long run it is smart business.

Understatement is the more common temptation. Home inspectors who are perceived by real estate agents as being too picky or alarmist get a reputation as a deal killer. These home inspectors may get fewer real estate agent referrals, and make less money as a result. The home inspector might be tempted to downplay a deficiency in order to maintain the referral stream from a real estate agent. **Good real estate agents understand that it is in everyone's best interest, including the agent's, to deal with facts up front** to avoid litigation later. Good home inspectors want to work with good agents, and avoid agents who want friendly reports.

Overstatement can also be a temptation. Defensive reporting involves reporting in a manner that is unduly alarmist or recommends further evaluation of almost everything, so that the home inspector perceives he/she is safe from litigation. **Defensive reporting is not necessary and does not serve anyone's interest, even the home inspector's.**

Inspection Result Disclosure Usually, many parties want to know the results of a home inspection, but the only party that has the right to know the results is the client. The home inspector should not share the inspection results, including the report, with anyone other than the client without the client's written permission. This includes the client's real estate agent, the listing (seller's) agent, and the seller. Many real estate sales contracts give the sellers the right to see the inspection report; however, the home inspector is not a party to that contract. **Distribution of the home inspection report to agents and sellers is at the client's discretion** and is the client's responsibility. Some jurisdictions that license home inspectors have interpretations of what is and what is not acceptable in this area.

Advertising and Marketing Advertising and marketing of home inspector services and qualifications should be truthful and accurate. The home inspector should not, for example, advertise or promote qualifications that the home inspector does not possess or membership in organizations to which the home inspector does not belong. The home inspector should not promote a business license as a home inspection license.

STARTING A HOME INSPECTION BUSINESS

Introduction

A new home inspector must do two things to start a home inspection business. The home inspector must **comply with the legal requirements for starting and operating** a home inspection business. These requirements vary depending on where the home inspector lives and where the home inspector intends to work. After complying with the legal requirements, the home inspector must **convince people to use the home inspector's services**. We will briefly discuss marketing home inspection services at the end of this section, but there is much more to marketing home inspection services than we will cover in this book. Most home inspectors should get additional training about marketing home inspection services. **Marketing is probably the most difficult and often the most poorly implemented part of running a home inspection business.** A new home inspector, and some experienced home inspectors, might consider hiring someone to help with marketing. The home inspector could then dedicate time to inspecting and learning.

The material in this section is not included in the National Home Inspector Examination content outline. It is unlikely that exam questions will be based on this material. This material is presented to help home inspectors.

The Business Plan

Failing to plan equals planning to fail. It often takes at least **five years to establish a viable home inspection business**, and many home inspection businesses fail during those first five years. An often cited reason for this failure rate is lack of financial resources to sustain the home inspector through the first few lean years. If the home inspector has properly planned for this normal situation, the home inspector has budgeted the necessary funds, or structured the home inspector's income stream so as not to rely solely on the home inspection business. It could be argued, therefore, that **the real failure is lack of planning**.

A detailed discussion of business planning is out-of-scope for this book. New home inspectors, and experienced home inspectors who want to grow their business, are encouraged to look for the many good sources of information about business planning that are available. What follows is an outline for a business plan and some basic plan contents.

A basic business plan begins with the following elements. The plan may be developed in a different order than is presented here, but the following order may help a new home inspector determine if starting a home inspection business is a viable endeavor.

- **Market Analysis** What is the size of the home inspection market in the proposed service area? Is the market expanding, shrinking, or stable? Who are the potential customers? What is their income level? Who are the potential referral sources? What do the customers really want?

- **Competitor Analysis** How many home inspectors are serving the market? What are their strengths and weaknesses?

- **Self-Analysis** What are your strengths and weaknesses? How will you differentiate yourself from your competition? How will you provide better value for your customers compared to your completion? (Hint: **do not compete on price.**) What are your goals for the business and for yourself?
- **Financial Analysis** How much will it cost to obtain the licenses, permits, training, certifications, insurance, and tools necessary to start the business? What are the realistic projected revenues and expenses for the first three to five years? How will you fund business startup costs and living expenses during the first three to five years?
- **Marketing Plan** How will you communicate your value proposition to your target markets?

Types of Business Ownership

Introduction How the home inspector organizes and owns the business can have a significant impact on the business and on personal success or failure. The following is a brief introduction to the common ways of organizing and owning a business. The home inspector should consult with a local attorney or accountant about the benefits, risks, and costs of different business ownership types in the home inspector's location. This discussion is based on practices in the United States.

Sole Proprietorship This is the simplest form of business ownership, in which one person owns and operates the business. The business may use the proprietor's name, or it may use an assumed (fictitious) name. There are few government requirements for registration. Separate business accounting records are required both for management and for tax purposes. Taxes are reported and paid through the owner's individual tax filing (IRS Form 1040 Schedule C). The primary advantage is simplicity and low cost to form and operate the business. The primary disadvantage is that the **owner's personal assets are at risk** if a claim is made against the business.

Partnership This is a more complex form of business ownership. There are many types of partnerships. In its most basic form, two or more people own the business and share in the profits and losses. One or more of the partners usually operate the business. The business usually operates under an assumed name. The partnership must register with some state governments, must file a partnership tax return with the IRS (Form 1065), and must file a return with some state governments. Taxes are reported and paid by the partners as individuals. Separate accounting records are required and a partnership agreement is strongly recommended. The primary advantage is simplicity and low cost to form a partnership compared to corporations. The primary disadvantages are that the **partner's personal assets are at risk** if a claim is made against the partnership, and that **each partner is responsible for liabilities incurred by the other partners**. This ownership form is uncommon in modern business, especially in states that allow limited liability companies.

Limited Liability Company (LLC) This is a newer form of business ownership that is available in most states. A LLC is a separate legal entity owned by one or more persons. The LLC operates under its registered name, usually with the letters LLC as part of the name. The LLC owners, called **members**, file forms with the state to create the LLC. Annual forms and reports (and fees) are usually required by the state to maintain the existence of the LLC. Taxes for single member LLCs and for LLCs owned by a married couple are usually reported and paid by the member(s) as individuals (Form 1040 Schedule E). The tax treatment of other LLCs is usually as a partnership, but can vary. **Separate accounting records are essential to maintaining the separate legal status of the LLC**, including the protection of member's assets. The primary advantages of a LLC are that the member's individual assets may not be at risk if a claim is made against the LLC, and the comparative ease and low cost of forming a LLC. The primary disadvantage is additional fees and paperwork involved in forming and maintaining a LLC. Many home inspectors form a LLC if it is allowed in their state.

<u>Corporation</u> This is a traditional form of business ownership that is available in all states. A corporation is a separate legal entity owned by one or more persons or entities. This form is used mostly by larger businesses that need to have many shareholders or a complex capital structure. The corporation operates under its registered name, usually with the designation Inc. or Corp. after the name. The corporation owners (called **shareholders**) file forms with the state to create the corporation. Annual forms and reports (and fees) are required by the state to maintain the existence of the corporation. A corporation files a separate tax form with the IRS (Form 1120) and must file with some states. Taxes for corporations with a few shareholders (**S Corporations**) are paid by the shareholder(s) as individuals. Taxes for other corporations (**C Corporations**) are paid by the corporation. Separate accounting records are essential to maintaining the separate legal status of the corporation, including the protection of shareholder's assets. The primary advantage of a corporation is that the member's individual assets may not be at risk if a claim is made against the corporation. The primary disadvantage is the higher cost of forming a corporation (an attorney is usually involved), the additional fees and paperwork involved in maintaining a corporation, and double taxation of corporate dividends (C Corporations).

Government Licensing and Registration

<u>Introduction</u> **Few businesses**, even a sole proprietor, **can avoid some type of government licensing and registration requirements.** This discussion presents common requirements that apply in most jurisdictions. The home inspector should become aware of the requirements where the home inspector lives and intends to work. A good place to start is with the **Secretary of State's** office in the home inspector's state of residence. Home inspectors who work in multiple states may need to obtain business and professional licenses in each state, and may need to register the business in each state. Some states have registration requirements in multiple counties or cities.

<u>Home Inspection Professional License</u> As of the date of this book, almost two-thirds of the states have some form of mandatory regulation of home inspectors. Some states call it **licensing**; some call it **registration**. The effect is the same. We will refer to mandatory regulation as licensing. Some states have professional practice acts that are neither licensing nor registration and may define the profession only, some with prohibited acts.

It is important to note that **home inspectors who intend to perform home inspections in license states must comply with the state licensing laws where the house is located**. This is true even if the home inspector lives in and is licensed in another state. A possible exception is if the states have a reciprocity agreement in which the states recognize each other's licenses. In many cases, reciprocity only makes the process of obtaining a license easier in the state where the home inspector does not live.

Requirements for obtaining a license vary between states and usually include some combination of classroom training, experience, and **passing the National Home Inspector Exam** or an exam designated by the state. Experience can sometimes be obtained by riding along with a licensed home inspector for a certain number of home inspections. Having an existing license in a related field such as a contractor, architect, or structural engineer can often be substituted for home inspection experience and may be substituted for a home inspector license in some states.

Requirements for renewing a license vary among states. All license states require renewal, usually at one or two year intervals. Most states have mandatory continuing education requirements.

Business (Privilege) License A business license is often required by a government for the privilege of doing business within the government's jurisdiction. This license is often required for every business including sole proprietors. **A business license is different from and in addition to a professional license.**

Business license requirements vary significantly between states and between jurisdictions within states. In some states, a business license is required only in the jurisdiction where the business is physically located. In some states, a business license is required in every jurisdiction where the business operates.

Federal Employer Identification Number (EIN) An EIN is like a social security number for a business. All businesses that have employees must have an EIN for filing employment tax returns. Businesses that must file tax returns, such as corporations and some LLCs and partnerships, must have an EIN. Sole proprietors do not usually need an EIN unless they have employees. LLCs that are not required to file a tax return usually do not need an EIN; however, an LLC might wish to obtain an EIN because (like social security numbers) they are sometimes necessary for conducting business. Obtaining an EIN is free and is done online at the IRS website.

Sales Tax Registration As of the date of this book, sales taxes on home inspection services are uncommon. Sales taxes may be assessed on other products or services that a home inspector may offer. A home inspector may be required to register as a sales tax collection agent as part of the requirements for other licenses or registrations such as a contractor's license.

Business Name Registration Businesses that operate under an assumed name (not the owner's name) **may be required to register this name** with a government department. This requirement applies mostly to sole proprietors and partnerships. Searching for the proposed business name in government records is wise, regardless of whether registration is required, in order to avoid picking a name that someone is already using. It would be unfortunate to spend money on business formation and marketing materials only to find that someone else has prior rights to the name. This search can be accomplished online in many states.

Office in Home Registration Many home inspectors operate their business from their home. Many local governments require that businesses register home offices with the local government. Registration usually requires completion of a form and payment of a small fee. There is usually no problem if the business has no employees working in the home (other than family members), and if clients usually do not come to the home to conduct business (which they rarely do).

Accounting and Financial Management

Introduction There is more cash in the bank at the end of the year than at the beginning. The business made a profit; right? Perhaps, but the business may not be as profitable as it should be. The business could be losing money. Some home inspectors, especially new home inspectors, do not understand how to determine real profit and loss, and how to establish an accounting system to determine real profit and loss. A good accounting system is essential for operating a home inspection business (or any business).

There is much more to establishing an accounting system and to determining business profit and loss than can be presented in this book. A home inspector who has a minimal background in accounting should hire a bookkeeper to establish an accounting system, and train the home inspector how to use it. This investment will likely pay large returns over time in terms of increased profits and reduced problems with government tax collectors.

The material in this section is not included in the National Home Inspector Examination content outline. It is unlikely that exam questions will be based on this material. This material is presented to help home inspectors.

Types of Accounts Everyone (businesses and individuals) has five types of accounts that comprise their financial life. (1) Assets are things owned. Examples include cash, stocks, vehicles, buildings, and tools. (2) Liabilities are amounts owed to others. Examples include loans, mortgages (a type of loan), and credit card debt. (3) Revenue is money received. Examples include wages, payments for services, interest, and dividends. (4) Expenses are money paid to others. Examples include vehicle expenses (gas, maintenance, insurance), professional association dues, continuing education expenses, and government fees and taxes. (5) Equity is the difference between assets and liabilities. Equity increases when revenue exceeds expenses (income/profit). Equity decreases when expense exceeds revenue (loss).

Types of Accounting Statements There are three types of accounting statements. The balance sheet shows the assets, liabilities, and equity at a point in time. The income statement shows the revenues and expenses incurred over a period of time. The cash flow statement shows why cash increased or decreased over a period of time. It does this by adjusting net income (from the income statement) for non-cash expenses, like depreciation, and for increases and decreases in assets and liabilities. Most home inspectors do not need a cash flow statement. These statements are more useful for larger and more complex businesses.

An important concept for understanding accounting statements, and an accounting system, is that the balance sheet and income statement are linked through the equity section of the balance sheet. As previously stated, equity increases when there is a profit and decreases when there is a loss. All five account types are, therefore, linked together through the system of double-entry accounting.

Double Entry Accounting Double-entry accounting has been the basis for accounting systems for hundreds of years. It is based on a simple concept. A transaction is recorded twice, once as a debit entry and once as a credit entry. If all entries are properly recorded, the net debit and credit entries should be equal.

Debits increase assets and expenses. Credits increase liabilities, equity, and revenue. Debits decrease liabilities, equity, and revenue. Credits decrease assets and expenses.

The following examples illustrate how double-entry accounting works. A client gives you a check for $400 for a home inspection. The check is recorded as a debit to cash (an increase) of $400, and a credit to revenue (an increase) of $400. The debit and credit are equal, so the transaction is properly recorded. You pay for $40 cash for gas. The cash is recorded as a credit to cash (a decrease), and a debit to vehicle expense (an increase). The debit and credit are equal, so the transaction is properly recorded. Instead of paying cash, you charge the gas on your credit card. The charge is recorded as a credit to credit card debt payable (an increase in a liability), and debit to vehicle expense (an increase in an expense). The debit and credit are equal, so the transaction is properly recorded.

Cash and Accrual Accounting In order to determine if a business is actually profitable, it is necessary to match revenues with the expenses required to generate the revenue. This matching principal is very important and we will discuss it more next.

There are two ways to account for revenues and expenses. The easiest way is called cash basis accounting. Many home inspectors and other small businesses use cash basis accounting. When using cash basis accounting, revenue is recognized when cash is received, and expenses are recognized when cash is spent. Cash basis works reasonably well for small service businesses like home inspectors. Most home inspectors do not have much in the way of accounts receivable and payable and inventory that might distort a cash basis income statement. For management purposes, however, cash basis accounting should be adjusted for material (significant) distorting factors.

Depreciation can be a distorting factor in **cash basis accounting**. Depreciation is an attempt to match the cost of assets that have a long life (vehicles, computers, reporting software, expensive tools) with the revenue they help produce. A vehicle provides a good example of depreciation. Assume a vehicle that used solely for business costs $30,000 and the expectation is to trade it in on a new vehicle in five years. At trade in time the expected vehicle value is $10,000. The net cost of the vehicle is $20,000. The vehicle will contribute to generating revenue for five years, so the cost of the vehicle should be allocated over those five years. This allocation is called depreciation and in this example $20,000/5 years equals an annual depreciation expense of $4,000 per year.

Continuing our double-entry accounting example, assume you paid $30,000 cash for the vehicle. The initial entry would be a debit to an asset account for the vehicle of $30,000 and a credit to cash for $30,000. Each year you would make a depreciation entry that reduces the value of the vehicle by $4,000 (a credit to the vehicle asset account) and an increase in the vehicle expense account by $4,000 (a debit to vehicle expense).

The other accounting system is called **accrual accounting**. Accrual accounting rigorously attempts to match revenue and expense during the reporting time period. A couple examples illustrate the difference between cash and accrual accounting.

Assume that a home inspector carries the home inspection fee to closing (the home inspector does not receive cash until the house closes). In a cash basis accounting system, the revenue for the home inspection is not recognized until the cash is received. In an accrual accounting system, the revenue for the home inspection is recognized when the home inspection is performed by debiting accounts receivable and crediting revenue. If the cash is received during the reporting period when the home inspection was performed, there is no impact on the income statement for that period. If the cash is received in a different period, the income statements for both periods are inaccurate. The revenue for the period when the home inspection was performed is less than it should be, and the revenue for the later period is more than it should be.

The previous depreciation example provides another example of accrual accounting. Allocating the cost of long life assets over their service life matches expenses with the revenues they help generate.

Setting Fees Assume that a can of peas costs a grocery store $ .50. Assume that all other expenses involved in running the store (labor, utilities, insurance, etc.) are $0.45. If the store wants a 5% profit, it needs to sell the peas for $1.00. Determining how to price purchased goods is relatively easy. Determining how to price services, such as home inspections, is more difficult. Performing this calculation is essential to running a successful and profitable home inspection business.

Home inspection fees are, to a significant extent, market driven. Home inspectors usually know, or can find out, what other home inspectors are charging and set their fees competitively. Some home inspectors can set fees higher than the market. These are usually experienced home inspectors with an established following and with significant credentials. Some home inspectors attempt to set their fees below the market. At best, this is a strategy that will involve lots of work and increased risk for little profit. At worst, this strategy will eventually cause business failure. The best way to set fees is to know the expense of running the business and the local market fees for home inspection services. With this information, the home inspector can set competitive fees that allow a fair profit.

One of the best ways to know the expense of running a home inspection business is to allocate a portion of operating expenses to each home inspection. To do this you need to know or to estimate the total expense of running the home inspection business and the total number of home inspections.

Certain expenses of running a business are fixed expenses. These are expenses that are necessary to keep the doors open and do not vary, or vary only a little, regardless of the number of home inspections performed. These expenses include: utilities (phone, internet), professional association dues, government licenses and fees, continuing education expenses (including travel), interest (if money is borrowed to start the business or to buy assets), insurance (GL, E&O, vehicle), and depreciation on long life assets.

Certain expenses of running a business are variable expenses; expenses that go up or down, at least somewhat, depending on the number of home inspections performed. These expenses include: vehicle expenses (gas, maintenance), small expendable tools and home inspection supplies (screwdrivers, flashlights), office supplies and expenses (paper, postage, software maintenance), marketing expenses, and legal and accounting expenses.

To begin the analysis, assume some number of home inspections performed in a year. Two hundred fifty home inspections per year is five per week over fifty weeks. If the sum of the fixed and variable expenses at 250 expenses per year is $25,000, then the expense allocated to each home inspection is $100 ($25,000/250). If the average home inspection fee is $300, that leaves $200 profit per home inspection, before taxes ($300-$100). The profit in this example is $50,000 ($200 x 250). Profit is the return on the home inspector's time. Assuming 2,000 working hours per year (40 hours per week times 50 weeks), the hourly rate that the home inspector makes for all the time spent inspecting and running the business is $25/hour ($50,000/2,000 hours).

It is important to remember that a self-employed person's profit comes without any benefits. There are no paid sick days, paid vacation days, and paid health and disability insurance premiums. There is no pension or employer sponsored retirement plan. A self-employed person must pay self-employment taxes that an employer would pay as the employer contribution. It is important, therefore, for the home inspector to set fees so that the home inspector makes a reasonable return on the time and risk involved in running a home inspection business.

HOME INSPECTION MARKETING

Introduction

There are two types of home inspectors when it comes to marketing. One has been in business for many years and has developed a network of real estate agents, clients, and other contacts that refer a regular stream of business. This home inspector may not have to actively market his/her business, at least not much, because the home inspector may rely mostly on referrals. This home inspector is the exception. Everyone else **must** continually market the business to survive, and market even more to grow. A home inspector who is not prepared to devote time to planning and executing this critical task should do himself/herself a big favor, work for a home inspector who is willing to market the business.

The following is a very brief introduction to a few of the most basic concepts involved in marketing home inspection services. New home inspectors should attend additional training and read books about marketing, especially about marketing home inspection services.

The material in this section is not included in the National Home Inspector Examination content outline. It is unlikely that exam questions will be based on this material. This material is presented to help home inspectors.

What is Marketing?

Marketing is a planned effort to communicate a message to a target market. The target market for home inspection services includes buyers and sellers of resale homes, buyers of homes under construction, and owners of existing homes. The message is that your inspection services are different from and provide a better value than your competitor's services. The message should be constant in order to make it memorable through the noise of competing messages, and consistent to avoid confusing people with different messages.

Marketing consists of advertising and public relations, both of which should be a part of all marketing plans. Advertising is the paid placement of a message in anything from print media to pay-per-click internet advertising. Brochures, business cards, and advertising specialities are forms of advertising. Advertising specialities are products such as pens with a company name printed on them. The home inspector has more control over the advertising message because advertising is paid for, however, that control can be costly.

Public relations is the unpaid placement of information about your company in various media. It lets people know who you are. It is your reputation within the community. Being interviewed as an expert by news media is one of the best forms of public relations, but any positive story is good. Blogging, article marketing, and social media such as Facebook and Twitter are the new forms of public relations that provide you with control over the content that you post. By not paying, considerable control is lost, but a larger audience can be reached for minimal out-of-pocket cost.

The objective of marketing is to motivate the target market to buy your home inspection services. If the target market is not motivated to act and to buy your home inspection services, then the marketing efforts and the marketing budget are wasted. In order to craft a message that will motivate people to act, the home inspector must understand the needs and wants of the target market. This requires looking at home inspection services from the perspective of the target market, not from the perspective of the home inspector.

Because a home inspection is usually needed in such a tight timeframe, it wise to cross market your services to allied professionals in the real estate transaction, such as, real estate agents, appraisers, pest control companies, lawyers, title agencies, etc. These allied professionals have been working with the client to this point in the real estate transaction and are able to refer your company to the client. A home inspector should never offer or accept any compensation for a referral.

Marketing the Intangible

Marketing home inspection services is challenging because, unlike tangible products, home inspection services are intangible. Products are much easier to market because products are tangible. People can see products and in many cases touch them before they buy. Most products have features and benefits that people can understand and compare to the features and benefits of competing products. Buying a product that can be seen, touched, and compared feels less risky.

People cannot see or touch a home inspection before they buy. It is more difficult to compare home inspection service features and benefits because it is more difficult to compare home inspectors. A home inspection is an intangible promise. The client purchases this promise on faith that the home inspector will perform a good home inspection. Buying a promise that cannot be seen, touched, and compared feels risky. This risky feeling is why credibility is so important for home inspectors. Credibility is an important part of a home inspector's marketing message.

Features and Benefits

Features are attributes of a product or service. A feature is important only insofar as it provides a benefit to the person buying the product or service. Any feature, no matter how fantastic, is worthless unless it provides a benefit to the person buying the product or service. For example, a guarantee is a feature when offered with an inspection service.

Benefits fulfill a want or a need. When buying a product or a service, a person is mostly interested in how that product or service benefits him/her. For example, the benefit of a home inspection guarantee is that it reduces the feeling of risk in buying the inspection service; it helps make the intangible promise more tangible.

A home inspector should not lead with features when crafting a marketing message, and should not assume that the target market will make the leap from a feature to a benefit. It is better to lead with benefits and use features to support how the benefits will be delivered.

Elements of a Marketing Plan

The home inspector should analyze five important elements when developing a good marketing plan: demand, supply, differentiation, message, and channels. Demand involves estimating the number of potential inspections in the service area and identifying wants and needs of the target market. Supply involves identifying the other home inspectors in the service area and analyzing their strengths and weaknesses. Differentiation involves analyzing the features and benefits of your inspection services and determining how to use them to stand out from the other home inspectors. Message involves crafting a message that will motivate people to buy your inspection services. Channels involves identifying the methods of communicating the message to the target market and deciding which channels to use, how and when to use them, how much to spend in time and money, and, perhaps most important, how to track and analyze the results from each channel.

Marketing Resources

Many books have been written about marketing. A few of these specifically address marketing home inspections. The smart home inspector should consider reading some of these books to gain more insight into marketing in general, and home inspection marketing in particular.

Classes about marketing are often given at community colleges. Classes about marketing home inspections are often given at home inspector training events. The smart home inspector should consider attending some of these classes.

Many, if not most, home inspectors do not have the training to be effective at marketing. Good resources exist to provide this training and the smart home inspector will avail himself/herself of these resources. To do otherwise is to increase the chance that the home inspection business will fail.

Please visit https://nationalhomeinspectorexam.org/prepare-for-the-exam/ and take advantage of the practice quizzes. The questions in the practice quizzes are designed to reflect the difficulty of the questions on the actual exam. The questions on the practice quizzes are not questions on the National Home Inspectors Exam. Passing the practice quizzes does not guarantee that you will pass the National exam. You will still need to study all topics to be prepared for the National exam.

GLOSSARY

½ Bathroom (half bath): a bathroom with a sink and a toilet; also called a powder room.

¾ Bathroom: a bathroom with a sink, toilet, and a shower.

AAV: see **Air Admittance Valve (AAV)**.

Aerator: a device that introduces air into a water stream, usually attached to the outlet of sink and lavatory faucets.

Adapter: a fitting that allows connection of different pipe types or different pipe sizes.

AFUE: see **Annual Fuel Utilization Efficiency (AFUE)**.

Air barrier: any material or combination of materials that prevents the flow of air from unconditioned areas into the thermal envelope.

Air Admittance Valve (AAV): an air pressure operated one-way valve used in place of an atmospheric plumbing vent; this device is different from a check (cheater) vent which contains a spring loaded gasket and is not approved for use in site-built houses.

Air conditioning: this term, broadly defined, includes heating, cooling, humidification, dehumidification, ventilation, and air filtration. Air conditioning, as the term is typically used in residential construction, refers to the cooling, dehumidification, ventilation, and air filtration functions.

Air conditioning system (central): a system that includes an air handler or a furnace, an evaporator coil, and a condenser unit that cools a house by removing heat from the house and moving the heat outside. See also **Heat pump** and **Split (air conditioning) system**.

Air gap: the vertical distance between a water supply discharge, such as a faucet, and the flood rim level of a fixture such as a sink; an air gap is one method of preventing a cross-connection between the water supply and drainage systems.

Air handler: the inside unit of a heat pump containing a fan, evaporator coil, and associated control and operating parts; air handler is sometimes used to describe a fuel-fired forced air furnace.

Ampacity: the maximum current that a conductor or device may carry continuously without exceeding its temperature rating.

Annual Fuel Utilization Efficiency (AFUE): a ratio of heat generated by a heating system versus the energy used; the minimum AFUE for most gas furnaces is 80 meaning that the furnace converts 80% of the fuel to heat and 20% is lost through the vent or by other means.

Appliance, plumbing: an appliance connected to the plumbing system that uses energy to perform its function, such as a clothes washing machine, dishwashing machine, food-waste disposer, or a water heater.

Arm, shower: the generally horizontal pipe that connects the shower riser to the shower head; usually curves down at about a 30° angle near the shower head.

Attic: a usually uninhabitable space above the ceiling of the highest habitable area and below the roof framing. Also called a crawl space in some markets.

AWG: the abbreviation for American Wire Gauge, a system for identifying the diameter of electrical wires; larger numbers identify smaller diameter wires; #14 (pronounced number 14 or 14 gauge) is the smallest wire used in house wiring, and 4/0 (pronounced four-oh) is usually the largest.

Axial force (load): the vertical force acting on a structural member such as a column or a beam, which places the member under compression at the loading point.

Backflow: the flow of a contaminate from an unintended source into the potable water supply system from an unintended source. See **Backpressure** and **Backsiphonage**.

Backflow preventer: a device or other means used to prevent backflow into the water supply system.

Backpressure: an uncommon condition that can occur when the pressure at a point outside the water supply system is greater than the water supply pressure. Example: the weight of water in a swimming pool located above the water supply system pipes can create enough pressure to force water back into the water supply pipes.

Backsiphonage: an uncommon condition that can occur when there is negative pressure in the water supply or distribution pipes; contaminants can be sucked into the pipes. Backsiphonage usually occurs because of a sudden loss of water pressure combined with rapid drainage of the water supply pipes.

Backwater valve: a device installed in the building drain pipe to prevent the flow of sewage from a public sewer into the house. A backwater valve is recommended when plumbing fixtures in a house are located below the nearest upstream manhole cover of the public sewer.

Balcony: an outdoor platform that is located at the second story or above. A balcony may be supported by posts, or it may be cantilevered.

Barrier, access (child): a fence, wall, house wall, or similar structure that is designed to limit access to the pool or spa area by unauthorized persons, especially children. A natural barrier such as a large body of water, a hill, or a cliff may also serve as a barrier, with approval.

Basement (cellar): a story that is partially or completely below grade; often has a ceiling height of 7 feet or more, but sometimes less in older houses.

Basement (daylight basement, walk out basement): a basement that has a door to the exterior.

Basement wall: a wall with at least (≥) 50% of its area below grade (covered by earth on the outside) and encloses conditioned space.

Beam (girder): a structural member that carries loads from other members, such as joists, rafters, and other beams.

Bed molding: a thin decorative molding that covers the seam between the soffit and the frieze and between interior walls and ceilings; also used for shadow boxes and for other decorative purposes.

Bend: a fitting that changes the direction of flow in drainage pipes. Bends are identified by the angle of the direction change either by a fraction or by the number of degrees of the direction change. Common bends include: 90° (¼ bend), 60° (1/6 bend) 45° (⅛ bend), and 22½° (1/16 bend). The fraction describes how much of a 360° circle that the bend angle sweeps. See **Elbow** and **Sweep**.

Bonding: the process of connecting, both physically and electrically, metal components of the electrical system that are not intended to carry electrical current to provide a low resistance return path to the circuit breaker or fuse to clear ground faults; bonding is an electrical safety system.

Boot (HVAC distribution system): sheet metal formed into a rectangle or circle that connects an air duct to a grille or a register.

Boot (flashing): the flashing surrounding a roof penetration such as a plumbing vent or a fuel-burning appliance vent; also called a roof jack.

Bow (bowed): a condition where a structural member is curved along its long axis.

Branch circuit: conductors that begin at a circuit breaker or fuse and serve one or more outlets.

Branch circuit, multiwire: a branch circuit in which two energized conductors share one neutral conductor; examples can include clothes dryers, ranges and other cooking appliances, and split-wire receptacle circuits; 240 volt water heaters and condensers for air conditioners and heat pumps are not usually multiwire branch circuits.

Braced wall: see **Shear wall**.

Branch drain (fixture branch): a pipe that receives material from two or more fixture drains or from other branch drains; branch drains are usually horizontal pipes that may have some vertical sections; a branch drain usually flows into a stack or into the building drain.

Brazing (silver soldering): a method of joining metal pipe and fittings (usually copper) by fusing them together with an alloy made mostly from sliver at a temperature above 800° F; makes a stronger connection than soldering. See **Soldering (sweating)**.

British thermal unit (Btu): the amount of heat required to increase the temperature of 1 pound of water by 1° Fahrenheit; this is a common description of the size or cooling capacity of an air conditioning system. See **Ton (of refrigeration)**.

Building drain: usually the lowest drainage pipe in the house; it extends 30 inches from the house exterior wall where it connects to the building sewer. See **Sewer (building)**.

Building thermal envelope: the conditioned (heated and cooled) area of the building. The envelope boundary between conditioned and unconditioned space includes walls, ceilings, floors, basement walls and slab-on-grade foundations. The thermal envelope may include the attic and the crawl space if these areas are designed and built as conditioned space.

Bulkhead door: a horizontal or inclined door that provides access to an area under the house or to a storage area, such as a cellar; sometimes referred to by the brand name Bilco.

Bus (buss, busbar): the heavy, rigid metal part of a panelboard on which circuit breakers or fuses are mounted; sometimes used to describe metal terminals to which the neutral and equipment grounding conductors (EGCs) are connected.

Cable (electrical): two or more conductors encased in sheathing; examples include non-metallic sheathed cable (often referred to by the brand name Romex) and armored cable (often referred to by the brand name BX).

Cantilever: a structural member (such as a floor joist) that extends horizontally beyond the vertical support (usually a wall) and has no other posts or supports.

Ceiling joist: a horizontal structural member that forms the ceiling of a room below an attic.

Ceiling, vaulted: a ceiling that extends at an angle above the top of a full-height wall; the ceiling finish (drywall) is usually attached directly to the rafters.

Ceiling, tray (or trey): a horizontal ceiling raised above the top of a full-height wall; the ceiling is often raised in one or two risers and decorated with crown molding or bed molding.

Chimney: a generally vertical structure containing one or more flues that conducts combustion products from a fuel-burning appliance to a point outside the house; chimneys are constructed using masonry and metal pipes.

Chimney cap (crown): the water-tight component at the top of a chimney; a masonry chimney cap should be made using concrete, metal, or stone; a factory-built chimney cap (pan) is usually made using metal.

Chimney connector: a component that conducts combustion products from a fuel-burning appliance to a chimney. See **Vent connector**.

Cinder block: a concrete masonry unit made using coal ash or other residue of combustion. Cinder blocks are less common in modern residential construction. Cinder blocks may contain corrosive materials. See **Concrete masonry unit (CMU)**.

Circuit breaker: see **Overcurrent protection device (OPD)**.

Cleanout (ash dump): an opening in a fireplace hearth into which ashes may be swept into a pit below.

Cleanout (plumbing): an accessible opening in drainage pipes that allows clearing of blockages; a cleanout may be a fitting with a covered opening, or it may be a removable trap or a fixture such as a toilet.

CMU: see **Concrete masonry unit (CMU)**.

Collar (duct): a round sheet metal ring that connects a duct to a plenum or to a trunk duct.

Collar tie: a horizontal member (usually a 1x4 or a 2x4) installed in the upper third of the attic between two rafters to help tie rafters together at the ridge.

Column: a generic term describing a structural member designed to support a concentrated vertical load. A column is usually a tall and relatively narrow component. Also called a post, especially when used with decks. See **Pier** and **Pile**.

Commode: a regional term primarily used in the South and Southeast; see **Toilet**.

Compression: The force that crushes or shortens a structural member. A beam under a vertical load is under compression on the top. See **Tension force (load)**.

Compression fitting: a method of connecting water supply pipes and valves using a compression ring (ferrule) and a compression nut; commonly used to connect small size pipes and tubes to fixture shutoff valves and appliances such as ice makers.

Compressor: part of an air conditioning or heat pump condenser unit; this device compresses the gas refrigerant into superheated gas, and provides the energy to move the refrigerant through the system.

Concrete masonry unit (CMU): a usually rectangular block made from concrete, aggregate, and water and intended for installation with other blocks to form walls and other structures. See **Cinder block**.

Condensate: water that condenses into liquid when heat is removed from the air flowing over the evaporator coil; this water must be disposed of in an appropriate manner; significant amounts of water can be produced in humid environments. Condensate is also produced when heat is removed from combustion gasses in the heat exchanger of a high efficiency furnace or boiler.

Condenser (coils): part of an air conditioning or heat pump condenser unit; these are the tubes (coils) around the perimeter of the condenser unit.

Condenser (unit): the outside unit of a split air conditioning or heat pump system consisting of a compressor, condenser coils, a fan, and associated control and operating parts.

Condominium: a form of real property ownership in which the owner holds 100% ownership of a dwelling unit and shares ownership of the common elements. Condominium does not describe a type of building.

Conductor: a material, such as copper or aluminum, that permits electricity to flow with low resistance; wires are conductors.

Cooktop: a cooking appliance installed in an opening in a countertop.

Coping: the material at the edge of a concrete pool that covers the bond beam. Coping is not required; the deck may be installed up to the edge of the water.

Corbel: the outward horizontal projection of a masonry course beyond the course below; corbelling changes the shape of a chimney, usually for aesthetic reasons. Compare **Racking (back)**.

Cornice: the usually decorative exterior trim where the rafters and wall meet. Cornice usually encloses the eaves. Cornice often consists of the fascia, soffit, and bed molding.

Cornice return: the continuation of the cornice in a different direction, such as at a gable end.

Corrugated Stainless Steel Tubing (CSST): a flexible tube that is used to convey fuel gas.

Coupling: a plumbing fitting that allows two pipes to be connected in a straight line.

Crawl space: an accessible area within the foundation walls below the first habitable story, usually having a soil floor, and a small distance between the soil and the floor joists. Also used to describe an attic in some markets.

Creep: See **Deformed**.

Creosote: a flammable byproduct of improperly burning wood, such as burning wet wood, and burning wood without adequate combustion air.

Cricket (saddle): a small gable-shaped projection that is installed on the high side of where the roof intersects a chimney that is more than 30 inches wide parallel to the ridge; a cricket diverts water around the chimney.

Cross-connection: a connection between the water supply pipes and a potential contaminate source, such as the DWV pipes, that could allow contaminated water to flow from the contaminate source into the water supply pipes. A cross-connection can be intentional, such as the fill valve in a toilet tank. A cross-connection can be unintentional, such as a hand-held shower head hanging below the flood rim level of a bathtub. See **Backflow**.

Crown (camber): a condition where a board or beam is curved along the long axis. See **Bow (bowed).** Most dimensional lumber joists have a natural crown which should be installed with the high side vertical. Manufactured beams have a camber built into the beam. The crown or camber installed with the high side vertical usually becomes straight when a load is applied.

Crown molding: a decorative molding that covers the seam between the soffit and the frieze and between interior walls and ceilings; usually wider and more ornate than bed molding.

CSST: see **Corrugated Stainless Steel Tubing (CSST).**

Culvert: a below ground passage that allows water to flow, usually through a large diameter metal or concrete pipe. In residential construction, a culvert may be located at the end of a driveway to permit water to flow in a swale under the driveway.

Cup (cupped): a condition in which a board is curved along the face of the board.

Current: the amount of electricity in a circuit; (similar to gallons per minute water flow in a pipe); unit of measure is the Ampere (Amp); expressed as I in Ohm's Law and Watt's Law equations.

Damper (barometric): a device used to control draft in an oil-fired appliance vent connector when using a masonry chimney as a vent; the damper is a round metal plate that is mounted on two hinges. It opens and closes based on the pressure in the vent connector.

Damper (fireplace): an operable metal plate that opens to allow combustion gasses to flow into a chimney, and closes to restrict outside air entry into the house when the fireplace is not being used.

Damper (HVAC duct system): a plate or louvers installed in a duct system that permits control of how much air flows in a duct; a damper may be controlled manually or it may be controlled by a motor. Motor controlled dampers are one method of installing a zoned system where one HVAC system is controlled by two or more thermostats.

Dead front cover: a panel that is removed to gain access to the energized components inside an electrical enclosure; the dead front cover is usually behind a door that must be swung or lifted in order to gain access to the dead front cover.

Deadman: a buried component, such as a railroad tie or landscape timber, that serves as an anchor to keep a retaining wall from rotating; a deadman is connected to the retaining wall using a tieback.

Deck: an outdoor recreational area that is usually, but not always, attached to the house. A deck is supported by posts. A deck is usually not covered. See **Balcony** and **Patio.**

Deflect (deflection): a condition where a structural member bends from its normal shape or position, such as when a joist bends under a load. Deflect implies a temporary condition wherein the member will return to its normal shape or position when the load is removed.

Deformed (deformation): a condition where a structural member changes shape or dimension from its normal shape or dimension. Permanent deformation occurs when the member will not return to its normal shape or dimension when the load is removed. Permanent deformation is called creep.

Developed length: the length of a pipe measured along the pipe including all fittings. For pipes that convey material under pressure (water pipes and gas pipes), an amount is sometimes added to the developed length of the physical pipe to account for pressure loss caused by friction at the fittings.

Dew point (temperature): the temperature at which water vapor in the air may condense into liquid water. A higher dew point temperature indicates that the air contains more water vapor.

Direct exhaust appliance: a fuel-burning appliance that obtains combustion air from inside the house and expels combustion products outside the house. These are usually high efficiency appliances with a sealed combustion chamber. Some appliances can be configured in the field as a direct vent appliance or a direct exhaust appliance. Also called a non-direct vented appliance.

Direct vent appliance: a fuel-burning appliance that obtains combustion air from outside the house and expels combustion products outside the house. These are usually high efficiency appliances with a sealed combustion chamber.

Dishwashing machine (dishwasher): a plumbing appliance that is used to clean eating and cooking utensils.

Disposall (Disposal): See **Food-waste disposer (disposal)**.

Diverter: (1) a valve in a bathtub spout that directs water from the spout to the shower riser. (2) Any valve that directs water flow from one pipe to other pipes, such as a valve in a shower that directs water from the shower head to body spray heads.

Dormer: a projection above a sloped roof that usually contains a window. A dormer usually has two sidewalls and a gable roof, but it may have any style roof.

Downdraft exhaust (vent): a fan located under a cooktop which pulls the cooking odors and moisture down and exhausts them to the outdoors through a duct located under the floor or in the foundation. A downdraft exhaust is sometimes used when a cooktop is located in an island, a peninsula, or other space where installing a hood is impractical or expensive.

Draft (forced): a method of expelling combustion gasses from gas-fired and oil-fired appliances that uses a fan (blower) to force the gasses through the vent under pressure; also referred to as positive pressure draft. Forced draft fans are installed at the beginning of the vent system, usually inside the appliance. Forced draft vents must be sealed to prevent combustion gasses from escaping through the vent.

Draft (induced): (1) the process of using negative pressure created by a fan to pull combustion gasses through a heat exchanger; draft inducers do not place combustion gasses in a chimney or vent under positive pressure; most medium efficiency gas furnaces are induced draft appliances. (2) the process of using negative pressure created by a fan to pull combustion gasses through a vent; this vent system may be used when the vent system for a natural draft appliance cannot be installed to operate using the stack effect; mechanical draft inducers are installed at the vent termination.

Draft (mechanical): a vent system that uses an electrically powered fan to assist in expelling combustion gasses through a chimney or vent; mechanical draft may be forced draft (positive pressure) or induced draft (negative pressure).

Draft (natural): the tendency of combustion gasses to rise in a chimney or vent due to the gasses being hotter and at a lower pressure than the surrounding gasses (also known as the stack effect); fireplaces and most gas-fired and oil-fired appliances rely on natural draft to expel combustion gasses.

Drain, waste, and vent pipes (DWV): see **DWV system**.

Drain (soil) pipe: a pipe that conveys feces and urine. Contrast **Waste pipe**.

Drainage pipe: a generic term that refers to a drain pipe or a waste pipe.

Drainage (storm water): a system intended to capture water and direct it away from the house and ultimately off the property. A drainage system may include components such as gutters and downspouts, swales, underground drains, and grading.

Driveway: a private road that is intended for vehicle use between a public road and a building.

Duct (branch): a duct that runs between a trunk duct or a plenum and one supply or return boot.

Duct (stack): a (usually) sheet metal duct that runs in a wall cavity; it terminates in a stack head instead of a boot. See **Boot** and **Stack head**.

Duct (trunk): a large duct that serves multiple branch ducts.

DWV system: an abbreviation used to describe the plumbing drain, waste, and vent pipes and associated fittings and fixtures.

Eaves: the extension of the rafters beyond the exterior wall of the building. See **Cornice**.

EGC: see **Grounding conductor, equipment (EGC)**.

EIFS: an acronym for Exterior Insulation and Finish System, a type of wall covering that looks like stucco. EIFS is not stucco and should not be described as such.

Elbow: a water supply fitting that changes the direction of flow in pipes. Elbows are identified by the number of degrees of the direction change. Common elbows include: 90°, 45°, and 22½°. Elbow is frequently used when discussing DWV fittings, but bend is the more technically correct term for DWV fittings. See **Bend**.

Enclosure (electrical): a case or a cabinet intended to prevent accidental contact with energized parts; a panelboard is housed inside an enclosure.

Energy recovery ventilator (ERV): a whole house mechanical ventilation system that transfers heat and moisture between the incoming ventilation air and the outgoing exhaust air. Compare **Heat recovery ventilator (HRV)**.

Equipment Grounding Conductor (EGC): see **Grounding conductor, equipment**.

ERV: see **Energy Recovery Ventilator (ERV)**.

Evaporator coil: part of an air conditioning or heat pump system; this device is located in the air handler of a heat pump or is attached to a furnace after the combustion chamber; an evaporator coil should not be located before a furnace combustion chamber because the moist air from the evaporator coil will damage the furnace.

Evaporative (swamp) cooler: a type of cooling system that reduces air temperature by pulling air through media soaked with water; these systems were once common in dry climates in the west, but have usually been replaced by a central air conditioning system.

Exhaust: air removed from a specific location by mechanical means; examples include bathroom exhaust fans, kitchen exhaust fans, and clothes dryers.

Exhaust hood (vent): an appliance that is installed above a range or cooktop to remove or filter cooking odors and moisture. An exhaust hood should be ducted to the outdoors; however, an exception allows for a hood that recirculates the exhaust back into the house if an operable window exists in the kitchen area or if the house is served by a system such as an ERV or HRV. See **Downdraft exhaust (vent)**.

Extruded Polystyrene (XPS): a type of insulation that is manufactured in sheets.

Fascia (eaves): vertical trim at the end of the eaves, usually part of the cornice.

Faucet: a type of valve that allows water to flow through the air from an outlet. See **Fixture, supply**.

Feeder conductors: conductors from the service equipment or from a panelboard that supply electricity to another panelboard such as a subpanel.

Fenestration: openings in the wall and roof of a house, such as windows, doors, and skylights.

Firebox: the firebox of a fireplace consists of the hearth and the walls from the hearth to the throat of the fireplace. See **Hearth**.

Fireplace: an opening at the base of a chimney in which a solid-fuel, such as wood may be burned.

Fitting: a part that allows two or more pipes to be joined together; commonly used to describe components that connect plumbing pipes.

Fixture drain (trap arm): a pipe that conveys material from a fixture trap to another drainage pipe.

Fixture, drainage: a receptacle (such as a floor drain, bathtub, or sink) or a device (such as a toilet) that receives water from the water supply system and discharges the water and other material into the drainage pipes.

Fixture, supply: a device (such as a faucet or hose bibb) from which water flows in the plumbing system. The term fixture is often used to describe a supply fixture, a drainage fixture, or both.

Flared fitting: a method of connecting annealed copper water supply tubing and gas tubing and their associated valves by enlarging the end of the tube and securing the tube on a flare fitting using a nut.

Flood rim level: the highest level water can rise in a drainage fixture before the water flows out from the fixture to an unintended area, such as the floor or the countertop.

Floor drain: a plumbing fixture recessed in a floor; floor drains in houses are usually located in the basement and receive water from sources such an as air conditioning condensate drain.

Flue: this term most accurately describes a generally vertical passageway inside a chimney; a chimney has at least one flue and may have several flues. See **Vent (combustion)**.

Food-waste disposer (disposal): a plumbing appliance that is used to grind and dispose of soft food waste matter into the plumbing system. This appliance is often called a disposal based on a brand name Disposall. Brand names should not be used to describe systems and components. This appliance is sometimes called a garbarator in Canada.

Footing (footer): the part of a foundation that transmits loads directly to the soil, usually made from concrete in modern houses.

Frieze: vertical trim that connects or covers the top course of wall covering with the bottom of the cornice. A frieze board usually hides the termination of wall covering such as brick or stone.

Functional drainage: when the water drainage rate from the fixture is approximately equal to the maximum water flow rate into the fixture; water should not be able to reach the flood rim level of the fixture when the drain is fully open.

Functional flow: a water flow rate at a water supply fixture (in gallons per minute, [gpm]) that is equal to the minimum recommended flow rate at the fixture supply pipe (with no fixture attached), or to the maximum recommended flow rate at the fixture, whichever is less. Examples: bathtub, 4 gpm:, sink or lavatory, 2.2 gpm; shower, 2.5 gpm: hose bibb, 5 gpm.

Fuse: see **Overcurrent protection device (OPD).**

GEC: see **Grounding electrode conductor (GEC).**

Girder: see **Beam (girder).**

Grade: the elevation or level of the ground outside the house.

Grading: the act of moving soil or other material to form a desired elevation on the property. The term is often used in conjunction with drainage to describe shaping land to affect water flow.

Gray water: liquid waste from lavatories, bathtubs, showers, clothes washers, and laundry trays. Gray water may be processed and recycled to flush toilets and for landscape irrigation. Gray water recycling may not be allowed in some jurisdictions or there may be different regulations.

Grille: a cover with louvers or perforations that are not adjustable and may not be closed; a grille usually covers a return air opening, but may cover a supply air opening.

Grounded: a conductor that is intentionally connected to ground; this describes what is often called the neutral conductor.

Grounding: providing an intentional connection to the earth; grounding provides an alternate path for current to return to its source; in an electrical power system, the source is the utility's transformer and ultimately the power plant. See **Grounding electrode** and **Grounding electrode conductor (GEC).**

Grounding conductor, equipment (EGC): a bare or green insulated conductor that provides a ground fault current path (a bonding connection) for equipment with metal cases and parts; these have been installed in most house branch circuit wiring since around 1960.

Grounding electrode: metal that is in direct contact with the earth and serves as the electrical system grounding connection; examples include copper rods, galvanized steel pipes, water service pipes and well pipes, and reinforcing steel encased in the footings.

Grounding electrode conductor (GEC): a conductor that runs between the grounding electrode and an accessible point downstream from where the grounded service entrance conductor connects to the service drop or lateral; the GEC connection is usually at the service equipment.

Ground fault: an event that occurs when metal that should not conduct electricity, such as a metal water pipe, becomes energized; if the metal is properly bonded, current flow should increase in the circuit and trip the circuit breaker or fuse.

Ground fault circuit interrupter (GFCI): a circuit breaker or receptacle that detects a ground fault by monitoring the imbalance in current flow between the energized and neutral conductors and stops current flow (opens the circuit) when a ground fault is detected.

Ground snow load: the estimated weight of accumulated snow on a surface; used when determining rafter span distance and fastening requirements for ceiling joists to rafters and ceiling joists to each other. Also used when determining cantilevered floor joist and deck floor joist span distance.

Grout (masonry): mortar with a high water content and a fluid-like consistency; used to fill the cores of masonry such as CMUs.

Header: a beam above an opening in a wall, such as a door or a window.

Hearth: the floor of a fireplace upon which the fire burns. See **Firebox**.

Hearth extension: the area directly in front and at the sides of a fireplace opening; it is intended to provide a safe, noncombustible, place for embers to land when they escape from the hearth.

Heat pump: a heating and air conditioning system that removes heat from a house in cooling mode and moves heat from outside the house to inside the house in heating mode. See **Air handler** and **Condenser (unit)**.

Heat recovery ventilator (HRV): a whole house mechanical ventilation system that transfers heat between the incoming ventilation air and the outgoing exhaust air. See **Energy recovery ventilator (ERV)**.

Heat seasonal performance factor (HSPF): a measure of the efficiency of a heat pump in heating mode; obtained by dividing the heating output of a system over a heating season by the electric energy used; HSPF ratings range between about seven and ten.

High loop: a backflow prevention method that helps prevent the flow of contaminated water from the plumbing waste system into a dishwasher. A high loop involves securing the dishwasher drain tube as high as possible in the kitchen sink base cabinet.

Hose bibb (bib): a plumbing supply fixture designed for attachment of a garden hose. See **Spigot**.

HRV: see **Heat Recovery Ventilator**.

HSFP: see **Heat seasonal performance factor (HSPF)**.

Hub (bell): the enlarged part of a pipe or fitting that accepts insertion of a pipe; cast iron pipes usually have a hub that accepts the spigot end of the pipe.

Humidity, relative: the amount of water vapor that is actually in the air compared to the amount of water vapor that could exist in the air at a given air temperature, expressed as a percentage. More moisture can exist in warm air than in cold air, so raising the air temperature while keeping the water vapor constant reduces relative humidity. Conversely, lowering the air temperature and keeping the water vapor content constant increases relative humidity.

HVAC: an abbreviation meaning heating, ventilation, and air conditioning; this is a common abbreviation used to describe cooling and heating systems.

Hydronic heating: a heating system that circulates hot liquid or steam through pipes; the pipes may be installed in the floor or may serve radiators or similar devices.

Joist: a horizontal structural member that supports a floor or ceiling.

Joules Law: a formula for calculating heat in an electrical circuit expressed as Heat = Current^2 X Resistance X Time.

Keyway: a slot or groove used to secure concrete or masonry walls to each other that are built at different times. A keyway is cut into the footing during finishing to help keep concrete or masonry walls from sliding off the footing.

Kicker: a piece of lumber, usually a 2x4, that is connected to a rafter and to a ceiling joist to reduce rafter thrust that could move the wall on which the rafter bears. A kicker serves the same function as a rafter tie. See **Rafter tie**.

Knockouts: stamped openings in an electrical enclosure where conduit or cable clamps are installed in order to secure conductors or cables. See **Tabs (twistouts)**.

Landscape (garden) block: a manufactured solid concrete block used to construct a landscape wall.

Landscape wall: a short height structure (usually 2 feet or less) that holds soil or fill on one side and keeps it from moving beyond the wall; a short height retaining wall.

Latent load: the amount of heat energy that an air conditioning system must remove from the air inside a home because of water vapor in the air; contributors to latent load include people breathing, activities such as cooking and bathing, and air infiltration from the outside; latent load is usually less in a desert location than in a coastal location. See **Sensible load**.

Laundry tray: a deep sink usually located in a laundry area; more commonly called a deep sink or a laundry sink.

Lavatory: a sink located in a bathroom.

Line set (refrigerant): the tubes in which refrigerant flows between the condenser and the evaporator coil in an air conditioning and heat pump; the line set consists of the liquid line and the suction line.

Lintel (angle iron): a horizontal structural component that carries the load from above. Lintels are used in masonry construction over openings such as windows and doors. Lintels are usually made from L-shaped steel, but may be made from steel reinforced concrete or wood.

Lintel (fireplace): a noncombustible material, usually iron or steel, that supports stone or masonry, and is installed above the fireplace opening.

Liquid line (tube): part of the refrigerant line set; the smaller, usually an uninsulated copper tube.

Load center: see **Panel (panelboard, load center)**.

Load (dead): the downward force on a structure imposed by the building materials and by permanently attached fixtures such as HVAC equipment.

Load (live): the downward force on a structure imposed by occupants and their belongings. Live load does not include environmental loads, such as wind and earthquakes.

Lug: a connection point where conductors are inserted and secured; examples include the connection points on panelboards for service entrance and feeder conductors, on terminal bars for neutral and EGCs, and on circuit breakers for branch circuit conductors.

Manifold (plumbing): several fittings spaced close together to which branch pipes or tubes are connected; can be a manufactured device or field-assembled; used to distribute water or gas to individual fixtures or appliances or to a group of fixtures or appliances; common uses include PEX water distribution systems and CSST gas distribution systems.

Mainfold (vent connector): a type of vent connector in which two or more vent connectors are joined together before being connected to the vent.

Mantel: the decorative facing around a firebox opening; it may consist of a horizontal shelf above the firebox opening and vertical trim at the sides of the firebox opening. The vertical trim is sometimes called the legs.

Mass wall: above-grade walls made from concrete masonry units, concrete, insulated concrete forms, masonry cavity, brick (structural, not veneer), adobe, compressed earth block, rammed earth, and solid timber logs.

Microwave oven (microwave): a cooking appliance that uses high frequency electromagnetic radiation to heat food; microwaves installed above ranges and cooktops usually have a built-in exhaust fan and light. A microwave may include a convection oven.

Offset (chimney): a change in the direction of a chimney or flue from vertical.

Ohm's Law and Watt's Law: expressions of the relationship between current, voltage, power, and resistance; expressed as Power = Volts X Amps and Resistance = Volts/Amps.

OPD: see **Overcurrent protection device (OPD).**

Outlet: a place where current is taken for use; examples include receptacles, light fixtures, and connections at electric appliances such as water heaters.

Oven: an enclosed cooking appliance intended for baking and broiling food. An oven may be mounted in a cabinet (a wall oven), or it may be part of a range.

Oven (convection): an enclosed cooking appliance intended for baking and broiling food. Cooking speed is enhanced by using a fan to circulate air inside the oven.

Overcurrent protection device (OPD): a fuse or a circuit breaker; overcurrent protection devices interrupt the flow of electricity when a set current flow is exceeded (an overload), or when a short circuit fault is detected; these devices prevent conductors and devices from overheating and causing fires.

Package (air conditioning) system: an air conditioning system or heat pump in which an evaporator coil and fan are contained in one cabinet; package units are usually located outside on the ground or on the roof, but may be located inside.

Panel (panelboard, load center): the equipment on which circuit breakers or fuses are mounted; panels include associated terminal bars; a panelboard is contained in an enclosure; the first and usually the largest panel is often referred to as the main panel or the service panel; there are, however, no generally accepted terms to identify panels.

Parapet wall: the section of a wall that is above the roof; often seen where a low slope roof is installed; also seen as an extension of a firewall in multi-family dwellings.

Patio: a flat outdoor recreational area adjacent to a house, usually but not always on grade.

Permeability: the ability or property of a material to resist or allow the diffusion of water vapor through the material. Permeability (perms) is expressed as a number greater than zero. For example, glass is a very low permeability material and fiberglass batt insulation is a high permeability material.

PEX: Cross-linked polyethylene, a type of water distribution pipe and water service pipe.

Pier: a column designed to support a concentrated vertical load, often installed above ground, but may be installed below ground.

Pilaster: a column that supports a concentrated vertical load. A pilaster may be on the interior or the exterior of a building, and may be taller and more decorative than a pier.

Pile: a column installed in the ground that is designed to support a concentrated vertical load. A pile is part of the foundation of a house, and is usually found where the soil has poor load-bearing capacity or is unstable.

Pipe, water service: the pipe beginning at the water meter or at the well head and ending at the main water shutoff valve.

Pipes, water distribution: pipes beginning at the main water shutoff valve that convey potable water to fixtures and appliances in the house.

Pitch (of a roof): the ratio of the total vertical height of a roof to the total horizontal distance that the roof covers. For example, if the total height of the roof from the top plate to the ridge is 12 feet and the total horizontal distance between the ridge and the edge of the eaves is 24 feet, the roof has a ½ pitch. See **Slope (of a roof)**.

Plenum: an enclosed space through which air flows in an air conditioning system; a plenum supplies air to or receives air from branch ducts; a plenum is usually installed on the supply and return side of a furnace and air handler; a distribution plenum is a plenum that receives air from a duct and distributes the air to branch ducts.

Plumb: vertical.

Plumb cut: a vertical cut of a rafter at the ridge or at a hip and valley rafter; also the vertical cut of a stair stringer at its support.

Porch: an outdoor area that is attached to the house. Porches are usually covered, which is a way to distinguish a porch from a deck.

Potable water: water that is safe to drink; taste and visual appeal are not considerations.

Power: a measure of the work performed by electricity; unit of measure is the Watt.

Press-connect fitting: a proprietary method of connecting copper water supply tubes and valves that uses specially designed fittings and a crimping tool to seal the fitting; sometimes called a compression fitting.

Pump: a device that moves water through the circulation system. A pool pump consists of three parts, a basket strainer, a pump, and an electric motor that provides the mechanical energy to move the water through the pump.

Purlin: a brace installed near the midpoint of a rafter that transmits the rafter load to a load-bearing wall, and allows the rafter to span a greater distance. A purlin consists of a purlin that is at least as wide as the rafter and a purlin brace that is at least a 2x4 and bears on a load-bearing wall. Purlin braces should be installed at least every 4 feet.

Push-connect (push-fit) fitting: a proprietary method of connecting water supply tubes that allows the tube to be pushed into the fitting, securing the tube without the use of solder, washers, nuts, or similar components (e. g., Sharkbite, Probite).

Raceway: enclosed metallic or nonmetallic components designed and listed for holding conductors or cables between points in the electricity distribution system of the house; examples include various types of conduit and tubing.

Rack (racking): the distortion or movement of a structure or its components; usually caused by wind or seismic loads.

Racking (back): the horizontal placement of a masonry course inward from the course below; racking is usually done to narrow the width of a chimney above the fireplace. Contrast **Corbel**.

Radiant cooling: a cooling system that circulates cool liquid through pipes; pipes are often installed in the ceiling, but may be installed in the floor; these system only address the sensible load, so they are not recommended for high humidity environments; these systems are uncommon in houses, but are sometimes encountered in adobe houses. Contrast **Hydronic heating.**

Rafter: an inclined roof structural member that supports the roof sheathing and roof covering.

Rafter (common): an inclined roof structural member that runs between the ridge and the top plate.

Rafter (fill-in): a dimensional lumber rafter used with trusses and I-joist rafters to construct parts of the roof system where trusses and I-joists are not practical.

Rafter (hip): an ascending rafter formed at the intersection of two hip roof sections. Hip rafters may need to be supported at a ridge board by a brace to a load-bearing wall.

Rafter (jack): a rafter that runs between a hip or valley rafter and the ridge, or between two rafters. Rafters that run between a hip rafter and the ridge are hip jack rafters and rafters that run between a valley rafter and the ridge are valley jack rafters. Rafters that run between valley and hip rafters are cripple jack rafters.

Rafter (valley): a descending rafter formed by the intersection of two roofs. Valley rafters are load-bearing members. Valley rafters may need to be supported at a ridge board by a brace to a load-bearing wall.

Rafter tail: the part of a rafter that extends past the exterior wall top and forms part of the eaves.

Rafter tie: a horizontal member running between rafters on opposite sides of the roof when ceiling joists run perpendicular to the rafters. Rafter ties act like ceiling joists to keep the rafters from pushing the walls out.

Rain cap: a cover over a chimney flue that protects from water entry into the flue, often combined with a spark arrestor; rain caps are not required. See **Spark arrestor**.

Range: a cooking appliance that combines a cooktop and an oven into one cabinet.

Rangetop: a cooking appliance that is similar to a cooktop, but is usually heavier and larger with commercial-type features. Rangetops usually use gas as the fuel.

Receptor, shower: a term sometimes used to describe a shower pan.

Receptacle: an outlet designed to accept a plug that supplies electricity to an appliance.

Resistance: the property of a material to allow or restrict the flow of electricity; materials with low resistance are conductors and materials with high resistance are insulators; unit of measure is the Ohm.

Refrigerant (coolant): the substance that flows through an air conditioning and heat pump system liquid and suction tubes; this substances was Freon (R-22) in older systems, but because of its negative environmental effects Freon has been phased out of production; the current refrigerant is R-410A.

Register: a cover with louvers or perforations that are adjustable or with a damper that may be opened and closed; a register usually covers a supply air opening. Contrast **Grille**.

Retaining wall: a structure that holds soil or other fill on one side and keeps it from moving beyond the wall; usually applied to walls more than 2 feet tall.

Ridge: the top horizontal board or beam of a roof. Most roofs use a ridge board that is a place to fasten rafters and does not provide structural support. Roofs supporting vaulted ceilings should usually have a ridge beam designed to provide structural support. Ridge boards and ridge beams should be deep enough so that the entire plumb cut of the rafter bears on the ridge.

Riser: (1) a vertical plumbing pipe that extends one story or more; (2) a vertical plumbing pipe that connects a valve to a water faucet. Examples: a shower riser connects the shower valve to the arm that supports the shower spray head, a fixture riser connects the shutoff valves to the faucet.

Rotate (rotation): a condition where a structural member moves laterally from its normal position relative to vertical, such as when a foundation wall moves inward due to pressure from soil.

Rumford fireplace: a fireplace with a tall opening and a shallow hearth that is designed to reflect more heat into the room; these fireplaces are most likely to be found in houses built in the first half of the 19th century, but may be found in any house; these fireplaces have different hearth and firebox dimensions compared to traditional masonry fireplaces.

R-value: the ability or property of a material to slow heat transfer. A higher R-value number equals a higher ability to slow heat transfer. R-value is expressed as a number greater than zero. R-value is used to compare the insulation value of materials.

Schedule 40 and Schedule 80 pipe: this refers to the thickness of pipe walls. Schedule 40 pipe has a thinner wall than Schedule 80 pipe. Schedule 40 pipe is more commonly used. Both have the same outside diameter; Schedule 80 pipe has a smaller internal diameter.

Schrader valves: valves at a condenser unit where technicians attach a gauge set to measure pressures in the refrigerant lines; similar to valves on automobile tires.

Seasonal energy efficiency ratio (SEER): see **SEER**.

Seat cut: the horizontal rafter cut at a wall top or a valley. Also the horizontal cut at the end of a stairway stringer.

SEER (seasonal energy efficiency ratio): a measure of the efficiency of a cooling system and a measure of the efficiency of a heat pump in cooling mode; obtained by dividing the cooling output of a system over a cooling season by the electric energy used; the minimum allowed SEER is currently 14 for most of the United States, and the maximum available is around 20; older systems may have SEERs of 10 or less. These ratings may be different in some states.

Sensible load: the amount of heat energy that an air conditioning system must remove from the air inside a home because of the temperature of the air, contributors to sensible load include heat gain through walls and ceilings, solar heat gain through windows, equipment operation such as ovens and lights; sensible load is usually greater in a southern location than in a northern location. Contrast **Latent load**.

Septic tank: a vessel that receives sewage from the building sewer pipe, allows the solids to settle and decompose, and allows the liquid to drain off into drain (leach) field. Septic tanks are usually made from concrete, but some are made from corrosion-resistant metal and from plastic.

Service drop and service lateral: the conductors between the transformer belonging to the utility and the house; a service drop is above-ground and a service lateral is below ground.

Service entrance conductors: the conductors between the service drop or the service lateral and the service equipment.

Service equipment: the circuit breakers, switches, or fuses that shut off power to the house; all power should be shut off using six or fewer circuit breakers, switches, or fuses; often called the main shutoff or main disconnect.

Service point: the place where the service drop or service lateral conductors end and the house service entrance conductors begin; this is usually at the drip loops for service drops; the service point for service laterals is more difficult to distinguish, but is often at the meter.

Sewage: liquid and solids in drainage or sewer pipes that contains animal or vegetable matter or any other impurities.

Sewage disposal system, (individual/private): an on-site system that disposes of sewage from a house. A modern system usually consists of a septic tank and drain field, but mechanical systems (such as mound systems) are also available. See **Septic tank**.

Sewage ejector pump: a pump that drains a sump filled with sewage and pumps the sewage into the building drain. Contrast **Sump pump**.

Sewer (building): a pipe that conveys sewage from the building drain to the public sewer or private sewage disposal system; begins 30 inches beyond the house exterior walls where it connects to the building drain; sometimes called the sewer lateral. See **Building drain**.

Sewer (public): a system that conveys sewage from houses to a central treatment plant, usually owned and operated by a local government.

Shear: the deformation of a structural member (such as a beam) in which parallel planes slide relative to each other.

Shear wall: a wall designed not to change shape (rack) under loads such as wind and earthquake; also called a braced wall. See **Rack (racking)**.

Sheathing: (1) the material covering the top of the rafters; (2) the material covering the top of the floor joists, also called the subfloor; (3) the material covering the exterior wall structural components.

Single phase electrical service: electrical service consisting of two energized 120 volt conductors and one grounded conductor; this is by far the most common residential electrical service.

Short circuit: this event occurs when current flows between conductors in an unintended manner, such as between the hot and neutral conductors.

Slip joint: a plumbing drainage connection, usually at a sink trap, that is secured by a gasket under a nut, and can be removed by hand or with a tool such as pliers; slip joints must be accessible.

Slope (of a roof): the number of inches that a roof increases in height (rise) for every 12 inches of horizontal distance (run). The slope is usually expressed as 4/12 or 4:12 where the first number is the rise and the second number is always 12, the run. The terms pitch and slope are sometimes used as synonyms. This is not technically correct. See **Pitch (of a roof)**.

Smoke chamber: the area between a masonry fireplace throat and the flue; it helps direct the combustion gasses toward the flue.

Soffit (eaves): the horizontal trim that covers the rafters, usually part of the cornice.

Solar heat gain coefficient (SHGC): a measure of the amount of solar radiation that passes through a window. A lower SHGC means that less solar radiation passes through a window.

Soldering (sweating): a method of joining metal pipe and fittings (usually copper) by fusing them together with an alloy made mostly from tin at a temperature below 800° F. See **Brazing (silver soldering)**.

Span: the horizontal distance between structural supports. Overspan is an informal term that refers to a joist or a rafter that is longer than allowed between structural supports. Rafter span is measured horizontally, not along the length of the rafter.

Spark arrestor: a screen around the perimeter of a chimney flue termination that helps keep hot embers from escaping and causing a fire, often combined with a rain cap; spark arrestors are required in some areas that are prone to wildfires. See **Rain cap**.

Spigot: (1) the un-enlarged end of a pipe that is inserted into a hub; (2) a hose bibb.

Split (air conditioning) system: an air conditioning system or heat pump in which an evaporator coil and fan are located inside, and a condenser unit is located outside; this is the most common type of air conditioning system.

Square (squared): a condition that occurs when intersecting walls form a 90° angle. Squared walls can be determined by measuring and applying the formula $A^2 + B^2 = C^2$ to the right triangle formed by the walls.

Stack: a vertical drainage pipe or vent pipe that extends more than one story.

Stack vent: an extension of a drainage stack that serves as the vent for the stack and fixtures connected to the stack.

Stack effect: the tendency of warmer, more boyant air to rise by displacing cooler air. The stack effect allows natural draft to occur in vents and chimneys and affects air flows inside buildings.

Stack head (HVAC distribution system): sheet metal formed into a rectangle or circle that connects a stack duct to a grille or a register. See **Boot** and **Duct (stack)**.

Standpipe: (1) a pipe used to receive liquid waste from a fixture or appliance, usually a clothes washing machine; (2) a system of pipes and fire department connections intended to provide water for fighting fires; fire fighting standpipes are found in commercial and industrial buildings.

Stoop: a small platform that serves as a landing on the exterior side of a door.

Stove: a device that uses an energy source to produce heat. In modern usage, the term stove sometimes refers to a range when used to describe a cooking appliance. The term is also used to describe a space heating appliance such as a wood-burning stove.

Street bend (elbow): a bend with a hub on one end and a spigot on the other end.

Stud: (1) a grade of lumber used in wall construction rated below #2 grade and approximately equal to #3 grade; (2) a vertical structural member in a wall.

Stud (cripple): a less than full height vertical structural member usually found under windows and in partial height walls.

Stud (jack): a less than full height vertical structural member placed under a header to provide bearing support for the header.

Stud (king): a full height vertical structural member placed on the sides of a header.

Subdrain: a drain pipe located below the building drain; usually occurs when basement plumbing is located below the building drain; the sewage is pumped up to the building drain by a sewage ejector pump. See **Sewage ejector pump.**

Subpanel: a panelboard that receives power from an upstream panelboard, usually the main panelboard; also called a downstream or a distribution panel; however, there are no generally accepted terms to identify panels.

Suction line (tube): part of the refrigerant line set; the larger, insulated copper tube. See **Line set (refrigerant)**.

Sump (crock): a vessel or pit that receives sewage, waste, storm water, or ground water from around the house foundation; a sump is installed below a level where it could drain by gravity, therefore it must be drained by a pump.

Sump pump: a pump that drains a sump filled by storm water or by ground water from around the house foundation. Contrast **Sewage ejector pump**.

Surcharge (earth): earth located above the top of a retaining wall.

Sweep: a DWV fitting with a 90° direction change; the term is more commonly used when referring to cast iron DWV fittings. A sweep may be a long sweep or a short sweep. A long sweep has a larger curve radius than a short sweep. A long sweep may be used in all direction changes whereas there are limits on how a short sweep may be used.

Swale: a depression or channel in the soil intended to direct water in a particular direction.

Tabs (twistouts): rectangular metal pieces on the dead front cover that are removed before installing a circuit breaker; tabs must be replaced by a filler plate if a tab has been removed and no circuit breakers is installed. See **Knockouts**.

Tailpiece (also tail piece): a vertical pipe installed between a sink outlet and trap, or between a sink outlet and a fitting that runs to a trap.

Tension force (load): The force that pulls or stretches a structural member. A beam under a vertical load is under tension on the bottom. Contrast **Compression**.

Terminal bars: metal bars associated with a panelboard on which neutral and equipment grounding conductors are mounted; called a neutral bar when neutral conductors or neutral and equipment grounding conductors are connected; called a ground bar if only equipment grounding conductors are connected.

Thermal expansion: the tendency of water to expand in volume when heated; 50 gallons can expand by ½ gallon or more when heated to about 115° Fahrenheit.

Thermal expansion tank: an enclosed vessel containing air that absorbs the water which has expanded when heated in a storage-type water heater or a hot water boiler.

Three phase electrical service: electrical service consisting of three energized conductors and one grounded conductor; this service type is mostly for commercial and industrial buildings.

Throat: the opening between a fireplace hearth and the smoke chamber. See **Damper (fireplace)**.

Tieback: a device used to resist the lateral force on a retaining wall. See **Deadman**.

Toilet (commode, water closet, WC): a plumbing fixture that receives human excrement and discharges it into the drain pipes.

Ton (of refrigeration): a measure of the size or cooling capacity of an air conditioning system equal to 12,000 Btu per hour; a 3 ton air conditioning system has a cooling capacity of 36,000 Btu. See **Brittish thermal unit (Btu)**.

Townhouse: a single family attached dwelling with all of the following: (1) three or more dwellings in one building, (2) dwelling extends from the foundation to the roof, (3) a yard or public way on at least two sides. A townhouse is a type of building, not a form of real property ownership.

Trap: a component that maintains a water seal to prevent sewer gas from entering the house; a trap may be a separate fitting or it may be integrated into a fixture such as a toilet.

Trap arm: see **Fixture drain**.

Trap primer: a device or pipe that conveys water to a trap to maintain the water seal; usually associated with floor drains because these fixtures often do not receive enough water to maintain the trap water seal.

Urea-Formaldehyde Foam (UFFI): a type of spray foam insulation.

U-value (factor): the ability or property of a material to allow heat transfer. U-value is the inverse of R-value (R-value = 1/U-value). U-value is expressed as a number greater than zero. A larger number equals a higher rate of heat transfer and a lower R-value. U-value is primarily used in residential construction to compare the thermal performance of fenestration. For example, metal such as aluminum has a high U-value; this is why higher quality aluminum windows have a thermal break in the frame to slow heat transfer.

Valve: a device used to activate and deactivate the flow of a liquid or gas; some valves can control the flow rate of the liquid or gas.

Valve, full open (full flow): a valve that has minimal resistance to water flow when open; ball and gate valves are the most common examples in houses.

Valve, quick closing: a valve that closes rapidly to stop the flow of water; typically found on clothes washing and dishwashing machines. Quick closing valves can cause water hammer.

Valve, service (main shutoff): the valve that activates and deactivates the water flow to the water distribution pipes.

Vapor barrier: a technically questionable term often used when the term **vapor retarder** is intended. Class I vapor retarders are effectively vapor barriers, but the term vapor retarder is preferred.

Vapor diffusion: the process by which water vapor passes through a permeable material from an area of greater vapor pressure to an area of lower vapor pressure.

Vapor drive: a condition that occurs when heat and vapor pressure cause increased vapor diffusion. One example is when water vapor diffuses through permeable building materials from heated interior areas in the winter. Another example is when solar radiation heats wet bricks forcing water vapor through permeable building materials in the summer. Vapor drive is usually less of a factor than vapor flow by convection through openings in the building envelope.

Vapor retarder: a material that restricts the flow of water vapor. A Class I vapor retarder is rated at 0.1 perms or less. Polyethylene sheeting is an example. A Class II vapor retarder is rated at between 0.1 and 1.0 perms. Kraft paper used as the facing on some batt insulation is an example. A Class III vapor retarder is rated at between 1.0 and 10.0 perms. Latex and oil paints are examples.

Veneer: a decorative surface applied over the exterior walls of a house. The term is usually applied to wall coverings such as brick and natural stone.

Vent, branch: a vent pipe that connects two or more individual vents to a vent stack or stack vent.

Vent (combustion): the final vertical component in a vent system; this term most accurately describes manufactured products such as metal pipes.

Glossary 443

Vent connector: a component that conducts combustion products from a fuel-burning appliance to a vent; vent connectors are single-wall or double-wall metal pipes.

Vent, pipe (plumbing): a pipe that conveys air.

Vent, plumbing: a pipe system that conveys air to help equalize pressure in the drain and waste pipes. The vent system protects the trap water seal from siphoning and blowout.

Vent stack: a vertical plumbing vent that extends more than one story.

Vent system: a passageway that conducts combustion products from a fuel-burning appliance to a point outside the house; the vent system begins at the appliance draft hood or flue collar and ends outside the house; the vent system consists of a vent or chimney and a vent connector, if one is used.

Ventilation (building): the process of supplying outside air to a house or removing inside air from a house by natural or mechanical means; ventilation can be random and uncontrolled (air leaks), or it can be designed and controlled (outside air ducts, heat recovery ventilators, energy recovery ventilators).

Vertical pipe (plumbing): a pipe that is 45° or more relative to horizontal.

Voltage: the pressure of electricity in a circuit; similar to water pressure in a pipe; unit of measure is the Volt.

WC: see **Toilet**.

Walkway: a private path on private property that is intended for pedestrian use.

Wall covering (cladding): a non-load-bearing material or assembly that is applied over the exterior walls of a house.

Waste: liquid in drainage pipes that does not contain feces or urine.

Waste pipe: a drainage pipe that does not convey feces or urine.

Water closet (WC): see **Toilet**.

Water hammer: a thumping or banging noise caused by the sudden stopping of water flow. Water hammer can damage pipes and fixtures.

Water hammer arrestor: a device that absorbs the hydraulic shock caused by the sudden stopping of water flow, usually installed near clothes washing machine and dishwasher water supply connections.

Water flow rate: the amount of water that comes from a plumbing fixture, usually measured in gallons per minute. Water flow is a function of the pipe type, pipe internal diameter, pipe length, and the number of elbows between the water source and the fixture. Increasing the water pressure past the point where a pipe is full will not increase the water flow rate, but it may burst the pipe.

Water pressure: the amount of force that water exerts on the walls of a pipe, usually expressed in pounds per square inch (psi). The minimum water pressure is 40 psi and the maximum pressure is 80 psi. Water pressure exceeding 80 psi should be reduced by installing a water pressure regulator in the water service pipe.

Water pressure regulator: a usually bell-shaped device installed on the water service pipe near where the pipe enters the house and downstream from the water shutoff valve of the house; it is adjustable and reduces water pressure.

Water (weather)-resistive barrier (WRB): a material that resists penetration of liquid water; usually describes materials such as asphalt-impregnated building paper (e. g., #15 felt) and house wraps.

Watt's Law: see **Ohm's Law and Watt's Law.**

WC: see **Toilet.**

Wiring methods: cables and raceways approved for distributing electricity from the service point to panelboards and outlets; examples include armored cable, nonmetallic sheathed cable, and various types of conduit and tubing.

WRB: see **Water (weather)-resistive barrier (WRB).**

Wythe (withe): (1) a course of masonry (usually brick) that separates flues in a masonry chimney; (2) a vertical masonry wall that is one masonry unit thick. A typical brick veneer wall is one wythe thick.

XPS: see **Extruded Polystyrene (XPS).**

INDEX

A

Access
  appliances in attics 262
  attic 261
  crawl space 192
  reporting limitations 380
  swimming pool and spa 1
Accounting, business operation 395
Acoustic ceiling 327
Adhered masonry veneer 30
Adobe walls 235
Air barrier 272, 277, 280, 281, 284, 288, 320
Air sealing 267, 271, 290
Algae
  asphalt shingles 125
  wood roof covering 142
Aluminum siding 34
Artificial stone 30
Asbestos
  reporting 381
  shingles 122
  siding 35
  textured ceilings 326
  vermiculite insulation 281
Asphalt, driveways and walkways 18
Asphalt shingles 123
Attic
  access opening 261
  appliance access 262
  escape openings 80
  inspection 391
  pull-down stairs 263
  unventilated 312
  vapor retarder 273
  ventilation 307
Auxiliary structures, inspection scope 1

B

Backer blocks, I-joists 210

Backspan
  cantilevered deck 101
  cantilevered floor 203
Backsplash 358
Baffles, attic ventilation 309
Balcony. *See also* Deck
  cantilevered 90, 202
  flashing 91
  materials and construction 89
Balloon framing 196
Balusters
  deck guards and stairs 99
  interior guards and stairs 352
Base flashing. *See* Flashing
Basement
  cold room 86
  columns 178
  cracks, floor 195
  cracks, walls 186
  definition, energy efficiency 268
  description 181
  draftstopping 213
  efflorescence 189
  escape opening 80
  foundation drains 184
  inspection 392
  insulation 320
  repairs 190
  suspended ceilings 327
  wall materials 182, 233
  water problems 9, 155, 187, 321
  waterproofing & dampproofing 184
  window wells 80
Bathroom
  exhaust fan 305
  safety glazing 81
Batt insulation 277

Beam
　bearing on support 199, 205
　deck 92, 103
　deflection 197
　engineered lumber 208, 209
　header 65, 76, 220
　in crawl space 192
　lumber grade 198
　notches and holes 204
Bed molding 62
Bedrooms, escape and rescue openings 80
Bifold doors 333
Bilco door. *See* Doors, exterior
Bird's-mouth cut, rafters 244
Blacktop 18
Blocking, floor framing 201
Block walls. *See* Wall, above ground; *See* Wall, below ground
Bolts
　deck 94
　foundation anchors 200
Bond, business 407
Boot, flashing. *See* Flashing
Bracing, trusses 255
Bracing, walls 223. *See also* Wall framing
Branch circuits. *See* Receptacles, Switches, and Wiring methods
Breach of contract 398
Brick veneer
　description 36
　flashing 60, 161
　mortar joints 38
　support 37
　terms 39
Brick wall, structural 230
Bridging
　ceiling joists 243
　floors 201
Built-up roof covering 144
Bulkhead door. *See* Doors, exterior
Bushes. *See* Plants

Business operation
　accounting 395
　business law 395
　ethics 409
　insurance 407
　licenses 414
　marketing 419
　planning 412

C

Cabinets, kitchen and bathroom 354
Camber. *See* Crown, lumber
Cantilever
　balcony 90, 202
　deck 102
　floor framing 202
Carpet 335
Cased opening 331
Cast stone 30
Catch basin 11
Caulk 45, 58, 75, 90, 94, 156, 161, 183, 237
　draftstopping 213
　fireblocking 217
Ceiling joists. *See* Roof framing
Cellulose insulation 279
Chimney
　cricket/saddle 159
　fireblocking 216
　flashing 58, 159, 161, 247
　opening in floor framing 203
Cinder blocks. *See* Columns; *See* Wall, above ground; *See* Wall, below ground
Clothes dryer exhaust 298
CMU. *See* Retaining walls; *See* Wall, above ground; *See* Wall, below ground
Code of ethics, inspection 409
Collar ties 242
Columns
　balcony 89
　deck 103
　foundation 177, 178
　porch roofs 86
　screw jack 178
Composite wood siding 46

Concrete
  control joints 18
  defects 18
  slab defects 196
Concrete blocks. *See* Wall, above ground;
    See Wall, below ground
Concrete slabs, defects 195
Condenser, plants nearby 14
Condominium 171
Contracts 401
  breach of 398
Control joints 18
Corner boards 56
Cornice 62
Corporation 414
Cosmetic defects 324, 329, 334, 338, 339, 364
Counterflashing. *See* Flashing
Countertops 357
Cracks
  basement walls 175, 186
  basement walls, repairs 190
  control in concrete slabs 18, 182, 194
  driveways, walkways, patios 19
  footings 179
  interior walls 329
Crawl space
  access 192
  clearance to wood 192
  columns 178
  description 192
  foam plastic insulation 219, 281
  inspection 378, 392
  piers 178
  unventilated 318
  ventilation 314
  wall materials 192, 233, 234
  water problems 9, 155, 276, 321
Crazing, concrete 196
Cripples 76, 220
Crown, lumber 204, 208
Cultured stone 30
Culvert 16

D

Dampers
  exhaust fans 298, 303
  ventilation, outside air 292, 296

Dampproofing 184
Deadman. *See* Retaining walls
Deck. *See also* Stoops, Porches, and Balconies
  beams 103
  bracing 103
  flashing 92
  flooring 102
  footings 103
  guards 99
  handrails 98
  joists 101
  lateral load connectors 95
  ledger attachment to house 94
  materials 92
  posts and columns 103
  stairs and landings 96
Deflection, floor 199
Developed length, clothes dryer exhaust duct 299
Dew point 268
Dirt. *See* Soil
Doors, exterior
  Bilco 67
  bulkhead 67
  egress (front door) 68
  escape openings 77
  fire separation 217
  flashing 58
  hinged, exterior 64
  landings 68
  safety glazing 69
  sliding (patio), exterior 64
  swimming pool barrier 23
Doors, garage vehicle 114
  automatic openers 118
Doors, interior
  bifold 333
  cased opening 331
  pocket 333
  side-hinged 331
  sliding 333
Dormer 244
Downdraft, kitchen exhaust 303
Downpipe. *See* Gutters
Downspouts. *See* Gutters
Draftstopping 213

Drainage
  at foundation 8
  catch basin 11
  culvert 16
  dry bed 10
  expansive soils 8
  foundation problems 8
  French drains 10
  minimum slope 9
  swales 10
  underground drains 10
Drains, foundation drains 11
Driveway
  construction 17
  cracks 19, 196
  materials 17
  slope 18
  width 15
Drop ceiling 327
Dry bed 10
Dryvit 50
Drywall 325
Duct
  clothes dryer 298
  kitchen exhaust 303
Dusting, concrete 196

E

Earth. *See* Soil
Eaves 62, 124, 128, 137, 140, 143, 155
Eaves trough. *See* Gutters
EDPM roof covering 152
Efflorescence
  adhered masonry veneer 31
  basement 189
  brick veneer 39
  CMU walls 232
  foundation slabs 195
  stucco 49, 51
Egress openings 80
EIFS 50
Electrical circuits. *See also* Wiring methods
Energy recovery ventilation system 293
Engineered wood floor covering 336
Engineered wood siding 47
Engineered wood, types of 207

Errors and omissions insurance 407
  claims 396
Escape openings 80
Ethics, inspection code of 409
Exhaust. *See also* Bathroom exhaust fan
  local 292, 298, 303
Expanded polystyrene insulation 280
Expansive soil 8
Extruded polystyrene insulation 280

F

Fan
  attic ventilation 308
  bathroom exhaust 305
  kitchen exhaust 303
  whole house 297
Fascia 62
Fence, swimming pool 22
Fiber cement
  roof covering 131
  siding 42
Fiberglass insulation
  batt 277, 320
  loose fill 279
Filler blocks, I-joists 210
Fireblocking 216
Fire separation
  between buildings 218
  garage 217
  townhouses 218
Flashing
  appliance vent 160
  brick veneer 60, 161
  chimney 161
  deck 93
  doors & windows 58
  exhaust duct 160
  kick out 47, 162
  plumbing vent 159
  roof penetrations 114
  sidewall & headwall 161, 163
  siding 59, 161
  skylight 166
  stucco 162
  transition between wall coverings 60
  wall penetrations 61
Flashing cement 125

Flat roofs 144
Floor framing
   bearing on foundation 199
   bridging 201
   cantilever 202
   defects 204, 213
   deflection 199
   description 196
   dimensional lumber 197
   draftstopping 213
   foundation anchors 200
   holes and notches 204, 209
   I-joists 206
   joist span 198
   loads 197
   openings in framing 203
   sheathing 198, 204
   trusses 212
Foam insulation 280
Foam plastic 219
Foam roof covering 150
Footings
   building 176
   deck 103
Foundation
   anchors 200
   basement 181
   columns 177
   cracks 186, 196, 231
   crawl space 192
   footings 176
   piles & piers 177
   post-tensioned 194
   slab 192
   stem wall 193
   stone 183
Foundation drains 11, 184
Fraud 400
French drains 10
Frieze 62

G

Gabion retaining wall 3
Gable roof 239

Garage
   fire separation 217
   inspection 391
   vehicle door 114
   vehicle door opener 118
Garden walls. *See* Retaining walls
Gate, swimming pool 23
Girder. *See* Beam
Glass, safety. *See* Safety glazing
Glue laminated beams 208
Grade
   around building 8, 31, 176, 181
   lumber 197
Green drywall 325
Ground snow load 90, 199, 202, 240
Grout 176, 178, 182, 231
Guardrails. *See* Guards
Guards
   deck 99
   interior 352
Gusset plate, trusses 254
Gutters 155
   underground drains 11
Gypsum board, interior 325

H

Handrails
   deck 98
   interior 350
Hardboard siding 46
Header. *See* Beam
Heat recovery ventilation system 293
Heat transfer 270
Hills, slope of grade 10
Hip roof, description 239
Holes in framing materials. *See* Floor, Roof, or Wall framing
Home inspection
   business 412
   contracts 401
   descriptions, reports 374
   ethics 409
   habitability 373
   insurance 407
   liability 398
   limitations 364, 379
   objective 363

procedures 389
reportable conditions 363
report contents, other 382
report deficiency statements 367, 371
standards of practice 365
threats to people and property 373
tools 384
Humidity, relative 268

I

Ice dams 143
Ignition barrier 219
I-joists
   defects 208
   description 207
   filler, backer, squash blocks 210
   roof/ceiling 239, 261
Infrared cameras 386
Inspection procedures 389
Inspection reports. *See* Reporting
Insulating concrete forms 232
Insulation
   basement 320
   batt 277
   crawl space 318
   foam 280
   history 266
   how it works 269
   loose fill/blown in 278
   perlite 281
   radiant barriers 289
   sheets 279, 320
   urea-formaldehyde 282
   vapor retarders 272
   vermiculite 281
Insulbrick siding 48
Insurance
   bond 407
   errors and omissions 395, 407
   general liability 408
   homeowner's 409
   vehicle 409
   worker's compensation 408
Interlayment, shakes 140
Internet of things 359
Isolation joint 18

J

Jack studs 65, 76, 220
Joist, floor. *See* Floor framing
Joists, deck 101

K

Keyway 182
Kicker 242
Kick out flashing 162
King studs 65, 76, 220
Kitchen
   cabinets and countertops 354
   exhaust duct 303
Kraft paper 277

L

Laminate countertops 357
Laminated Strand Lumber (LSL) 208
Laminated Veneer Lumber (LVL) 208
Laminate floor covering 336
Landings
   deck 96
   doors, exterior 68
   flight of stairs 343
   patio 17
   stoops 85
Landscape wall. *See* Retaining walls
Lap cement 125
Lateral load connectors. *See* Deck
Law, business 395
Leader. *See* Gutters
Ledger. *See* Deck
Licenses 414
Limited liability company 413
Linoleum floor covering 338
Lintel
   brick veneer 38
   CMU walls 231
Load
   basement walls 182
   CMU walls 231
   floor system 197
   footings 176
   headers 222
   insulating concrete form walls 233

live and dead loads 174
roof system 238, 240, 242
roof trusses 255
wall system 215
wind 221
Locks
door 65, 66
window 77
Log houses 237
Lumber. See Wood

M

Manufactured stone 30
Marketing home inspections 419
Metal roof covering
panels 134
shingles 132
Microlam beams 208
Mineral wool insulation
batt 277
loose fill 279
Modified bitumen roof coverings 147
Moisture meters 385
Mold
causes 275
reporting 381
Molding, interior 328
Moss
asphalt shingles 125
wood roof covering 142

N

Nail pops 329
Nails, types of 222
Negligence 399
Negligent misrepresentation 400
Notches in framing materials. See Floor, Roof, or Wall framing

O

OSB
floor sheathing 198, 204
roof sheathing 246
wall sheathing 223

P

Parallel Strand Lumber (PSL) 208
Partnerships 413
Patio 13, 17, 19, 85
Perlite insulation 281
Pickets. See Balusters
Piers 86, 174, 177, 178, 191
Piggyback trusses 259
Piles 174, 177, 178
Pitch of a roof 141, 172
Plants
location 13
scope of inspection 13
Plaster
exterior 48
interior 326
Platform framing 196
Plumb cut 96, 244
Plumbing vents, flashing 114
Plywood
floor sheathing 198, 204
siding 53
wall covering 53
wall sheathing 223
Pocket doors 333
Point loads 227
Polymer roof coverings 143
Popout, concrete 196
Porch 85
Post-and-beam framing 235, 238
Posts. See Columns
Post-tensioned slab foundation 194
Preservative treated wood
balconies 89
decks 92
retaining walls 4
Pull-down stairs
fire separation 217
installation 263
Purlins 245

Q

Quartz countertops 358

R

Racking, walls 170, 175, 215, 221, 329
Radiant barriers 289
Rafters. *See* Roof framing
Rammed earth walls 235
Ramps 349
Readily accessible 364
Receptacles, test instruments 384
Reporting
    deficiency statements 367
    description statements 374
    inspection limitations 364, 379
    report writing 366
    scope of inspection 363
    standards of practice 365
    types of deficiencies 371
Retaining walls
    common materials 3
    deadman 6
    footings 6
    garden walls 2
    landscape walls 2
    scope of inspection 2
    tieback 6
    weep holes 7
Roof coverings
    asbestos cement shingles 122
    asphalt shingles 123
    built-up membrane 144
    EDPM 152
    fiber cement 131
    foam 150
    ice dams 143
    low slope 144, 239
    metal panels 134
    metal shingles 132
    modified bitumen 147
    polymer 143
    roll mineral 146
    shakes, wood 139
    shingles, wood 139
    single-ply membrane 152
    slate 136
    tile 127
Roof drainage
    low slope 157
    steep slope 155

Roof framing
    ceiling joists 207, 231, 238, 241, 242, 249, 261
    collar ties 242
    holes and notches 244
    I-joists 207
    joist & rafter spans 240
    kicker 242
    purlins 245
    rafters 167, 175, 238, 244
    rafter ties 242
    ridge board 244
    sheathing 246
    trusses 254
Roofing cement 125
Roof jack 159
Roof styles 239
R-value 266, 269, 270, 271, 272, 276, 290
R-value requirements table 291

S

Safety glazing
    bathroom 81
    labeling 81
    near doors 69
    near stairs 83
    skylights 165
    swimming pool 81
    windows 81
Screw jack column. *See* Columns
Scupper 158
Sealants 58. *See* Caulk
Security bars, escape openings 77
Shakes
    roof covering 139
    siding 54
Sheathing
    floor 196, 198, 204, 213
    roof 218, 240, 246, 255
    wall 223, 246
Shed roof, description 239
Sheetrock 325
Shingles
    asbestos cement 122
    asphalt 123
    metal 132
    siding 54
    slate 136
    wood 139

Shrubs. *See* Plants
Sidewalk. *See* Walkway
Siding. *See* Wall coverings, exterior
Sill plate 220
Skylights 165
Slab foundations
   defects 195
   description 192
   post-tensioned 194
Slate roof covering 136
Sliding doors, interior 333
Slope
   driveways, walkways, patios 18
   foundation, away from 9
   grade near hills 10
   low slope roof coverings 144
Slope of a roof 173
Smart home
   definition 359
   inspection scope 324, 360
Soffit 62
Soil. *See also* Drainage
   expansive soil 8
   types of 174
Solar heat gain coefficient
   definition 269
   glazing requirements table 291
Sole plate 220
Sole proprietor 413
Spa. *See* Swimming pool
Spalling
   basement 189, 232
   brick veneer 39
   definition 196
   driveways, walkways, patios 18
   stucco 49, 51
   tile roof coverings 128
Span
   floor framing 197, 204
   roof framing 240, 246
   trusses 255
Sprial stairs 348
Squash blocks, I-joists 210
Stairs
   deck 96
   flight of 343
   guards, deck 99
   guards, interior 352
   handrails, deck 98
   handrails, interior 350
   headroom 348
   names of components 343
   nosing 346
   opening in floor framing 203
   riser, deck 97
   riser, interior 345
   safety glazing 83
   sprial 348
   stringers, deck 98
   stringers, interior 344
   treads, deck 97
   treads, interior 346
   treads, winder 347
   walkways 17
   width 348
Standards of practice 365
Standing seam metal roof covering 134
Steel siding 34
Steel wall framing 236
Stem wall foundation 193
Stone, artificial. *See* Adhered masonry veneer
Stone countertops 358
Stone floor covering 339
Stone foundations 183, 233
Stone, natural 30, 36
Stone walls, above ground 237
Stoop
   materials & construction 85
   separation, cracks 87
Straw bale wall 237
Structural insulated panels 234
Structured wiring 359
Stucco 48. *See also* Adhered masonry veneer
   EIFS 50
   flashing 162
Stud
   cripple 220
   jack 220, 222
   king 220
Stud shoe 230
Sump pump, exterior drainage 11
Sump pumps
   exterior drainage 11
Surcharge. *See* Retaining walls
Suspended ceiling 327
Swale 10, 16

Sweep, doors 66
Swimming pool
   fences and gates 22
   safety glazing 81

T

T-111 siding 53
Tar and gravel roof covering 145
Technically exhaustive 364
Tempered glass. See Safety glazing
Termites 226
Test instruments 384
Thermal barrier 219
Thermal bridging 272
Thermal envelope, definition 268
Thimble 159
Threshold, doors 66
Tieback. See Retaining walls
Tile
   countertops 357
   floor covering 339
   roof covering 127
Timber frame walls 238
TJI joists. See Floor framing, I-joists
Townhouse 217, 218
Trees. See Plants
Trim, exterior 56
Trim, interior 328
Trimmer studs 220
Trusses
   floor 212
   roof 254
Tubular skylights 165
Type X drywall 325

U

U-factor requirements table 291
Underground drains 10
Underlayment
   asphalt shingles 124
   fiber cement roof covering 131
   flashing 161
   shingles, wood 140
   tile roof covering 128
Unified soil classification system 174
Urea-formaldehyde insulation 282

V

Vapor retarders
   crawl space, unventilated 318
   crawl space, ventilated 315
   how they work 272
   unventilated attic 313
   ventilated attics 273
   walls 273
Vegetation. See Plants
Vent, bathroom. See Bathroom, exhaust fan
Vent, clothes dryer. See Clothes dryer exhaust
Ventilation, building
   attic 307
   bathroom exhaust 305
   clothes dryer exhaust 298
   crawl space 314
   energy recovery ventilation system 293
   heat recovery ventilation system 293
   kitchen exhaust 303
   outside air duct 292
   whole house fans 297
Vent, kitchen. See Kitchen exhaust
Vents, attic 308
   vaulted ceilings 309
Vents, flashing, plumbing 159
Vermiculite insulation 281
Vertical load paths 227
Vines. See Plants
Vinyl floor covering 338
Vinyl siding 51, 56, 59, 62

W

Walkway
   construction 17
   cracks 19, 195
   materials 17
   slope 18
   width 16
Wall, above ground
   adobe 235
   block & brick
      defects 231
      description 215, 230
   insulating concrete forms 232
   log houses 237
   post-and-beam walls 238

rammed earth 235
steel 236
stone 237
structural insulated panels 234
timber frame 238
wood-framed 220
Wall, below ground
   basement walls 181
   crawl space walls 192
   repairs 190
   slab foundation 193
Wall covering, exterior
   adhered masonry veneer 30
   aluminum siding 34
   asbestos cement siding 35
   brick veneer 36
   EIFS 50
   fiber cement siding 42
   flashing 59
   hardboard siding 46
   insulbrick siding 48
   steel siding 34
   stone, natural 36
   stone natural, adhered veneer 30
   stucco 48
   trim 56
   vinyl siding 51
   wood planks, shingles, shakes 54
   wood structural panels 53
Wall covering, interior
   drywall 325
   plaster 326
   trim molding 328
   wood 327
Wall framing
   bracing 222, 223
   defects 224
   fireblocking/fire separation 216
   headers 222
   holes and notches 224
   lumber grades 222
   lumber size/spacing 222
   material types 215
   plates 222
   sheathing 223
   terms 220
Waterproofing 184

Water-resistive barrier 58
   adhered masonry veneer 30
   installation 288
   purpose of 30
   vapor retarder 272
Water stains and damage 226, 329
Weather stripping 66, 77
Web stiffeners, I-joists 210
Weep holes
   adhered masonry veneer 31
   brick veneer 39, 60
   retaining wall 7
   wall coverings 30
Whole house fans 297
Winder treads 347
Wind loads 221
Windows
   components 75
   energy efficiency 75, 290
   escape openings 80
   fall protection 83
   flashing 58
   locks, hardware 77
   parts of 75
   safety glazing 81
   scope of inspection 78
   types 73
   window wells 80
Wood
   dimensional lumber characteristics 197
   floor framing 197
   foundation, permanent 183
   roof covering 139
   roof framing 240
   wall covering, exterior 53, 54
   wall covering, interior 327
   wall framing 220
Wood destroying organisms 226
Wood floor covering 341
Worker's compensation insurance 408
Wythe 29, 231